DISCARD

Cornel West:
A Critical Reader

BLACKWELL CRITICAL READERS

The *Blackwell Critical Readers* series presents a collection of linked perspectives on continental philosophers, and social and cultural theorists. Edited and introduced by acknowledged experts and written by representatives of different schools and positions, the series embodies debate, dissent, and a committed heterodoxy. From Foucault to Derrida, from Heidegger to Nietzsche, *Blackwell Critical Readers* address figures whose work requires elucidation by a variety of perspectives. Volumes in the series include both primary and secondary bibliographies.

Cornel West:
A Critical Reader

Edited by
George Yancy

BLACKWELL
Publishers

Copyright © Blackwell Publishers Ltd 2001

First published 2001

2 4 6 8 10 9 7 5 3 1

Blackwell Publishers Inc.
350 Main Street
Malden, Massachusetts 02148
USA

Blackwell Publishers Ltd
108 Cowley Road
Oxford OX4 1JF
UK

Library of Congress Cataloging-in-Publication Data

West, Cornel.
  [Selections. 2001]
  Cornel West: a critical reader/edited by George Yancy.
    p. cm—(Blackwell critical readers)
Includes bibliographical references and index.
  ISBN 0–631–22291–X (alk. paper)—ISBN 0–631–22292–8 (pbk. : alk. paper)
1. Afro-Americans—Intellectual life. 2. Afro-American intellectuals.
3. West, Cornel—Political and social views. 4. Afro-Americans—Politics and government.
5. United States—Politics and Government—1989—Philosophy. 6. Pragmatism. 7. United States—Civilization—Philosophy. 8. Afro-Americans—Religion. 9. United States—Race relations. I. Yancy, George. II. Title. III. Series.
  E185.86 .W4383 2001
  973—dc21   00–012342

British Library Cataloguing in Publication Data

A CIP catalogue record for this book is available from the British Library.

Typeset in 10 on 12pt Bembo
by Kolam Information Services Private Limited, Pondicherry, India
Printed in Great Britain by MPG Books, Bodmin, Cornwall.

This book is printed on acid-free paper.

To Susan and Gabriel,
Deo Gratias

Contents

Part IV   Cultural Studies   293

Acknowledgments

First and foremost I would like to thank Cornel West for his synoptic and synthetic conceptual corpus, a critical body of work that embodies historico-philosophical turns, boldness, and a complex weaving, often leaving the reader in a state of creative vertigo, of African-American, Anglo-American, and Continental thought. And far from working within the confines of a Cartesian paradigm, West is painfully aware of his historical facticity and finitude, his raciated identity, the sociopolitical implications of this identity, and his groundedness within a world that forever teeters on existential and epistemological precariousness and uncertainty. But within the crucible of this ever-present fallibilism, West is empowered by an indefatigable *hope*. It is precisely this hope that fuels his political praxis. Hence, I also thank him for his demonstration of the embodied lived reality of theory and practice. Lastly, West's Afterword is both philosophically engaging and critically dialogical.

Second, I would like to thank the contributors to this text. Each is aware of West's importance as a significant intellectual. Yet this understanding is not expressed in empty praises and vacuous apotheosis; rather, like the New York Society of Black Philosophers, which was crucial for West's development, each contributor gives West the benefit of being wrong, challenging him to take a metaphilosophical look at his rather prodigious work.

Third, I give a very special thanks to Jeff Dean, philosophy editor at Blackwell, for immediately recognizing the significance of this project, and to Beth Remmes, senior development editor of books, for her assistance in the production of this important text. John Taylor, my copy editor, is to be thanked for his meticulous work on the text, and Lisa Eaton is to be thanked for her cover design insights.

Barbara Karasinski, West's assistant, I would like to thank for her help and cordiality. Scholars Moni McIntyre, Fred Evans, Tom Rockmore, Nicholas Rescher, Wilfrid Sellars, Adolf Grunbaum, Eugene Fitzgerald, Wilhelm Wurzer, and Linda A. Kinnahan are thanked for their insights and for encouraging me to exceed beyond my grasp. A special thanks goes to Moni McIntyre for her liberationist theological insights and her personal demonstration of the synthesis of theory, practice, existential concern, and kindness. I would also like to thank McIntyre and Evans for their meticulous reading of my introduction.

I extend a deeply personal thanks to the Hadley family – Geoff and Lillian (my loving in-laws), Peter and Jennifer (ethnomusicologists), Emma, Thomas, and Sonya – and the Sutherland family – Ruth, Michael, Charles (a gentle and promising young man), Megan, Geoffrey and Susan. To Ruth Yancy, Brother EL, and Artrice, I give my love. To Gabriel Miles Yancy (who finds wonder in ordinary things and is a profound blessing to me), Adrian Brice Yancy (who has so much goodness in his heart), and Susan J. Hadley, my wife, faithful friend, intellectual companion, supporter of my work, co-equal partner, and one who constantly shows patience toward my often quixotic ways, I extend a special embodied love of dedication.

To my friends, Charles Williams, Francis Albert Lotuaco (a burgeoning historian), and my late dear friend Robert Houston, I extend a warm thanks for the many hours of dialectical engagement. William L. Banks, thanks for the support and encouragement. Leandre Jackson, thanks for your photographic talents. To historian and cultural theorist James G. Spady, whom I first met when I was only 18, thanks for your many years of encouragement, time, and intellectually spirited and rigorous discussions. You perform an invaluable service as you continue to train young promising intellectuals.

Lastly, my hope is that this text will provide readers with a critical guide to West's work. The aim is that readers will come to appreciate the critical intelligence of West and the historical importance of his contributions; moreover, to appreciate the many praised and contested aspects of his intellectual corpus. Most of all, however, my hope is that readers will come to experience West's work as an invitation to embrace a morally transformative life and to unsettle the moral decay of their culture and society.

Notes on Contributors

Victor Anderson is a graduate of Princeton University and former student of Cornel West. He is the Associate Professor of Christian Ethics at Vanderbilt Divinity School, Associate Professor of African American Studies and Associate Professor of Religious Studies in the College of Arts and Sciences. Anderson's books include *Beyond Ontological Blackness: An Essay in African American Religious and Cultural Criticism* (1995, 1999), *Pragmatic Theology* (1997), and an edited volume entitled *African American Religious Thought and Pragmatism* (1998).

James H. Cone is Charles A. Briggs Distinguished Professor at Union Theological Seminary in New York, and is the author of numerous books on Black theology, including *Black Theology and Black Power*, *A Black Theology of Liberation*, *God of the Oppressed*, and *Martin and Malcolm and America: A Dream or a Nightmare*. His most recent book is *Risks of Faith*.

M. Shawn Copeland is Associate Professor of Systematic Theology at Marquette University, Milwaukee, Wisconsin, and (adjunct) Associate Professor of Systematic Theology at the Institute for Black Catholic Studies, Xavier University of Louisiana, New Orleans. Professor Copeland is the author of more than sixty articles, reviews, and commentaries in professional journals and books on such topics as suffering, identity, and difference, and the common human good, social analysis, and freedom.

Nada Elia (PhD in Comparative Literature) is Scholar-in-Residence in the Afro-American Studies program at Brown University. Prior to that, she was Visiting Scholar at the Pembroke Center for Teaching and Research on Women, also at Brown University. She is the author of *Trances, Dances, and Vociferations: Agency and Resistance in Africana Women's Narratives*. Her articles on African, postcolonial, and women of color feminisms, identity construction in the diaspora, and visibility issues have been published in such journals as *World Literature Today*, *Research in African Literatures*, *Callaloo*, and *The Canadian Review of Comparative Literature*. Elia has taught African, African-American, and Women's Studies at Brown University, Tufts University, the University of Massachusetts–Dartmouth, and Western Illinois University. Lastly, she is Associate Editor of *Radical Philosophy Review: A Journal of Progressive Thought*.

Lewis R. Gordon is Chair of Africana Studies and Professor of Africana Studies, Contemporary Religious Thought, and Modern Culture and Media, at Brown University. He is also Ongoing Visiting Professor of Political Philosophy at the University of West Indies at Mona, Jamaica. He is author of several books, including *Her Majesty's Other Children: Sketches of Racism from a Neocolonial Age*, which won the Gustavus Myer Award for Outstanding Books on Human Rights, and *Existentia Africana: Understanding Africana Thought*. He is also editor of *Radical Philosophy Review: A Journal of Progressive Thought* and the Routledge book series *Africana Thought*.

Floyd W. Hayes III is Associate Professor of Multidisciplinary Studies and Political Science at North Carolina State University. He is the editor of *A Turbulent Voyage: Readings in African American Studies*, the third edition of which will be issued in 2000. Hayes has published numerous articles on Africana studies, public policy, and political theory. He is currently working on a book, entitled *Domination and Ressentiment: the Desperate Vision of Richard Wright*.

Clevis Headley is an Associate Professor of Philosophy at Florida Atlantic University. African philosophy is one of his major research areas. His work has appeared in *Philosophy Today*, the *Journal of Social Philosophy*, *Semiotica*, and *The Continental Philosophy Review*. Currently, he is working on a manuscript investigating Black subjectivity in the context of postmodernism and deconstruction.

Clarence Shole Johnson is Associate Professor of Philosophy at Middle Tennessee State University. His publications have appeared in books, in various scholarly journals, including *Dialogue: Canadian Philosophical Review*, *Journal of Philosophical Research* and the *Southern Journal of Philosophy*, and in the *Encyclopedia of African Religions and Philosophies*.

Peniel E. Joseph is Assistant Professor of History and African and Afro-American Studies at the University of Rhode Island. His work, which appears in *Souls*, *The Black Scholar*, and *New Politics*, deals with Black radicalism, race theory, and African-American political thought and practice during the twentieth century. He is currently completing a book-length manuscript on Black radicalism during the Civil Rights and Black Power eras.

Howard McGary, Jr is Professor of Philosophy at Rutgers University. He is author of *Race and Social Justice* and co-author (with Bill Lawson) of *Between Slavery and Freedom: Philosophy and American Slavery*. His articles have appeared in numerous journals, including *The Journal of Ethics*, *The Journal of Philosophy*, *Philosophical Forum*, and *The American Philosophical Quarterly*.

Eduardo Mendieta is Assistant Professor of Philosophy at the University of San Francisco. He is the editor and translator of Enrique Dussel's *The Underside of Modernity*, which also contains essays by Karl Otto Apel and Paul Ricouer. He co-edited *Liberation Theologies, Postmodernity and the Americas* and *The Good Citizen*. He is the author of several essays on liberation philosophy, ethics, globalization, and the critical theory of Jürgen Habermas. Currently, he is writing a book entitled *The Geography of Utopia: Modernity's Spatio-temporal Regimes*.

Charles W. Mills is Professor of Philosophy at the University of Illinois at Chicago. He works in the area of radical political theory, and has recently published two books on race: *The Racial Contract* (1997) and *Blackness Visible: Essays on Philosophy and Race* (1998).

Lucius Turner Outlaw, Jr is Professor of Philosophy and Director of the African American Studies Program at Vanderbilt University. Outlaw has been a member of the faculties of Haverford College, Morgan State University, and Fisk University, and a visiting professor at Spelman College, Howard University, Hamilton College, and Boston College. Born in Starkville, Mississippi, he is a graduate of Fisk University (BA in philosophy, 1967) and of the Graduate School of Arts and Sciences of Boston College (PhD in philosophy, 1972). His essays have been published in a number of journals, including *Philosophy and Social Criticism*, *Philosophical Forum*, *Journal of Social Philosophy*, *Man and World*, *Graduate Faculty Philosophy Journal* (The New School), *The Journal of Ethics*, and a number of anthologies. A collection of several of his essays, *On Race and Philosophy*, was published by Routledge. His current book project is a collection of essays on social and political philosophy.

John P. Pittman teaches at John J. College of Criminal Justice in New York City. He edited *African-American Perspectives and Philosophical Traditions*. Pittman is also co-editor, with Tommy Lott, of the *Blackwell Companion to African-American Philosophy*.

Hilary W. Putnam is Cogan University Professor Emeritus at Harvard University. His books include *Reason, Truth and History, Realism with a Human Face, Renewing Philosophy, Words and Life, Pragmatism*, and *The Threefold Cord: Mind, Body and World*.

George Yancy is McAnulty Fellow at Duquesne University. His published work appears in numerous journals and books, including *The Journal of Social Philosophy, Hypatia: A Journal of Feminist Philosophy, The Western Journal of Black Studies*, the *College Language Association Journal, Radical Philosophy Review: A Journal of Progressive Thought, Social Science Quarterly, Popular Music and Society, The Cornel West Reader, Women of Color and Philosophy*, and *The Encyclopedia of Feminist Theories*. Yancy's book, *African-American Philosophers, 17 Conversations*, won the *Choice* Outstanding Academic Book Award for 1999. Yancy has also published over 80 articles and 50 book reviews in *The Philadelphia Tribune* and *The Philadelphia Tribune Magazine*, respectively.

Iris M. Young is Professor of Political Science at the University of Chicago. Her research interests are in contemporary political theory, feminist social theory, and normative analysis of public policy. Her books include *Justice and the Politics of Difference, Throwing Like a Girl and Other Essays in Feminist Philosophy and Social Theory, Intersecting Voices: Dilemmas of Gender, Political Philosophy, and Policy*, and *Inclusion and Democracy*.

Josiah Ulysses Young III is Professor of Systematic Theology at Wesley Theological Seminary. He is the author of several books, including *No Difference in Fare: Dietrich Bonhoeffer and the Problem of Racism, A Pan-African Theology: Providence and the Legacy of the Ancestors*. He is also the author of several essays in theology and Africana Studies.

Cornel West: The Vanguard of Existential and Democratic Hope

George Yancy

To evade modern philosophy means to strip the profession of philosophy of its pretense, disclose its affiliations with structures of powers (both rhetorical and political) rooted in the past, and enact intellectual practices, i.e., produce texts of various sorts and styles, that investigate and unsettle one's culture and society.

Cornel West

The displacement and transformation of frameworks of thinking, the changing of received values and all the work that has been done to think otherwise, to do something else, to become other than what one is – that, too, is philosophy.

Michel Foucault

Without doubt, Cornel West, a self-ascribed New World African, influenced by African-American, Anglo-American, and Continental traditions, has become one of the most significant and recognized Black philosophers and, indeed, American philosophers and public intellectuals in the United States. A prolific intellectual, West has written and co-written numerous books, including *Race Matters* (1993), which was a nonfiction bestseller; a two-volume work entitled *Beyond Eurocentrism and Multiculturalism*, which was awarded the 1993 American Book Award; the provocative dialogical text *Breaking Bread: Insurgent Black Intellectual Life* (with womanist and cultural theorist bell hooks, 1991); and his widely acclaimed *The American Evasion of Philosophy: A Genealogy of Pragmatism* (1989). If there is a contemporary scholar who deserves to be described as an intellectual *par excellence* – a Black philosopher deeply critical of the profession of philosophy, a man of letters, radical democrat, humanist, race-transcending prophet, spiritual gadfly,

social and cultural critic, advocate on the side of "the least of these," political
activist (combining elements of *theoria* and *praxis*), astute critic of our postmodern
moment, cognoscente of the intertextuality of Western intellectual traditions, and
more – then that person is Cornel West.

While many contemporary academics remain comfortably insulated behind the
walls of academia, West, for twenty years, has lectured almost 150 times a year,
reconfiguring and effectively utilizing public spaces as sites of important intellectual
exchange and critical dialogue. Speaking in a profound, intense, and passionate
voice, which is often structured by a rich tradition of African–American homiletic
style, and manifesting bodily articulations that suggest that he speaks with his entire
being, West immediately establishes a symbiotic relationship with his audience.
Whether speaking at universities, churches, synagogues (such as the audience of
1,700 at Congregation Emanu-El in San Francisco), or small coffee shops, West is
often responded to with thunderous applause as he effortlessly moves through, and
discursively interlaces, philosophy, postmodernism, history, social criticism, ethics,
religion, cultural studies, African–American aesthetics, legal theory, economic
analysis, coalitional politics (Black–Jewish relations), and contemporary political
theory. This demonstrates both a critical mind ensconced in the thickness of
history (not confined to ethereal armchair philosophizing) and a mind driven
with passion, an erotic desire, to know about the world and one's place within
it. Also indicative of West's rejection of narrow academicism, he demonstrates that
critical dialogue and profound learning are not simply confined to the academy;
indeed, one often finds that the development of critical intelligence, "to think
otherwise" and "invigorate and unsettle one's culture and society," involves a
process of unlearning sedimented and often stultifying patterns of behavior, normative rules and paradigms of "intellectual excellence." Moving beyond the
academy is part of West's enactment of democracy; philosophizing with everyday
people is his attempt to dehierarchize, decompartmentalize and thereby democra-
tize knowledge; his is an inclusive project which is designed to engage with
multiple voices, not a single oracle voice. In the spirit of the Italian Marxist
Antonio Gramsci, West "takes the life of the mind seriously enough to relate
ideas to the everyday life of ordinary folk."[1] "An academic," according to West,
"usually engages in rather important yet still narrow scholarly work, whereas an
intellectual is engaged in the public issues that affect large numbers of people in a
critical manner."[2] Moreover, in this respect, West is preeminently a modern
intellectual. For "to be modern is to have the courage to use one's critical
intelligence to question and challenge the prevailing authorities, powers and
hierarchies of the world."[3] And West is aware that to philosophize with everyday
people, often with those who have been socially and economically derailed, will
require radically different discursive tools that are not themselves alienating, and
"that have not been bequeathed to us by philosophy departments."[4] Instead, for
West, given his interdisciplinary or de-disciplinary approach to knowledge, it will

be necessary to draw from the fruits of cultural criticism, historical works, and social theory. Like literary critic Lionel Trilling, West draws from a multitude of domains of inquiry for combat; he does not rely on a single hermeneutic lens through which to contest injustices. Philosophy, for West, reminiscent of Dewey's impatience with philosophy's narrow professionalism and epistemological centrality, is not limited to a cerebral affair "where intricate puzzlelike problems are solved, resolved, or dissolved";[5] rather, "the crucial element is the ability for rigorous thought, clear exposition, and investment of one's whole self in one's thinking."[6] In short, for West, philosophy is intimately linked to existential concreteness and the normative dimensions of an exemplary life, not mere cleverness.[7]

What makes West's project even more difficult and dangerous is the fact that he is a raciated Black male. His very presence is a challenge to the various mythopoetic constructions of what a Black male should look like, speak like and act like. His very presence is a disruption and is a threat to the white racist knowledge/ power lens through which he is viewed and profiled. As a thinker, as a Black male demonstrating critical subjectivity, West is already operating against the regime of white racist theorizations of the Black male body; his presence is iconoclastic, shattering white lies that overdetermine the Black body as devoid of *Geist*, naturally inferior, and criminal by nature. West, however, is no Promethean thief; he demands recognition for his humanity and his fully embodied Blackness. West is very much aware of how the regime of whiteness operates to criminalize the Black male body where he relates:

> Years ago, while driving from New York to teach at Williams College, I was stopped on fake charges of trafficking cocaine. When I told the police officer I was a professor of religion, he replied 'Yeh, and I'm the flying Nun. Let's go, nigger!' I was stopped three times in my first ten days in Princeton for driving too slowly on a residential street with a speed limit of twenty-five miles per hour.[8]

Moreover, through the bio-politicization of the Black body, it was/is believed that Black males of African decent were/are rapists and imbued with sexual madness.[9] European philosophers David Hume and Immanuel Kant would have found West to be an aberration; for they held that Blacks were naturally inferior to whites.[10] Voltaire, the great French philosopher, man of letters, and powerful voice of the Enlightenment, was seduced by the normative structuration of whiteness where he claimed that "they [Blacks] are not capable of any great application or association of ideas, and seemed formed neither for the advantages nor the abuses of philosophy."[11]

To be a philosopher under Black skin, from the perspective of white racist America, is to be a chimera. Not only is one's very capacity for critical intelligence called into question, but one is conceptualized, *ontologically*, as a problem, a problem whose citizenship and humanity, from the perspective of white normativity and white hegemony, are placed seriously in doubt. According to West:

> The notion that black people are human beings is a relatively new discovery in the modern West. The idea of black equality in beauty, culture, and intellectual capacity remains problematic and controversial within prestigious halls of learning and sophisticated intellectual circles. The Afro-American encounter with the modern world has been shaped first and foremost by the doctrine of white supremacy, which is embodied in institutional practices and enacted in everyday folkways under varying circumstances and evolving conditions.[12]

Although West has been criticized, and I think rightly so, for the neo-conservative overtones of his claim that it is partly Black nihilism that is the aetiology of the lovelessness and hopelessness so prevalent within neocolonial Black urban spaces, he is more on target where he maintains that "to engage in a serious discussion of race in America, we must begin not with the problems of black people but with the flags of American society – flags rooted in historic inequalities and long-standing cultural stereotypes."[13] To begin from this angle of analysis, Black people are deproblematized. They are no longer essentialized as a problem, but seen as having problems imposed upon them as a result of being enslaved and transported to geographical sites of anti-Blackness, Black bodily "thingification," dehumanization, and death.

Given the above, *Cornel West: A Critical Reader* is a political act: it is a book engaged in textual and existential combat; for it honors and *recognizes* the complexity, critical subjectivity, humanity, intellectual productivity, and fecundity of this prominent Black scholar. Existing and thinking within academic spaces that deny Black critical subjectivity, and reject the Black experience as a significant *locus philosophicus*, places Black people within an existential and intellectual war zone. Is this not an accurate description, given the reality that Black people live in a country that continues to assault "black intelligence, black moral character, and black possibility"?[14] Indeed, what does it mean to exist as a "black possibility" under the historical facticity and weight of white hegemony? Existentially, how can Black people freely choose themselves in their own being within an oppressive (white) *Herrenvolk* cultural and sociopolitical matrix? Pertinent here is West's question: "What does it mean to be a philosopher of African descent in the American empire?"[15] Fighting to be intellectually productive within a discursive field and institutional context dominated by *Bell Curvese* logic, Black philosophers may come to believe that they "are not 'philosophers,' or 'serious philosophers,' 'rigorous philosophers,' 'precise philosophers.' "[16] Seduced by white racist lies and imaginative myth making, they may undergo what Ruth Frankenberg has called a process of "epistemic violence," coming to *know* themselves and their work as inferior.[17] While many contemporary philosophers are debating the issue of whether or not we inhabit a post-philosophical historical moment, Black philosophers still struggle to be *recognized* as philosophers. And now that the white gaze has legitimated our existence, as if it really has this power, we must not co-opt the transformative and conceptually explosive possibilities of African-American philosophy through the process of inertial compartmentalization. The trick is to utilize white spaces within the academy without becoming a prisoner to those spaces. The reader should note that West's critical obsession with white racism, and his emphasis on the cultural aesthetics, intelligence, and historical reality of Black people, does not make him a Black nationalist ideologue; rather it is evidence of his humanist outlook that protests the oppression, "epistemic violence," and degradation of Black people and accents the humanity and dignity of all people. West is critical of any form of Black nationalism governed by a closing-of-ranks mentality and the postulation of an ("authentic") Black ontological essence which exists beneath the top layer of social reality.

As a political act, *Cornel West: A Critical Reader* is a variation on the theme of moving the center of conversation raised and developed in my first book, *African-American Philosophers, 17 Conversations*. The idea here, one consistent with West's historicist and pragmatist sensibilities, is that philosophy is not an ahistorical project. Rather, philosophy is deeply embedded within particular configurations of racial, gendered, class, and cultural experiences. To raise the issue of moving the center of conversation of much modern (especially, European) philosophy is consistent with West's motif of "evasion," of stripping the profession of philosophy of its pretense. Undergirding the theme of moving the center of conversation is the recognition of the deep historical, experiential embeddedness and radical contingency of philosophical systems; hence, it is to recognize the reality of multiple philosophical voices and the importance of their being heard. This, of course, raises the "whose knowledge?" or "whose experience?" question. Within the history of Western philosophy, many white male philosophers theorize as if from an Archimedian point, a site of unquestioned absolute normativity and institutional power. Once their philosophical systems and modes of philosophical discourse become institutionalized and canonized – that is, cut off, as it were, from their raciated and gendered value-laden foundation – we often assume that they are beyond critique, deconstruction, and reformulation. This is what I call the ritualization of whiteness or philosophical acts of whiticization. Whiteness and maleness, as normalizing historical constructs, are then rendered incognito and silent. Given the above, West's question with regard to African-American philosophy is key. He asks, "how does philosophy relate to the Afro-American experience? This question arises primarily because of an antipathy to the ahistorical character of contemporary philosophy and the paucity of illuminating diachronic studies of the Afro-American experience."[18] Asked if there is anything called African-American philosophy, West is quite consistent:

> So much would hinge upon what we mean by "philosophy." If we understand philosophy as a type of autonomous discourse that somehow transcends history, I would say "no," because I don't think that there is such a thing in general. If, however, we understand it as a certain cultural response to the world and trying to come up

with holistic views, synoptic visions, and synthetic images of how things hang together, then certainly there is an Afro-American philosophical tradition.[19]

The reader should note that, for West, African-American philosophy is not the same as Afrocentricity. He sees African-American philosophy as a historically emergent discursive field and a sociohistorical and existential response within a context of deep cultural and historical hybridity. Moreover, he sees African-American philosophy as consistent with the "humanist tradition" of refusing to romanticize African-American culture. African-American philosophy, a tradition which West has fundamentally helped to shape, is not an epidermal project. Rather, as West has indicated, it is a deeply experiential and cultural response to the world. African-American philosophy grows out of our historical experiences within the so-called New World. It is partly linked to our experiences of exile, exclusion, and struggle. The lived experiences of the Black body within a hegemonic context of whiteness act as valid conduits of meaning through which the Black-self-and-world get articulated. We can transmute, theorize, and articulate those experiences – what West refers to as "that guttural cry"[20] – in the form of critical oppositional discourses, and a constructive, enhancing, sociopolitical, and cultural ontology. As West concludes:

> In this way, Afro-American philosophy reconstructs the Afro-American past and critically evaluates Afro-American responses to crucial challenges in the present. It attempts to understand the Afro-American experience in order to enhance and enrich the lives of Afro-Americans; it demands personal integrity and political action.[21]

It is important to note, however, that African-American philosophy is not, and certainly should not be, limited to struggle. No one will deny the physically and psychologically hostile and existentially absurd American context within which Blacks have been thrown. Nevertheless, African-American philosophy is also born of the free play of the imagination; it also involves improvisational, active modes of cultural creation, discursive and nondiscursive insightful productions that are not simply tethered to *struggling against* white hegemony, always in the reactive mode; for to remain within the reactive mode is to become a prisoner to whiteness. In this way, though taking West somewhat out of context, whiteness does not dictate "the terms of what one thinks and does."[22]

There is no single or final approach to Cornel West. First, his variegated philosophical corpus does not allow for a *single* hermeneutic lens through which to understand the man and his work. His writing style, reflective of a propensity toward synoptic and synthetic modes of analysis, is often improvisational, a conceptual democratic blending of ideas (after all, he is a jazz man in the life of the mind[23]); it is deeply steeped in the thickness of history; it is de-disciplinary; and embedded in a process of what he calls "worldliness," which involves his attempt to render his own values and presuppositions explicit. Second, West is still very much in process, protean and metastable. One of the great assets of this text is that it comes to terms with West's intellectual development *in medias res*. But this does not mean that getting a critical conceptual hold on West is impossible.

I met West while I was a graduate student at Yale University. Prior to meeting him, I was told that he was a brilliant Black scholar who taught philosophy of religion. Given my love of philosophy of religion, I thought that it would be great to talk to a brother about issues in the area of philosophy of religion. I saw him by accident one day. We talked of getting together, but for reasons that I cannot now recall, that meeting never took place. The next time that I saw West, he was being arrested, and subsequently jailed. As I recall, he was involved in both the movement for clerical unionism at Yale and the movement against Yale's investments in South Africa. Seeing him arrested was a powerful example of how the intellectual life of the mind can be deeply ensconced in the realities of political everydayness. Blending critical reflection and political praxis, however, was not new to West. At ten, he participated with his family in a civil rights demonstration in Sacramento in 1963, which was the first and only time he heard Martin Luther King, Jr, speak in person. And early on, he was exposed to the Marxist tradition and revolutionary ideas. A branch of the Black Panther Party was located next door to the Black Baptist church attended by West; he was an avid reader of Black Panther literature. Moreover, while still in high school, then class president, he and a friend, Glenn Jordan, "organized a strike of students demanding courses in black studies. The strike was city-wide and brought positive results."[24] And while an undergraduate at Harvard, West assisted in helping out at the Black Panthers' prison outreach and breakfast programs. In short, West had already begun to enact the vocation of an organic intellectual, one who is an activist and engaged, not hermetically detached

West is fundamentally concerned with the reality of evil and the experience of the absurd. Throughout his writings, issues of finitude, evil, absurdity and our existential contingency are accented. This grows out of what he calls his Chekhovian Christian conception of what it means to be human-in-the-world. West writes:

> To be human is to suffer, shudder and struggle courageously in the face of inevitable death. To think deeply and live wisely as a human being is to meditate on and prepare for death. The quest for human wisdom requires us to learn how to die – penultimately in the daily death of bad habits and cruel viewpoints and ultimately in the demise of our earthly and temporal bodies.[25]

West does not suggest that we passively brood over the facticity of our finite lives and our encounter with evil. Rather, as Foucault would say, this reality of human existence presents itself as a possibility for us to think wisely and strive "to become other than what one is." On West's historicist view, which places emphasis on contextualism and revisionism, while attempting to avoid subjectivist nihilism, there are no ultimate foundations according to which we might appeal that might guide our selection of self-images. There are only contingent vocabularies, historical narratives, and useful metaphors. There is no escape from radical choice. He writes:

> To choose a tradition (a version of it) is more than to be convinced by a set of arguments; it is also to decide to live alongside the slippery edge of life's abyss with the support of the dynamic stories, symbols, interpretations and insights bequeathed by communities that came before.[26]

West's existentialist, though not Sartrean, sensibilities are quite apparent. West writes that he is "not an existentialist like the early Sartre who had a *systematic grasp of human existence*" (emphasis added).[27] The impact of his early reading and partiality toward Søren Kierkegaard is evident where he says: "It [reading Kierkegaard] gave me a profoundly Kierkegaardian sensibility that required then that philosophizing be linked to the existentially concrete situations, wrestling with decision, commitment, actualized possibility and realized potential."[28] So, although we make decisions "alongside the slippery edge of life's abyss," in Emersonian fashion, according to West, we are not completely curtailed by our social and existential situatedness. In short, there is always our capacity for Promethean constancy and radical choice. Though our situation is existentially and socially bleak, West does not suggest a passive ironic consciousness:

> To be human, at the most profound level, is to encounter honestly the inescapable circumstances that constrain us, yet muster the courage to struggle compassionately for our own unique individualities and for more democratic free societies. This courage contains the seeds of lived history – of memory, maturity and melioration – in the face of no guaranteed harvest. Hence, my view of what it means to be human is preeminently existential – a focus on particular, singular, flesh-and-blood persons grappling with dire issues of death, dread, despair, disease and disappointment.[29]

Not only does West place emphasis on human courage, he is also a prisoner of hope. In his heart, West is no Jeremiah. For West, it is not despair and calamity that will have the last word, but hope.[30] Not only is West a blues man in the world of ideas, but he also adopts, through his emphasis on affirming life in the midst of tragedy, a blues ontology, a mode of being which is affirmative in the face of existential and social adversity. He lives and moves within an existential space full of possibilities. West implies that there is a measure of virtue in our historical situatedness (or hermeneutic circle), "because we never transcend or complete the circle. Like Sisyphus, we go endlessly up and down with noble aims and aspirations, but no ultimate harmony or achieved wholeness."[31]

For West, hope is that existential posture that enables one to endure precisely when there is no evidence to support an optimistic outlook. Coupled with West's emphasis on the power of hope is his emphasis on *Caritas*, the urgent significance of demonstrating charity toward others in a world saturated and dominated by a market mentality obsessed with titillation and hyperreality. For West, the urgency for *Caritas* is fueled by a kind of "*kairos* time" *vis-à-vis* the oppressive conditions within which we live, move, and have our being. It is not just white racism that West critiques, but all forms of oppression. His is a synthetic and synoptic approach to evil, an approach which is shaped by a broad moral vision, a vision which critiques injustices in the form of racism, classism, androcentric domination of women, the commodification of women's bodies, homophobic violence, ecological exploitation, multinational oligarchic power, deindustrialization and the displacement of vital job resources, and the disparity in the distribution of wealth in the United States.

Cornel West, Fikre Selassie ("Spirit of Love"), the name given to him while in Ethiopia, is an unusual, principled, and exceptional contemporary intellectual. Given his academic status and intellectual prominence, he neither makes a fetish of criticism nor desires to be shaped in the image of Harvard, Princeton, or Yale. He would rather, despite the profound risk involved, bank "his all . . . on the courage to love enacted by a particular Palestinian Jew named Jesus, who was crucified by the powers that be, betrayed by cowardly comrades and misconstrued by corrupt churches."[32] His is a love ethic grounded in resistance to evil and injustice which involves "trying to leave the world a little better than you found it,"[33] and requires a great deal of hope and endurance. Reminiscent of Tertullian's dictum, *credo quia absurdum est*, West writes: "It is the love ethic of Christian faith – the most absurd and alluring mode of being in the world – that enables me to live a life of hope against hope without succumbing to a warranted yet paralyzing pessimism or to an understandable yet miserable misanthropy."[34]

Coupled with his religio-existential hope and love ethic is West's prophetic pragmatism. Although, for West, prophetic pragmatism is not necessarily linked to a religious foundation, it is compatible with, and intricately related to, his Christian and political outlook. He writes:

> Like James, [Reinhold] Niebuhr and to some extent Du Bois, I hold a religious conception of pragmatism. I have dubbed it "prophetic" in that it harks back to the Jewish and Christian tradition of prophets who brought urgent and compassionate critique to bear on the evils of their day. The mark of the prophet is to speak the truth in love with courage – come what may. Prophetic pragmatism proceeds from this impulse.[35]

Moreover, West's unique form of prophetic pragmatism involves profound risks and is self-reflexive. He stresses the "strenuous mood," signifying the subjunctive, protean dimensions of human agency. In short, there are always innovative possibilities for human agency and transformation. West: "Therefore, the distinctive features of prophetic activity are Pascalian leaps of faith in the capacity of human beings to transform their circumstances, engage in relentless criticism and self-criticism, and project visions, analyses, and practices of social freedom."[36] West's prophetic pragmatism involves deep cultural criticism that is marked by Ralph Waldo Emerson's sense of vision, his utopian drive; John Dewey's conceptual notion of creative democracy; and W. E. B. Du Bois's "social structural analysis of the limits of capitalist democracy."[37]

In the spirit of Reinhold Niebuhr, Paul Tillich, and others, West's Christian sensibilities exist alongside a "very deep commitment to democratic socialist politics."[38] And in the tradition of James Cone, Gustavo Gutierrez, Leonardo Boff, and others, West's liberationist theological standpoint emphasizes "that Christian thinkers should employ elements of various social analyses of power, wealth, status, and influence that look at the world from the situation of the 'least of these,' the various kinds of victims in the world."[39] Though West emphasizes the importance of Pascalian leaps of faith and the importance of his love ethic, and though he describes himself as a non-Marxist socialist, he also emphasizes the importance of "Marxist theory as an indispensable intellectual weapon for freedom fighters in the present."[40] He elaborates as follows:

> The Marxist intellectual tradition remains indispensable in order to keep track of certain forms of social misery, especially these days in terms of oligopolies and monopolies that take the form of transnational corporations that have a disproportionate amount of wealth and power, not just in America but around the world.[41]

Cornel West: A Critical Reader is a collection of essays that attempt to come critically to terms with the complex, synthetic, and synoptic writings of Cornel West. Given West's prolificity, and the sheer diversity of issues about which he writes, including popular culture, architecture, music, and painting, I decided to divide the text into four parts that effectively cover the more general range of West's intellectual areas of concern: pragmatism; philosophy of religion; political philosophy; and cultural studies. These four sections are by no means exhaustive in terms of dealing with West's intellectual corpus; rather, they allow for a schematically manageable and helpful way of approaching his work. Moreover, West has written substantially in each of these areas. The parts are also rather fluid. For example, it is difficult to write about West's political philosophy without invariably invoking his nuanced pragmatism, his cultural theorizations, and the religious, prophetic dimensions of his work. Each contributor is aware and respectful of West's importance and prominence as a contemporary intellectual, but not blinded by his status. Thus, each contributor takes West to task, critically and honestly examining his work.

Part I, on Pragmatism, begins with Hilary Putnam's insightful reading of West's *The American Evasion of Philosophy: A Genealogy of Pragmatism* in relationship to Dewey's injunction that philosophy should deal with the problems of human beings. In his close and skillful reading, Putnam argues that at the core of West's work is an emphasis placed on the inseparability of the personal and the political, the self's fundamental power of moral vision and action, and the importance of personally and existentially bearing witness to democratic faith. Lewis Gordon's chapter not only argues for the underemphasized presence of an existential motif operative in West's work, but critically argues that West tends to suppress the Black revolutionary tradition, which, according to Gordon, constitutes a very significant *fourth* tradition that transcends West's conceptual trinity of Pragmatism, Christianity, and Marxism. Gordon argues that if West were to give adequate attention to the importance of this fourth tradition, this would have profound implications not only for West's work, but for Black intellectual production more generally. Clevis Headley provides a critical evaluation of West's prophetic pragmatism, moving the reader through recent construals of pragmatism, its main themes, West's take on pragmatism, and West's own unique prophetic pragmatism. Headley's conclusion is that West fails to make a plausible case for prophetic pragmatism. Headley also provides an insightful appendix where he contrasts Richard Rorty's neopragmatism with West's attempt to graft prophecy onto pragmatism. Eduardo Mendieta locates the emergence of pragmatism in part as a response to the question: what is the United States or what should it become? In this way, Mendieta's chapter understands West's genealogy of pragmatism not as a project steeped in the history of ideas, but as a normative intervention into the national discourse of what the American Republic ought to be. Mendieta concludes with an exposition of prophetic pragmatism as the embodiment of tragedy; political, existential, and spiritual engagement as committed praxis; anamnestic and historical situatedness; and post-humanist, post-universalistic cosmopolitanism.

Part II, on Philosophy of Religion, opens with James Cone's (partly personal narrative) chapter where he shares his memory of having first met the 24-year-old West and being captivated by his intellectual brilliance. Cone explicates some of the mutual influences that he and West had on each other and some of their shared conclusions. For example, both came to accept that Black theology and the Black church needed Marxism to gain an understanding of various sociopolitical structures that are in need of change. Yet both of them held the conviction that the Black church provided deep cultural and spiritual power to resist. George Yancy's essay maintains that West has yet to explore fully the implications that his historicism and antifoundationalism have for issues of religious truth, religious pluralism, religious experience, and a metaphysically realist conception of God. On Yancy's view, given West's historicism and antifoundationalism, what is to prevent the conclusion that "religious truth" is simply a question of what a particular religious community, steeped in a rich tradition, allows us to say? Yancy draws attention to an overlooked tension between the social constructionist implications of West's historicism and antifoundationalism, and the possibility of a form of Kantian transcendentalism (i.e. God as a noumenal reality) implicit in his work. Victor Anderson's chapter explores the issue of where West stands among the theologians.

Central to Anderson's challenging critique of West is the latter's minimalist conception of transcendence, which, according to Anderson, "tends to identify Christian faith and radical democracy under an ethical reductivism." Even West's acceptance of the Hegelian term *Aufhebung* does not lead to a maximalist conception of God, and tends to reduce Christianity's truths to a calculus of existential satisfaction. For Anderson, this calculus misses the "MORE" that Christian narratives point to and leaves West's religious cultural and social criticism, though open to the divine, with a mere shadow of the divine. M. Shawn Copeland sees West as a gadfly who critically questions certain apolitical tendencies in theology. She situates West within a jazz and blues ontology that affirms life in the very midst of oppression and evil, and she explores what it is that a theologian might find of interest in the work of West. She locates common concerns in terms of "rethinking Christian theological and religious praxis from the side of the victims of history," which creates spaces for political praxis and theological reflection that are subversive and liberatory. Copeland also raises key questions regarding theologians who commit to the critical transformation of the social and cultural racist structures embedded within America. For example, "What might it mean for despised women and men of color to grasp themselves as subjects?" Josiah Young draws upon West's categories of "existential aptness" and "epistemological correctness," maintaining that individual rights to self-expression involve existential aptness and that democratic structures championed by Marxist praxis involve epistemological correctness. Consistent with other liberation theological standpoints, for Young, God plays a significant role in West's project of speaking truth to power. Hence, Young sees West's "theo-praxic" position as counter to the *atheology* of Ludwig A. Feuerbach. Lastly, Young links his concerns with the devastation of the African world within the context of West's exposition of "post-industrial cosmopolitan American culture," where a humane God and a humane form of human interaction have been marginalized.

Part III, on Political Philosophy, begins with Iris Marion Young's diachronic examination of West's recent political writings and how they relate to his earlier more visionary ideology critique. She finds his genealogical materialist prophetic pragmatism to be in tension with his social and political analyses, particularly as set forth in his recent books, *The Future of American Progressivism* (with Roberto Unger) and *The War Against Parents* (with Sylvia Ann Hewlett). Young argues that the program put forward by West and Unger is "thin on policy specifics and tactics for achieving them." From a feminist perspective, Young criticizes West and Hewlett for their retrograde and anti-feminist solutions regarding the family, for they look for "remedies for pressures on parents in a nostalgic idea of family." In Charles Mill's analytically rich essay, he elucidates and analyzes various aspects of West's political philosophy, i.e. prophetic pragmatism, which Mills sees as awkwardly situated "in a standard taxonomy of liberal or conservative, Marxist or Black nationalist" philosophy. Locating tensions in West's "political philosophy,"

against the background of a certain construal of what constitutes political philosophy, Mills wonders about West's prophetic pragmatism, which is not intended to
guide a political movement. Mills insightfully argues with great irony, despite
West's writings on white supremacy, that in West's political corpus there is little
or no analysis of the racial state and the racialization of the economy. John
Pittman's reading of West's *The Ethical Dimensions of Marxist Thought* points out
some of the problematics with West's grafting onto Marx's view his own "radical
historicism." Pittman wonders if West has taken too much interpretative liberty
with Marx. He notes that West's conceptualization of radical historicism "and the
conceptions related to it . . . are conceptions drawn from the 'metaphilosophical'
discourse of the second half of the twentieth century." Pittman feels that applying
these conceptions to Marx's youth, "in the second quarter of the nineteenth
century," indicates an aprioristic dimension in the organizational body of *The
Ethical Dimensions of Marxist Thought.* Examining West's distinction between theory and philosophy, which West sees as key to Marx's radical historicist turn,
Pittman finds slippage in West's philosophical/theoretical bifurcation. He notes
how persistently "what can only be described as philosophical questions seem to
resist West's attempts to outrun them." Lastly, Pittman examines, within the
context of West's appraisal of Frederic Jameson's work, the extent to which West's
attitude to Marxism has shifted. Floyd W. Hayes takes a critical look at West's
article entitled "Nihilism in Black America." Hayes points out that for West the
essential problem facing Black America is *"the nihilistic threat to its very existence."* He
sees West's conceptualization of the Black life-world in nihilistic terms as constituting a narrow and conservative vision. Not that Hayes rejects a form of Afro-
nihilism; rather, he sees this nihilism as a death of faith in the promise of American
democracy. It is not that Black communities are simply plagued by intracommunal criminality, rather, they show outrage against American social injustice.
Finding contradictions and dilemmas in West's ideological leanings, Hayes moves
the reader through Nietzsche, Max Scheler, and Albert Camus to support his
contention that nihilism is "induced by white supremacy and capitalist exploitation
[which] gives rise to *ressentiment*." Lucius Outlaw raises critical hermeneutic questions with regard to interpreting West's work. Through an insightful use of
immanent critique of West's "Black Strivings in a Twilight Civilization," which
also raises issues concerning the "accuracy" and "honesty" of autobiographical
representation, Outlaw argues that West's problem with Du Bois possibly masks
West's own aim to best Du Bois as a more important historical intellectual
endowed with insight into the human condition. Outlaw is also troubled by
West's lack of argument for criteria with regard to what constitutes "the human
condition"; for West claims that Du Bois failed to grasp the ("genuine") absurdity
of "the human condition." Outlaw also offers a challenging critique of West's
assumption that writers such as Dostoyevsky, Turgenev, Leo Tolstoy, Franz Kafka,
and especially Anton Chekhov have a monopoly on the existentially tragic, and of

West's assumption that it was important for Du Bois to have read their works. Furthermore, Outlaw wonders why there is no reciprocal requirement for "Russians and Central European Jews" to read the "*world*-historical works" produced by Black intellectual figures. Howard McGary explores West's political philosophy and his humanist orientation. McGary examines how humanism has been understood in the Renaissance, and how humanism gets defined within modern frameworks like communism and existentialism. He notes that West's humanism champions a (non-atomistic) conception of human autonomy, one based on the existentialist assumption that humans fashion themselves. As a pragmatist, however, as McGary reminds us, West does not argue for the apriority of his brand of humanism. McGary also sees West's active role in the Democratic Socialists of America, and his call for interracial coalitionary politics, as expressive of his humanist framework, though, according to McGary, West does not endorse Frederick Douglass's biological amalgamationism. West's humanism, however, does not result in a form of Black nationalist ideology; for West's humanism does not deem African-American culture superior to all others. On the critical side, McGary faults West for failing to provide "us with compelling reasons for thinking that a humanistic perspective is the only perspective that will allow us to frame laws and policies that will address the needs of all." Indeed, "Why," according to McGary, "are those who believe that we can achieve a more egalitarian and democratic society, by acting from enlightened rational self-interest, wrong?"

Part IV, Cultural Studies, opens with Peniel Joseph's assessment of West's cultural politics within a broader political, theoretical, and cultural context. Joseph argues that West demonstrates a misunderstanding of the Black nationalist tradition, and that West's critique of contemporary Black leadership and intellectuals "effectively silences Black radicalism by ignoring alternative interpretations of Black cultural production in post-industrial American society." He observes that West's critique of so-called "Black nihilism" is devoid of a corresponding critique of the state. Lastly, Joseph compares West's apocalypticism with rapper DMX's discourse and concludes that both espouse a form of political defeatism. Clarence Johnson's chapter understands West as a cultural critic *par excellence* and as one who is sociopolitically moved to alleviate the "numbing crisis" of our time. Part of that crisis has to do with the "Otherization" of people (Blacks, women, Jews, etc.), thus depoliticizing and excluding "their members from so-called mainstream society." According to Johnson (though critical of West's assessment of early Black cultural critics) this is what West's new cultural politics of difference, which is fueled by West's affirmation of all people and his passionate project of expanding the scope of freedom and democracy, attempts to do. At the core of West's new cultural politics of difference, Johnson locates West's *humanism* in both rhetoric and practice. Nada Elia calls into question West's feelings of alienation and his understanding of the Black intellectual as "inescapably" alienated. Though she praises West for both his persistence in fighting against oppression and his intellectual criticality, she critiques his narrow definition of the intellectual, arguing that it "fails to recognize genius outside the elite academy." By deploying the work of Edward Said, where the notion of "exile" suggests greater freedom, Elia maintains that West need not suffer from a sense of existential angst *vis-à-vis* his intellectual status. She says West conflates the terms scholar and intellectual. She believes that in order to come to expand our appreciation of Black intellectualism, we must "change the criteria by which 'intellectualism' is gauged." Elia draws from the work of feminists Nell Painter, bell hooks, and Joy James to support her position that intellectualism and alienation are not synonymous. Taking West to task on the issue of intellectualism is Elia's way of sending "a wake-up call for all our academic leaders of the left."

There is no better way to honor the work of Cornel West. Free of mean-spirited critique, intellectual obscenity, and vulgarity, this text engages in serious inter-textual dialogue. This text also bears the mark of modernity, for it pursues the "treacherous trek of dialogue," and wagers "on the fecund yet potentially poison-ous fruits of fallible inquiry, which require communicative action, risk-ridden conversation, even intimate relation."[42] Lastly, this text is partly the expression of a sort of personal freedom, resulting from following my own pattern of intellectual wonder. As Edward W. Said might say, I have experienced this text as a unique pleasure, a pleasure steeped in the courage not to follow a prescribed path. Within the confines of many philosophy departments, Cornel West is neither studied nor considered as an important *philosophical* figure. Therefore, one must have the courage to see beyond the normative limits of what philosophy departments deem significant, and take the path least traveled. And though this may very well place one in a state of exile, removed from established patterns of academic valuation and canonization, there is great pleasure to be gained from living the life of an intellectual exile.

Notes

1   Cornel West, *Prophetic Fragments* (Grand Rapids, MI: William B. Eerdmans Publishing Company, 1988), p. 271.

2   bell hooks and Cornel West, *Breaking Bread: Insurgent Black Intellectual Life* (Boston: South End Press, 1991), p. 29.

3   Cornel West, *The Cornel West Reader*, ed. Cornel West (New York: Basic Civitas Books, 1999), p. xvii.

4   Fred Lee Hord and Jonathan Scott Lee, *I Am Because We Are: Readings in Black Philosophy* (Amherst, MA: University of Massachusettes Press, 1995), p. 357.

5   Cornel West, *Prophesy Deliverance! An Afro-American Revolutionary Christianity* (Phila-delphia: The Westminster Press, 1982), p. 43.

6   Ibid., pp. 23–4.

7   Richard Shusterman, *Practicing Philosophy: Pragmatism and the Philosophical Life* (New York: Routledge, 1997), p. 17.

8   Cornel West, *Race Matters* (Boston: Beacon Press, 1993), p. x.
9   George M. Frederickson, *The Black Image in the White Mind: The Debate on Afro-American Character and Destiny, 1817–1914* (Hanover, NH: Wesleyan University Press, 1971), p. 279.
10   *The Cornel West Reader*, pp. 83–4.
11   *Prophesy Deliverance!*, p. 62.
12   Ibid., p. 47.
13   *Race Matters*, p. 3.
14   Ibid., p. 86.
15   *I Am Because We Are*, p. 356.
16   Ibid., p. 357.
17   Ruth Frankenberg, *The Social Construction of Whiteness* (Minneapolis: University of Minnesota Press, 1993), pp. 16–17.
18   Cornel West, "Philosophy and the Afro-American experience," *The Philosophical Forum*, 9(2/3), 1977/8, p. 117.
19   George Yancy, *African American Philosophers: 17 Conversations* (New York: Routledge, 1998), pp. 37–8.
20   Ibid., p. 38.
21   *Prophesy Deliverance!*, p. 91.
22   *Race Matters*, p. 99.
23   *The Cornel West Reader*, p. xv.
24   Jessie Carney Smith, *Black Heroes of the Twentieth Century* (Farmington Hills, MI: Gale Research, Inc., 1997), p. 854.
25   *The Cornel West Reader*, p. xvi.
26   Ibid., p. 14.
27   Ibid., p. xvii.
28   *African American Philosophers*, p. 33.
29   *The Cornel West Reader*, pp. xvi–xvii.
30   Cornel West, *Restoring Hope:Conversations on the Future of Black America*, ed. Kelvin Shawn Sealey (Boston: Beacon Press, 1997), p. xii.
31   *The Cornel West Reader*, p. xviii.
32   Ibid., p. xvii.
33   *Breaking Bread*, p. 17.
34   Cornel West, *Keeping Faith: Philosophy and Race in America* (New York: Routledge, 1993), p. xi.
35   *The Cornel West Reader*, p. 171.
36   *Prophetic Fragments*, p. 38.
37   Cornel West, *The American Evasion of Philosophy* (Madison: University of Wisconsin Press, 1989), p. 212.
38   Peter Osborne, *A Critical Sense: Interviews with Intellectuals* (New York: Routledge, 1996), p. 130.
39   *Prophetic Fragments*, p. 122.
40   *The Cornel West Reader*, p. 13.
41   *African American Philosophers*, p. 41.
42   *The Cornel West Reader*, p. xvii.

Part I

Pragmatism

1

Pragmatism Resurgent: A Reading of *The American Evasion of Philosophy*

Hilary W. Putnam

Philosophy recovers itself when it ceases to be a device for dealing with the problems of philosophers, and becomes a method, cultivated by philosophers, for dealing with the problems of men.

John Dewey

I met Cornel West when he was still an undergraduate, at the end of the 1960s. Today those years are often remembered simply as the years of "protest against the Vietnam War," which they were, but they were also much more. They were watershed years in American life. The great civil rights struggles of the early 1960s were only a few years in the past – in fact, only four years separated Martin Luther King's great speech in Washington, DC to a quarter of a million people in 1963 and the public draft refusals of 1967 (and it was at a meeting of the New England Resistance, an organization of draft resisters centered in Boston, that I myself heard the terrible news of King's assassination in 1968). Moreover, the first powerful rumblings of the renewed power and energy of feminist protest were being heard, and at times disturbed even the patriarchy that controlled such radical groups as Students for a Democratic Society (SDS, whose almost wholly male leadership was at times outspokenly contemptuous of the women in the movement). If anything has characterized life in the United States since the 1960s it has been, on the one hand, the sense that irreversible changes have taken place – changes in how "white Anglo-Saxon" Americans are called upon to relate to African-Americans, Hispanics, and other still oppressed groups, changes in how men are called upon to relate to women, and significant changes in the way in which many citizens respond to demands by their government that they support this or that military action or adventure – and, on the other hand, the appearance of a powerful backlash, a backlash that always shouts "this has gone too far," and that seeks to turn back the clock in race relations (by undoing affirmative action) as well as in gender relations, and to enforce the old style of jingoistic "patriotism."

One of the classes that Cornel West took with me in the late sixties, in the middle of the political storms of the time, was a course in Marxism, and this led to a dialogue between us which has continued to this day. (In spring 2000, at the end of my last year at Harvard before retirement, West and I co-taught a course on "Pragmatism and neo-pragmatism," which offered us an opportunity to continue and extend that dialogue in front of more than a hundred students.) In the decades since that dialogue began West has matured from an idealistic undergraduate to one of the most impressive thinkers (as well as one of the most impressive human beings) that I know. His penetrating intelligence, his breadth of knowledge, the brilliance of the connections he draws between the most diverse areas of literature and scholarship are obvious to all who know him. If West wished to be no more than an "ivory tower intellectual," nothing could be easier, given these talents. But West has never forgotten Dewey's injunction to "deal with the problems of men [human beings]" and not simply with "the problems of philosophers." It is in this light that I want to examine West's book-length engagement with the American pragmatist tradition, *The American Evasion of Philosophy*.[1]

As I remember, the book received mostly favorable reviews. But it seems to me that even some of the most favorable reviewers missed just what West achieved – not because the book isn't clear; it could hardly be clearer! – but because its agenda is foreign to the way academic reviewers think (just as John Dewey's was). Consider, for example, the contrast between the two "blurbs" printed on the back cover of the University of Wisconsin's paperback edition of West's text. The blurb by Paul Boyer (a professor of history) seems to me right on target when Boyer writes that "What shines through, throughout the work, is West's firm commitment to a radical vision of philosophic discourse as *inextricably linked to cultural criticism and political engagement*" (emphasis added). Rorty's blurb is equally friendly, but the emphasis is markedly different. Thus Rorty writes, "I believe that *The American Evasion of Philosophy* will be widely read and respectfully reviewed, and that it may well become a standard account of the role of Pragmatism in American thought." Here the emphasis is on the book as, so to speak, an academic *credential*. For what aspiring academic doesn't hope that her book will be "respectfully reviewed" and that it will become "a standard account" of so-and-so? I wish to argue that to see the book in these terms is necessarily to miss its real contribution. For to appreciate any of West's contributions requires just what it requires to appreciate the contributions of the thinkers he writes about and (critically, to be sure) applauds – Emerson, Dewey, James, Du Bois, or Gramsci – namely *to experience the writing as a challenge, a challenge to one's whole mode of life*.

But Why Pragmatism?

It is in part because the American transcendentalist movement of which Emerson was the universally recognized leader *was* in its time seen as a challenge to the personal as well as the collective lives of Americans that West pays so much attention to Emerson. (Even more important is the fact that West finds in Emerson themes which he believes the American Left needs to reincorporate in its philosophical and political vision.) Moreover, West is right to see the classical Pragmatists as "standing, in part, on Emerson's shoulders."[2] Although Stanley Cavell has recently attempted to draw a line in the sand between Emerson (whom he praises as a pure teacher of the individual in search of the betterment of her private soul) and Dewey (whom he patronizes, as a — worthy, to be sure, but hardly unique — social reformer),[3] such a dichotomy is, in my opinion, something that both Dewey and Emerson opposed throughout their respective careers. As the transcendentalist minister O. B. Frothingham later testified,[4] among the transcendentalists, and among those whom the transcendentalist preachers inspired (in 1854):

> The antislavery agitation was felt to be something more than an attempt to apply the Beatitudes and the Parables to a flagrant case of inhumanity — it was regarded as a new interpretation of religion, a fresh declaration of the meaning of the Gospel, a living sign of the purely human character of a divine faith, an education in brotherly love and sacrifice; it was a common saying that now, for the first time in many generations, the essence of belief was made visible and palpable to all men; that Providence was teaching in a most convincing way, and none but deaf ears could fail to understand the message. ... Then, if ever, we ascended the Mount of Vision.

And even more tellingly, Frothingham adds (loc. cit.):

> It was a great experience; not only was religion brought face to face with ethics, but it was identified with ethics. It became a religion of the heart: pity, sympathy, humanity and brotherhood were its essential principles. At the antislavery fairs all sorts and conditions of men met together, without distinction of color or race or sex. There was really an education in the broadest faith, in which dogma, creed, form, and rite were secondary to love, and love was not only universal, but was warm.

Moreover, the living faith, the "original revelation" that Emerson famously called for, was not something felt only in transcendentalist circles: it had meaningful political impact. As Albert Von Frank has recently written,[5] "Without the general encouragement of Transcendentalism, without its assault on institutions or its invitation to subjectivity and authentic action, antislavery might never have been seen as an occasion for religious renewal or become popular on that basis."

It is not particularly hazardous to guess that "an education in the broadest faith, in which dogma, creed, form, and rite [are] secondary to love, and love [is] not only universal, but was warm" is part of what West means by the phrase "prophetic pragmatism" that he uses to designate his personal combination of pragmatist, socialist, and Christian ideas. But West also finds more particular insights and inspirations in both transcendentalism and pragmatism, and particularly in the writings of Ralph Waldo Emerson and John Dewey, insights which he believes the American Left needs to reincorporate in its philosophical and political vision. I shall concentrate on the special contribution of Dewey, as I think both West and I see it.

The Distinctiveness of Pragmatism

When West repeatedly praises pragmatism for "the evasion of epistemology-centered philosophy" he is using the word "epistemology" as a pejorative, just as Dewey did (for instance, in his Presidential Address to the American Philosophical Association in 1905).[6] In epistemology, Dewey said there, "philosophy has dreamed the dream of a knowledge which is other than the propitious outgrowth of beliefs that shall develop aforetime their ulterior implications in order to recast them, to rectify their errors, cultivate their waste places, heal their diseases, fortify their feebleness – the dream of a knowledge that has to do with objects having no nature save to be known." Evidently Dewey associated the term "epistemology" with transcendental epistemology, not just in the technical sense of Kantian epistemology, or the sense of Hegelian epistemology (from which he had made his break known, to James at least, only two years before), or in the sense of Platonic epistemology or Aristotelian epistemology, but more broadly with the whole project of finding indubitable "foundations of knowledge," foundations which, once the philosopher had ascertained them, would permit her to say with unshakeable confidence what could and what could not be known and how to go about knowing it. Even empiricist epistemology, Dewey tells us in *The Quest for Certainty*, has its aprioristic aspect: the empiricist thinks that the form of the *data* (namely, that they are all, in the last analysis, describable in the language of "ideas and impressions," or, to use the term made popular by Russell's writings, the language of "sense data") is fixed once and for all, in advance of investigation, whereas in fact, Dewey teaches, the right language for "instituting" data is one of the hardest things to discover, and one of the things that science constantly revises.

The "evasion of epistemology-centered philosophy" might thus be described, in more familiar language, as the rejection of all foundationalisms and the espousal of a thoroughgoing fallibilism. The term "evasion of philosophy" that West uses (I conjecture that the language reflects his sympathies with Rorty at that time, sympathies which have considerably moderated as Rorty's pronouncements against philosophy have grown increasingly extreme in the more than a decade that has followed) is misleading, however, even with the qualifier "epistemology-centered," because (as West indeed makes clear) there is a topic which is usually lumped under the rubric of "epistemology" which is not only *not* rejected by Dewey, but absolutely central to his enterprise – namely, the topic of *inquiry*. By all accounts, *Logic: The Theory of Inquiry* is a major work – some would consider it Dewey's *magnum opus*, and Ruth Anna Putnam and I, at least, are quite willing to call it "epistemology" even if Dewey wouldn't.[7]

The "theory of inquiry" that Dewey develops as a replacement for the aprioristic and foundationalist epistemologies of both empiricism (I have just explained why Dewey considers empiricism to be marred by apriorism) and rationalism is obviously inspired by the previous writings of Pierce and of James. I myself would say that it involves at least the following four important claims:[8]

1 Knowledge of facts (true singular statements) presupposes knowledge of "theories" (i.e. true statements about what is true in general, or in most cases).
2 Knowledge of "theories" (of what is true in general, or true in most cases) presupposes knowledge of facts.
3 Knowledge of facts presupposes knowledge of values.
4 Knowledge of values presupposes knowledge of facts.[9]

While this is not the place for a detailed explanation of these claims, I *will* say that the reference to "knowledge" in these claims is, of course, a reference to fallible, revisable, but nonetheless "warrantedly assertable" judgments, which is what the theory of inquiry (in Dewey's sense) is concerned with. It will be seen from even these few too-brief remarks that while pragmatism shares with positivism a repudiation of all non-empirical or would-be *trans*-empirical metaphysics, it rejects positivism's sharp fact/value dichotomy. It would not be an exaggeration to say that while both positivism and pragmatism thought there were deep lessons to be learned from the success of the new empirical way of "putting questions to nature" practiced by science from Bacon on, they differed profoundly over what those lessons were. For positivists, the moral of the success of science was that one should try to make every respectable field of inquiry *look like physics*. If that was obviously unrealistic in the case of ethics or aesthetics, that showed that ethics and aesthetics were not really fields of inquiry at all; what we mistakenly take to be "judgments" in ethics and aesthetics are really just expressions of emotion or volition or something of that sort. For pragmatists, the moral (or rather the morals) was quite different. Science succeeded not because it all looks like physics (which it does not, if one actually looks at the motley of the sciences), but because it has learned a number of lessons, particularly the lesson of *fallibilism*, the lesson that the successful pursuit of knowledge involves *cooperation*, and the lesson that that cooperation must provide opportunity to challenge accepted hypotheses by challenging the evidence upon which they were accepted, or by criticizing the application of the norms of scientific inquiry (which must themselves be open to challenge and revision!) to that evidence, or by offering rival hypotheses. And these lessons, pragmatists believe, are just as relevant – indeed, even more crucially relevant – to ethical and political inquiry as they are to natural science. Far from abandoning ethical inquiry as a contradiction in terms, as positivism would have it, we must learn to apply the genuine lessons of the scientific revolution to ethical inquiry, as Dewey argued early and late.

The Distinctiveness of Dewey

What I have written about the distinctiveness of pragmatism applies as much to James's pragmatism or to Mead's or (with an important qualification)[10] to Peirce's as it does to Dewey's. But Dewey is distinctive in other ways, ways which make it natural that he should (in spite of certain shortcomings that West detects in Dewey's political strategies) be an exemplary figure for West. West is, after all, the very opposite of a "compartmentalized" intellectual. Religious (a lay preacher), politically active to an extent that would exhaust a dozen ordinary "political activists," a serious philosopher, West is at the same time a person who refuses to believe that one's literary and aesthetic sensibilities are simply a matter of recreation, something to be kept apart from one's philosophy or one's religion or one's politics. And in these respects he resembles Dewey. Although Dewey lost his Christian faith before his turn from Idealism to pragmatism, he remained someone for whom ideals and the willingness to sacrifice for ideals were central.[11] In *Ethics*, co-authored with Tufts, he could approvingly quote George Eliot in *Romola*:

> It is only a poor sort of happiness that could ever come by caring very much about our own narrow pleasures. We can only have the highest happiness, such as goes along with being a great man, by having wide thoughts and much feeling for the rest of the world as well as ourselves, and this sort of happiness often brings so much pain with it, that we can only tell it from pain by its being what we would choose before everything else, because our souls see it is good.

Again like West, Dewey valued democracy while refusing to shut his eyes to the distance we have to travel if we are to achieve real democracy. For real democracy, Dewey consistently taught, is not just a matter of counting votes; it is the ideal of real participation in the decision-making process by those affected by the decisions to be made, and it requires a new kind of education,[12] a new way of applying intelligence to social problems,[13] and what he called a "democratic faith,"[14] an attitude toward individuals that manifests itself in all of one's personal relations and not just in "public life." In addition, the centrality of aesthetic experience to what we may call Dewey's "philosophical anthropology" is obvious. (My friend Steve Wagner has remarked that Dewey's *Art as Experience* could as well have been named *Experience as Art*.) While there are aspects of Dewey's philosophical anthropology that West finds troubling (he sometimes finds a lack of the sense of the tragic, an insensitivity to the existential dimensions of life, in Dewey), the idea that the philosopher must above all *integrate* and not *compartmentalize* is common to both West and Dewey. Dewey is the supreme example in American life up to the present day that one does not have to choose between being a cultured and sensitive human being, a professional philosopher, and a politically committed public intellectual.

The Purpose of *The American Evasion of Philosophy*

If, then, there are many reasons why West should find the thought and legacy of American pragmatism (as well as, as has been mentioned, Emersonian transcendentalism), and of John Dewey in particular, well worth engaging, it is important to understanding *how* he chose to engage it. Although West is a trained philosopher, he did not choose to write a straight philosophical text, although, as he says, the book certainly "tries to get inside the formulations and arguments of American pragmatists so that the social roles and functions of ideas do not exhaust their existence or curb intellectual curiosity." The method he chose instead, as he tells us, is that of "a social history of ideas" (p. 6). But, as I explained at the outset, that does not mean that he intended to write a merely academic history, although Rorty was not wholly wrong to think the book could be read (and deserves praise) as such a history. The book is a call to arms, an attempt to, as it were, *reissue* the pragmatist challenge, after critically analyzing that challenge.

That West's "social history of ideas" has a political aim is made quite explicit in the Introduction. Thus, after the disclaimer that "The turn to the American heritage – and especially American pragmatism – is neither a panacea for our ills nor a solution to our problems," the author continues (p. 5): "Rather it should be an attempt to reinvigorate our moribund academic life, our lethargic political life, our decadent cultural life, and our chaotic personal lives for the flowering of many-sided personalities and the flourishing of more democracy and freedom."

To briefly describe the book, for those who have not read it: what is unique about *The American Evasion of Philosophy* as a social history of ideas is how widely it casts its net. What West does is to show us how tremendously *influential* Deweyan pragmatism was, how wide and deep an impact it made, especially in the years of Franklin Roosevelt's New Deal, but also during the years that followed – the "Cold War" years. "Influential" does not, however, mean, *successful*. And part of the question West wants us to think about is how a movement could have "influenced" so many prominent thinkers while accomplishing so little of what John Dewey wanted it to achieve. For example, the figures discussed in the chapter titled "The dilemma of the mid-century pragmatic intellectual" – Sydney Hook, C. Wright Mills, W. E. B. Du Bois, Reinhold Niebuhr, Lionel Trilling – were among the most prominent "public intellectuals" of their time, and, as West shows, even those among them who started out by attacking Dewey and what they thought he stood for ended up far more influenced by Dewey than they perhaps themselves appreciated. Indeed, by analyzing a thinker like Niebuhr (or a thinker like C. Wright Mills) in this way, West gives us a far richer vision of his intellectual, personal, even existential, trajectory than I have seen anywhere else.

The fact that all of these thinkers except Du Bois (who ended as a despairing Marxist) became, at least intermittently, "Cold Warriors" shows, however, that the story West is telling is not a success story. It is true that in his Introduction, West tells us (p. 4), "My basic aim in this book is to chart the emergence, development, decline, and resurgence of American pragmatism." The "resurgence" he speaks of here is described in chapter 5, "The decline and resurgence of American pragmatism: W. V. Quine and Richard Rorty." There is no question that Quine is a philosophic genius, and that he owes *some* debt to pragmatism, although, as West rightly points out, "Quine's evasion of modern epistemology[15] is not as thorough as Dewey's. This is so owing to the residues of logical positivism in Quine's monumental breakthrough: namely his ontological allegiance to physics and his need for minimally foundationalist (though radically underdetermined) 'observation sentences' in his Skinnerian behaviorist psychology" (p. 186). But politically, Quine is a conservative (he was extremely hostile to the antiwar protests of the late 1960s, for example), and Rorty is criticized by West for "political narrowness" (p. 207). "Rorty leads philosophy to the complex world of politics and culture, but confines his engagement to the transformation of the academy and to apologetics for the modern West" (p. 207). So the "resurgence" West describes in this chapter is a resurgence of *academic* interest in pragmatism, not a resurgence of pragmatism as a left political force. The latter sort of resurgence remains a hope and a program ("prophetic pragmatism").

Cornel West's Diagnosis of Dewey's Political Ineffectiveness

As Robert Westbrook relates, Dewey arrived to take up his professorship at the University of Chicago in the middle of a great labor struggle, "for he found himself on a train to the city at the height of the Pullman strike." As Westbrook explains, the strike was provoked by a "severe wage cut at the Pullman car works – a cut unaccompanied by any reduction in the rents, food prices, and service rates George Pullman charged his workers in the model company town he had built for them just north of Chicago in the 1880s." The strikers won the support of Eugene Debs's recently formed American Railway Union, while Pullman received the support of the General Managers Association of the twenty-four railroads with Chicago terminals, and "by July the strike had escalated from a local dispute to an effort by these powerful corporate managers to break the union and assert the superior power of capital."[16]

Dewey was whole-heartedly on the side of the strikers,[17] but he published nothing directly in support. As Westbrook describes his stance at the time, "Dewey couched [social criticism] in language carefully designed to avoid giving offense to the powerful."[18]

Cornel West makes a similar remark on Dewey's political caution in this period (p. 83):

> [Dewey] moved in 1894 to John D. Rockefeller's University of Chicago (a move engineered by his friend and former colleague James H. Tufts), where his work in Jane Addams' Hull House became a focus of his activities. From then on, Dewey practiced professional caution and political reticence. He remained deeply engaged in civic affairs, but shunned controversy.

Neither Westbrook nor West suggests that Dewey was actually *co-opted* by the corporate managers, however. West writes, "I am suggesting neither that opportunism motivated Dewey's behavior in Chicago, nor that he lacked the courage of other colleagues. Rather I am claiming that his high-falutin left-Hegelian rhetoric of a few years earlier had simmered back down into professional research and respectable activism" (p. 83). In fact, some of that rhetoric had been anything but "high-falutin." For example, in an article Dewey wrote for the first volume of the *International Journal of Ethics* titled "Moral theory and moral practice" Dewey had written:

> Let us take then a specific case. Here is a streetcar conductor, and the question is whether he should (ought to) join in a strike which his Union has declared.... The man thinks of his special work, with its hardships indeed, and yet a work, an activity, and thus a form of freedom or satisfaction; he thinks of its wage, of what it buys; of his needs, his clothing, his food, his beer and pipe. He thinks of his family...; his need of protecting and helping them on; his children that he would educate and give an evener start in the world than he had himself; he thinks of the families of his fellows; of the need that they should live decently and advance somewhat; he thinks of his bonds to his Union; he calls up the way in which the families of the corporations which employ him live.[19]

Moreover, Dewey was later to position himself conspicuously to the left of the New Deal liberal consensus, as the most prominent intellectual who publicly supported Norman Thomas's Socialist Party.

West *does* take Dewey to task for neglecting Marxism. As West well knows from our conversations, I find his own version of Marxism rather too rosy to be attributed to the actual Marx. Thus, West writes (p. 110): "Dewey remains unable to conceive of Marxism as anything but a 'uniformitarian theory' that 'throws out psychological as well as moral considerations' in the name of 'objective forces.' He goes so far as to say that this is true of 'Marx and every Marxist after him.' This is blatantly false." I would reply "Cornel, you are right that there are Marxists *after* Marx who gave much more weight to psychological and moral considerations (even if, like Lukács, some of them were also able to function as vicious communist functionaries!). But Marx himself was openly hostile to psychology ('I need no psychological premises,' he writes in *The German Ideology*). Moreover, the whole *point* of the laborious mathematical model of capitalism in the third volume of *Capital* is supposedly to show that capitalism must *inevitably* suffer worse and worse economic crises because of, in effect, a mathematical law of 'the falling rate of profit.' I do not find Dewey's take on Marx as an economic determinist at all incorrect." But this it not the place for this conversation, which I am sure West and I will continue to have.

In the end, however, West's central criticism of Dewey – and it is a just one – is that he has no sense of real politics, of a politics that goes beyond gentle persuasion and appeals to good will and enters the arena of actual struggle and confrontation. "The point here is not that Dewey possesses a deep nostalgia for a lost golden age of harmonious *Gemeinschaft*, but rather that he believes that social conflict can be resolved and societal problems overcome by a widely held consensus more characteristic of artisanal towns or farming communities than of industrial cities or urban capitalist societies" (pp. 101–2). And West adds (p. 102):

> This focus does permit Dewey to see more clearly than most – especially his Marxist [*sic*] and liberal contemporaries – the cultural dimensions of the crisis of American civilization, yet it also distorts his view regarding the role of critical intelligence in dislodging and democratizing the economic powers that be. Thus, Dewey's central concern is to extend the experimental method in the natural sciences to the social, political, cultural, and economic spheres *rather than to discern the social forces and historical agents capable of acting on and actualizing (i.e. approximating) his creative democracy*. His relative confinement to the professional and reformist elements of the middle classes makes such discernment unlikely.[20] (Emphasis added)

The sympathetic reference to Dewey's insight into "the cultural dimensions of the crisis" is not accidental. Even in this chapter, West clearly sympathizes with Dewey's aim of "the cultural enrichment and moral development of self-begetting individuals and self-regulating communities by means of the release of human powers provoked by novel circumstances and new challenges" (p. 103), and in the closing chapters the centrality of this aim to West's own prophetic-pragmatist vision becomes ever more clear. Yet he trenchantly summarizes his criticism of Dewey when he writes (p. 107):

> Contrary to popular opinion, Dewey's project never really got off the ground. Like Emerson's moralism, Dewey's culturalism was relatively impotent. Why? Principally because his favored historical agents – the professional and reformist elements of the middle class – were seduced by two strong waves of thought and action: managerial ideologies of corporate liberalism and bureaucratic control, and Marxist ideologies of class struggle.

Dewey *and* Gramsci

The Marxist thinker who, more than any other, is described as an influence on West's own "prophetic pragmatism," especially in the last two chapters of *The American Evasion of Philosophy*, is Antonio Gramsci, and it is of value, I believe, to reflect on the ways in which, in those chapters, West does and does not find him superior to Dewey. Certainly those aspects of Marx's thought that I find reductionist (and whose presence in Marx's thought West seemed to want to deny or at least minimize in a sentence I quoted above) are *not* aspects that West admires in Gramsci. I refer, of course, to the idea of iron laws of history ("laws of motion" of capitalism, for example), or a fatal (and *mathematically* demonstrable) contradiction in the capitalist "mode of production" as such. Gramsci was, to be sure, a "Marxist-Leninist" for all his originality and iconoclasm, and West criticizes him for this. But it is not even Gramsci's *theoretical* revisions of Marxism that West, in the end, values, but rather his innovative conceptions of how one should go about mobilizing popular energies for struggles against oppression, conceptions which do not depend at all on Marxist "supertheory."

West's main discussion of Gramsci begins in the section of the penultimate chapter of the book devoted to Roberto Unger. I want to call attention to this section, because in it, and continuing to the end of the book, we find a much more positive valuation of Dewey than we seemed to find in the earlier chapter (chapter 3) devoted explicitly to Dewey. It is as if West came to appreciate Dewey more and more as he approached the end of the book!

West describes Unger's project as a "third-wave romanticism," a description that he explains thus:

> I shall argue three claims concerning Unger's project. First, I shall suggest that his viewpoint can best be characterized as the most elaborate articulation of a *third-wave left romanticism* now [1989] sweeping across significant segments of principally the first world progressive intelligentsia (or what is left of this progressive intelligentsia!). Second, I will show that this third-wave left romanticism is discursively situated between John Dewey's radical liberal vision of socialism and Antonio Gramsci's

absolute historicist conception of Marxism. Third, I shall highlight the ways in which this provocative project, though an advance beyond much of contemporary social thought, remains inscribed within a Eurocentric and patriarchal discourse that not simply fails to theoretically consider racial and gender forms of subjugation, but also remains silent on the antiracist and feminist dimensions of concrete progressive political struggles.

What West means by speaking of successive "waves" of left romanticism is this: the liberatory rhetoric of Jefferson and Rousseau certainly deserves to be dubbed "romanticism," and it certainly helped to inspire the French and American Revolutions. As West says, "it unleashed unprecedented human energies and powers, significantly transformed selves and societies, and directed immense human desires and hopes towards the grand moral and credible political ideals of democracy and freedom, equality and fraternity" (p. 216). Yet, West tells us, we need to be "disturbed." For first-wave left romanticism also "reinforced and reproduced barbaric practices," including white supremacy, slavery, imperial conquest over indigenous peoples, male supremacy, and "excessive business control and influence over the public interest" as seen in, for example, laws against unions.

The second "wave" of left romanticism, in West's chronology, "is manifest in the two great prophetic and prefigurative North Atlantic figures: Ralph Waldo Emerson and Karl Marx." (Here we should remember that West's Marx is the Marx of the *1844 Manuscripts* and the 1848 *Manifesto*, rather than the author of *Capital* or *The German Ideology*.) This second wave leads to Emersonian ideals of American democracy and to Marxist conceptions of socialism. But here again, West tells us, there was a disturbing side. For, by the end of the Second World War,

> the second wave of left-romanticism began to wane. The dominant version of the Marxist legacy – Marxist-Leninist (and at the time led by Stalin) – was believed by more and more left romantics to be repressive, repulsive and retrograde. And the major mode of the Emersonian legacy – Americanism (led then by Truman and Eisenhower) was viewed by many left romantics as racist, penurious, and hollow. (p. 216)

We see in these paragraphs a certain architectonic, and we are not to be disappointed. Each "wave" is led by two giant figures, and each wave leads to certain disappointment. But since the third wave is only a gleam in Unger's eye, the disappointment is not going to be that it has been played out, or degenerated in a way that reveals that certain shortcomings were there all along. Instead West is going to caution Unger that if he does not improve his views (and his politics) in certain ways the "third wave" *will* inherit the defects of the second. The two figures that West sees Unger as steering between are, as already noted, John Dewey and Antonio Gramsci. And in this entire section, somewhat surprisingly (in the light of what West writes in chapter 3), Unger is consistently criticized for being insufficiently critical of Gramsci and being too neglectful of Dewey (whom Unger has recently come to value as highly as West himself does, by the way). There is no question but that in this section Dewey wins a significant victory over Gramsci.

West's procedure is first to describe Unger's debts to Gramsci in some detail, ending with the sentence: "In short, the major lesson Unger learns from Gramsci is to be a more subtle, nuanced and sensitive supertheorist than Marx by building on elements in Marx and others" (p. 220). (Although this might sound positive, we will soon see that it is "left handed" praise.) This sets the stage for a remarkably laudatory paragraph about Dewey. In the paragraph in question, West first chides Unger: "Dewey is virtually absent in Unger's text.[21] Furthermore, the one reference to Dewey is a rather cryptic and misleading statement." The passage in question is one in which Unger first writes that it is wrong to associate the sort of theory he advocates (Unger calls it "ultratheory") with "Leftist or modernist intellectuals." He asks rhetorically, "Why not John Dewey? (despite the gap between the commitment to institutional experimentalism and the slide into institutional conservatism)."[22]

Here is West's response to this passage:

> This passage is perplexing for three reasons. First, is Unger implying that Dewey was neither a leftist nor a modernist intellectual? Second, is Unger drawing a distinction between his own social experimentalism and Dewey's institutional experimentalism? Third, in what sense and when did Dewey slide into institutional conservatism? If Unger answers the first question in the affirmative, he falls prey to a misinformed stereotypical view of Dewey as a vulgar Americanist. For as we saw earlier, Dewey's sixty-five year political record as a democratic socialist speaks for itself.[23] And no argument is needed for Dewey's being a modernist intellectual when he stands as the major secular intellectual of twentieth-century America. If Unger is making a distinction between his form of experimentalism and that of Dewey, its validity remains unclear unless one remains fixated on Dewey's educational reform movement and neglects the broader calls for fundamental social change put forward during the years Dewey concentrated on progressive education as well as afterward, in the late twenties, thirties, and forties. And the implausible notion that Dewey slid into institutional conservatism holds only if one wrongly views his brand of anti-Stalinism in the forties as conservatism, for his critique of American society remained relentless to the end.

This is all-out defense of Dewey (not to say fulsome praise)! And the praise continues: after two more paragraphs of praise of Dewey's "linkage of scientific attitude (as opposed to scientific method) to democracy as a way of life," Dewey's insistence on "respect for the other and accountability as a condition for fallibility," and his admonition to use theories "as any other instruments or weapons we have, and to use them when they serve our purposes and criticize or discard them when they utterly fail us," West delivers the *coup de grace*: "The significant difference between Gramsci and Dewey is not that the former accepts Marxist theory and the latter rejects it, but rather that *Gramsci tenaciously holds onto Marxist theory in those areas where it fails, e.g., politics and culture.* Dewey accepted much of the validity of Marxist theory, and simply limited its explanatory scope and rejected its imperial, monistic, and dogmatic versions" (p. 221).

Ten pages later, however (in a different section of this chapter), we get an appreciation of what West sees as the positive contribution of Gramsci. What seems most important to West is that Gramsci demanded that left intellectuals give up their elitist contempt for all ways of thinking that are not secularized through and through.[24] West gives this demand his own ringing endorsement. West condemns the "arrogant scientistic self-privileging or haughty secular self-images of many modern thinkers and intellectuals," and continues (p. 232):

> The point here is not that serious contemporary thinkers should surrender their critical intelligence; but rather that they should not demand that all peoples mimic their version of critical intelligence, especially if common efforts for social change can be strengthened. . . . For Gramsci, ideologies of secularism or religion are less sets of beliefs and values, attitudes and sensibilities and more ways of life and ways of struggle manufactured and mobilized by certain sectors of the population in order to legitimate and preserve their social, political, and intellectual powers. Hence the universities and churches, schools and synagogues, mass media and mosques become crucial terrain for ideological and political contestation.

West goes on to write that philosophers are not exempt from "this fierce battle," even within the walls of the university; a thought that was not alien to Emerson or James or Dewey. West makes the comparison explicitly, when he writes (loc. cit.) that "Similar to the American pragmatist tradition, Gramsci simply suggests that philosophers more consciously position these battles themselves as objects of investigation and thereby intervene in these battles with intellectual integrity and ideological honesty."

What Cornel West Means by "Prophetic Pragmatism"

Up to this point – the middle of page 232 – West has proceeded as he said he would, by the method of a "social history of ideas." Since only seven and a half pages remain in the book, it is clear that this history – and the critical comments that West has made throughout his attempt to "chart the emergence, development, decline, and resurgence of American pragmatism" – is supposed to carry the burden of telling the political lessons that West wants the reader to learn. The book is not at attempt to sell a very specific program, and indeed West tells us that "There is – and should be – no such thing as a prophetic pragmatist movement" (p. 232). Nevertheless, its aim is to "inspire progressive and prophetic social motion" (p. 234). These final seven and a half pages, brief as they are, are clearly the point at which *The American Evasion of Philosophy* draws morals and recommendations from its "social history of ideas."

I have already remarked that the "resurgence" of pragmatism in the story that West tells is, paradoxically, more a resurgence in the academy than in America's political life, and this is clearly something that he wants to change. If we review the positives and negatives in the history as West has told it, the bottom line might look something like this (I omit many central figures in West's story in this summing up, in order to highlight what seem to me to be the main conclusions of the story as a whole):

Emerson: West sympathizes with what he in one place (p. 216) describes as the "Emersonian themes of the centrality of the self's morally laden transformative vocation; the necessity of experimentation to achieve the self's aims of self-mastery and kinship with nature; and, the importance of self-creation and self-authorization." But he also tells us (p. 212) that Emerson's concerns with "power, provocation, and personality" need to be rechanneled "through Dewey's conception of creative democracy and Du Bois' social structural analysis of the limits of capitalist democracy." In short, West shares Emerson's sense that human individuals have Promethean possibilities. He sees Emerson as a figure who was "unable to engage honestly in sustained activities with agitators or reformers" (p. 22), but he is aware of the way in which transcendentalism was able (as we saw above), if only for a short time, to unleash moral energies to extraordinary effect. West, like Unger, thinks that leftist politics must value human aspirations to self-creation and self-realization, not denigrate or despise them as "petty bourgeois."

If we modify Emerson by thinking in Deweyan terms of a whole *culture* of creative democracy, then, West tells us (p. 212), the first step is to give some sense of the process by which it can be created. Here West builds on what he perceives as Emerson's *anti-foundationalism.* As West interprets him (pp. 212–13), Emerson sees the traditional philosopher's belief in formal thought, foundations, certainty as a way of creating detached abstractions "which command their creators and thereby constrain their creators' freedom." "This consequence is both anti-libertarian and antidemocratic," West writes, "in that human potential and participation are suppressed in the name of philosophic truth and knowledge." Thus Emerson sets the stage for Dewey's strategy of connecting the rejection of apriorisms of all kind with the valorization of democracy. The positive aim is to be (p. 213), "a society and a culture where politically adjudicated forms of knowledge are produced in which human participation is encouraged and for which human personalities are enhanced. Social experimentation is the basic norm, yet it is operative only when

those who must suffer the consequences have effective control over the institutions that yield the consequences, i.e., access to decision-making processes."

Not only must Emerson's important insights – his optimism about the Promethean potentialities of human beings, his anticonformity, his antifoundationalism – be rendered political by being set in the framework of Deweyan aspirations for creative democracy, but they must also "confront candidly the tragic sense found in Hook and Trilling" (p. 212). What West means by this, if I am not mistaken, is that "Promethean possibilities" include Promethean potentialities for evil as well as good, and that a realistic left must never fall into the error of imagining that human beings can or ever will be angelic beings. (I hope that West will sometime write at more length about just how – and how far – he views the Christian emphasis on our "fallen" condition as compatible with Emerson's calls for self-realization and self-empowerment.)

Dewey: since most of this chapter has been about West's reading of Dewey, I can be brief. I have emphasized that in the course of *The American Evasion* West's appreciation of Dewey as a man and as a thinker obviously grows; but an important criticism still remains. That criticism is that Dewey *called* for social change from below but did not, in fact, pay any real attention to that "below," to mass movements and political developments outside of the white American middle class. The moral is clear!

Du Bois: Du Bois (who received an honors degree in philosophy at Harvard in 1890) was strongly influenced by James. The influence of pragmatism was joined by the influence of Marxism especially after the Russian Revolution. In West's beautiful words, "Du Bois provides American pragmatism with what it sorely lacks: an international perspective on the impetus and impediments to individuality and radical democracy, a perspective that highlights the plight of the wretched of the earth, namely the majority of humanity who own no property or wealth, participate in no democratic arrangements, and whose individualities are crushed by hard labor and harsh living conditions" (p. 148). And after showing how Du Bois is superior in this respect to James ("who did not see social structures, only individuals"), Dewey (who "saw social structures and individuals yet primarily through an American lens"), Hook (whose "cold war sentiments give a tunnel vision of the third world as a playground for the two superpowers"), and C. Wright Mills (who comes closer, but for whom "postmodern historical agency resides almost exclusively in the Western (or Westernized) intelligensia"), West writes that "Du Bois goes beyond them all in the scope and depth of his vision: creative powers reside among the wretched of the earth even in their subjugation, and the fragile structures of democracy in the world depend, in large part, on how these powers are ultimately exercised."

In the end, however, after suffering tremendous persecution during the McCarthy years, Du Bois gave up all hope that racism in American could ever be overcome (he died in 1963, the very day that Martin Luther King delivered the

"I have a dream" speech). Obviously, West has *not* given up hope; yet he soberly concludes the section on Du Bois with the words: "though Du Bois may have lost his own ideological 'sight' owing greatly to national neglect and limited political options, there is no doubt that what he did 'see' remains a major obstacle for an Emersonian culture of radical democracy in America."

Quine and Rorty: As we have seen, Quine is valued by West not for his politics but for his contribution to the overthrow of foundationalism and apriorism in all their forms. Surprisingly (and I believe West has subsequently revised this estimate), so is Rorty: "Rorty strikes a death blow to modern North Atlantic philosophy" (p. 201).

Gramsci: Gramsci sees the need to bring political struggle into the church (West adds the synagogue and the mosque), and, indeed, into all cultural forms and institutions, especially popular ones. In late twentieth-century America, the example of Martin Luther King, Jr, was a powerful example of how a religious figure who spoke the language of prophecy (not in the sense of prediction,[25] but in the sense in which the transcendentalist sermons that Albert Von Frank describes might be said to have spoken the language of prophecy) – the language of moral vision and absolute moral exhortation – can have enormous political impact and mobilize undreamed of popular energies. Moreover, as a Christian thinker, West can say that, "unlike Gramsci, I am religious not simply for political aims, but also by personal commitment." He adds, "Needless to say, without the addition of modern interpretations of racial and gender equality, tolerance, and democracy, much of the tradition warrants rejection. Yet the Christian epic, stripped of static dogmas and decrepit doctrines, remains a rich source of existential empowerment and political engagement when viewed through modern lenses (indeed, the only ones we moderns have!)" (p. 233).

When we put together the lessons that West has drawn in the course of telling this story, we already get a picture of what he describes as his own prophetic pragmatism, namely a "democratic faith" that resembles Dewey's but goes beyond it in both existential depth and political consciousness. I will close with one more quotation from *The American Evasion of Philosophy*, because I want to give West the last word. But before this quotation, let me say my own "last word" on this book: what West has produced is obviously an extraordinary work, personal and political at once (in keeping with the Emersonian idea that any politics worthy of the name must be personal), one which connects in its large sweep the history of the rise and decline of America's most promising intellectual movement to date and a program for its "resurgence," and which concludes with what I can only call an act of "witness" to a democratic faith. If much of the story is cautionary, at the end of the day it is for us who share that faith to heed those cautions as we add our own acts of witness to West's.

Here is my last quotation (pp. 233–4):

on the political level, the culture of the wretched of the earth is deeply religious. To be in solidarity with them requires not only an acknowledgment of what they are up against but also an appreciation of how they cope with their situation. This appreciation does not require that one be religious; but if one is religious, one has wider access into their life-worlds. This appreciation also does not entail an uncritical acceptance of religious narratives, their interpretations, or, most important, their often oppressive consequences. Yet to be religious permits one to devote one's life to accepting the prophetic and progressive potential within those traditions that shape the everyday practices and deeply held perspectives of most oppressed peoples. What a wonderful privilege and vocation this is!

Notes

1   *The American Evasion of Philosophy* (Madison: University of Wisconsin Press, 1989).
2   *The American Evasion*, p. 6.
3   "What's the use of calling Emerson a pragmatist?" In Morris Dickstein (ed.), *The Revival of American Pragmatism* (Durham, NC: Duke University Press, 1998).
4   O. B. Frothingham, *Recollections and Impressions, 1822–1891* (New York, 1891), pp. 49–50 (cited in Albert J. Von Frank, *The Trial of Anthony Burns* (Cambridge, MA: Harvard University Press, 1999), who gives no publisher).
5   In *The Trial of Anthony Burns*, p. 268.
6   "Beliefs and existences [beliefs and realities]." In Jo Ann Boydston (ed.), *The Middle Works of John Dewey, volume 3* (Carbondale: Southern Illinois University Press, 1977).
7   See Hilary Putnam and Ruth Anna Putnam, "Dewey's *Logic:* epistemology as hypothesis." In Hilary Putnam, *Words and Life* (Cambridge, MA: Harvard University Press, 1994).
8   See my *Pragmatism: An Open Question* (Oxford: Blackwell, 1995), p. 14.
9   For an explanation of why pragmatists accept (3) and (4) see, in addition to the work cited in the previous note, my "Pragmatism and moral objectivity" in *Words and Life*.
10 The important qualification referred to is that Peirce, at least in certain moods, did not think that one should apply reasoning to practical decisions of a moral, religious, or political nature. Here, he thought, one should rely on sentiment and tradition, especially the latter.
11 John Dewey, *Ethics* (1908), volume 5 in Jo Ann Boydston (ed.), *The Middle Works of John Dewey* (Carbondale: Southern Illinois University Press, 1975).
12 On Dewey's educational philosophy, see Hilary Putnam and Ruth Anna Putnam, "Education for democracy" in *Words and Life*.
13 See Hilary Putnam, "A reconsideration of Deweyan democracy." In *Renewing Philosophy* (Cambridge, MA: Harvard University Press, 1992).
14 See Dewey's *A Common Faith* (1934), volume 9 in Jo Ann Boydston (ed.), *The Later Works of John Dewey* (Carbondale: Southern Illinois University Press, 1986), particularly pp. 35 and 58. See also p. 428 in Westbrook, *John Dewey and American Democracy*.

15 Here it is important to remember the special (and pejorative) Deweyan inflection of the word "epistemology" in *The American Evasion of Philosophy*.

16 Robert B. Westbrook, *John Dewey and American Democracy* (Ithaca, NY: Cornell University Press, 1991), p. 86.

17 See ibid., pp. 86–8.

18 Ibid., p. 91.

19 John Dewey, "Moral theory and practice." *International Journal of Ethics*, 1, 1891, p. 191; reprinted in Jo Ann Boydston (ed.), *The Early Works of John Dewey, volume 3* (Carbondale: Southern Illinois University Press, 1969). In *Ethics* (1908), pp. 450–1, Dewey again makes his sympathy with labor and the unions very clear.

20 Yet, when West comes to examine Dewey's writing about Marxism and Stalinism at the end of the chapter from which I have been quoting (chapter 3), he makes it clear that if Dewey had an unrealistic view of the social forces capable of actualizing his project, that does not mean that he had an unrealistic view of the forces opposed to it: "Dewey is often accused of either assuming a pluralist-interactionist view of society that overlooks the larger structural forms of power or promoting an explanatory nihilism that fails to give more weight to one factor over another, and therefore yields no explanation. I think Dewey is innocent of both charges. In fact Dewey approaches Marxism in highlighting the economic, though he is actually closer to Charles Beard's Madisonian economic determinism than that of Marx" (p. 110).

21 The text West quotes from is Roberto M. Unger, *Politics – A Work in Constructive Social Theory* (Cambridge: Cambridge University Press, 1987).

22 Unger, *Politics*, p. 237.

23 What West wrote earlier was that "it seems that Dewey adopted this label ['socialist'] more by default than by choice" (p. 103).

24 West also writes that "Gramsci's work is historically specific, theoretically engaging, and politically activistic in an exemplary manner." This may seem hard to square with the statement only ten pages earlier that "Gramsci tenaciously holds onto Marxist theory in those areas where it fails, e.g., politics and culture," but I think that the contradiction is only apparent; different sorts of theory are involved. The "theory" that Gramsci is criticized for tenaciously holding on to is Marxism-Leninism; but the historically specific analyses that ground Gramsci's recommendations for political activism do not presuppose "industrial strength" Marxism-Leninism, but only the sensitivity to questions of economic power that we also find in Dewey.

25 James Kugel points out that "prediction" is not what the biblical prophets typically or primarily engaged in either! See his *The Great Poems of the Bible* (New York: The Free Press, 1999), pp. 107–28.

2

The Unacknowledged Fourth Tradition: An Essay on Nihilism, Decadence, and the Black Intellectual Tradition in the Existential Pragmatic Thought of Cornel West

Lewis R. Gordon

Several years ago, I was a graduate student in the world of academic philosophy. That world, in spite of the many wonderful intellectual challenges it offered, was an isolating world under the cold, wintery daylight of white normativity. Whiteness pervaded that world in every direction – in teachers, in course texts, and in the majority of the students. The result was a dizzying atmosphere of selective vision. To be a Black graduate student in philosophy requires constant suspension of the contradictory reality that pervades one's world: to study with people the majority of whom ultimately refuse to see you; to learn to write texts that may be read if and only if it is not made known that you have written them; to study with many people who ultimately consider your venture into the life of the mind to be illegitimate. I was fortunate in my career to have had several teachers who were not that way, but at the time of being a graduate student, that reality was not readily apparent beyond the wonderful, committed spirit of my mentor, Maurice Alexander Natanson. Company was needed beyond the social world that mirrored my white colleagues' and my white teachers' realities as *reality*. As most graduate students are wont to do, I enjoyed the practice of perusing bookstores for recently published developments in my fields. In Book Haven, the special kind of "serious readers" bookstore that tends to pop up in college communities here and there, I was often assured surprises. One day, that surprise came in the form of four important texts: *Prophesy Deliverance!*, *Post-Analytical Philosophy*, *Prophetic Fragments*, and *The American Evasion of Philosophy*. I looked at the back of *Prophetic Fragments* and was immediately struck by an image that was to become iconic in American public intellectual life: a slender Black man with a goatee, an Afro, large glasses, and a black three-piece suit. Strange attire for such a young Brother, I thought. It was clear to me that the Brother was trying to look *old*, and in subsequent years, as we met here and there, it became clear that he was paradoxically a youthful elder, an old spirit, as they are wont to say about sages in traditional African religions such as among the Akan. As I read through the pages of each of those books, their author's name burned its way into my memory, into that special file catalogued as *extremely important:* Cornel West.

I ended up advising a senior essay at Yale on Cornel West's thought. The young lady who wrote the thesis was enthusiastic and energetic, and she managed to achieve high honors for the work that required her working through a variety of metaphilosophical and contemporary political issues. It was during that period that West came out with a spate of writings that catapulted him to superstar status and the unfortunate position of someone more seen than heard and understood. Readers of this volume are no doubt familiar with the enthusiastic responses of many fans who have heard West speak. They speak of being moved; they speak of West's charisma; they speak of his eloquence. But when asked about the content of his speeches, they provide seldom a word and often lack a single clue.

In a Forest of Minds

West is an unusual mind. By "mind" I also mean here the presence of a person. There are people whose presence is such that they permeate their environment in a positive way. Think of how the world is lived, for instance, through the ongoing presence of a loved one. His or her eventual absence marks a transformation of the world. Every crevice, every artifact, every building is marked by an absence of that spirit. When people live in their environments negatively, their presence could be compared to a cancerous growth eating away at the social world to the point of a barren landscape. They are people who take the "there" out of places, as Virginia Woolf might say. When such people permeate places, the result is claustrophobic. With them and their ego there is no, in a word, room. West is of the opposite type. He is one of those rare souls whose permeation of a room, an auditorium, or a campus is patently *inclusive*. There is always room for others, signaled not only by his warm, inviting smile, but also by the enthusiastic attention of his eyes and the odd gait of his embodiment – one that never pushes away but always says "welcome." It is perhaps the ecumenicism of his very being that is a source of the most problematic dimensions of his thought; can one really welcome Sista Souljah (the African-American hip hop activist and critic) and Brother David Duke (the Klansman politician) without suppressing one's critical resources or worse: failing to admit, in the end, that there *is* evil in the world and that there is a good versus a bad position to take?

Decadence

In the literature of praise and criticism of West, there emerges, as well, concern for assessment and classification. What is he, by way of intellectual tradition? There is a mistaken view of his work connected, no doubt, to several fallacious tendencies in American thought. The first one is premised on the tendency to subordinate a Black intellectual to whatever *white* thinker he or she studies. Thus, it becomes nearly impossible for Black thinkers to comment on, say, Hegel, Nietzsche, Heidegger, Sartre, or Foucault without being considered Hegelian, Nietzschean, Heideggerian, Sartrean, or Foucauldian. At the heart of this tendency is the credo that white thinkers bring thought to what Black thinkers are struggling through. And what do Black thinkers bring? In a word, *experience*.[1] Because Black intellectual production is pushed to the wayside as nontheoretical, the search, then, for, say, an authentic American philosophy collapses into a search for white upsurges of philosophical reflection. The standard candidate that emerges is American pragmatism. I say "American" because it is often forgotten that pragmatism was a movement in other countries as well – for example, England, as found in the work of F. C. S. Schiller.[2] American pragmatism dominates American intellectual history as the authentic American philosophy to the point of a collapse of consequence and cause: one studies pragmatism because it is supposedly the authentic American philosophy, one studies the authentic American philosophy because it is supposedly pragmatic. West took on the study of pragmatism, as is well known among the growing group of scholars who might also be called "West scholars," because he saw it as a fundamental dimension of American valuative life which as a consequence must be addressed in any search for the transformation of American society. What is more, his efforts in this regard led to his articulation of *prophetic pragmatism*, which made its way full swing into American intellectual history by the time of his *The American Evasion of Philosophy: A Genealogy of Pragmatism*.[3] For some readers, this route made all the sense in the world because it was laying foundations for the *American* dimension of African-American philosophy – to the point where it seemed inconceivable to talk of African-American philosophy as anything other than a form of pragmatism.[4] The consequence was twofold: West has to be a pragmatist because he is an American; and he has to be a pragmatist because he has devoted so much attention to pragmatism in his writings, including coining a new form in the literature.

The odd thing is that when one actually reads West's sources of valuative inspiration, they are hardly pragmatic ones. Like that of Richard Rorty, who exercised much influence on his ideas, West's inspiration is patently existential. Rorty, however, wants to be so American that he fails to see the implications of wedding a European philosopher like Heidegger to John Dewey and working through a European literary figure like Nabokov to establish his claims (why couldn't Faulkner, Wright, or Ellison do?). Readers of Rorty should try, for a moment, to read Richard Rorty's recent *Philosophy and Social Hope* from an existential perspective and ask themselves why recent pragmatism seems to look more like existentialism than pragmatism.[5] The power and consistency of West's thought is that he has been aware of the existential roots of his project from his early works onward. In his own words from George Yancy's interview of him in *African American Philosophers*:

> I think early on I was just in some sense seized by a certain kind of terror that struck me as being at the heart of things human and a profound sadness and sorrow that struck me as being at the core of the human condition. And so in reading Kierkegaard from the Bookmobile, and here was someone who was seriously and substantively wrestling with a certain level of melancholia, I was struck by his very honest and candid – I want to stress candid – encounter with what he understood to be this terror, this suffering, and this sadness and sorrow.[6]

When asked about the impact of Kierkegaard on his later philosophical development, he responded:

> I think that it was decisive. It gave me a profoundly Kierkegaardian sensibility that required then that philosophizing be linked to the existentially concrete situations, wrestling with decision, commitment, actualized possibility and realized potential. And so I tended then to have a deep suspicion of what Arthur Schopenhauer calls "university philosophy" or "academic philosophy" that tended to be so much concerned with abstract concepts and forms of universalizing and always in track of necessity as opposed to the concrete, the particular, the existential, the suffering beings, and the loving beings that we are and can be. You have to realize that I was coming out of the church. . . . So in that sense I think that the Black church and its profound stress on the concrete and the particular – wrestling with limit-situations, with death, dread, despair, disappointment, disease, and so on – has been influential on my Kierkegaardian outlook. (p. 33)

The motif of "death, dread, despair, disappointment, and disease" is a constant feature of West's thought.[7] It is clear that West is guided more by the lived reality of these features of late twentieth-century American society than by the ideology of philosophical nationalism. That reality situates him as an existential pragmatist, which in the end questions the supremacy of pragmatism in his thought. A pragmatic existentialist would, for example, center pragmatism and thus render problems of existence *pragmatic*. In the existential pragmatist designation, pragmatism is advanced as an *existential* encounter. Look at how West describes pragmatism in his work from the late 1980s and early 1990s. In *The American Evasion of Philosophy*, he writes:

> My own version of prophetic pragmatism is situated within the Christian tradition. Unlike Gramsci, I am religious not simply for political aims but also by personal commitment. To put it crudely, I find existential sustenance in many of the narratives in the biblical scriptures as interpreted by streams in the Christian heritage.[8]

He adds:

> My kind of prophetic pragmatism is located in the Christian tradition for two basic reasons. First, on the existential level, the self-understanding and self-identity that flow from this tradition's insights into the crises and traumas of life are indispensable *for me* to remain sane. It holds at bay the sheer absurdity so evident in life, without erasing or eliding the tragedy of life. Like Kierkegaard, whose reflections on Christian faith were so profound yet often so frustrating, I do not think it possible to put forward rational defenses of one's faith that verify its veracity or even persuade one's critics. Yet it is possible to convey to others the sense of deep emptiness and pervasive meaninglessness one feels if one is not critically aligned with an enabling tradition. One risks not logical inconsistency but actual insanity; the issue is not reason or irrationality but life or death.[9]

Four years later, he declares:

> Prophetic criticism rests on what I understand to be the best of Euro-American modernity – the existential imperative to institutionalize critiques of illegitimate authority and arbitrary uses of power; a bestowal of dignity, grandeur and tragedy on the ordinary lives of everyday people; and an experimental form of life that highlights curiosity, wonder, contingency, adventure, danger and, most importantly, improvisation.... Chekov's drama of the everyday and Kierkegaard's unique Christian perspective, are exemplary European expressions of the personal aspects of existential democracy.[10]

In the final quotation, where his existential pragmatism exemplifies a commitment to "existential democracy," we see a feature of West's thought that will be of concern throughout this chapter. In spite of West's existential struggle for the soul of Black humanity, his thought carries great resistance to the normative force of

Black ideas. Existential foundations are for him a patently *European* phenomenon and consequently an understanding drawn from Euro-American reality. On the positive side, it suggests a realization that pragmatism cannot, then, be the only source of American philosophy. But on the negative side, there is a failure here to recognize the impact of Africana existential challenges without European dependence. Struggles over existence and existential dimensions of struggles against oppression both preceded and were exemplified in the thought of Black folks prior to and throughout encounters with Europeans.[11] The tendency to keep both existentialism and pragmatism "Euro," which renders contemporary Africana innovations as Black adaptations, creates some serious misrepresentations of Black intellectual history and a failure to explore some creative possibilities in West's thought.

West's existential proclivities emerge most poignantly in his discussion of nihilism in his 1994 bestseller *Race Matters*, although the theme has been a subtext of all his work: "The liberal/conservative discussion conceals the most basic issue now facing black America: *the nihilistic threat to its very existence*."[12] The theme of nihilism raises anew the question of what type of existentialism is West's prophetic existential pragmatism. Although Kierkegaardian influences are explicit, the theme would at first suggest possible Nietzschean influences. To some extent that would be possible insofar as there is some affinity between Nietzsche and Kierkegaard on a particular dimension of nihilism that they both abhor: its leveling tendencies. For Kierkegaard and Nietzsche, the value of equality nurtures a disastrous, leveling cancer that eats at the human spirit and serves as a harbinger of a passionless world.[13] West is, however, right for placing his bets with Kierkegaard, for Kierkegaard saw redemption in Christ, and since West is a Christian, the affinity is obvious. Nietzsche, however, regarded Christianity as a manifestation of values born of decadence, the inevitable consequence of which is nihilism. Equality, or at least its value, is after all a hallmark of the modern age, and it makes perfect sense why West – a philosopher struggling with issues pertaining primarily to people whose ancestors were slaves and who are dealing with legacies of slavery and US apartheid – adheres to the value of equality in his conceptions of freedom; what would a struggle against slavery be without such values? The result is a conception of nihilism that Nietzsche would find absurd: "Nihilism is to be understood here not as a philosophic doctrine that there are no rational grounds for legitimate standards or authority; it is, far more, the lived experience of coping with a life of horrifying meaninglessness, hopelessness, and (most important) lovelessness."[14] It would be absurd for Nietzsche because it is guided by the project of achieving an eventual victory of the values that cultivate nihilism in the first place. That is why "lovelessness" is a most important feature for West, even though an equally distributed love hardly stands as the most valuable; it is a political love that affords a dignity premised upon equality. Thus, even if the equality sought by West were achieved, the irony is that, if Nietzsche is right, the problem of nihilism would be intensified. The result has many reasons. A Black person who desires to be *equal* to whites is, in the end, as Frantz Fanon has shown in *Black Skin, White Masks*, pathetic.[15] The damage achieved by racism is such that even equality may not be enough. A more complex response is needed. Ironically, Nietzsche offers some insight into this response:

> Nihilism. It is *ambiguous*:
>   A. Nihilism as a sign of increased power of the spirit: as *active* nihilism.
>   B. Nihilism as decline and recession of the power of the spirit: as *passive* nihilism.[16]

Passive nihilism renders Black people reactive. A response that involves setting up whites as the measure of equality to be achieved leads to a bittersweet victory, an equality that loses on two counts: (a) it centers whites as the source of value that occasions Black value by raising Blacks "up" to whiteness; and (b) it renders a degenerate category ("whiteness") as worthy of equality. In the end, is not the true desire to be *better* than whites? But if whiteness is a function of degeneracy – decay, or better, *decadence* – then at the heart of whiteness is a separate but equal form of equality, which renders whiteness, as well, nihilistic. If this is correct, then active nihilism, as a response to racism/passive nihilism, is constituted by acts that render whiteness meaningless and consequently not worthy of Black equality. But to do so would be *reactive*. The active response, then, would be acts that chip away at whiteness as value; it requires rejecting not only whiteness, but also the value of equality with whites. Since inferiority to whites is untenable as a healthy value (passive nihilism), a value superior to whiteness is needed, a value that renders whites, in the end, irrelevant.[17] Such an analysis, from Nietzsche's point of view, hinges upon recognition of the values that are a consequence of decadence, not its cause.[18] It requires taking a position that would be too harsh for West, who has great faith in American society, and it is this: that American society is in decay, is decadent, and that what he analyzes as a condition of Black life in America is in reality symptomatic of American society in general – a society in decay and as a consequence nihilistic. A look at Nietzsche's reflections on decadence in *The Will to Power* is a striking, opposing mirror of West's portrait of the nihilistic threat:

> *The concept of decadence.* – Waste, decay, elimination need not be condemned: they are necessary consequences of life, of the growth of life. The phenomenon of decadence is as necessary as any increase and advance of life: one is in no position to abolish it. Reason demands, on the contrary, that we do justice to it.
>   It is a disgrace for all socialist systematizers that they suppose there could be circumstances – social combinations – in which vice, disease, prostitution, distress would no longer grow. – But that means condemning life. – A society is not free to

remain young. And even at the height of its strength it has to form refuse and waste materials. The more energetically and boldly it advances, the richer it will be in the failures and deformities, the closer to decline. – Age is not abolished by means of institutions. Neither is disease. Nor vice.

Basic insight regarding the nature of decadence: *its supposed causes are its consequences.* (p. 25)

The fact that decay pervades American society leaves no room for an optimism that is not paradoxically a nihilism. Americanism sold its soul to a form of mass consciousness that makes the most rigorous formulation of its ethos, simply put, this: freedom to be as mediocre as the majority of those in power have had the luxury of being. If one thinks about the debate over affirmative action from the perspective of many Blacks, this credo is all too true: justice is a matter of no longer having to be twice – and at times four times – as good as whites for the sake of equal treatment; thus genuine achievement of affirmative action would be opportunities, as well, for mediocre Blacks. That is why the myth of "underqualification" is so precious in many white communities; it enables them to hide from their own mediocrity. The best response is not optimism but active nihilism. Ironically, such a position has been a feature of African-American thought for more than a century. It is called "double consciousness." It is an awareness of American society from an active recognition of what it cannot achieve. It is what has for more than a century haunted the consciousness of whites in America – an awareness deep down that from the standpoint of most Black Americans, whites suffer from the naivete of arrogance and the false belief that their epistemic condition is, in a word, ontological.

West's political predilections are such that these Nietzschean possibilities may be unpalatable for him. The irony here is that in spite of Nietzsche's anti-Black racism (he considered it degrading to seek recognition from Blacks), his counsel would require West's taking seriously the Black intellectual tradition as a manifestation of active nihilism against white supremacy (passive nihilism).[19] Oddly enough, when West appeals to that tradition, it is primarily as a reactive one. For example:

New world African modernity attempts to institutionalize critiques of white-supremacist authority and racist uses of power, to bestow dignity, grandeur and tragedy upon the denigrated lives of ordinary black people and to promote improvisational life-strategies of love and joy in black life-worlds of radical and brutish contingency. . . . Billie Holiday's artistic sensibility and Howard Thurman's religious sentiments are exemplary New World African expressions of the personal aspects of existential democracy. W. E. B. Du Bois's early pragmatism (and democratic socialism) is a leading New World African example of the political aspects of existential democracy.[20]

In West's universe, Kierkegaard offered a proactive conception of existential democracy, but Holiday, Thurman, and Du Bois are reduced to its personal aspects with a politics premised primarily on responses to white supremacy. There is much more in the history of Black intellectual production than the struggle against white supremacy. Such an exploration also requires struggling through the creative, constructive projects of, for instance, developing a philosophical anthropology without essentialism and taking seriously the African contributions to the constitution of the Black self in the New World.[21]

That Most Adventurous of the Spirit

The tendency to write out the Black intellectual tradition as a major component of developing theoretical foundations for a revolutionary vision of and position on American society has been a feature of West's work from the beginning. The consequence has been great primarily because his earliest works have served a foundational role in his thought. They have been what he has either adhered to or revised throughout the years. This is certainly the case with his most philosophically creative and systematic work, *Prophesy Deliverance! An Afro-American Revolutionary Christianity*. That work set not only the outline of West's philosophy, but also the role Black intellectual production would play in his thought. Although the text is layered with discussions of Black intellectuals, they never achieve the status of an intellectual tradition at the text's reflective, metatheoretical level. This is ironic for a work that is a genuine classic of African-American philosophy.

The argument is straightforward: philosophy is advanced as a textual enterprise through which the revolutionary task of the intellectual is to advance or write texts that could create a counternarrative to the hegemonic texts that militate against a humane world. Since African-Americans live in the United States, this means adopting the best texts offered by the intellectual resources of that society. For West, this means three traditions: the pragmatist, Marxist, and Christian traditions. The basis for advancing the pragmatist tradition is, as we have already seen, its unique place as *the* American philosophy. But more, in pragmatism – in West's case, highly saturated with existential motifs – is a commitment to historical analysis and social criticism and the value of intellectual production in the service of social change. The Marxist tradition offers messages of class revolt, egalitarianism, and revolution. It should be borne in mind that the Marxist tradition to which West here refers is what he calls "left-wing Marxism," which for him means a highly Americanized Marxism. West considers vanguardism – communism – to be "right-wing" Marxism. Thus, although he adopts Antonio Gramsci's model of the organic intellectual, he rejects the rest of Gramsci's critical philosophy – for example, "the Modern Prince"/the Communist Party – as undemocratic. Radical egalitarianism or radical participatory democracy is West's conception of the "left" here. Since West's Marxism is not the focus of this chapter, I will not go into detail about the objections I have for this characterization of Marxist strains of thought. Suffice it to say that a Marxism devoid of the threat of an organized proletariat as an institution (a party) lacks not only the dialectical insights on civil society offered by G. W. F. Hegel but also Marx's dialectical point of that class being the contradiction of the bourgeoisie.[22] In the end, how can bourgeois democracy work as the more rigorous Marxism? Or worse, if Americanism is bourgeois democracy, is not the project of a rigorously Americanized Marxism doomed at its inception? We press on. The Christian element is added primarily because of its egalitarian values, but West adds "prophesying" to the equation to bring the Christian critic to the fore. In stream with the pragmatist social critic and Marxist ideological critique, the prophetic voice occasions the Christian critic as social critic to emerge. But more, the initial situating of philosophical activities in terms of textual analysis enables the emergence of the critic of texts to emerge as well, and hence the creation of the textual production of African-American revolutionary Christianity.

Now, the obvious concern at this point is the absence of Black contributions to these theoretical foundations of Black revolutionary thought. The heroic theorist of pragmatism is John Dewey; the hero of Marxism is obviously Marx; and although Jesus' race has been subject to debate, he is, in the end, clearly not African-American and clearly not Christian. African-American thinkers seem not to have contributed to African-American *thought*. A response to this objection could be that West was not aware of there having been such thinkers, but for the presence of two peculiar chapters in the text: chapter 3, "The four traditions of response"; and chapter 4, "Prophetic Afro-American Christian thought and progressive Marxism."

As with Black existential democracy, the four traditional responses are responses to white supremacy. They are the exceptionalist, assimilationist, marginalist, and humanist traditions. The exceptionalist tradition "*lauds the uniqueness of Afro-American culture and personality*" (p. 70, emphasis in original). The assimilationist tradition "*considers Afro-American culture and personality to be pathological*" (ibid.). The marginalist tradition "*posits Afro-American culture to be restrictive, constraining, and confining*" (p. 71, emphasis in original). And the humanist tradition "*extolls the distinctiveness of Afro-American culture and personality*" (ibid.). That West is a humanist pretty much stacks the decks against the first three. One may wonder about the distinction between "uniqueness" and "distinctiveness." The former refers to *sui generis* features whereas the latter is ambiguous. It means both "different from" and "high achievement" or "mark of honor." The difference between the two becomes evident in West's criticisms of the former. The problem with the exceptionalist tradition is that it cultivates an environment of race representatives and narcissistic self-lauding. In this camp, he locates such African-American intellectuals as the early W. E. B. Du Bois, James Weldon Johnson, the Honorable Elijah Muhammad, in addition to the Black Arts Movement advanced by Imamu Baraka, Hoyt Fuller, Addison Gayle, and "weak" versions in Marcus Garvey and the early Martin Luther King, Jr. The upshot of his criticism is that there is an appeal to "Black genius" and Black nationalist sentiments that in the end foster an environment of progress through the cultivation of a Black elite in place of a white one. "Results for the Afro-American poor," he reminds us, "have been minimal" (p. 77). Thus, "The exceptionalist response to the challenges of self-image and self-determination is this: a romanticization of Afro-American culture that conceals the social mobility of an emerging opportunistic Afro-American petite bourgeoisie" (ibid.).

It was indeed courageous, if not hypocritical, for West, a future member of Harvard's "dream team," to have made the last claim so early in his career. How he stands by this conclusion – if he still does – will no doubt serve as inspiration for America's and Europe's Black academic elites. In the end, however, *ad hominem* attacks will not shake the validity of his point. It is a point that received its classic treatment in Frantz Fanon's *The Wretched of the Earth*, but whose early formulation was, ironically, through the work of one of the intellectuals in the assimilationist tradition: E. Franklin Frazier.[23] Frazier argued that a limitation of the Black intelligentsia is its link to a political economy of race representation instead of genuine capital. What has emerged is a class of people who look like a bourgeoisie but lack material transformations that should be a function of their status. Capital for them is political clout, garnered through race representation, which leads to an elite that does not translate into the building up of their nation. Neither grand nor petit, they are a new breed – a "lumpen-bourgeoisie."

The problem with the assimilationist response, led by E. Franklin Frazier, is that it renders African-Americans and African-American cultures pathological. "The assimilationist tradition, like the exceptionalist one, is a rash reaction against a hostile white society rather than a responsible response to particular challenges. Both traditions represent the peculiar predicament of the Afro-American middle class" (p. 80). In other words, they are two sides of the same reactionary coin, and both lack an organic connection to the Black poor, the overwhelming majority of Black people. These traditions are rejected on all of West's grounds, but especially so by virtue of his commitment to radical democracy. How democratic is a world whose values are designed only for its elites? Besides, as any one who moves through Black and white worlds knows, the failure of assimilation and its connection to exceptionalism are that only Blacks who are considered exceptions are, in the end, those who are considered assimilatable.

West's analysis of the marginalist tradition may surprise some readers of his later work. Its model is the alienated artist, which means that quite a number of the most influential writers and avant garde musicians, painters, sculptors, and the like would be situated here. It is what might be called the Black Bohemians, but also those who are nearly all in the atheistic existentialist tradition. Here we see a conflict between a Christological existentialist (West) and nihilistic existentialists, such as Richard Wright – *the* quintessential alienated Black man. West reads Wright as a twofold attitude toward African-America: "a conscious embodiment and rejection of it" (p. 82). Because of this, Wright is in "perennial limbo" (p. 84), which renders his route a politics that leads to inaction and in effect leads nowhere. Gifted writers ensnared in this "tradition" (in quotation marks here since it resists identification with *tradition*) are Gayl Jones, James Baldwin, and Toni Morrison. Baldwin's and Morrison's location here betrays a limitation of the typography, as is evident in their shifted status in West's thought by the 1990s.[24] Here is how West sums up his rejection of that response: "the marginalist response to the challenges of self-image and self-determination is this: a candid acceptance of personal marginality to both Afro-American culture and American society plus moral sermonizing to all Americans" (p. 85).

Finally, there is the humanist tradition, which is best exemplified by its music. So jazz musicians from Louis Armstrong through to Miles Davis fare well. Even bebop and avant garde musicians like Charlie Parker and Dizzie Gillespie on one hand and the later John Coltrane and Ornette Coleman on the other come out well in spite of their historical connections to Bohemia after dark, as the saying goes. By way of writers, Langston Hughes, Zora Neale Hurston, and Ralph Ellison are exemplars here. So we have West's brand of humanism: "a promotion of an individuality strengthened by an honest encounter with the Afro-American past and the expansion of democratic control over the major institutions that regulate lives in America and abroad" (p. 90). A Nietzschean, West is not.[25]

A strange Manicheanism is clearly evident in this aspect of West's thought. The themes are familiar, although West does not avow an essentialist reading: whites produce theory; Blacks produce art, expressions of the soul, in a word, *experience*. The essentialist reading, often attributed to Léopold Senghor, is well known: *L'émotion est nègre, comme la raison hellène* ("Emotion is Negro, while reason is Greek").[26] Appeal to music, which indirectly refers to the world of affect, becomes prime domain for Black folk. Much is elided in appeals to music – for instance, the difference between those who were composers and those who primarily improvised, the complex political economy of the distribution of certain arts that both permit and restrict Black aesthetic expression, the overarching decadence that renders sites of intellectual production beyond the aesthetic realms utterly hostile, the reality that the value of aesthetic production versus theoretical production is not evenly distributed in modern Western civilization. In a civilization that has set itself up as the Promethean bearer of the fire of science, "Kant or Mozart" and "Hegel or Beethoven," although obvious instances of apples and oranges, don't function as equal but different terms. Without the theorists (reason, science), the aesthetic realm would simply stand as a marvel without interpretation.

The problem is that West does not seem able to recognize Black intellectual production as a major interpretive resource through which to make sense of experience. This is explicit in the later *Keeping Faith*, especially in the essay, "The dilemma of the Black intellectual."[27] What he says there warrants a lengthy quote:

> I would suggest that there are two *organic* intellectual traditions in African American life: *the black Christian tradition of preaching* and *the black musical tradition of performance*. Both traditions, though undoubtedly linked to the life of the mind, are oral, improvisational and histrionic. Both traditions are rooted in black life and possess precisely what the literate forms of black intellectual activity lack: institutional matrices over time and space within which there are accepted rules of procedure, criteria for judgment, canons for assessing performance, models of past achievement and present emulation and an acknowledged succession and accumulation of superb accomplishments. The richness, diversity and vitality of the traditions of black preaching and black music stand in strong contrast to the paucity, even poverty, of black literate intellectual production. There simply have been no black literate intellectuals who have mastered their craft commensurate with the achievements of Louis Armstrong, Charlie Parker or Rev. Manuel Scott – just as there are no black literate intellectuals today comparable to Miles Davis, Sarah Vaughn or Rev. Gardner Taylor. This is so not because there have been or are no first-rate black literate intellectuals, but rather because without strong institutional channels to sustain traditions, great achievement is impossible. And, to be honest, black America has yet to produce a great literate intellectual with the exception of Toni Morrison. There indeed have been superb ones – Du Bois, Frazier, Ellison, Baldwin, Hurston – and many good ones. But none can compare to the heights achieved by black preachers and musicians. (pp. 72–3)

How does one respond to this? Given the argument that makes institutions a necessary condition for the achievement of greatness, the die is cast against Black intellectuals and in favor of white intellectuals from the outset because of the latter's institutions. The talents, the creativity, and the energy of Black intellectuals do not matter; however first-rate they might be, the upshot is that greatness is not achievable for them. Toni Morrison is no doubt the exception not because of what she has written – which in many instances might even be inferior to the production of some "first-rate" Black intellectuals who do not count here – but because of her achieving the Nobel Prize and the Pulitzer Prize; in other words, *white institutional recognition*.

It was most fortunate that I had not read that essay until after completing my graduate degree. The argument leads to the obvious question: why bother? It is a reactive nihilistic document. The best counsel to a Black intellectual at this point would be either to exercise some innate musical abilities or go preach.[28]

Yet, in truth, those are not the only options. Another option is that West is just plain wrong, and that he has inadvertently exemplified the exceptionalist-assimilationist tradition he had criticized little more than a decade before. For if *white* institutional recognition is the key to greatness, then developing Black ones would fail by virtue of their being *Black*. Could there, however, be another possibility – that the world is such that the highest corridors of white recognition often come with a price? Recall our discussion of decadence. If white civilization (America) is indeed in decay, then would not the highest works be those that actively transcend its nihilistic effects through paradoxically conceding them? Put differently, if there is no hope for *great* Black intellectuals in contemporary American and European societies, would not the reality for them, those who are "first rate" and in the present, be, as in the case of Nietzsche in the nineteenth century and Fanon in the twentieth, their future? Isn't a hallmark of a great thinker the focus on the work being produced, not the search for greatness?

I say that West could be "just plain wrong" because of some obvious figures that came to mind as I read his sequence of jazz greats. Consider the contrast in this passage from Paget Henry's *Caliban's Reason*:

> An outstanding novelist, playwright, and critic from Jamaica, [Sylvia] Wynter's creative and world-constituting activities have been both reconstructive and trans-formative. Their primary focus has been the practical problems created by the internal contradictions of the postcolonial ideologies of the region. The originality of Wynter's contribution derives from her invitation to both historicists and poeticists to make an epistemic turn. ... Wynter makes both brilliant and playful use of these semiotic appropriations, producing strikingly original ideas, which are elaborated with virtuoso performances of metaphorical play. Wynter's playful elaborations of very serious ideas can only be compared to the exquisitely decorated notes of Sarah Vaughn's singing. She is in so many ways "the Divine One" of Caribbean letters. (p. 118)

American race politics is such that Wynter's Caribbean origins may make some readers concede West's point about US Black reality, but such a position would fail to address Wynter's primary self-designation as a *Black* woman and her contributions as a former chair of Black studies and her work as a professor in Spanish and Portuguese literature at Stanford University throughout the last quarter of the twentieth century until her retirement. The artificial narrowing of who counts as Black in the American context fails to deal with the complex mixtures – racially, regionally, culturally, and linguistically – of the Black diaspora in the United States. Wynter actively engages New World political reality as hemispheric, spanning from

northern Canada to the southern tip of Chile. *She* is Sarah Vaughn's intellectual
correlate. What is the Harlem renaissance without Alain Locke's axiology and his
activist work around the arts and philosophy in the academy?[29] What is odd about
the dismissal of Black intellectual greatness in West's work is its double standard. Not
all great white intellectuals receive the Nobel Prize or the MacArthur "genius"
prize, nor the Pulitzer Prize, etc. Sometimes, the institutions and networks are so
specialized that most white people go through their everyday lives having never
heard of these intellectuals. Alain Locke had received recognition in contexts that
ranged from his invited contribution to highly specialized anthologies of best work
in his fields, to the recognition he received through his efforts at Howard University
and his work in the cultivation of subsequent generations of Black intellectuals. We
should remember that the white-owned Cotton Club provided a space for Duke
Ellington, true, but Atlanta University had its moment during Du Bois's tenure
there, and Howard was making the effort, however elitist its aspirations, to set the
stage for Locke (and a litany of other Black intellectuals, including Toni Morrison).
Is it not obvious that Du Bois was Ellington's correlate, except that whereas
Ellington was made European royalty, Du Bois took the eventual route of
working-class hero through at first white Soviet Union recognition, but eventually
Black revolutionary efforts in Ghana?[30] In some cases, and in some art forms, there
are also no correlates with the *Black intellectual* who emerged in that region. Who,
among the musicians and the preachers, is the equivalent of Frantz Fanon not only in
Martinique but in Algeria during his time? Only in poetry is there someone close:
Fanon's teacher, Aimé Césaire. Fanon, after all, wrote texts that made thinkers of
such stature as Jean-Paul Sartre, Simone de Beauvoir, and Maurice Merleau-Ponty
his European "equals." The notion of institutions of white recognition as necessary
conditions for the evaluation of Fanon's greatness is absurd on its face. To this list, we
could also add C. L. R. James, whose influence continues to grow in the Western
academy but whose importance has been understood all along in what West would
consider fringe circles. For James, the musical correlate would have to be the Mighty
Sparrow in Trinidad. Similarly, there is Walter Rodney, whose influence on Third
World political economy and the complexity of theorizing politics through the
realities of the lumpen-proletariat puts him in the company of giants. Given his
influence on Rastafari, his obvious musical correlates are Bob Marley and Peter
Tosh.[31]

   What is missing from the claim about music is a failure to see the complex
marginalization of Black music even when it seems as though it is being valorized.
The music world has a double standard in which the ultimate desire is for Black
music with white performers. Where Black geniuses are recognized it is usually with
the provision that the art form itself is of less value than white ones. Think of the
pages Harold Cruse devoted to the national debate over whether Duke Ellington
should receive the Pulitzer Prize for lifetime achievement in music.[32] That many

forgotten, and ultimately second rate, white composers of European classical music have stood in the place of the great Black composers mentioned by West is a testament to the reality that, in the end, there is the reassertion of "reason," "universality," and "history" in European music rather than African descended music. Deep down, the anti–Black racist consolation is that at least whites had Bach, Mozart, Beethoven, and Tchaikovsky. We should remember that it is part of American cultural history to know that George Gershwin supposedly "made a lady out of jazz."

Black musical talent can be accepted in American society because the society values composers more than performers. It is similar to athletics. Ultimately Black athletes win the day because the society does not value the body, the biological, as it does only a single element of it: the brain. The same applies to speech. The oral skills of Black preachers pose no threat in a world that accepts the speaker–audience relation as a fundamentally cathartic instead of reflective one. Where writing is more valued, and Black people are not valued, there will always be a so-called "Black oral tradition."

What would West's texts look like if, instead of declaring second-place citizen-ship to Black intellectual production in his work, *he* were to move them to full, intratextual engagement? Would not, given West's popularity and stature, a dif-ferent conception of the value of Black intellectual production emerge? Would not such texts themselves function as the exemplification of that value? That West devotes considerable energy to minor white thinkers in addition to great ones raises the question of what his thought might look like if he were to take the minor white thinkers out and replace them with (in his view) minor Black ones. Perhaps a discovery might be made that the Black ones are not so minor after all. How about major Black ones? How would West's Americanism look through a sus-tained engagement with C. L. R. James's *American Civilization*?[33] How about the articulation of nihilism? Although our early discussion was through Nietzsche's formulations, the most influential theoretical exploration of the Black intellectual's struggle with nihilism is surely Frantz Fanon's *Black Skin, White Masks*. Fanon fits the model of the active nihilist in that he has no faith in Western civilization's ability to recognize the humanity of Black people. For him, decay has gone full swing. What is needed is not reformation but a different civilization – one in which the concepts and material conditions, and consequently *the people*, would be utterly different.[34] In some ways, that speaks more to the problem of constructing a Black revolutionary philosophy than do the tripartite of Pragmatism, Marxism, and Christianity. It suggests taking seriously the suppressed *fourth*: the Black revolu-tionary intellectual tradition, a tradition that has always centered the question of the value and meaning of the humanity of Black folk and consequently the human being. West is part of that tradition, as is evident by his preference for the *humanist* response. It is the hallmark of philosophical reflection across the Black diaspora that philosophical anthropology or human-centered concerns are primary. Having rejected the position that Black people have to be essentially base, thinkers in this tradition find themselves facing a human world without an essence, a world without the reductive trappings against which West's generation of intellectuals have come to regard themselves as their chief opposition.

Conclusion

Perhaps the best way to conclude this piece is where I began. Cornel West inspired me as a student. I have found him inspirational as a friend. So much love. So much devotion to the project of demonstrated humanity. He clearly wants to *be* a possibility. In older parlance, this is called a moral and intellectual role model. There is irony here. For the complexity of his project is such that he needs to abandon such a project for the intellectual greatness he admires, but such an abandonment would also eliminate the moralism he cherishes, for he would have to reject his struggle to live as being no better than anyone else. To not care whether he is great, equal, or less but instead simply focus on the important work to be done come what may goes against the grain of West's populism. This makes him, in ways, a tragic figure, for in the end, he wants Black achievement in a world in which, when it comes to Blacks, its resources of assessment are bankrupt and decadent. Saving American civilization is the folly that makes West popular but, in the end, perhaps the most passively nihilistic thinker in the negative, dialectical moment of a recent, active, nihilistic past.

Acknowledgments

Thanks are due to Jane Comaroff Gordon and Rowan Ricardo Phillips for conversations and critical examinations of this chapter.

Notes

1   I provide a developed critique of this tendency in Lewis R. Gordon, *Existentia Africana: Understanding Africana Existential Thought* (New York: Routledge, 2000), chapter 2.
2   See, for example, F. C. S. Schiller, *Logic for Use: An Introduction to the Voluntarist Theory of Knowledge* (New York: Harcourt, Brace, and Company, 1930) and his *Our Human Truths* (New York: Columbia University Press, 1939). See also Ralph Barton Perry's *The Thought and Character of William James* (New York: George Braziller, 1954), p. 302, for

some examples of Schiller and James conspiring for the victory of pragmatism on both sides of the Atlantic.

3 Cornel West, *The American Evasion of Philosophy: A Genealogy of Pragmatism* (Madison: University of Wisconsin Press, 1989).

4 I discuss some of the debates around this conception of African-American philosophy and Cornel West's thought in my essay on Cornel West in Lewis R. Gordon, *Her Majesty's Other Children: Sketches of Racism from a Neocolonial Age* (Lanham: Rowman & Littlefield, 1997), pp. 193–206, "Black intellectuals and academic activism: Cornel West's 'Dilemmas of the black intellectual.'"

5 Richard Rorty, *Philosophy and Social Hope* (London: Penguin, 1999). Given, as well, Rorty's forays into deconstruction, I don't see how this was avoidable. Deconstruction could be read as the semiotizing of existentialism, and since one cannot *live* by texts alone, the rest follows.

6 "Cornel West." Interview in George Yancy (ed.), *African American Philosophers: 17 Conversations* (New York: Routledge, 1998), p. 33.

7 For example, "On the one hand, this commitment [of prophetic vision and practice] looks the inescapable facts of death, disease and despair in the face." Cornel West, *Keeping Faith: Philosophy and Race in America* (New York: Routledge, 1993), p. x.

8 *The American Evasion of Philosophy*, pp. 232–3.

9 Ibid.

10 *Keeping Faith*, pp. xi–xii. See also Cornel West, *Prophesy Deliverance! An Afro-American Revolutionary Christianity* (Philadelphia: Westminster, 1982), p. 18, where existential democracy is foreshadowed as "existential freedom."

11 For multiple positions on this aspect of black intellectual history, see Lewis R. Gordon (ed.), *Existence in Black: An Anthology of Black Existential Philosophy* (New York: Routledge, 1997), Lewis R. Gordon, *Existentia Africana*, and Paget Henry, *Caliban's Reason: Introducing Afro-Caribbean Philosophy* (New York: Routledge, 2000).

12 Cornel West, *Race Matters* (Boston: Beacon, 1993), p. 12.

13 See, for instance, Søren Kierkegaard, *Two Ages: "The Age of Revolution" and "The Present Age": A Literary Review*, ed. and trans. with intro. and notes by Howard V. Hong and Edna H. Hong (Princeton, NJ: Princeton University Press, 1978), and Friedrich Nietzsche, *The Will to Power*, trans. by Walter Kaufman and R. J. Hollingdale, and ed. with commentary by Walter Kaufmann (New York: Vintage, 1968).

14 *Race Matters*, p. 14, emphasis in original.

15 Frantz Fanon, *Black Skin, White Masks*, trans. Charles Lamm Markman (New York: Grove, 1967), introduction and chapter 1.

16 *The Will to Power*, p. 17.

17 Whether conservative racist or liberal racist or Marxist progressivist racist, it has been my experience that few attitudes agitate such whites more than their irrelevance. Such a turn of events lead to the most hostile efforts of reinstating Hegelian dynamics of lordship and bondage. For discussion, see Lewis R. Gordon, *Bad Faith and Antiblack Racism* (Amherst, NY: Humanity Books, 1999), pp. 117–23, "Exoticism." There are similar dynamics at work, I suspect, with the controversy over Afrocentrism in the

Northeastern United States. White critics are too passionate for issues of "correct" versus "revisionary" history to be at stake. There is a desire to get Afrocentric scholars to *submit* to the previous order of things and recognize the legitimacy of white scholarship as normative. There is something powerful about rendering whiteness irrelevant. Because it does not reject the existence of white people, nor does it mean trying to eradicate white people, it is immune to the "dependency argument." Since black people are a function of a world in which there are white people and vice versa, the elimination of white people means the elimination of black people; to desire being black without whites requires a world of continued blackness, but in relation to whom? For some recent discussion of the dialectics of this phenomenon, see Slavoj Žižek, *The Ticklish Subject: The Absent Center of Political Ontology* (London: Verso, 2000), pp. 70–119. See also Wendy Brown, *States of Injury* (Stanford, CA: Stanford University Press, 1996), p. 36.

18 For recent discussions of Nietzsche on decadence, particularly with regard to problems of values, see Jacqueline Renee Scott, "Nietzsche and decadence: the revaluation of morality," *Continental Philosophy Review* (formerly *Man and World*), 31 (January), 1998, pp. 59–78, and "Nietzsche and the revaluation of women's bodies." *International Studies in Philosophy*, 31, 1999, pp. 65–75.

19 See William Preston, "Nietzsche on blacks" in *Existence in Black*, pp. 165–72.

20 *Keeping Faith*, p. xii.

21 Such projects have been a feature of black intellectual production throughout the modern period. See B. Anthony Bogues, *Africana Heretical Intellectuals: A Study in Africana Political Thought* (New York: Routledge, forthcoming). On the African roots of African-American (and Afro-Caribbean) existentialism, see Paget Henry, "African and Afro-Caribbean existential philosophies" in *Existence in Black*, pp. 11–36, and *Caliban's Reason*, especially chapter 1.

22 See Hegel's discussion of "estates" in his *Philosophy of Right*, trans. by T. M. Knox (Oxford: Clarendon Press, 1967). See Marx and Engels's discussion of the meaning of revolutionary class in *The Communist Manifesto*, with an intro. by Martin Malia (New York: Signet Classic/Penguin, 1998), but see especially p. 63 of part I (special sesqui-centennial edition). The main point is that for Hegel and Marx, a radicalized mass – that is, West's notion of radical democracy – suffers from a failure of political appearance. Only *organized* groups can appear in the political world. Masses are amorphous without rational organization. Thus, a working-class "mass" requires a working-class organization as the rational manifestation of its struggle. For discussion, see Ross Harrison, *Democracy* (London: Routledge, 1993), pp. 119–22.

23 Frantz Fanon, *The Wretched of the Earth*, trans. Constance Farrington (New York: Grove, 1963), "The pitfalls of national consciousness." E. Franklin Frazier addressed this issue several years earlier, in Paris, in *Les Bourgeoisie noir* (Paris: Librairie Plon, 1955).

24 See, for example, p. 43 of *Race Matters*.

25 Although he shares some intellectual affinity with Nietzsche through Michel Foucault's adoption of Nietzsche's genealogical method, which is evident in chapter 2 of *Prophesy Deliverance!* and in his various excursions through Foucauldianism as recently as *Keeping*

Faith, it is clear that West's existential situation – a black Christian in America – has placed a limit on what he could take from Nietzsche. Ironically, taking the *method* exemplifies what Nietzsche has argued is a peculiar aspect of modern nihilism, as suggested by his observation that "It is not the victory of science that distinguishes our nineteenth century but the victory of the scientific method over science," *Will to Power*, p. 262.

26   Léopold Senghor, *Liberté: I* (Paris: Seuil 1964), p. 24. See also "La contribution nègro-africaine à l'édification d'une civilisation mondiale," *Liberté de l'Esprit*, 41 (June/July), 1953, p. 143. I wrote "attributed to" since, according to Jacques Louis Hymans, the source of Senghor's infamous comparison is Arthur Compte de Gobineau's *Essai sur l'Inegalité des Races Humaines* (*Essay on the Inequality of Human Races*): "Senghor adopted Gobineau's phrase 'emotion is Negro, while reason is Hellenic.' Gobineau, quoted by Senghor had written that '... the Negro is the human being most energetically involved by artistic emotion.' He also stated that artistic genius only developed when Whites crossbred with Negroes," Hymans, *Léopold Sédar Senghor: An Intellectual Biography* (Edinburgh: Edinburgh University Press, 1971), p. 66. The full citation for Gobineau's work is *Essai sur l'Inegalité des Races Humaines*, présentation de Hubert Juin (Paris: P. Belfond, 1967), volume 2, chapter 7. There is much debate over Senghor's claim. Hymans provides a good outline of Senghor's intent, which was to argue that rationality is not the sole basis of reason and that we should consider affective reason. There are, however, recent, less forgiving, interpretations and critical evaluations; see, for example, Tsenay Serequeberhan, *The Hermeneutics of African Philosophy: Horizon and Discourse* (New York: Routledge, 1994), pp. 42–53.

27   My criticisms of that essay can be found in *Her Majesty's Other Children*, pp. 193–206.

28   Preaching, of course, is the other black "humanist" tradition emphasized in *Prophesy Deliverance!*

29   A recent testament of Locke's importance can be found in the collection of scholars gathered to assess his work in The Alain Locke Society and in Leonard Harris (ed.), *The Critical Pragmatism of Alain Locke: A Reader on Value Theory, Aesthetics, Community, Culture, Race, and Education* (Lanham, MD: Rowman and Littlefield, 1999). For Locke's writings, see Leonard Harris (ed.), *The Philosophy of Alain Locke: Harlem Renaissance and Beyond* (Philadelphia: Temple University Press, 1989).

30   West is guilty of continuing to confine our memory of Du Bois to the first third of his life. That Du Bois took a road to communism and then Ghana under the Marxist revolutionary Kwame Nkruma's African philosophical version of Marxism challenges the adage: radical in youth, conservative in old age. A retort is, however, as we have already seen, that West considered communism right-wing, which rendered the elderly Du Bois, in his view, a conservative Marxist. That Du Bois is the Duke Ellington of the black intellectual tradition is evident not only by his well known prefix "the dean of black scholars," but also by the many studies of his life and work, the most influential of which is David Levering Lewis's *W. E. B. Du Bois: Biography of a Race (1868–1919)* (New York: Holt, 1993). See, as well, *Existentia Africana*, pp. 62–95.

31 For a study of Rodney's contributions, see Rupert Charles Lewis, *Walter Rodney's Intellectual and Political Thought* (Detroit: Wayne State University Press, 1998). Rodney's influence extends also to setting the framework for formulating African-American radical politics. Think of how his *How Europe Underdeveloped Africa*, revised edition, postscript by A. M. Babu (Washington, DC: Howard University Press, 1982) and *The Groundings with My Brothers* (London: Bogle L'Ouverture Publications, 1969) were taken up by Manning Marable in *How Capitalism Underdeveloped Black America* (Boston: South End Press, 1983), which includes the chapter "Groundings with my sisters: patriarchy and the exploitation of black women."

32 Harold Cruse, *The Crisis of the Negro Intellectual: A Historical Analysis of the Failure of Black Leadership* (New York: Quill, 1984), pp. 107–9.

33 C. L. R. James, *American Civilization* (Oxford: Blackwell, 1993). For an appreciation of James's contribution, see *The C. L. R. James Reader*, ed. and introduced by Anna Grimshaw (Oxford: Blackwell Publishers, 1992), B. Anthony Bogues, *Caliban's Freedom: The Early Political Thought of C. L. R. James* (London: Pluto Press, 1997), and Paget Henry, *Caliban's Reason*, passim, but especially pp. 47–67.

34 Frantz Fanon, *Black Skin, White Masks*, chapter 1. See also the conclusion of *The Wretched of the Earth*. For a longer version of this reading of Fanon, see *Existentia Africana*, chapter 2, and for a discussion of how it relates to crises and limitations in Western civilization, see Lewis R. Gordon, *Fanon and the Crisis of European Man: An Essay on Philosophy and the Human Sciences* (New York: Routledge, 1995).

3

Cornel West on Prophesy, Pragmatism, and Philosophy: A Critical Evaluation of Prophetic Pragmatism

Clevis Headley

Pragmatism, from its very beginnings, has been the focus of much controversy. Even Charles Peirce, long credited as the father of pragmatism, recommended substituting " 'pragmaticism' – a name ugly enough to be safe from kidnappers" – for "pragmatism" to distance himself from those thinkers who identified themselves as pragmatists. Hence, it is not surprising to discover that pragmatism is not known for having any kind of rigid and exclusionary definitional status. Indeed, as recently stated, "the pragmatic movement has always been characterized by a conflict of narratives and metanarratives. 'Pragmatism' has always been an essentially contested concept."[1] Even the current resurgence of pragmatism, as is to be expected, is as controversial and contestable as the early days of pragmatism. What is particularly interesting about the current resurgence is that it is captive to a certain interpretive conflict, which emerges from the struggle over different narrative reconstructions of the very history of pragmatism.[2] And, in this regard, pragmatism is not so much different but, instead, proves itself similar to other philosophical movements that must contend with the stresses and frustrations commonly afflicting intellectual traditions. "A tradition," according to MacIntyre, "not only embodies the narrative of an argument, but is only to be recovered by an argumentative retelling of the narrative which will itself be in conflict with other argumentative retellings."[3] The relevance of this statement emerges from the main goal of this essay: a critical examination of Cornel West's argumentative retelling or, rather, reconstruction of pragmatism.

West quite recently presented his own historiography of pragmatism; that is, his own argumentative retelling of pragmatism as well as what he considers a prophetic recovery of the progressive commitments of this tradition. Not surprisingly, his narrative reconstruction culminates in his novel conception of prophetic pragmatism. In this chapter, the case is made that West's prophetic pragmatism really does not offer much by way of an improvement on earlier construals of pragmatism. The first section offers a brief review of recent construals of pragmatism. The second section is a general discussion of the main themes of pragmatism. This section is followed by an examination of West's general take on pragmatism and his prophetic pragmatism. Next, there is a more detailed exposition of West's prophetic pragmatism. Finally, there is a critical evaluation of some of the structural flaws of West's prophetic pragmatism. This critical examination proves that, despite the dialectical interactions among the several elements constituting prophetic pragmatism, West fails to make a plausible case for prophetic pragmatism. I have added an appendix in which I discuss Richard Rorty's take on prophecy and pragmatism.

Varieties of Pragmatism

One popular construal of pragmatism that has captured the attention of many is Richard Rorty's aesthetic pragmatism. Rorty offers his own retelling of pragmatism from the perspective of the linguistic turn, and hence emphasizes the significance of language to any plausible construal of pragmatism. Viewing language as tool – that is, rejecting the traditional representationalist view of language as primarily referential – he maintains that we should stress and more aggressively exploit the metaphorical capacity of language. Instead of seeking to fulfill the dreams of the philosophical tradition, Rorty urges us to engage in a certain playfulness. We should see ourselves as now being free to create redescriptions of ourselves, as well as other aspects of our existence. While engaging in these activities we should fully appreciate the fact that, in changing our vocabularies – that is, fashioning linguistic redescriptions – we are creating ourselves anew, not offering more accurate descriptions of our human essence. Similarly, we create new descriptions of the physical world not for the purpose of obtaining more accurate descriptions of nature, but to predict and control phenomena more effectively and efficiently. Three additional brief examples suffice to illustrate the contestability of pragmatism.

Richard Shusterman argues that pragmatism emphasizes the practicality of philosophical activity, meaning that, roughly speaking, philosophy is the pursuit of knowledge for instrumental reasons. We seek knowledge not for its own sake but for something higher, such as happiness or virtue. Shusterman writes:

Pragmatism . . . represents a return to this practical perspective and thus deserves its Jamesian description as "a new name for old ways of thinking." It is no "evasion of philosophy," but the revival of a tradition that saw theory as a useful instrument to a higher philosophical practice: the art of living wisely and well.[4]

Susan Haack endorses the more sober pragmatism of Peirce but shuns what he describes as the "vulgar pragmatism" now being championed by Stephen Stich and Richard Rorty. According to Haack, Stich and Rorty disastrously "repudiate the idea that criteria of justification should be judged by their truth-indicativeness. Rorty thinks that the idea makes no sense; Stich, that it is narrow-minded and parochial."[5] Haack adds that, "Referring to Rorty and Stich as 'vulgar pragmatists' is intended as an implicit challenge to their claim to be the philosophical descendants of the classical pragmatists."[6]

And, finally, Richard Posner, supporting a form of pragmatic jurisprudence, stresses the scientific heritage of Pierce and Dewey. He writes:

Pragmatism in the sense that I find congenial means looking at problems concretely, experimentally, without illusions, with full awareness of the limitations of human reason, with a sense of the "localness" of human knowledge, the difficulty of translations between cultures, the unattainability of "truth," the consequent importance of keeping diverse paths of inquiry open, the dependence of inquiry on culture and social institutions, and above all the insistence that social thought and action be evaluated as instruments to valued human goals rather than ends in themselves. These dispositions, which are more characteristic of scientists than of lawyers (and in an important sense pragmatism is the ethics of scientific inquiry), have no political valence.[7]

This brief sampling of views clearly represents the contestability involved in any argumentative retelling of the pragmatic tradition. Our next task is to flesh out some of the main ideas constituting the tradition of pragmatism.

The Main Themes of Pragmatism

Despite its contestability, we can isolate core themes of pragmatism. First, pragmatists reject the idea that philosophy needs secure, fixed foundations that can be known with absolute certainty. This view represents pragmatism's commitment to antifoundationalism, although not all antifoundationalists are pragmatists. Indeed, pragmatists generally do not believe that any form of inquiry rests upon sure, secured, and *a priori* foundations. In conjunction with antifoundationalism, pragmatism also advocates a contextual conception of reality and values. Second, pragmatism embraces fallibilism. Believing that all inquiry is fallible, pragmatists tend to adopt a certain epistemological liberalism, which acknowledges that each knowledge claim is subject to revision or, rather, is not immune to criticism. Epistemological incorrigibility is not a pragmatist trademark. Connected with the recognition of the fallibility of inquiry, pragmatists, starting with Peirce, stress the importance of a community of inquirers to test and criticize knowledge claims instead of depending upon the authority of the consciousness of the individual. Third, pragmatism shuns deterministic conceptions of the universe, and actively underscores the ineradicable presence of chance, contingency, and novelty as features of the universe. Perhaps, without too much exaggeration, we can construe this tenet as evidence in favor of pragmatists acknowledging the plasticity of the universe. Hence, pragmatism rejects metaphysical closure in the sense of holding that we can obtain some absolutist conception of the universe that is not limited by the temporal flux of things, a conception that answers determinately to some principle or concept. Peirce insists upon the importance of understanding that any complete understanding of the universe should admit indeterminacy and chance. Dewey similarly emphasizes contingency and chance, and refers to what he called "the precariousness of existence," "the world [as] a scene of risk," and being "uncannily unstable."[8] And, finally, pragmatism readily supports a radical pluralism. James in particular made the theme of pluralism philosophically respectable. Pragmatic pluralism celebrates the plurality of traditions, cultures, perspectives, cognitive schemes, and philosophical orientations.

In terms of their respective individual accomplishments in defining pragmatism, Peirce receives credit for dismantling Cartesian-centered philosophy. He specifically rejects Descartes's claim that philosophy begins with a universal, radical doubt; that the foundations of knowledge are sets of self-evident principles found in the individual consciousness; and, finally, that philosophical theory should be a singular thread of inference. It warrants quoting his statement that philosophy's "reasoning should not form a chain which is no stronger than its weakest link, but a cable whose fibers may be ever so slender, provided they are sufficiently numerous and intimately connected."[9] James receives credit for articulating a radical holism, along with his pluralism. Forever skeptical of a priori, rationalistic, metaphysical, and transcendental notions, James, while not embracing naive relativism or subjectivism, constructively and insightfully argues for the importance of understanding things from the perspective of human thought. He reminds us of the inescapable human contribution to philosophical activity in his apt saying: "the trail of the human serpent is over everything." In short, he fully embraces the humanistic principle: "you can't weed out the human contribution." Finally, Dewey receives credit for his emphasis on the practical, specifically his insistence on the importance of critical intelligence, experimentation, human adaptation to the physical world, and, more importantly, the idea that reality possesses a practical character. According to this last view, human knowing creatively participates in shaping and transforming the world.

But it is important that we avoid the temptation of imposing misleading interpretations upon the above mentioned themes. We should be especially wary of viewing pragmatism as irresponsibly courting either relativism or a complacent skepticism. As a matter of fact, we can safely avoid these mistakes once we acknowledge that pragmatism is antirepresentationalist, in that it rejects what Dewey calls the "spectator theory of knowledge" and the referentialist view of language; that is, language as "mirroring" or "picturing" the world. Indeed, Dewey asserts that the traditional representationalist view of knowledge rendered knowledge as the passive copying of the world and, in some cases, the passive gathering of facts. This move by pragmatists to reject this traditional picture of knowledge, meaning, and language leads to the rejection of the God's eye view of things, described by Bernard Williams as the aim to "represent the world in a way to the maximum degree independent of our perspective and its peculiarities."[10] In evading this God's eye view, pragmatists, particularly James and Dewey, claim that the purpose of language is not to represent the world but rather to enable us to cope with the challenges of an unruly environment. The real position of the pragmatists, then, is not a rejection of truth, knowledge, and rationality, etc. Rather, while wisely avoiding involvement with seemingly inept concerns, they recognize that the "task becomes one of developing an account of inquiry that is sensitive to human finitude, fallibility, and contingency."[11] We can now turn to West's position.

West on pragmatism

First, let us briefly examine West's philosophical take on pragmatism and then gradually narrow the scope of our focus to his construal of prophetic pragmatism. Although Emerson is a source of great inspiration and motivation for West, West, nevertheless, names Dewey as his favored pragmatist. He states:

> When philosophers talk about pragmatism, they are talking about Charles Peirce, William James, and John Dewey. For me, it is principally Dewey. Three theses are basic: (1) anti-realism in ontology, so that the correspondence theory of truth is called into question and one no longer can appeal to Reality as a court of appeal to adjudicate between conflicting theories of the world; (2) anti-foundationalism in epistemology, so that one cannot in fact invoke non-inferential, intrinsically credible elements in experience to justify claims about experience; and (3) de-transcendentalizing of the subject, the elimination of mind itself as a sphere of inquiry. These three themes (mainly Dewey's) are underpinned by the basic claim that social practices – contingent, power-laden, structured social practices – lie at the very center of knowledge. In other words, knowledge is produced, acquired, and achieved.[12]

West claims that pragmatism represents an evasion, not in the sense of a cautious avoidance but rather a deliberate displacement of "epistemology-centered philosophy." Pragmatism, according to West, is the attempt "to evade a specifically Cartesian epistemological problematic."[13] That is, pragmatism ignores the search for absolute standards of knowledge and truth. What West particularly likes about pragmatism's encounter with the philosophical tradition is the attempt by pragmatists to substitute cultural criticism in place of *a priori* philosophical inquiry. Describing his prophetic pragmatism in the most general terms, he states that:

> [it] rests upon the conviction that the American evasion of philosophy is not an evasion of serious thought and moral action. Rather, such evasion is a rich and revisable tradition that serves as the occasion for cultural criticism and political engagement in the service of an Emersonian culture of creative democracy.[14]

We should note that West's take on pragmatism emerges from his broad understanding of philosophy. "Philosophy," he states, "is cultural expression generated from and existentially grounded in the moods and sensibilities of a writer entrenched in the life-worlds of a people."[15] Hence, it comes as no surprise to learn that he favors a form of pragmatism not centered on traditional *a priori* philosophical concerns and sensibilities.

West hammers at the idea of pragmatism transitioning to a prophetic pragmatism in light of what he calls the American evasion of philosophy. Indeed, West's historiographical organic emplotment of pragmatism reads pragmatism as ultimately culminating in his (West's) own conception of prophetic pragmatism. West writes:

> Prophetic pragmatism understands the Emersonian swerve from epistemology – and the American evasion of philosophy – not as a wholesale rejection of philosophy but rather as a reconception of philosophy as a form of cultural criticism that attempts to transform linguistic, social, cultural, and political traditions for the purpose of increasing the scope of individual development and democratic operations. Prophetic pragmatism conceives of philosophy as a historically circumscribed quest for wisdom that puts forward new interpretations of the world based on past traditions in order to promote existential sustenance and political relevance. [It] views truth as a species of the good, as that which enhances the flourishing of human progress.[16]

Even if the earlier pragmatists did not take seriously the idea of evading technical philosophy, and despite West's claim that they did not reject serious thinking, West comes very close to a literal evasion, in the sense of a deliberate renunciation, of professional philosophy. For he favors a narrative redescription of pragmatism purposefully saturated with deep religious themes. West boldly states:

I hold a religious conception of pragmatism. I have dubbed it "prophetic" in that it harks back to the Jewish and Christian tradition of prophets who brought urgent and compassionate critique to bear on the evils of their day. The mark of the prophet is to speak the truth in love with courage – come what may. Prophetic pragmatism proceeds from this impulse. It neither requires a religious foundation nor entails a religious perspective, yet prophetic pragmatism is compatible with certain religious outlooks.[17]

In another context, he offers the following statement on his new brand of pragmatism. He writes:

My own kind of pragmatism – what I call prophetic pragmatism – is closely akin to the philosophy of praxis. ... [M]y focus on the theoretical development in emerging forms of oppositional thought – feminist theory, antiracist theory, gay and lesbian theory – leads me to posit or look for not an overarching synthesis but rather an articulated assemblage of analytical outlooks to further more morally principled and politically effective forms of action to ameliorate the plight of the wretched of the earth.[18]

And so it is that West invokes a conception of pragmatism that borrows from the pragmatic tradition but which ultimately leads to a literal evasion of philosophy and to the embrace of a religiously inspired pragmatism. West's evasion is literal and his enthusiastic appeal to the idea of the prophetic does not serve merely as a metaphorical model of the philosopher. Indeed, West employs all the idiosyncrasies of the prophet. First, he denies being a professional philosopher. Responding to the question posed by the philosopher George Yancy – "Do you see yourself as a professional philosopher?" – West responds as follows:

No, not at all. I think that my concern has always been just trying to make sense of the world and trying to leave the world a little better than I found it. I think that if I were to call myself anything it would be a man of letters who's deeply immersed in philosophical texts, in literary texts, deeply concerned also with scientific texts, but science much more as one element in the quest for wisdom rather than science as a way of gaining knowledge in order to dominate nature. So, in that sense, I have an intellectual curiosity that is quite broad, but I've never viewed myself as an academic or professional philosopher in the narrow sense.[19]

This passage is characteristic of West the prophetic pragmatist and not what one would expect from a philosopher deeply concerned with offering arguments, adequately complemented with advancing deep and probing analytical engagement with issues. Rather, West, the prophet, while situating himself in what he calls "the Black Christian tradition of preaching and the Black musical tradition of performance,"[20] evades the disciplinary standards of philosophy. Desiring to reach both a professional and a nonprofessional audience, West invests in the theatricality of "rhetorical motivation." Hence, he offers an "acrobatic style of argument," and "bursts of rhetorical flight" rivaling the performance of the Baptist preacher. For his style "sounds more like a Baptist sermon than a sober philosophical analysis."[21] The result of these various strategies is "sketchy, journalistic 'mapping' of broadly conceived intellectual terrains."[22]

West is certainly honest about his intentions when he confesses his efforts to avoid seduction by philosophical distractions that are capable of leading one to unproductively focus on the disciplinary matrix of philosophy. Indeed, he castigates Rorty, one of his intellectual heroes, for not being courageous enough in following through on the radical implications of his project. He maintains that Rorty "refuses to give birth to the offspring [his project] conceives . . . his demythologizing retreats into the philosophical arena as soon as pertinent sociopolitical issues are raised."[23] West, full of inspiration, confidently follows through on the sociopolitical implication of his own project. Let us now turn to this project.

Describing prophetic pragmatism

West does not offer a systematic or a carefully argued account of his prophetic pragmatism. Instead he favors an "assemblage of analytical outlooks." Although he does not explicitly state that he models his prophetic pragmatism on the idea of cultural pluralism, there is the appearance that he favors a certain theoretical integration, without assimilation, of various political positions. This theoretical equivalence of cultural pluralism is at odds with philosophy, for it would seem that philosophy should not support this kind of uncritical pluralism without some kind of critical evaluation. Philosophy, on West's view, is seen as not allowing certain "voices" to be heard, whereas West wants to give an equal hearing to as many progressive points of views as possible. Nevertheless, it will become obvious that West really does not effectively assemble analytical outlooks, but rather weaves various rhetorics of liberation for the purpose of building progressive coalitions. The result of this theoretical generosity is that West presents his prophetic pragmatism by attempting to seduce the reader into accepting his insights through the use of passionate and motivational rhetoric. He substitutes intellectual seduction in place of rational persuasion. Since West's strategy evades suspect disciplinary-specific philosophical criteria, we are forced to develop our own interpretive reconstruction of his position. There are varied construals of prophetic pragmatism.

First, West describes prophetic pragmatism as a form of inquiry centered on democratic practices. Prophetic pragmatism, he states, is "an intellectual inquiry constitutive of existential democracy – a self-critical and self-corrective enterprise of human 'sense-making' for the preserving and expanding of human empathy and compassion."[24] To the extent that West claims that prophetic pragmatism is a form of inquiry, we would expect that he would describe the methodology of this form of inquiry. But there is no such methodological clarification forthcoming from West.

Prophetic pragmatism, West tells us, also emerges from the Christian tradition. Here West maintains that the religious dimension of prophetic pragmatism springs from his own embrace of Christianity. Accordingly, then, his claim is that the personal satisfaction he has enjoyed and continues to receive from being Christian leads him to welcome others to embrace this tradition. He writes:

> My own version of prophetic pragmatism is situated within the Christian tradition. [I] am religious not simply for political aims but also by personal commitment. To put it crudely, I find existential sustenance in many of the narratives in the biblical scriptures as interpreted by streams of the Christian heritages.[25]

Of course, the challenge confronting West is to show precisely how he is going to persuade others that they too can similarly find existential sustenance in biblical narratives. He asserts his own conviction without considering the need to provide reasons to the reader. However, although West offers personal testimony for the religious element of his prophetic pragmatism, he intimates that it is also rooted in the African-American tradition of liberation theology.

Next, West describes prophetic pragmatism as a form of cultural criticism, committed to the realization of a democratic culture. Again, we must ask, how does a prophetic pragmatism, construed as a form of cultural criticism, connect to highly contested interpretations of biblical narratives? Regarding prophetic pragmatism as a form of cultural criticism, West writes:

> [it] is a new kind of cultural criticism [and it] must confront candidly the tragic sense found in [various thinkers in the pragmatic tradition]. Prophetic pragmatism ... constitutes the best chance of promoting an Emersonian culture of creative democracy by means of critical intelligence and social action.[26]

Transitioning from construing prophetic pragmatism as a form of cultural criticism and as religiously inspired, West turns to describe prophetic pragmatism as an emancipatory political project. The focus of this construal of prophetic pragmatism is, once again, on the prospects of securing a greater realization of democracy. Indeed, West boldly admits that there is a clear political motivation to his prophetic pragmatism. He writes:

> The political motivation of the American evasion of philosophy is not ideological in the vulgar sense; that is, the claim here is not that philosophy is a mere cloak that

conceals the material interests of a class or group. Rather, the claim is that once one gives up on the search for foundations and the quest for certainty, human inquiry into truth and knowledge shifts to the social and communal circumstances under which persons can communicate and cooperate in the process of acquiring knowledge. What was once purely epistemological now highlights the values and operations of power requisite for human production of truth and knowledge.

Prophetic pragmatism makes this political motivation and political sustenance of the American evasion of philosophy explicit . . . it understands pragmatism as a political form of cultural criticism and locates politics in the everyday experiences of ordinary people . . . prophetic pragmatism promotes a more direct encounter with the Marxist tradition of social analysis . . . prophetic pragmatist politics closely resembles the radical democratic elements of Marxist theory.[27]

One cannot help but underscore the fact that, if we were to accept as true the claim that a turn away from epistemology-centered philosophy leads to an investigation of the social and political conditions sustaining the production of knowledge, it still does not follow that a passionate or motivational rhetoric should replace the need to justify knowledge claims. Certainly, a naturalized epistemological project need not jettison the most minimal philosophical requirement for normative restraints.

West, in further developing the political element of prophetic pragmatism, nuances his stress on institutional democracy by focusing on the freedom of the individual. The political thrust of prophetic pragmatism is consistent with West's concern to maximize democratic possibilities, which should extend greater agency to those with meager political resources. Again, describing prophetic pragmatism as a form of third wave romanticism, he writes, "It consists of an emancipatory experimentalism that promotes permanent self-development for the purpose of ever-increasing democracy and individual freedom."[28] The political core of prophetic pragmatism is an embrace of the various social movements currently dominating the political landscape. West favors a spiritual coalition involving these various movements ranging from racial, ethnic, religious, class, gender to anti-homophobic movements. West does not distinguish between these movements but writes as though they occupy a common egalitarian political space regardless of intragroup and intergroup differences. Indeed, his prophetic pragmatism embraces difference without qualification, claiming that prophetic pragmatism is politically centered on democracy and individuality. He states:

Prophetic pragmatism purports to be not only an oppositional cultural criticism but also a material force of individuality and democracy. By "material force" I simply mean a practice that has some potency and effect or makes a difference in the world. There is – and should be – no such thing as a prophetic pragmatist movement. The translation of philosophic outlook into social motion is not that simple. In fact, it is possible to be a prophetic pragmatist and belong to different political movements, e.g., feminist, Chicano, black, socialist, and left-liberal ones. The distinctive hall-marks of a prophetic pragmatist are a universal consciousness that promotes an all-embracing democratic and libertarian moral vision, a historical consciousness that acknowledges human finitude and conditionedness, and a critical consciousness which encourages relentless critique and self-criticism for the aims of social change and personal humility.[29]

The final component of the political construal of prophetic pragmatism deals with the issue of power. Here, West announces that prophetic pragmatism will unmask the different power structures that present themselves as natural. Along with this, he favors a genealogical strategy that will similarly unearth the relevant practices and systems of beliefs inappropriately dependent upon questionable moral values. Confessing to his Foucauldian connections, he states that "Prophetic pragmatism shares with Foucault a preoccupation with the operation of powers. It also incorporates the genealogical mode of inquiry.... [P]rophetic pragmatism promotes genealogical materialist modes of analysis similar in many respects to those of Foucault."[30] West finally construes prophetic pragmatism as a form of tragic thought, although not a "doomsday" form of thinking. To the extent that prophetic pragmatism evades involvement with *a priori* epistemological concerns but instead focuses on the everyday concerns of human beings, West cautions that, despite our efforts to better our existential condition, both personal and social evil are persistent realities not immediately submissive to our intentions to do good. Evil's evasion of the good that we seek to do will continue. West's focus on the presence of evil is not an invitation to concede defeat but rather one to force us to become humble as we realize that our best intentions are not immune to failure. Prophetic pragmatism, according to West, "is a form of tragic thought in that it confronts candidly individual and collective experiences of evil in individuals and institutions – with little expectation of ridding the world of *all* evil."[31]

As with his other construals, West links his conception of prophetic pragmatism, as a form of tragic thought, with democracy. What he seems to be getting at here is the idea that it is misleading to assume that we can totally and completely realize the absolute ideal of democracy as a historically manifested reality. Democracy remains an ideal that we must constantly pursue while realizing that we are not pursuing an illusion. The dynamics of human existence and the dialectical tensions between human beings and the natural world continually give rise to various obstacles and challenges as we seek a more socially enriching existence. Nevertheless, in acknowledging the constant struggle to improve things, West warns against surrendering to pessimism or yielding to the seductive idea of perfectibility. Hence, he maintains:

Prophetic pragmatism denies Sisyphean pessimism and utopian perfectionism. Rather, it promotes the possibility of human progress and human impossibility of paradise. Human struggle sits at the center of prophetic pragmatism, a struggle guided by a democratic and libertarian vision, sustained by moral courage and existential integrity, and tempered by the recognition of human finitude and fragility.[32]

Clearly, West focuses persistently upon the importance of creating "new possibilities for human agency." He even briefly describes his prophetic pragmatism as a form of historical consciousness attuned to the struggles of the past as well as appreciative of the alternative forms of life based upon the best of the past. But he quickly interjects the theme of the tragic, stating that the praxis of prophetic pragmatism "is tragic action with revolutionary intent."[33] Finally, forever straddling two modes of thought at once, West reiterates that prophetic pragmatism is not blind to the fact that utopian schemes cannot escape the limitation presented by the unfortunate condition of individuals and the structures of injustice normally sustained by social, economic and political institutions. So, even if prophetic pragmatism evades pessimism, it still cautiously embraces utopianism. According to West:

> Prophetic pragmatism . . . tempers its utopian impulse with a profound sense of the tragic character of life and history. This sense of the tragic highlights the irreducible predicament of unique individuals who undergo dread, despair, disillusionment, disease, and death *and* institutional forms of oppression that dehumanize people.[34]

Now that we have some understanding of West's impressionistic conception of prophetic pragmatism, we can offer an evaluation of it. We should keep in mind, however, that this task is complicated by West's preference for a method of reading that emphasizes moving the reader through passionate and motivational rhetoric rather than persuading the reader through the dispassionate execution of arguments. Hence, in criticizing West, we must focus on the vision at the heart of his prophetic pragmatism and not treat it as a systematic body of truths.

Evaluating Prophetic Pragmatism

From a progressive perspective, West says all the right things, meaning that he covers all the necessary bases in proclaiming his support for various political causes. Indeed, he presents a defused enough prophetic pragmatism quite capable of reaching as many targeted groups as possible, ranging from the theist to the secular Marxist. But, despite all his efforts at intellectual diplomacy, prophetic pragmatism functions, at best, as an impressive collage of political slogans. To this extent, what West offers us can best be described as a performative pragmatism; that is, pragmatism infused with the improvisational use of language. Let us turn to more detailed critical reactions to West's position.

First, we can start by critically considering whether or not West's prophetic pragmatism is consistent with the pragmatism of Peirce, James, and Dewey. Clearly, there is some agreement in substance, but little in terms of philosophical specificity. Although the pragmatists were critical of certain traditional philosophical claims, they endeavored to engage with issues regarding truth, knowledge, reality, inquiry, and the philosophical relation between philosophy and democracy, to name but a few. Hilary Putnam recently rehearsed the centrality of inquiry to pragmatism. He states that:

> What the pragmatist thinkers . . . had in common was the conviction that the solution to the "loss of the world" problem is to be found in action and not in metaphysics. . . . Peirce and James and Dewey would have said that democratically conducted inquiry is to be trusted; not because it is infallible, but because the way in which we will find out where and how our procedures need to be revised is through the process of inquiry itself.[35]

In accepting that pragmatism is minimally committed to the idea of a community of inquirers who test and criticize validity claims, West's prophetic pragmatism does not include any notion of critical inquiry situated within a community of critical inquirers. He also announces his commitment for greater democratic possibilities, but he does not even attempt to describe how he proposes to link this goal with the pragmatic tradition of open inquiry guided by critical intelligence, which I understand roughly as indicating the need for some notion of normative constraints.

But the real problems with prophetic pragmatism are to be found elsewhere. Closely connected with the above mentioned concern is West's appropriation of the Black homiletic tradition in the service of his evasion of philosophy. West deserves credit for seeking to establish dialogue between these two traditions. The Black homiletic tradition is a very respectable and resourceful tradition in its own right.[36] Its incredible historical persistence certainly renders it capable of positively influencing the dominant philosophical tradition. I do not want, at this time, to describe the specifics of this possible influence. However, what I want to expose is West's casual assumption that one can integrate the Black homiletic tradition, with its stress on what he calls passionate and motivational rhetoric, with the dominant philosophical tradition. The fact that West even desires to go further than integration and achieve a more intimate assimilation of these two traditions betrays his blindness to the issue of incommensurability. He in no way indicates just how the different rhetorical strategies of the Black homiletic tradition would either be incorporated within the disciplinary matrix of philosophy or replace the critical and analytical demands of the institution of philosophy and its emphasis on the claims of Reason. Certainly, it is going to be quite difficult for West to make any significant impact upon the discipline of philosophy by urging that it is possible to evade the epistemologically centered concerns of philosophy and turn to a rhetoric that is supposed to be true to the speaker's heart. Indeed, West's project comes dangerously close to urging that one should speak from the convictions of one's heart while seemingly remaining skeptical of the corrosive effect of reason on what one holds with deep conviction.

Finally, we learn much about West's prophetic pragmatism when he applies his prophetic framework to actual social issues; for, despite all his declarations of affirming individual freedom, West offers no serious analysis detailing the precise manner in which prophetic pragmatism concretely promotes individual freedom. Uncontested evidence of West's intent to link his prophetic pragmatism with social issues emerges from his claim that the solutions to many social problems are to be found in a new framework for thought and practice: prophetic thinking.[37] Like the prophets of the Old Testament who warned about impending danger, West is today's prophetic pragmatist equivalent, warning about the specter that haunts us. This specter, according to West, is Black nihilism. Let us consider nihilism from two perspectives: one philosophical and the other social. Let us start with the philosophical issue.

Nihilism construed as a philosophical position roughly holds that there are no objective principles of right and wrong, and that since we lack objective ethical principles, there is no objective truth in morality. Moreover, since there are no objective truths in ethics, it follows that no moral position is better than another; we have an "anything goes" situation. It is commonly known that many critics have argued that pragmatism leads to nihilism to the extent that pragmatists have attacked the traditional philosophical concern with a definition of truth, an analysis of knowledge, and *a priori* justification. The specific claim is that if we accept the claim made by pragmatists, such as Dewey, that truth and knowledge are not discovered but socially agreed upon, then any belief can be socially justified in the absence of *a priori* normative constraints. Some philosophically feasible notion of normative rationality or objectivity must survive in order to safeguard the notion of objective truth-indicativeness.

Now, since West develops a new form of pragmatism, one would at least expect him to defend his version of pragmatism against charges of nihilism. However, while evading this challenge, he claims that his position is the solution for a certain form of cultural and psychological nihilism. He remains silent on the issue of philosophical nihilism.

Prophetic pragmatism and Black existence

In his book *Race Matters*, West focuses on the alleged nihilism and meaninglessness experienced by many African-Americans and the crisis of Black leadership. The problem here is that West, in his desire always to avoid extremes and seek a merging of what he considers to be the more reasonable and correct synthesis of two opposing positions, allows his prophetic pragmatism to become undermined by a certain "semantic infiltration." With regard to the condition of African-Americans, West appropriates a discourse that has been framed by those who he would consider his political adversaries. In his analysis of inner-city problems, West does not focus on structural and institutional factors but rather on the spiritual and psychological conditions of African-Americans. To the extent that West does this, his prophetic pragmatism is participating in the "pejorative tradition"[38] of explaining Black personality and culture in terms of pathology, or rather what Albert Murray calls the "fakelore of black pathology." His prophetic pragmatism takes as its point of departure the specter of pathological nihilism currently undermining African-American culture from within.[39] Indeed, he employs his prophetic pragmatism in the service of deciphering the enigma of the Black soul. West describes his concern as centered on *the lived experience of coping with a life of horrifying meaninglessness, helplessness, and (most important) lovelessness. The frightening result is a numbing detachment from others and a self-destructive disposition toward the world. Life without meaning, hope, and love breeds a coldhearted, mean-spirited outlook that destroys both the individual and others.*[40] West here is not talking about institutions but about the inner life of individuals. He bluntly announces his position when he states that the most basic issue confronting African-Americans is *the nihilistic threat to its very existence.*[41] He also claims that the Black "underclass embodies a kind of *walking nihilism* of pervasive drug addiction, pervasive alcoholism, pervasive homicide, and an exponential rise in suicide."[42] Moreover, West goes on to tell us just what he means by the threat of nihilism corroding the fabric of Black existence. He writes:

> This threat is not simply a matter of relative economic deprivation and political powerlessness – though economic well-being and political clout are requisites for meaningful black progress. It is primarily a question of speaking to the profound sense of psychological depression, personal worthlessness, and social despair so widespread in black America.[43]

It is clear where West intends to go with his analysis of Black life. Functioning as the prophetic pragmatist, he locates the problem within the victim. Consequently, but not surprisingly, he urges, like certain biblical prophets of the Old Testament, that it is only by turning from some subjective spiritual malady that an individual can find spiritual and moral redemption. However, the story does not end here. West wants to understand what has happened to the "cultural structures that once sustained black life in America" and "are no longer able to fend off the nihilistic threat." He claims that market forces have undermined these structures, but this is not the whole story. To the extent that Blacks are more susceptible to the coercive effects of market forces than others, West attributes this susceptibility to "a limited capacity to ward off self-contempt and self-hatred"[44] by Blacks.

Another cause for the nihilism threatening Black existence, according to West, is the failure of Black leadership. He attributes the lack of good Black leadership to "the gross deterioration of personal, familial, and communal relations among African-Americans."[45] This last claim is another manifestation of the tendency to explain Black subordination as a result of the pathological family practices of Blacks. West's focus is not on material forces such as the economy. Indeed, while berating those "liberal structuralists" who focus only on the political and the economic, West claims that "Culture is as much a structure as the economy or politics; it is rooted in institutions."[46] Hence, what he is after is the claim that nihilism is not reducible to wretched material conditions. Rather, nihilism is intimately embedded within the "cultural structure." So West redefines the problem, substituting the spiritual ills of individuals in place of structural explanations. The Black community is the cause of its own bitter affliction. Only now the sin is not necessarily the worship of a false God but rather the embrace of pathological social traits. And West is impeccably clear that the curse of nihilism inhabits the souls of the victim. He supports a "politics of conversion" in order to slay the existential dragon of "concrete nihilism." Continuing with his prophetic pragmatic mission against pathology, West's model for nihilism is that it is a disease. "Like alcoholism and drug addiction," West asserts, "nihilism is a disease of the soul. It can never be completely cured, and there is always the possibility of relapse."[47] Here is one case where West's emphasis on agency conflicts with his take on Black existence. Given West's claim that nihilism is never completely cured, the reformed nihilist can never claim full agency and autonomy because nihilism can always make its presence felt. Obviously, then, pathological souls will produce a pathological culture. How should we deal with nihilism to the extent that, according to West, we can only tame it? West claims that there is hope with regard to taming and managing nihilism, but that philosophy is ill-equipped to aid in efforts to conquer nihilism. According to him:

> This chance [the chance of conversion from nihilism] rests neither on an argument about what justice consists of nor on an analysis of how racism, sexism, or class subordination operate. Such arguments and analyses are indispensable. But a politics of conversion requires more.[48]

Once we get a clear grasp of West's vision of the role of the prophet, it is not at all surprising that he rejects argumentation and critical analysis. His proposal to contain nihilism is to convert the nihilist through nonphilosophical means. He writes:

> Nihilism is not overcome by arguments or analysis; it is tamed by love and care. And disease of the soul must be conquered by a turning of one's soul. This turning is done

through one's own affirmation of one's worth – an affirmation fueled by the concern of others. A love ethic must be at the center of a politics of conversion.[49]

This conversion must take place from within for, like salvation, no other person can do it for you. Of course, West thinks that we can lead individuals to start the healing process through motivational and passionate rhetoric. He adopts the idiom of the preacher who mounts the pulpit, pounds the lectern, and enjoins his flock to "have the audacity to take the nihilistic threat by the neck and turn back its deadly assaults."[50] To the extent that West's prophetic pragmatism leads him to use a regime of medical and pathology metaphors to describe Black existence, we must dismiss his project as misdirected. For despite his intentions, he does not offer a new paradigm that would better enable us to understand the problems that he seeks to clarify. Having to reach this conclusion is all the more disappointing after being told by West that "inspirational slogans cannot substitute for substantive historical and social analysis."[51] Furthermore, for all his commitment to fostering human agency, West's embrace of nihilism in the context of Black existence is glaringly contradictory. His flat account of nihilism essentially entails the absence of creative human agency on the part of Blacks, for he views them as being helpless in creatively adapting to and changing their environment. In another context, Eric Lott states that West's "versions of the struggle are pale because he demonstrates little actual faith in black working-class self-activity."[52] However, this develop-ment directly violates the pragmatist's claim that "Humans are not passive specta-tors of the world around them but actively interact with it in the very process of coming to understand it."[53] At this time, let us briefly consider West's views in the context of Dewey's pragmatism.

Unlike his pragmatist hero, Dewey, who stresses human praxis, human creative and radical intervening in the material world to adapt, adjust, and control problem situations, there is no trace of the core of Dewey's "moral and political philosophy [which includes] an ethical account of the individual self-realization through participation in collective forms of life."[54] Indeed, West's prophetic pragmatism, contrary to his claims about remaining optimistic with regard to democracy, is systematically silent on Dewey's idea of an ethics of democracy. Dewey was the leading "advocate of participatory democracy, that is, of the belief that democracy as an ethical ideal called upon men and women to build communities in which the necessary opportunities and resources are available for every individual to realize fully his or her particular capacities and powers through participation in political, social and cultural life."[55] We should add that Dewey infused his ethical theory, and specifically as it relates to democracy, with a conception of human flourishing. After all, Dewey thinks that the democratic character of the social environment should foster intelligent choice. Finally, instead of worrying about diagnosing the health of the souls of individuals outside the context of social existence in human communities, Dewey instead focuses upon developing a moral criterion by which to judge social, cultural and political practices. According to him:

> The moral criterion by which to try social conditions and political measures may be summed up as follows: The test is whether a given custom or law sets free individual capacities in such a way as to make them available for the development of the greatest happiness or the common good. This formula states the test with the emphasis falling upon the side of the individual. It may be stated from the side of associated life as follows: The test is whether the general, the public organization and order are promoted in such a way as to equalize opportunity for all.[56]

West advocates repairing the souls of individuals. But, once again, this focus is his undoing, especially with regard to his take on Black existence. Any faithful pragmatism should be especially alert to the intimate link between the individual and the community within pragmatism. Problems suffered by individuals are ultimately problems that must be resolved at the communal level. The condition of the inner life of the individual is as contingent on the health of the cultural community as is the social life of the individual. West's appeal to a politics of conversion that focuses on the souls of individuals is far removed from the pragmatist's insistence on solving the problems of individuals through creating communities that foster human flourishing. Dewey, once again, holds that it is through the dynamic of social interaction that "the self is both formed and brought to consciousness,"[57] and not in "spiritual isolation." West does not indicate how his focus on the individual will ultimately sustain institutional and communal transformation. Consequently, his pragmatism, far from being prophetic, is more correctly described as a "pragmatism of the dramatic" to the extent that its energies are devoted to eradicating the specter of nihilism. His prophetic pragmatism needs a good philosophical exorcism.

In conclusion, West would probably reply that his take on pragmatism, among other things, is a response to the current professionalization of philosophy that has resulted in the alienation of philosophy from the daily concerns of people. Indeed, West favors the idea of the philosopher as a public intellectual, in the tradition of Dewey, and not as a professional concerned with technical matters. I do not think that appealing to the sociological condition of philosophy immedi-ately warrants surrendering critical and analytical scrutiny in philosophical matters as well as in matters of more general public concern. Hence, despite West's admirable goals, he still needs to make a strong and compelling case for the strategy of using motivational rhetoric as a solution to the practical problems of human beings.

Appendix: Richard Rorty and West's Prophetic Pragmatism

I want to encourage critical engagement between West and Rorty because Rorty, describing himself as a neopragmatist, has flirted with both prophecy and pragmatism. However, unlike West, Rorty argues against linking prophecy with pragmatism; hence, he finds the notion of prophetic pragmatism problematic.

Rorty, of course, favors limiting philosophical pragmatism to its place within the academy; more specifically, within the philosophical domain. He claims that philosophical pragmatism, broadly understood as concern with presenting philosophical arguments, is banal outside the enclosure of philosophy.[58] Furthermore, he charges that lawyers and judges who are pragmatic in their activities are quite successful without depending upon philosophical pragmatism for any beneficial philosophical assistance. Rorty states, "I agree with Posner that judges will probably not find pragmatist philosophers — either old or new — useful."[59]

All the while, Rorty's main enemy is professional philosophy and not pragmatism in general. He drastically favors limiting the task of philosophers. Instead of offering *a priori* philosophical arguments for the purpose of justifying foundational principles of truth and knowledge, or anything else, they should understand their professional obligations as restricted to removing the philosophical obstacles created by other philosophers — or, to appropriate Posner's metaphor, "clear[ing] the underbrush."[60] Once the task of the philosopher is limited to clearing away obstacles, it will become more apparent that those working outside the philosophical arena are not in need of any philosophical support. Let us turn briefly to examine Rorty's take on prophecy.

Rorty maintains that Dewey, besides his involvement with pragmatism, also assumed the role of prophet. In describing Dewey as a prophet, he states that he is referring to "the Emersonian visionary rather than the contributor to *The Journal of Philosophy*."[61] So, although a philosopher can function as a prophet, his so functioning is not in need of any philosophical justification.

Rorty claims that there was a time when the term "pragmatism" escaped the burden of being identified with philosophical argumentation. Indeed, he links pragmatism with a prophetic tradition. This relation between pragmatism and a prophetic tradition was made possible at a time when efforts were made to justify oppressive institutions by employing impartial (philosophical) arguments, guaranteed to convince any reasonable person. According to Rorty, in the era of James and Dewey, there was "still some relation between pragmatist philosophical doctrines and attempts to overcome racial prejudice, to make labor unions seem morally respectable, and to subordinate property rights to social needs."[62] We have to be careful not to interpret Rorty as contradicting himself. He is not saying that there is a prophetic pragmatism that should use philosophical arguments to fight oppressive institutions. Rather, he is making a historical claim. On his view, there was once the practice of using philosophical arguments to justify oppressive institutions. During this time it made sense to use philosophical arguments to attack oppressive institutions. Currently, both political conservatives and liberal progressives are "pragmatic"; neither group employs arguments. Hence, in a culture where philosophy is disciplinarily potent but culturally marginal, philosophers are not needed to denounce oppressive practices. Now judges and lawyers are the ones who dismantle oppressive conventions. This development means that there is no role for philosophical prophets; that is, individuals who use arguments to fight oppressive conventions. And Rorty wastes no time announcing that, from the perspective of professorial pragmatism, the term "prophetic pragmatism" is no more meaningful than "charismatic trash disposal."[63] Let us see how the proceeding considerations bear on West's notion of prophetic pragmatism.

To be clear, Rorty thinks that philosophy, with its emphasis on normative integrity, is not going to be able to tell us anything substantive about justice. Instead of seeing justice as sharing philosophical parity with the Good in the sense of having a nature or essence that can be discovered through *a priori* philosophical inquiry, Rorty claims that there is a prophetic element to justice.[64] But he does not think that the prophetic side of justice is dependent upon pragmatism for any kind of substantive philosophical assistance. Pragmatism can, at best, play a minimal role in clearing away philosophical obstacles that may place unnecessary constraints on the utilization of imagination and prophecy. However, there is no intimate connection between prophecy and pragmatism. According to Rorty, "if you had the prophecy, you could skip the pragmatism."[65]

In his review of West's text,[66] Rorty rejects West's attempt to invigorate his prophetic agenda by appropriating themes from professorial pragmatism. Again, Rorty wants to deflate the role of philosophical pragmatism outside the philosophical arena. Hence, any social movement, firmly committed to attacking oppressive institutions, must draw upon some other nonphilosophical source. Rorty says, "I do not think that professorial pragmatism is a good place to look for prophecy, or for the sort of rich possibilities which the prophetic imagination makes visible."[67] Citing Martin Luther King, Jr, as one engaged in prophetic activity, Rorty maintains that King was able to function successfully with the aid of philosophy. "The philosophy professors," according to Rorty, "cheered from the sidelines, but were of no great use to the civil rights movement."[68] So, from Rorty's perspective, West's prophetic pragmatism is problematic because: (a) West's attempt to link the prophetic and philosophical is misleading – prophecy depends upon imagination and not philosophical arguments; and (b) West is mistaken in his attempt to mine prophetic possibilities from professorial pragmatism. Professorial pragmatism is most effective in the task of clearing the underbrush in the philosophical arena, not offering prophetic motivational resources.

We must accept as correct Rorty's view that prophecy and philosophical pragmatism need not be linked. The obviousness of this conclusion becomes inescapable when we consider the problems plaguing West's attempt to graft prophecy onto pragmatism. Nevertheless, the choice is not between Rorty who wants prophecy without pragmatism or West who wants a prophetic pragmatism. Rather, it seems that both West and Rorty have, in their own way, resurrected the issue of the philosophical merit of pragmatism. I am wary of their call to deemphasize the role of philosophy in culture. Certainly, one cannot assume that philosophy can miraculously make things better by providing arguments. Nevertheless, there appears to be no substitute for the kind of critical and analytical thinking that can provide various cognitive models to bear on our understanding of issues. Dewey skillfully appropriated clusters of evolutionary and naturalistic metaphors in his account of human agents as social organisms struggling to adapt to a precarious external world. Such a move enabled Dewey to view language, beliefs, culture, etc. as tools that serve instrumental purposes for human beings. Correcting the *a priori* excessive concerns of traditional philosophy need not lead us unnecessarily to embrace linguistic performativity in place of probing and critically informative thinking, which seeks a more profound understanding of human projects of world construction.

Notes

1   Richard Bernstein, "American pragmatism: the conflict of narratives." In Herman Saatkamp (ed.), *Rorty and Pragmatism: The Philosopher Responds to His Critics* (Nashville, TN; Vanderbilt University Press, 1995), p. 66.

2   For a detailed and interesting history of pragmatism, see John Diggins, *The Promise of Pragmatism: Modernism and the Crisis of Knowledge and Authority* (Chicago: Chicago University Press, 1994).

3   Alasdair MacIntyre, "Epistemological crises, dramatic narrative and the philosophy of science." *Monist*, 60(4), 1977, p. 461.

4   Richard Shusterman, *Practicing Philosophy: Pragmatism and the Philosophical Life* (Routledge: New York, 1997), p. 5.

5   Susan Haack, "Vulgar pragmatism: an unedifying prospect." In Saatkamp (ed.), *Rorty and Pragmatism*, p. 126.

6   Ibid.

7   Richard Posner, *The Problems of Jurisprudence* (Cambridge, MA: Harvard University Press, 1990), p. 465.

8   John Dewey, *Experience and Nature, The Later Works 1925–1953, volume 1*, ed. Jo Ann Boydston (Carbondale: Southern Illinois University Press, 1981), p. 43.

9   J. Buchler (ed.), *Philosophical Writings of Peirce* (New York: Dover Publications, 1955), p. 229.

10   Bernard Williams, *Ethics and the Limits of Philosophy* (Cambridge, MA: Harvard University Press, 1985), pp. 138–9.

11   Richard Bernstein, "The resurgence of pragmatism." *Social Research*, 59(4), 1992, p. 837.

12   Cornel West, *Beyond Eurocentrism and Multiculturalism, volume II* (Monroe, ME: Common Courage Press, 1993), p. 81.

13   Robert Gooding-Williams, "Evading narratives myth, evading prophetic pragmatism: Cornel West's *The American Evasion of Philosophy*." *The Massachusetts Review*, Winter 1991/2, p. 523.

14   Cornel West, *The American Evasion of Philosophy: A Genealogy of Pragmatism* (Madison: University of Wisconsin Press, 1989), p. 239.

15   Cornel West, *Prophesy Deliverance! An Afro-American Revolutionary Christianity* (Philadelphia: Westminster Press, 1982), p. 24.

16   West, *The American Evasion of Philosophy*, p. 230.

17   Ibid., p. 233.

18   Cornel West, "Theory, pragmatisms, and politics." In Robert Hollinger and David Depew (eds), *Pragmatism: From Progressivism to Postmodernism* (Westport, CT: Praeger, 1995), p. 324.

19   George Yancy (ed.), *African-American Philosophers: 17 Conversations* (New York: Routledge, 1998), p. 35.

20   Cornel West, "The dilemma of the black intellectual." In bell hooks and Cornel West, *Breaking Bread: Insurgent Black Intellectual Life* (Boston: South End Books, 1991), p. 136.

21   Bernstein, "The resurgence of pragmatism," p. 831.

22   Robert Gooding-Williams, "Review of *Keeping the Faith: Philosophy and Race in America*." *Philosophical Review*, 104(4), 1995, p. 601.

23   West, *The American Evasion of Philosophy*, p. 207.

24   Cornel West, *Keeping the Faith: On Race and Philosophy in America* (New York: Routledge, 1993), p. xi.

25   West, *The American Evasion of Philosophy*, pp. 232–3.

26   Ibid., p. 212.

27   Ibid., pp. 213–14.

28   Ibid., p. 214.

29   Ibid., p. 232.

30   Ibid., p. 223.

31   Ibid., p. 228.

32   Ibid., p. 229.

33   Ibid.

34   Ibid., p. 228.

35   Hilary Putnam, *Pragmatism* (Cambridge, MA: Blackwell, 1995), p. 2.

36   See Henry Mitchell, *Black Preaching: The Recovery of a Powerful Art* (Nashville, TN: Abingdon Press, 1991); Gerald L. Davis, *I Got the Word in Me and I Can Sing It, You Know: A Study of the Performed African-American Sermon* (Philadelphia: University of Pennsylvania Press, 1985).

37   Cornel West, *Race Matters* (New York: Vintage Books, 1994), p. 43.

38 Charles Valentine, *Culture and Poverty: Critique and Counter-Proposals* (Chicago: University of Chicago Press, 1968), pp. 20–1; and Jerry Watts, *Heroism and the Black Intellectual: Ralph Ellison, Politics, and Afro-American Intellectual Life* (Chapel Hill: University of North Carolina Press, 1991), p. 59. For an excellent study of the use of pathology in the study of Blacks, see Daryl Scott, *Contempt and Pity: Social Policy and the Image of the Damaged Black Psyche 1880–1996* (Chapel Hill: University of North Carolina Press, 1997).

39 For a radically different take on nihilism in the black context, see Nick De Genova, "Gangster rap and nihilism in black America: some questions of life and death." *Social Text*, 43 (Fall), 1995, pp. 89–132.

40 West, *Race Matters*, pp. 22–3.

41 Ibid., p. 19.

42 West, *Beyond Eurocentrism and Multiculturalism, volume II*, p. 90.

43 West, *Race Matters*, pp. 19–20.

44 Ibid., p. 27.

45 Ibid., p. 56.

46 Ibid., p. 19.

47 Ibid., p. 29.

48 Ibid.

49 Ibid.

50 Stephen Steinberg, "The liberal retreat from race during the post-Civil Rights era." In Wahneema Lubiano (ed.), *The House that Race Built* (New York: Vintage, 1997), p. 38.

51 West, *Race Matters*, p. 21.

52 Eric Lott, "Cornel West in the hour of chaos: culture and politics in *Race Matters*." *Social Text*, 40 (Fall), 1994, p. 43.

53 Sandra Rosenthal, "Democracy and education: a Deweyan approach." *Educational Theory*, 43(4), 1993, p. 381.

54 Matthew Festenstein, *Pragmatism and Political Theory: From Dewey to Rorty* (Chicago: University of Chicago Press, 1997), p. 24.

55 Robert Westbrook, *John Dewey and American Democracy* (Ithaca, NY: Cornell University Press, 1991), p. xv.

56 John Dewey, *Ethics* (with James Hayden Tuffs), 1st edn, in John Dewey, *The Middle Works, 1899–1924, volume 5*, ed. Jo Ann Boydston (Carbondale: Southern Illinois University Press), p. 431. Quoted in Matthew Festenstein, *Pragmatism and Political Theory: From Dewey to Rorty* (Chicago: University of Chicago Press, 1997), p. 59.

57 *Art as Experience*. In *The Later Works, volume 10*, ed. Jo Ann Boydston (Carbondale: Southern Illinois University Press, 1987), p. 286.

58 See "Banality of pragmatism and the poetry of justice." In Michael Brint and William Weaver (eds), *Pragmatism in Law and Society* (Boulder, CO: Westview Press, 1991), pp. 89–97.

59 Ibid., p. 92.

60 Ibid., p. 44.

61 Ibid., p. 92.

62 Richard Rorty, "The philosopher and the prophet." *Transition*, 52, 1991, p. 74.

63 Ibid.

64 "Banality of pragmatism and the poetry of justice," pp. 92–3.
65 Richard Rorty, "Afterword." *Southern California Law Review*, 63 (September), 1999, p. 1917.
66 See Rorty, "The philosopher and the prophet," pp. 70–8.
67 Ibid., p. 73.
68 Ibid.

4

Which Pragmatism? Whose America?

Eduardo Mendieta

Introduction

Pragmatism has once again become a worthy and formidable philosophical movement, after having been eclipsed during most of the twentieth century.[1] Yet the
revival and rescue of pragmatism is linked to some of the same reasons that have
made poststructuralism, deconstruction, postmodernism, and postcolonial theory
the vogue of the academy and the talk of highbrow journalism. So the revival is
neither fortuitous nor adroitly forced. There is a logic to it. Indeed, there is a
strong family resemblance between pragmatism's rejection of foundationalism,
logocentrism disguised as a philosophy of consciousness, a strong concept of theory
and philosophy, a correspondence theory of truth, a museum-like theory of
language (in which there are things, and language just names them, like labels on
dioramas in museums), and similar rejections by deconstruction, postmodernism,
and related philosophical and literary criticism currents. Such convergences and
elective affinities have been explored with great acuity and perspicacity by writers
like Rorty, Bernstein, Fraser, and West.[2] What has not been analyzed and made
explicit is that underlying the various projects of the refunctioning and renaissance
of pragmatism, whether as simple neopragmatism or prophetic pragmatism, is the
project of the reconstitution and reframing of national identity. Curiously, many
have noted that there is a relationship between the projects of the total critique of
reason and the criticism of the West.[3] The postmodern critique has been assimi-
lated to a critique of the West as such. The idea is that the totalitarianism of the
West is rooted in the totalitarianism of monological and instrumental reason, at
which is aimed the deconstructive onslaught of postmodern criticisms. Such

criticism arose from two sources: internally, from the demise of Western credibility and claim to historical privilege due to the horrors of the holocaust and two bloody World Wars; and externally, from the decolonizing countries that had suffered Western colonialism. To what extent, it should be asked, is the revival of pragmatism related to these crises and critiques of the "West," and the internal and external criticisms of the United States, which unquestionably has taken over the civilizing project of the West? Pragmatism emerged during the middle of the nineteenth century partly as a response to the question: what is the United States or what should it become after a traumatic and devastating Civil War? Today, when "American" philosophers reach back to nineteenth-century pragmatism as an autochthonous philosophical tradition, they do so in order to partly and sometimes covertly answer the question: what is the United States or what should it become at the end of a century and the beginning of a new one? In other words, and this is the core of these reflections, how American pragmatism is reconstructed and portrayed, which figures are foregrounded and given prominence, and what philosophical importance is attached to specific insights and arguments, seeks to develop and project a new national imaginary; that is, a new image of the nation. To use West's language, we might say that what genealogy we trace determines which America we are able to visualize and project. Which pragmatism thus also means, which America?

The title of this chapter is therefore to be taken as suggesting that there is a deep link between these two questions, that to attempt to answer one is, in a very unequivocal sense, to attempt to answer the other. The visions that we may possess of what "America" was, is, and should become, inform and guide our reconstructions and interpretations of its intellectual biography. By the same token, how we reconstruct and interpret the history of this intellectual, philosophical, and cultural inheritance will give a very concrete content to our own anticipatory and prospective images of who we are, and who we would like to become. It is precisely this entwinement that reveals itself in the contemporary debates concerning, let us say, Robert Westbrook's reading of Dewey, or John Smith's, in contrast to Richard Rorty's; or in the much broader debate between Richard Rorty's privately ironic and publicly solidaristic neopragmatism and West's publicly and privately prophetic pragmatism.[4] This subterranean connection between how we reconstruct our so-called autochthonous philosophical inheritance, and what we claim we have become as a nation, as a country, and as a culture which faces very unique problems, is precisely what is revealed in the debate about the canon and the debilitating, disempowering, fetishizing, and alienating images therein projected, legitimated, and made hegemonic. In this chapter, therefore, I argue that West's "genealogy of pragmatism" be read not just as a quaint philosophical and exegetical, or history of ideas, project. Rather, West's project should be read as a profound intervention in the national project and discourse about what and how it should define itself. Further, I want to argue that West's reading is not just politically charged, but also philosophically astute; that is, the suggestion is that West's reconstruction of North American pragmatism is philosophically constructive because it furthers the insights of classical pragmatism. And, finally, in this chapter I hope to offer warrants for the arguments that West's reconstruction of pragmatism offers us a "more useful" image of our intellectual traditions. In order to accomplish these goals, I proceed by way of a reconstruction of West's intellectual itinerary, and then I conclude with the discussion of four key rubrics that typify West's creative contribution to the rescue, renewal and transformation of American pragmatism.[5]

The Making of a Public Intellectual and the Project of Prophetic Pragmatism

West unquestionably has emerged as one of the most important public intellectuals in contemporary United States.[6] His rise to prominence can only be appropriately understood when contrasted with that of Richard Rorty. Earlier, Rorty seemed to occupy the place that West has assumed. *The New York Times Sunday Magazine*, for instance, dedicated its front page to Rorty, and a lengthy and sympathetic profile.[7] This profile, however, placed Rorty within the narrow horizon of intra-university struggles and transformations. Rorty is an apostate professor, a rebellious and disillusioned one, who tells of the crises internal to his own field. While announcing the obsolescence and anachronism of a particular form of doing philosophy, Rorty calls for the transformation of the profession, and its revitalization by means of a turn to certain elements within American's philosophical traditions. Rorty's intellectual biography and his recent rise to prominence in the intellectual life of "North Atlantic" cultures, then, must be understood as the history of the crisis of an institution, namely professional philosophy, and of a particular philosophical tradition, namely analytic philosophy, the professional philosophy which has been hegemonic in most philosophy departments at least since the Second World War, and the philosophies of science, mind, and language that evolved from it. Rorty's rise to prominence, at the same time, must also be understood against the background of the overall "crises" of upper, and one should also include secondary, education within the United States. It is not without surprise, or incidental, that within the past decade we have had the similar rise to prominence of conservative intellectuals like Bloom and Hirschman, who bewail the disintegration of cultural standards brought about by the inclusion of the barbarians within the sacred halls of the parthenon of United States' intellectual life, while on the left, as well, intellectuals like Russell Jacoby, for different reasons, also bemoan the institutionalization of left intellectuals whereby they are domesticated into professional academics. The "multiculturalism," the "canon," and "why Johnny can't add" debates have to do with the crises of the educational system in the United States. In short, we need to keep in mind the plethora of institutional and societal crises out of which Rorty arises. In another context, under different goals, it would perhaps be more relevant and pertinent to attempt a richer profile of the "thick" web of economic, social, political, and cultural factors and events that have conditioned the appearance of cultural phenomena like Rorty, Bloom, Hirschmann, and Jacoby. I would suggest that this picture, rich in tones and thick in consistency, would have to start, at least, with: the inclusion within the academy of an unprecedented number of minorities, i.e. Blacks, women, Hispanics, Asians, etc.; the decline of the United States as a World Empire; the deep and unhealed wound of the catastrophic failure of Vietnam, the return of the "Other America" in Michael Harrinton's words; the conservative dismantling of the welfare state (which affected the structures of education, to the point that higher education is turning more and more into a class privilege); the attack on democratic structures, or nominal presuppositions of its working principles, by the conservative elites (I am here thinking of Ronald Reagan's Iran–Contra Affair, the unconstitutional and undeclared war on Nicaragua, the Invasion of Panama, and, later, Bush's Iraq war, which was waged on the deceitful and coercive deployment of power at the international level through the United Nations – twelve years, in short, of conservative rule that have left a seriously undermined and politicized judiciary, a splintered legislative, and an overgrown and overpowering executive); and the transformation of the United States' economy from industry to a highly technical and service-oriented economy. Indeed, the elitism of a conservative government, a depoliticized body politic, the increasing demand for justice and inclusion by minorities, the struggles over the canon, and the similar struggles for the development of nonracist, non-Eurocentric curricula, and thus over what elements are included in the definition of our self-identity as citizens of the United States, as well as the need to meet the challenge of Japan and a post-industrial economy, are all one within the fabric that also determines the rise of intellectuals like Rorty, Hirschman, Bloom, et al.

West's case, if not entirely different, is at least one that cannot be easily subsumed under the internal dynamics of the crises of a particular institution or philosophical tradition. In contrast to Rorty, for instance, who has published most of his books with academic presses, West has published with popular and left presses, i.e. Pantheon, which generally published left liberal materials, South End Press, Monthly Review Press, Courage Press, and even Africa World Press, and the religious presses Orbis Books and Westminster Press. Similarly, although West received a philosophy PhD from Princeton University in 1980, he has taught for most of his professional career in either religion departments or theological schools, i.e. Union Theological Seminary, Yale Divinity School, Princeton University, and now Harvard. West has been no outsider, but by no means has he been an insider who needs to renounce and denounce a moribund institution. Most importantly, and in stark contrast to Rorty, West has been what in Gramscian terminology we call an "organic intellectual." The use of this denomination for

West is warranted by his close ties to the African-American churches. In addition, West has been active in Democratic Socialists of America (DSA), the socialist conference that takes place yearly in New York, and has participated in all kinds of locally based protest movements. West moves comfortably between the different dimensions and aspects of the North American public sphere: he can preach in the morning, teach a seminar on Wittgenstein, Heidegger, and Dewey in the after-noon, talk to a group of workers on the history of the labor movement in the United States, and spend the evening playing jazz with his music buddies. All of West's talents, at the same time, come to bear on his interventions in any public situation. As against Rorty, who would like to retreat behind the postfeminist realization that the private and the public are always co-determining and over-determining each other, West wants to mobilize private experience, which is always shot through with the public, in order to transform a public which has frozen and petrified into particular modes and forms of injustice, and dehumaniza-tion.

In any event, what I am trying to delineate very sketchily is the extent to which Rorty and West are different, while also keeping in mind how both emerge from the same constellation of societal problems that presently confront United States citizens. Later, after we have gone over some aspects of West's work, these contrasts will become more evident, and perhaps we will be able to see in greater detail how West's work is important in how it contributes to a self-understanding by and of the United States that is not reflected in or refracted through Rorty's work.

In order to obtain a substantive but not exhaustive characterization of West's work, I would like to focus on two of his major works. These two works mark the two major points of transition and solidification in West's own development. There are at least four other books which merit close discussion, but which in my analysis, since they are collections of essays, speeches, and reviews, can only indirectly contribute to our understanding of West's philosophical and intellectual program. Furthermore, I do not discuss the books produced during the nineties, mostly because they are applications of his insights and approach, rather than departures and transformations in his basic intellectual and philosophical orienta-tion. In any event, I will refer to them only in order to illustrate the cogency and coherence of West's project.

First, we need to note that West received his PhD from Princeton in 1980, where he submitted his dissertation: "Ethics, historicism and the Marxist tradition." This dissertation has since been published under the title *The Ethical Dimensions of Marxist Thought*.[8] Very succinctly, in this work, West sets out to demonstrate how Marx made a metaphilosophical move by means of which he overcame the classical form of doing philosophy. This metaphilosophical move consisted, in West's view and under the influence of Rorty, who was his professor at Princeton, in turning away from ontological, epistemological, and metaphysical questions towards historical, social, and ethical issues. West proceeds to show, through exegeses of Marx's *1844 Manuscripts*, the *German Ideology*, and his minor historical writings, how Marx was not interested in developing a grand system of philosophy that would set aright all prior philosophical systems. Marx was interested in thick historical narratives from the perspective of the need to transform social reality. Marx's social analytics had the concrete goal of empowering historical subjects to engage in the historical transformation of situations in which these same subjects are rendered inhuman. For West, above all, Marx's social analytics was a moral judgment on a dehumanizing world that demanded its abolition and transformation.

It is with Kautsky, Engels, and Lukács that Marx's metaphilosophical move of evading Platonist–Kantian–Hegelian type philosophy gets disarmed and his historical views become frozen systems. It is only with Gramsci that we see a return to the fundamental insights of Marx. Gramsci, in this sense, will become the true inheritor of the Marxist move which abolishes philosophy by transforming it into localized sociocultural criticism and engaged political practice. This view of Gramsci will become permanent in West's thought.

Between 1980 and 1982, when his next major work is published, *Prophesy Deliverance!*, West works on a series of essays on the relationship between Black theology of liberation and Marxism. These essays, however, are subsumed within *Prophesy Deliverance!*, as we will see. Nevertheless, it is important to keep in mind that this work emerges in many ways out of the discussions and debates around Black liberation theology which took place in the context of West's first and early teaching years at Union Theological Seminary, where James H. Cone (author of *Black Theology and Black Power* (1969)), James M. Washington (editor of Martin Luther King, Jr's speeches and writings), James Forbes (who was senior preacher at Riverside Church in Manhattan), Gustavo Gutierrez, Enrique Dussel, and many other theologians of liberation have taught. West was also a member of the editorial collective of *Social Text*, where he interacted with Jameson, Aranowitz, and other Marxist thinkers. In short, the context is one where Black religiosity, Black liberation theology, Latin American liberation theology, postmodern, post-communist Marxism intersect and overlap.

Prophesy Deliverance! is an ambitious, rich, challenging, and systematic work whose primary dual question is: what are the tasks for Afro-American thought, and what are the "intellectual, philosophical, cultural, religious, historical, etc." sources that Afro-American thought can take recourse to in order to address these tasks as they present themselves to the Afro-American in contemporary United States? The task, in fact, of Afro-American thought becomes that of discovering, reconstructing, and rescuing its own sources. This project, in other words, is archeological, destructive, reconstructive, and constructive. For West, two of the major sources of Afro-American thought are, first, prophetic Christian thought and religiosity, and, second, American pragmatism. Christianity is a major source because it combines the fundamental principle of self-realization, self-actualization, with the deeply ingrained awareness of the dynamic between tragedy and triumph. Christianity, viewed by West through the lens of Black Baptist evangelical Protestantism, is primarily a theodicy; that is, the perennial question after the origins of evil and suffering, and the tentative answer that God will redeem all suffering. It goes without saying that it is through this lens that slaves read Christianity, namely primarily as a theodicy. From this perspective, then, slaves were able to transform Christianity into a gospel of rebellion and liberation. Christianity as theodicy, as opposed to Christianity as theogony, or cosmogony, etc., can thus be understood as a type of optimism tempered by healthy skepticism and a long memory of defeat and failure. American pragmatism is a major source because it rejected Cartesianism, its monism and individualism, and its preoccupation with epistemology for a form of agency born out of intersubjectivity, and the reconceptualization of knowledge as a societal and communal affair. Above all, for West, the pragmatist's dethroning of epistemology meant the transformation of philosophy into an ethical practice of critique. To a certain extent, we may say, these two complementary sources related to a complementary division of labor. If prophetic Christianity, sobered by the theodicy perspective, contributes to the constructive function of Afro-American thought, American pragmatism contributes to its destructive function. One develops the prospective dimensions of the intellectual tradition, while the other helps undermine any kind of philosophical vision that would challenge or place in question the prospective project. Later this division of labor will not be as severe or parceled. West will move to a reading of pragmatism which places it already within the Christian tradition; he will read pragmatism more clearly and distinctly as a form of second and third wave romanticism, which will also bring it into a closer vicinity to Marxism, another variant of romanticism.

For West, there cannot be a serious and in-depth understanding of the tasks of Afro-American thought without an understanding of the historical situation in which Afro-Americans find themselves today, and the genesis of that situation. In this context, West suggests a periodization that attempts to provide us with a historical panorama filled with historical upheavals, and major dynamics. In West's historical canvas we have, first, the age of Europe that lasts approximately from 1492 through 1945, second, the end of Modernity as a consequence of the end of the age of Europe, and, third, the rise of dispersive and critical practices under the rubric of postmodernism. Part and parcel of these periods, more or less, are the dissolution of industrial provinciality, and the challenge to the overweening confidence in the supremacy and coherence of Western humanism, as well as the deployment of postindustrial cosmopolitanism, and the development of complementary inclusionary practices, demanded and attained if only partially, by the exploding Third World, and the empowered and embattled subjectivities of hitherto marginalized and occluded selves.

Of greatest importance in terms of this historical canvas that West paints is the character of postmodernity. West paints it in broad strokes in the following manner. First is the crisis of science, brought about by its pyrrhic victory, epitomized in two bloody and devastating world wars, the atom bomb, and the unleashing of ecological devastation and waste. This crisis, notes West, resembles the crisis of the church which was catalyzed by the Enlightenment. Second, with the delegitimation of Western humanism, and the rise of relativistic historicism, the cultural atmosphere of Europe gets saturated by paganism, skepticism, cynicism, fatalism, and hedonism. Third is the continuance and deepening of the attacks on the Cartesian and Kantian primacy of the subject. It is against this broadly characterized historical background that we need to understand the possibility for the development of a viable Afro-American thought tradition that addresses itself to its historical situation. In other words, it is precisely against the background of the twilight of Western humanism and the emergence of a discourse of Otherness that Afro-American thought makes its bid for self-identity and relevance.

Consonant with this historical periodization is West's genealogy of modern racism. Neither unsophisticated Marxist economic determinism nor broad cultural views will do in the task of understanding modern racism. One of the tasks, in fact, of Afro-American thought is to develop a set of analytical tools that will allow the Afro-American thinker, in particular, and society, in general, to explore the multiple levels at which racism is elaborated, produced, deployed, legitimated, and sedimented into sets of cultural norms and practices that permeate the entire social fabric. It is with this in mind that West rejects these unilateral, abstractive, insufficient perspectives and opts for the development of his own, one that he calls a genealogical perspective. This perspective, or methodology, above all, asks the question after the conditions of possibility of a particular set of discursive practices and their accompanying structures. Here West takes Foucault as his guide. Given this understanding of genealogy, West proceeds to ask: what are the structures of modern racial discourses, what are their grammars, how do they constitute the domains within which they locate their racialized subject-objects? In West's understanding of discursive practices, one must include not only metaphors, notions, categories, norms, but also the social structures that serve as the institutional space for the articulation of the former. West's genealogies, then, also attain greater "thickness" when they address themselves to the historical, economic, political, and social causes and effects of these discursive practices and institutions. These metaphors, norms, categories, and their corresponding institutions have been conditioned and are circumscribed by three major historical events: first, the scientific revolution; second, the Cartesian transformation of philosophy; and, third, the classical revival, or what Bernal has referred to as the "creation of the Greek" aesthetic myth. With science there emerges the primacy of evidence and observation which harmonizes and complements the Cartesian preoccupation with epistemological representability, which in turn also coordinates and harmonizes with the dominance of the Ocular metaphor within Greek aesthetic ideals. In short, modern discourses of raciality must be understood under the rubric of the hegemony of ocularity, representability, scientificity, and the Greek aesthetic ideal imposed by a return to Greece as a cultural model for beauty, of a particular type, proportion, moderation, etc. The convergence of these historical currents give rise to what West calls "the normative gaze." In a second stage in the development of modern racism, there appear, as concomitants of the "normative gaze," phrenology and physiognomy, pseudo-sciences that, in any event, came to receive the widest support, even by the most avid defenders of the Enlightenment: Hegel, Kant, Hume, et al. What West is arguing is that racism is not an aberration of modernity, but rather its *sine qua non*, its logical outcome and not one of its pathologies.

Given this periodization of modernity, and postmodernity, and this genealogy of modern racism, West proceeds to develop a typology of Afro-American responses to the experience of racism. In this typology, curiously, West presents himself as an internal but nevertheless serious and uncompromising critic of his own tradition(s), and in the process of characterizing these different responses his own counterproposal is adumbrated. West speaks of four major traditions: the exceptionalist, the assimilationist, the marginalist, and the humanist.[9]

The exceptionalist tradition lauds the uniqueness, particularity, and exceptionality of Afro-American culture and personality. This exaltation might assume either strong or weak forms depending on the emphasis and nature of the exceptional character of the Afro-American. West faults this tradition for romanticizing Afro-American experience and culture. At the same time, West also sees the origins of this type of cultural position in the emergence of a Black bourgeoisie for which the primary question was that of their own cultural identity. In their hypostatization of a cultural nucleus that is representative of all suffering Black humanity, the rising petit bourgeois is able to conceal its own class mobility, a class mobility that nevertheless leaves untouched, or barely calls into question, the overall structure of racism. To this tradition belong Du Bois, James Weldon Johnson, and Martin Luther King, Jr.

The assimilationist tradition began from the opposite proposition from the exceptionalist tradition. It considers Afro-American culture inferior, and a liability, a product of pathology and underdevelopment. This self-image is one of hate, shame, and fear. This perspective elaborates a sociological analysis that tries to explain the superstition, ignorance, self-hatred, and fear that plague Afro-American culture as consequences of institutional racism. It was this type of analysis that provided the intellectual framework for the legal and political argumentation for civil rights during the decades of the 1940s, 1950s, and 1960s. This tradition rejects *in toto* Afro-American culture, and calls for complete assimilation. To this tradition belongs someone like E. Franklin Frazier.

The marginalist tradition, like the assimilationalist tradition, also posits Afro-American culture to be constraining, confining, restrictive, and disabling, evidently as a consequence of the history of slavery and institutional racism. In contrast, however, whereas the assimilationalist tradition performed its critique of Afro-American culture from a sociological perspective, sensitive to historical determination, the marginalist tradition seems to read the negativity of Afro-American culture through existentialist, ontological, and metaphysical constructs. To this tradition belong Richard Wright and Charles Chesnut.

The humanist tradition begins with the taken-for-granted humanity of Afro-Americans and sees their culture as both rich and varied, but also filled with profound insights into humanizing attitudes. Instead of seeing Afro-American culture as an opiate, it sees it as a balm that heals, a repository of memories of struggle and hopes of liberation, and also a great testament for all humanity of the struggles against all inhumanity. This tradition, above all, values the cultural gains made by Afro-Americans. Despite all the odds, without romanticizing their experience, the humanist tradition sees Afro-Americans as products of humans interacting in history, in their own situations. In this sense, the projects for liberation and transformation can be and must be read through the very cultural documents left behind by Afro-Americans. The question of identity, too, can only be addressed through a serious engagement with Afro-American cultural traditions. To this tradition belong Ralph Ellison, Zora Neal Hurston, Langston Hughes, et al. Without question it is to this tradition that West himself subscribes, the one to which he feels closest.

Finally, West proceeds to delineate a history of the development of Black theology of liberation and what this has to say to both prophetic Christianity and progressive Marxism. In this last section, then, after he has given us characterizations of why, methodologically and substantially, Marxism and Christianity share many goals and presuppositions, and after he has sketched a history of Black liberation theology itself, West gives more substance to his own project of developing an autochthonous intellectual tradition that sets out to discover what both its sources and tasks are.

After this work, West continued to develop his notion of prophetic criticism through a series of essays and reviews, in which the major themes are Marxism, the Afro-American experience, religion, and contemporary social criticism, and especially Afro-American contemporary culture, which includes music, movies, and letters. We can say then that the first three-quarters of the eighties is the period in which West is primarily concerned with the development of a productive and mutually fruitful discourse between, above all, two major traditions: prophetic Christianity, as best expressed in Afro-American religiosity, and progressive Marxism, as best expressed in the thought of Gramsci, Jameson, and Williams. It is within the context of this encounter that we must place West's concern with postmodernity. Indeed, in many ways, postmodernism has a place within West's thought only as long as it is conceptualized as contributing to the methodological expertise and dexterity of deep and thick deconstructive and destructive practices that elaborate narratives and analytics of both struggle and oppression. Post-modernism is internal to Marxist critiques and is already a cultural presupposition of the cultural projects of modern Afro-American subjectivity. To this period belong the collection of essays *Prophetic Fragments*,[10] *Keeping the Faith: Philosophy and Race in America*,[11] and the book, which he co-authored with bell hooks, *Breaking Bread*.[12] This last book is noteworthy because in it West opens himself wholeheartedly to the problem of sexism within the Afro-American community, in general, and the gender blind spot in his own work, which up to then had privileged Black male intellectuals. This entire book, a collection of conversations between hooks and West, represents the execution of a public critical pedagogy, the living out of an ideal that both West and hooks have espoused since they have been public intellectuals.

With West's next major work, *The American Evasion of Philosophy: a Genealogy of Pragmatism*,[13] the focus changes, but not the project. As we have seen above, West considers pragmatism to be one of the main sources for a critical and prophetic criticism. In his early work, however, West only dealt with pragmatism tangen-tially, and not as extensively as he had dealt with the two other major sources, namely prophetic Christianity and progressive Marxism. In this major work of interpretive cultural criticism and history, West sets out to rescue by means of an avowedly political and ideological genealogy the most important intellectual and philosophical tradition that the United States has given birth to. West is clear and honest about the nature of his project, namely that it is a project that has to be understood against the background of our particular postmodern situation, which includes not only the internal crises of the academy and the crises of the left, but also the much more important national identity crisis. This crisis affects as much Afro-Americans as other members of the body politic, although it is clear that the point of entry into this crisis for West is precisely his belonging to the Afro-American community. With this in mind, West hopes to engage in a project of cultural reinterpretation and rescue so as to intervene directly and effectively in the mobilization of autochthonous cultural resources that would address this crisis in cultural identity. For West, this tendentious look at the history of American pragmatism is far from being an academic pursuit. It is, above all, a political gesture, one which assumes his project as a background. As West puts it, it is a political interpretation that hopes not to be ideological in the pejorative sense.[14]

Inasmuch, then, as West is primarily interested in rendering evident the cultural resources that gravitate around what is considered to be the most unique intellec-tual tradition of the United States, he reaches back to Emerson, in whom West locates the origins of that particular set of cultural, philosophical, and tempera-mental attitudes that characterized most broadly but specifically American prag-matism. In Emerson, whose "The American Scholar" is said to have been a declaration of intellectual independence of the United States, West discovers the formulations that will be again and again taken up by later North American thinkers as their guide. Emerson, according to West, elaborates a concept of the self which is at the center of the North American imperial self, namely the protean, exceptional, creative, courageous, voluntaristic, independent self. This self is also characterized by its idealism, and experimental character. Emerson also rejects tradition so as to free the exceptional American individuality to engage in its own project of creation. West, at the same time, is careful to note that this self, which must struggle against the market nonetheless, inasmuch as it lives from provocation, can easily align itself with the forces of the market place. The protean, imperial self can also fall into an anthropophagy, it literally feeds off of other people. Abstractly, the consequences of this mobile and creative self, as West notes pointedly, can lead to a kind of antihierarchism, egalitarianism, and populist democracy. In the concrete, however, it leads to elitism, to a disregard for the common person, and an unexpected classism. But most important is Emerson's "evasion" of philosophy; that is, that "he skillfully refuses (1) its quest for certainty and its hope for professional, i.e., scientific respectability; and (2) its search for foundations. It is from this refusal that the sensibilities and sentiments of future American pragmatism emerge."[15]

American pragmatism emerges, in West's account, when the Emersonian evasion of philosophy has to be justified within the professional parameters of academic philosophy. It is this evasion which Peirce, James, and Dewey, the classical philosophers of American pragmatism, are said to be justifying and explaining to their academic colleagues. Peirce, for instance, is read as carrying on one of the most devastating critiques of classical philosophy by means of a critique of Cartesianism. Above all, Peirce champions an intersubjective notion of the self, if not at least of knowledge, and a transformation of the scientific enterprise into a communal project. Here, Peirce, in West's view, is said to be also moving toward the same kind of religious and emotive sources that lay behind Emerson, namely a certain form of pietistic Christianity. Love, community, and the scientific method are woven in Peirce's thinking so as to provide us with a view of the world in which both our knowledge and the order of the cosmos are assumed to be on a path of convergence.

In contrast to Peirce, James emerges as the thinker of individuality and subjectivity. James's concern with cultural and experiential issues, to which he brings to bear the methodological insights which he credited Peirce for having discovered, makes him into the great popularizer of pragmatism. West creates an interesting parallel between Peirce and James. If the former gave greater primacy to convergence, harmony, oneness, and synthesis, the latter gave greater primacy to individuality, creativity, diversity, and plurality. Above all, also, these differences are temperamental. Peirce was interested in logic, mathematics, science, and the scientific method, to which he contributed in such significant ways that even today we are still discovering the importance of his contributions. James, on the other hand, was interested in religion, psychology, culture, and the constitution of subjective experience and its effects on practical life.

American pragmatism, however, comes of age with Dewey, West's greatest representative. West links this coming of age of pragmatism in Dewey with the particular historical juncture in which Dewey operates. This is the time when the United States is emerging on the world scene as a world power. In this sense, the United States is confronted with a new role. It must open itself to Europe in a new and unprecedented manner but, at the same time, it must articulate its own cultural identity.[16] The most important contribution and further articulation of pragmatism that Dewey makes is to bring to the Emersonian concern with futurity, creativity, individuality, and power the European discovery of historicity. In contrast, then, to Emerson, who thought of conditionedness in individualistic and subjective terms, and Peirce, who thought of conditionedness in terms of fallibilism and revisability of scientific theories and scientific knowledge in general, Dewey came to think of conditionedness in terms of historical contingency; that is, in terms of historical projects and processes. In short, Dewey introduces to pragmatism, via his early Hegelianism, and later via his concern with the consequences of Darwinism for science, a fully historical consciousness, a deep sense of contingency and historical fallibility. This will affect not only Dewey's perception of the fundamental issues with which philosophy concerns itself, but also his very conception of philosophy. According to West, with Dewey, pragmatism finally reaches the consequences of the Emersonian evasion of philosophy. For it is with Dewey that philosophy becomes a type of social criticism in which philosophical problems are societal problems, in which philosophical systems express particular social values, goals, concerns, and historical situations. In this way, the role of philosophers is to engage philosophical problems as social problems, and not as parts of ahistorical thought systems. West calls this final "metaphilosophical" move, first made by Emerson and now concluded by Dewey, a regicide. Dewey dethrones and beheads philosophy. For Dewey attacks, just as Peirce had attacked the Cartesian preoccupation with total doubt and self-evident truths, the obsession with epistemology, and its corollary, subjectivism, or the experience of the subject without the horizon of its possibility. In Dewey's move, then, the autarkic self, the epistemology industry, as Rorty will later call it, and the hegemony of science are all challenged and demystified. With this critique there also comes the critique of philosophy as the arbiter of truth and objectivity, rationality and normativity. Philosophy is finally dethroned, and in that sense it has been sublated, superseded into a type of social criticism with practical intent (as Habermas will talk about his own project of universal pragmatics).

For this genealogy of American pragmatism, West claims Sidney Hook, W. E. B. Du Bois, C. Wright Mills, Reinhold Neibuhr, and Lionel Trilling. The tradition continues, now challenged, broadened, put on the defensive, but still as a subtext, as a general horizon, a general set of presuppositions. In West's mind, Sidney Hook, who was a student of Dewey, and one of his points of contact with American left thought, contributes to pragmatism by historicizing tragedy. In contrast to Dewey, who had already historicized pragmatism's meliorism, and optimism, Hook historicizes Emerson's concern with evil. Hook, as a thinker deeply aware of the Marxist critique of capitalism, and, in general, of a thick understanding of the material constraints on human creativity, gives a substantive twist to Emersonian theodicy. Du Bois, a student of James and Dilthey, in West's opinion, contributes to pragmatism by providing Americans with thick narratives of the struggles for liberation and democracy in the United States. Du Bois's *Black Reconstruction*, for instance, is taken to be an exemplary work in that it shows the possibility of individuals assuming a democratic character, and how that same character can be thwarted and suppressed by the weight of history itself. C. Wright Mills, who wrote his dissertation on the rise of the social sciences, the institution-alization of social criticism, and research and pragmatism, concerned himself similarly with the constraints on democracy. Mills was concerned, throughout all his work, with the possibility for true democracy in a society which has organized itself around principles which lead it in the opposite direction, i.e. in the direction of elitism, political apathy, technocracy, and oligarchy. Trilling, one of the first Jews to be allowed into the academy, is said to have contributed to pragmatism inasmuch as he was interested in literature as a means to develop cultural con-sensus. For Trilling, just as for Matthew Arnold, the tradition of Western literature was the repository of Western humanism in which mass cultures and mass democ-racies can find the moral and cultural resources to confront popular kitsch, and totalitarian simple-mindeness.[17] Trilling, in West's view, would be the pragmatic equivalent of Lukács, the Marxist literary critic, minus the Stalinism, or Williams, without the unequivocal trust in the masses.

After this broad historical view on the effects of pragmatism in the general cultural life of the Unites States, West turns to pragmatism's fate within philosophy as an academic discipline. The story of pragmatism within the philosophical profession is one of both decline and resurgence or rediscovery. West notes three major factors as being the causes for the decline of pragmatism. First, there was pragmatism's unprofessionalism, which made it anathema to the overall turn toward professionalism and respectability within the academy. Second, there was the wave of European emigrants who brought with them logical positivism, analytical philosophy, and very specialized concerns with logic, mathematics, and science. Third was the overall turn in philosophy toward questions of logic, which was originally initiated by Russell and Whitehead. Obviously, one can take issue with all these factors. One may challenge each one of these factors as influencing the so-called decline of pragmatism. One may even challenge the whole narrative of a decline of pragmatism, as Richard J. Bernstein has done in an extremely insightful essay on the metanarratives of pragmatism.[18] The other side of West's narrative is the metanarrative of the hegemony of analytical philosophy, which in turn has come under attack. Nonetheless, the point is that classical pragmatism, that associated with James and Dewey, and partly with Mead, was eclipsed by the formalism and rigor of analytical philosophy. It is for this reason that West portrays the period between the fifties and seventies as a stage of decline and occlusion, but also a period of preparation and ferment. To this period belong, in West's narrative, principally Quine and Rorty, who, from within the analytic tradition, begin a process of dismantlement and criticism that will, if not augur, at least prepare the ground for the arguments that will allow the revival of pragmatism in the eighties in the work of critics and philosophers like Nancy Fraser, Richard J. Bernstein, and West himself. West's political and contentious rereading of American pragmatism closes with analyses of Antonio Gramsci, Roberto Unger, and Michel Foucault. The goal, however, of looking at these foreign figures (an Italian, an Americanized Brazilian, and a Frenchman) is to highlight the contemporary challenges of: how and why committed cultural criticism is possible; why we must and can still believe in the power of the people to rule themselves, and why if social theory is to be at the service of their cause they must contribute to the demystification of the false necessity of historical inevitability; and why forms of criticism of power and genealogies of regimes of control cannot and should not lead into a mere negative, nihilistic, and anarchistic type of great refusal. In short, the challenges concern the viability of tradition, the possibility of criticism, and the need for engaged praxis that is guided by visions of transformation that are not based on the hypostatization of false ideals, which have at the same time dispensed with historical and metaphysical certainties.

Achieving a New America: Tragedy, Memory, and Hope

As Richard J. Bernstein put it, "there is not only a conflict of narratives, but *a fortiori*, a conflict of metanarratives. There are better and worse narratives and metanarratives. And we can give good reasons in support of our claims for what is better."[19] A central thesis of this chapter is that West's metanarrative of pragmatism is not just one among many such metanarratives, but one of the best ones, and that "good reasons" can be offered for such a claim. I would like to devote this last section to this task.

It is quite clear that West is a great synthesizer, very much like Habermas and Rorty are also synthesizers. He fuses creatively and insightfully not just particular figures, but also traditions: Emerson, Dewey, Du Bois, Trilling, Unger, and Gramsci; but also American social democracy, romantic Marxism, ethically motivated postmodernism, Black liberation theology, and politically engaged literary criticism. In contrast to Rorty, and much like Habermas, West has a foothold in different public spheres: the Black church, political activism on behalf of the oppressed, excluded, and exploited. He is no mere academic, just as he is clearly not simply a preacher. This infuriates and perplexes many, as it also makes him highly attractive and seductive to many. To some, West's hybridity (professor, church speaker, media celebrity, political advisor, etc.), make him *de facto* suspect and unreliable. To many more, however, this is what makes him especially unique, relevant, and important in the contemporary context. But what is this new context? After the end of the Age of Europe, the end of the American century, and the end of decolonization, and the beginning of post-Occidentalism, post-Orientalism, and postmoderism, it is the time for beginnings. We are beyond the "end of" and the "posts." We are at the historical juncture in which we are in need of new visions and new projects. We are also at a particular juncture in the history of American public spaces. On the one hand, the American university is poised for major transformations. The end of the Cold War is beginning to register as the privatization of higher education and research. On the other hand, the rise of the "infotainment" sector, to use Benjamin Barber's phrase, has meant the hyper-corporatization of mass media and the concomitant commodification of popular culture, at levels unimaginable by the Frankfurt School theorists. These factors are combined with a general crises of the disciplines and areas of investigation that were housed in the ivory tower. The crises of both the West and the American empire have registered themselves in the interminable and trenchant debates about the future of the social sciences.[20] Another way of putting it is that the provincializing of Europe and the globalization of finance capitalism has meant that the disciplinary regimes that crystallized around such hegemonies are cracking under the power of external contestation and their own obsolescence. All of this, of course, at the very moment that obscene levels of capital accumulation in fewer hands is matched by growing levels of poverty in major cities, and across the land of the brave, free, racially segregated, and impoverished masses of a nation that peddles itself as the pinnacle of history. We live in a social situation that is framed by new forms of impoverishment, as the welfare state is rolled back, and the dynamics of racial apportionment shift with the influx of newer minorities. While race has not ceased to be a determinant in the political economy of the nation, Hispanics and Asians are shifting and modifying the character of this discourse. This, in broad strokes, is the contemporary context, and it is against this context that West's prophetic pragmatism offers itself as a "better" metanarrative of pragmatism, which is nevertheless a narrative about "America."

In West's prophetic pragmatism we find articulated at least four elements or themes. I will name them in the following way: (a) tragedy; (b) political, existential, and spiritual engagement as committed praxis; (c) anamnestic and historical situatedness; and (d) post-humanistic, post-universalistic cosmopolitanism. Each one of these themes or elements rescues, synthesizes, and reformulates elements from classical pragmatism and makes them speak to us in the context of post-imperial United States. With respect to the first, it does not need too much elaboration. One of the key ideas in West's prophetic pragmatism is the fore-grounding of the idea of tragedy, of misery, of evil and defeat[21] – not to undermine the idea of the amelioration and positive transformation so central to pragmatism, but precisely so as to temper and inform that sense of progress and hope. In West's view, the protean and Adamic character of the Emersonian pragmatist needs to be tempered by a profound sense of tragedy, of the inevitability of defeat and retreat behind accomplishments won at great pains and suffering. Tragedy is the name we give to fallibilism in history. There are no guarantees, and, furthermore, our best dreams will flounder on the shoals of historical resistance. Second, the quest for transformation, which is always guided by a dual vision that looks forward while never forgetting past defeats, can only result in a mass movement if it is able to combine political with spiritual and existential engagement. This means that a viable mass democratic movement can only succeed if it speaks to the existential fears, dreams, and hopes of the people as they are gathered up and preserved in a community's spiritual yearnings. As West does not tire of repeating, the culture of the oppressed is "deeply religious."[22] This culture of the oppressed is not just a palliative or opiate of the people; it is a compendium of memories and a peda-gogical resource. Communities are empowered by their religious traditions, espe-cially when these are prophetic and critical. Third, West speaks of the power of remembrance, or anamnesis, to keep us on track. How do we know we are going the right way when we have no guarantees from either reason or history, i.e. when we have dispensed with all metaphysical and historical alibis? "Subversive mem-ory" provides this guidance.[23] Subversive memory is memory of danger, a mem-ory of past suffering, of past defeat, but also of past triumph and success. And as such, subversive memory can serve as both a negative and a positive point of reference. "Memory without hope is blind, hope without memory is empty" could be one of the central aphorisms of West's prophetic pragmatism.[24] Evidently, if tragedy is what deflates all exorbitant claims to success or possibility for change, then anamnesis provides both guidance and impetus. Fourth, and finally, West offers the contours of a post-universalistic cosmopolitanism that is based on the recognition of differences, but does not seek to assimilate them or neutralize them with the acid of procedural homogenization so central to political liberalism. In contrast to Rorty, West does not speak of an abstract "we" that too easily can be confused with a type of tribal ethnocentrism. West localizes himself as a critic of American culture who speaks from the subversive memory of Black Americans, and who takes sides with the oppressed throughout the world. At the same time, he continues to provincialize himself in a gesture of solidarity with all those people who have suffered the underside of European modernity, and the riches and poverty of the American century. West speaks for and on behalf of the Enlight-enment, and its political bequest, but not as a great past accomplishment; rather, as something still to be achieved. In this sense, I think that West's type of cosmopolitanism is fueled not by abstract or procedural universalism, or a dehistoricized, deflated, and contingent "We," but is instead energized by a universality of diversity, or better, to use Walter Mignolo's term, a "diversality": the imperative of establishing a broader "we" on the greater appreciation, recognition, preservation, and respect for differences. For such differences are not only a challenge but also a source of creativity and hope.

Inasmuch as West has reread pragmatism in order to offer warrants for his prophetic pragmatism, then I think he has done a great service to both pragmatism and the broader US society. Pragmatism is the name, the American name, for a sense of moral outrage combined with a sense of hope and belief in the power of people to redeem and transform themselves. If academics reject West's revitilization of this unique American gospel, the worse for them. In an age in which Americans are forging a new identity, it is important to remember, as Rorty put it with respect to the political left, that the "moral identity" of our country's "we" is yet to be achieved.[25] But how can that moral identity be established if we also forget all the past injustices and suffering that weigh so heavily on the shoulders of so many Americans? Prophetic pragmatism is hope that refuses to forget. It is the name of a form of critical pedagogy on the side of the oppressed. It is what results when we do what Rorty, again, described so well in his review of West's *The American Evasion of Philosophy*, namely replace the reality-appearance distinction with one that juxtaposes instead "between the oppressor's descriptions of what is going on and the oppressed's descriptions, unsupplemented by the claim that the oppressed are on the side of the *really* real."[26] In the euphoria of the moment, speaking for and with the oppressed may strike many as out of tune and even un-American. But West's pragmatism rescues for most contemporary Americans that dream that was so central to so many paradigmatic Americans, including Douglass, Day, Jeronimo, Lincoln, the Grimke sisters, King, Parks, Steinem, Chavez, and many others: the dream of justice for the oppressed, exploited, and excluded. For them, America remains an ideal, something still to be achieved.[27]

Notes

1   See Morris Dickstein (ed.), *The Revival of Pragmatism: New Essays on Social Thought, Law, and Culture* (Durham, NC: Duke University Press, 1998); John Patrick Diggins, *The Promise of Pragmatism: Modernism and the Crisis of Knowledge and Authority* (Chicago: University of Chicago Press, 1994); James Livingston, *Pragmatism and the Political Economy of Cultural Revolution, 1850–1940* (Chapel Hill: University of North Carolina Press, 1994); see also Richard J. Bernstein, "The resurgence of pragmatism." *Social Research*, 59(4), 1992, pp. 813–40; see also James T. Kloppenberg, "Pragmatism: an old name for some new ways of thinking." *Journal of American History*, 83(1), 1996, pp. 100–38.

2   See Richard Rorty's *Philosophical Papers*, 3 volumes (New York: Cambridge University Press, 1991–8), and most recently the afterword to his collection of essays *Philosophy and Social Hope* (New York: Penguin, 1999); for Richard Bernstein, see his *Philosophical Profiles* (Philadelphia: University of Pennsylvania Press, 1986), and *The New Constellation: The Ethical-Political Horizons of Modernity/Postmodernity* (Cambridge, MA: The MIT Press, 1992); for Nancy Fraser, see *Unruly Practices: Power, Discourse, and Gender in Contemporary Social Theory* (Minneapolis: University of Minnesota Press, 1989). See also the excellent discussion volume Chantal Mouffe (ed.), *Deconstruction and Pragmatism* (New York: Routledge, 1996), with essays by Simon Critchley, Jacques Derrida, Ernesto Laclau, and Richard Rorty.

3   Gayatri Chakravorty Spivak's monumental *A Critique of Postcolonial Reason: Toward a History of the Vanishing of the Present* (Cambridge, MA: Harvard University Press, 1999) establishes once and for all, irrevocably and unequivocally, in almost in a manifesto fashion, the family relationship between postmodernism and postcolonialism.

4   On different versions of pragmatism, see James Kloppenburg T. Kloppenberg, "Pragmatism: an old name for some new ways of thinking?"

5   In a forthcoming book, I include an analysis and reconstruction of the context of the emergence of pragmatism in the nineteenth century, which I take to be important for a more thorough and in-depth understanding of why I think that West's brand of prophetic pragmatism is more appropriate to the challenges presented to us in times of globalization and the search for a new national identity.

6   For an overview of West's place within American cultural life, see the informative and thoughtful piece by Robert S. Boynton, "The new intellectuals." *The Atlantic Monthly*, March 1995, pp. 53–69. See also the special symposium on West's *The American Evasion of Philosophy* in *Praxis International*, 13(1), 1993, with essays by Robert B. Westbrook, Garry M. Brodsky, Lorenzo C. Simpson, and a response by West.

7   L. S. Klepp, "Every man a philosopher king." *The New York Times*, Late edition-final, Sunday, December 2, 1990, Magazines Section, pp. 57ff.

8   New York: Monthly Review Press, 1991.

9   A fairly recent text on Du Bois by Cornel West is again indicative of this uncompromising and unflinching self-criticism. See Henry Louis Gates, Jr and Cornel West, *The Future of the Race* (New York: Alfred A. Knopf, 1996).

10 Trenton, NJ: Africa World Press, Inc., and Grand Rapids, MI: William B. Eerdmans Publishing Company, 1988.

11 New York: Routledge, 1993.

12 Boston: South End Press, 1991.

13 Madison: The University of Wisconsin Press, 1989.

14 West, *The American Evasion of Philosophy*, p. 6.

15 Ibid., p. 36.

16 Ibid., p. 85.

17 Ibid., p. 169.

18 Richard J. Bernstein, "American pragmatism: the conflict of narrative." In Herman J. Saatkamp, Jr (ed.), *Rorty and Pragmatism: The Philosopher Responds to His Critics* (Nashville, TN: Vanderbilt University Press, 1995), pp. 54–67. See also Thomas Bender and Carl E. Schorske (eds), *American Academic Culture in Transformation: Fifty Years, Four*

Disciplines (Princeton, NJ: Princeton University Press, 1998), especially the pieces by Hilary Putnam and Alexander Nehamas.

19   Bernstein, "American pragmatism," p. 55.

20   See Immanuel Wallerstein, *The End of the World as We Know It: Social Science for the Twenty-First Century* (Minneapolis: University of Minnesota Press, 1999), and Walter Mignolo, *Local Histories/Global Designs: Coloniality, Subaltern Knowledges, and Border Thinking* (Princeton, NJ: Princeton University Press, 2000).

21   See Cornel West, *Beyond Eurocentrism and Multiculturalism. Volume 1: Prophetic Thought in Postmodern Times* (Monroe, ME: Common Courage Press, 1993), pp. 31–58, and "Pragmatism and the sense of the tragic." In *Keeping the Faith: Philosophy and Race in America*, pp. 107–18.

22   West, *The American Evasion of Philosophy*, p. 233; West, "Religion and the left." In *Prophetic Fragments*, pp. 13ff.

23   West, *Race Matters* (Boston: Beacon Press, 1993), p. 19.

24   On the relationship between memory and hope, see the discussion in the introduction to David Batstone, Eduardo Mendieta, Lois Ann Lorentzen, and Dwight N. Hopkins (eds), *Liberation Theologies, Postmodernity, and the Americas* (New York: Routledge, 1997), p. 15.

25   Richard Rorty, *Achieving our Country: Leftist Thought in Twentieth-Century America* (Cambridge, MA: Harvard University Press, 1998), p. 31.

26   Richard Rorty, "The philosopher and the prophet." *Transition*, 52, 1991, pp. 70–8, at p. 73.

27   See West, "Introduction." In *The Cornel West Reader* (New York: Basic Civitas Books, 1999), pp. xviii–xix in particular.

Part II
Philosophy of Religion

5

"Let Suffering Speak:" The Vocation of a Black Intellectual

James H. Cone

Cornel West is one of the most prominent African–American public intellectuals of our time. Author of more than a dozen books, including the bestseller *Race Matters*, West is a frequent television and radio pundit – debating with conservative, liberal, and left intellectuals, politicians, and other public figures of all races and ethnic origins. He lectures more than 150 times a year at churches and community groups, high schools, colleges, universities, and other educational institutions. His name is a household word throughout the United States and much of the world. Through his prolific writing and speaking, the African–American struggle for justice and dignity has become a central part of the discourse among progressive public intellectuals.

I first met West when he came to teach at Union Seminary in 1977 at the early age of 24 – the youngest in the history of the institution. What struck me about him were not only his youth but also his sheer intellectual brilliance. One of my white colleagues even suggested that he was too smart for Union students. Equally impressive was his deep commitment to justice for all and his unconditional love and care for Black people, especially the underclass and working poor – the ones Malcolm X called "the deepest in the mud." Combined with his political and intellectual commitment is his passion for play and humor, affirming life in all its complex and multifaceted dimensions. To encounter West is to meet a Black man who loves to have fun and who can laugh at himself, acknowledging his own strengths and limitations. His recognition of the latter keeps him on his toes; he is self-critical, humble, and open to the truth no matter who speaks or lives it. He never stops reading, listening, and thinking, drawing upon intellectual and cultural resources from many disciplines and cultures.

The moment I met West, we clicked, as it is for most people who meet him for the first time. It seemed I had known him for years, as a friend and a brother in the struggle for justice. He expressed his appreciation for and solidarity with my perspective on a Black theology of liberation. He told me about the impact of the "little red book" (the original color of my *Black Theology and Black Power*) on his life while he was just a teenager. While West often heaps inordinate praise on his colleagues and friends, he also challenges them to rethink their perspectives in the light of historical and existential realities absent in their thinking. As soon as he thanked me for *Black Theology*, he expressed his uneasiness about its one-sided accent on Blackness and its silence on class issues in the Black community and American society. Affirmation and critique are his trademarks in debate. His style of engagement kept me on guard, intellectually alert, and ready for an unexpected insight and critique. A dialectical tension was created between us, as we deepened our friendship and explored the various dimensions of our similarities and differences. We both became teachers and learners to one another as we walked the streets of New York and traveled the world together. We were always aware of our love and respect for one another because we both are sons of the Black church and equally committed to human liberation throughout the world.

Our mutual respect empowered us to explore our differences in public debates and private conversations. Our differences were not only intellectual but generational, geographical, and educational. I am fifteen years his senior. He grew up on the West Coast in the urban city of Sacramento, California, and I am a child of the rural South – born in Fordyce, Arkansas, and raised in Bearden. He went to Harvard and I attended Shorter Junior College (a small AME Church school) in North Little Rock, Arkansas, and then finished at Philander Smith College (United Methodist) in Little Rock. Growing up in Dixie during the 1940s and 1950s placed race at the center of my thinking in a manner quite different from West. In the segregated South, I encountered a barbaric expression of white supremacy that he could only read about in history books and view in documentary films. Coming of age in an urban city on the West Coast during the 1960s, West witnessed a kind of class conflict not self-evident in the rural South. He early acquired a "street smart" eloquence honed by sharp debate of urban Black culture. The racism he encountered was very different from the racism I knew in Arkansas.

Age, geography, and education provide clues for understanding our differences in the way we initially participated in and reflected on the struggle for justice in the USA and the world. West was concerned about the absence of class analysis in Black liberation theology, and I was determined to keep race at the center of the Black struggle for justice. What West said about class analysis was quite similar to the claims of progressive whites in the USA, Latin America, and Europe – all of whom were trying to get me to acknowledge that white supremacy was *secondary* to class contradictions in America and the world. Perhaps they were right, but I remained unconvinced. People who have not experienced white supremacy existentially are not in the best position to instruct its victims regarding the priority that race ought to have in the fight against oppression and the struggle for liberation.

Dialoguing with West was quite different. He is a brother not only in the flesh, but also in spiritual commitment to Black people. I could easily listen as he analyzed the significance of Marx and the importance of class in evaluating the life-chances of human beings. Our dialogues on race and class and their interlocking relationship enlarged my perspective on the nature and complexity of human exploitation and what is needed to eliminate it.

While I listened attentively to West and sought to incorporate many of his insights about class into my theological perspective, I did not alter my focus on racism and its priority in my analysis. I was not making a scientific claim that race was more important than class in analyzing the complexity of human oppression; rather, I hold race as my point of entry into the struggle for dignity and the analysis of justice. Others may choose other entry points – such as class, gender, and sexuality. While we enter the struggle at different points, we must incorporate such contradictions into our analysis if we are to gain a comprehensive understanding of human oppression and liberation. People do not change their perspectives on life and death issues simply by listening to erudite reflections. Intellectual debates inform and challenge perspectives but do not change them. People are changed through their struggle for life and fight against death.

To deepen our dialogue, West and I respectively wrote the essays "Black theology and Marxist thought" and "Black church and Marxism: what do they have to say to each other?"[1] We also decided to teach a joint course on the same theme. In our essays and the course, we explored the interrelationship of class and race in the history of the Black church, Black theology, and Marxism, showing the strengths and weaknesses of each. The central point of agreement was that Black theology and the Black church needed Marxism if they expected to gain a theoretical understanding of the sociopolitical structures they are seeking to change. Black theology and the Black church could teach Marxism something about the creative role religion and culture play in motivating people to resist injustice and to sustain their resistance. Where Marxism is strong on social analysis, Black theology and the Black church are weak; where Marxism is weak on cultural and spiritual resistance, Black theology and the Black church are strong. There can be no truly radical social change in America and the world unless economic issues are addressed, and Marxism is an indispensable tool for doing this. There is no way to empower and sustain a community in the struggle for justice without the cultural and spiritual power to resist. The differences between West and me on these issues were matters of nuance and emphases, largely determined by the various contexts in which we are speaking and the differences in age, geography, and education.

I was greatly impressed by the depth and range of West's knowledge of Marxism and leftist politics in Europe and America. To hear him reflect on race and class issues is like watching and listening to a classic jazz musician play an instrument. West's message is embodied as much in the rhythm of his lanky frame and the sound of his sermonic voice as in the content of his discourse. Lecturing without notes and responding spontaneously to questions in interviews are nowadays commonplace for West, because they allow him to experiment and improvise. Like a jazz musician, he surprises you with his spontaneity, rhythm, and the range of his intellectual competence. "Only Cornel West could write a book that contains essays on Marvin Gaye and Hans Frei that serve equally to illumine our current theological and cultural contexts," comments Stanley Hauerwas of Duke University on *Prophetic Fragments*.[2] There is much laughter when West engages an audience in dialogue. He transforms mean-spirited questions and comments into insightful conversations, amazing listeners at how he makes intellectual reflection look so easy and humorous.

Because West's lectures are entertaining, it is easy to think that he is playing an intellectual game and thus is not really serious. Nothing could be further from the truth. West's humorous style connects him with his Black roots, providing him the spiritual and cultural resources necessary to sustain himself in struggle. His struggle is intellectual, and he is determined to carve out a distinct Black intellectual style just like jazz man Charlie Parker in music and Reverend Gardner C. Taylor in preaching. That is why no white academic guild or Black nationalist rhetoric can limit his intellectual vision and style.

West is keenly aware of the white assault on Black intelligence and Black possibility and is fiercely determined to combat it. In the tradition of Black activist intellectuals before him (like W. E. B. Du Bois and Martin Luther King, Jr), West is deeply concerned about defending the humanity of Black people against the arrogance of white power. He is primarily focused on making justice and meaning for "the truly disadvantaged,"[3] as his Harvard colleague, William J. Wilson, called them. "The vocation of the intellectual," West tells Bill Moyers, is to "let suffering speak, let victims be visible, and let social misery be put on the agenda of those in power."[4] His love and care for the Black poor is evident not only in the content of what he writes and says but also in his improvisational and experimental style of speaking, his political activism, and his informal encounters with grassroots Blacks in churches, mosques, barbershops, schools, nightclubs, and on the streets of America's inner cities. "I'm just trying to make some sense of the world and love folks before I die,"[5] he said in another interview. West comes from that school of Black thought that believes in "giving back" to the community that nurtured you. Service to and sacrifice for others are for him the only ways to justify the privilege he possesses as a Harvard University professor. His main concern is not to become a great scholar in an academic guild. On the contrary, he views himself as a prophetic Christian freedom fighter who uses his intellect as a weapon against oppression in all its forms and to inspire ordinary people to believe in themselves, and their ability to make a difference in their lives and the world.

West is proud of his cultural roots and deeply pained by the profound suffering in America's poorest Black communities. His active participation in organized justice movements for the poor separates him from most Black and white university professors. West's Harvard colleagues are professional academics first – accountable to the scholarly guilds, for which they write and teach. They are specialists with a very narrow intellectual vision. Some may write about the poor and even speak on their behalf, but they are seldom found in the company of the poor. They usually keep themselves safely isolated in their offices at home and school, trying to stay ahead of their academic competitors. Not so with West. "Charlie Parker didn't give a damn,"[6] he spurted out in a media interview. Bird, as alto saxophonist Charlie Parker is commonly called, was just being himself, creatively expressing his humanity without reacting to whites. West seeks to embody in his intellectual work the same "self-evident creativity" found in Black music and the best of Black preaching. But it is not easy to embody Black creativity (like Parker and other jazz musicians) at Harvard and other white centers of academic power. I know something about this difficulty teaching at Union Seminary, which is a major center of white theological power. If, however, anyone can walk successfully this intellectual and cultural tightrope, West probably can do it. With one foot in Harvard and the other in Roxbury, West is pulled in opposite directions, each regarding the other as the enemy. Since Roxbury represents his cultural heritage and is most in need of affirmation and defense, West's Black Christian spirit pulls him mostly in that direction. It is commitment to the Roxburies of the world that prevents him from imitating the typical white academician.

West perceives himself as an intellectual freedom fighter who happens to be a university professor. Active solidarity with the poor – physically, spiritually, and psychologically – is his first priority. West is in his element speaking to, with, and for the underside of humanity. He feels their pain and joy in the depth of his being and seeks to embody in his relationship with the poor the old Black saying "But for the grace of God, there go I."

At Union and still today, justice, faith, love, hope, and courage shape West's philosophical and theological perspective. His understanding of these virtues derives not from Christian doctrines but from lived Christian stories. Doctrines are too static and rigid for West, whose fluid mind moves rapidly from one idea to the next, embracing his gift for public speaking and storytelling. While Christian stories shaped West's perspective, he also acknowledges the importance of stories in other religions and cultures. His thinking is eclectic and inclusive in every way.

Throughout West's work, justice is defined as fairness among people in society. It involves analyzing and transforming unjust social, political, and economic structures. There can be no successful achievement of justice without critical analysis of the structures of power and the willingness to fight injustice wherever it raises its ugly head. Oppressors do not relinquish power freely. Power must be taken. Nothing pleases West more than exposing and fighting the arrogance of power.

Faith is a religious resource that empowers people to fight for justice. It is a spiritual power that transcends the limits of reason and points to a divine reality that enables people to "keep on keeping on" even when the odds are against them. *Keeping Faith* is the title of one of West's books, which is reminiscent of *Keep the Faith, Baby!*[7] – a book of sermons and a popular saying by Adam Clayton Powell, Jr, the legendary Congressman and Harlem pastor. West consciously connects his work with the faith of the Black church and its great preaching tradition, which nurtured him as a child and today provides him with the "existential equipment to confront the crises, traumas, and horrors of life."[8]

West is a prophetic Christian Baptist – going back to the left-wing of the Protestant Reformation, the revolutionary tradition of Thomas Muntzer in the sixteenth century and Nat Turner in the nineteenth, and the love tradition exemplified in the life and writings of Martin Luther King, Jr.

As it was for Martin King, love is a paramount theme in West's faith perspective. There can be no Christian faith and no civil society without love and care for all human beings, compassion for enemies as well as friends. West will not tolerate the demonization of enemies, but insists that they must be treated as human beings no matter how inhuman they act. We must love enemies just as Jesus, Gandhi, and King did. The imperative to love enemies is what separates West from his Black nationalist and Jewish critics and friends. Radical Blacks and Jews often demonize one another, refusing to engage in civil conversation. West refuses to cut himself off from either group and is highly critical of their demonization of each other. His commitment to love – the center of his faith – demands his care for all as brothers and sisters, however misguided they may be.

Hope is confidence in the future. It is the belief that the world can and will be transformed. Nothing is more important to West than hope. The titles of several of his books reflect this emphasis: *Restoring Hope*, *The Courage to Hope*, and *The Future of the Race*. There can be no struggle for justice without hope. West's idea of hope is derived from African-American religion, especially as expressed in the songs and sermons of Black people. While he is discoursing on a complicated analysis of the power of market forces and the difficulty in effecting social change on behalf of the poor in corporate America and the world, West's listening and reading audience is sometimes prone to think that he has lost hope in the possibility of making a new world. When he encounters that response, he dispels it by turning to the traditions of hope in African-American history. In style and content, one can hardly distinguish his orations from those of a charismatic Black preacher. When speaking on justice and what must be done to achieve it, West becomes an erudite political philosopher who dazzles an audience with his brilliance. But when speaking of hope amid seemingly insurmountable odds, he puts on the mantle of a preacher, like the powerful writer James Baldwin, bearing witness to the great refusal to let evil have the last word.

Courage is essential for hope. Without it, one loses hope in the face of great odds. Courage is the power to be in the face of nonbeing, as Paul Tillich once said. It is the "in spite of," the willingness to confront death head-on, refusing to back down. Courage sent Malcolm and Martin to martyrs' deaths – both at the early age of 39. The same happened to Dietrich Bonhoeffer in a Nazi prison and a white Detroit housewife, Viola Liuzzo, on a dark night driving on an Alabama highway between Selma and Montgomery. Courage marginalizes one's message and gets one in trouble with the government and other centers of power.

West is at his best talking about courage, especially in African-Americans like Martin and Malcolm. One senses in his intellectual and sermonic reflections a deep yearning to embody this virtue in his own practice. Courage is profoundly difficult to embody, because standing up to power, speaking the truth bluntly and without compromise, makes people angry.

Like most intellectual and political leaders, West wants to be liked and considered worthy of respect by conservative, liberal, and left intellectuals, politicians, and community activists among all racial and ethnic groups. He wants to be perceived as inclusive and fair to all. But that is nearly an impossible feat. Nowhere has this struggle been more difficult than in his dialogues with Jews and Blacks. Extreme voices in both groups will not tolerate anyone who treats their enemies civilly.

West is a deep believer in dialogue as a means of breaking down the walls that separate people. No group is too far to the right or the left for West to exclude them from dialogue. I have seen him debate Justice Robert Bork, William Buckley on "Firing Line," Pat Robertson of the Christian Coalition, and Congressman Robert Barr of Georgia – white conservatives who seem completely unconcerned about respecting Blacks in a manner they presume Blacks should exhibit toward whites.

I know there are many Black nationalist leaders who make equally obscene assumptions about the humanity of whites. And I find dialogue with such Blacks, as with such whites, quite difficult, because to deny any group's humanity denies mine too. As Martin King said, "all life is interrelated." We are all "caught up in an inescapable network of mutuality, tied to a single garment of destiny. Whatever affects one directly affects all indirectly."

There is, however, a major political difference between the Black denial of white humanity and the white denial of Black humanity. Blacks lack the socio-political power to implement what many call "racism in reverse." Black supremacy may be morally as bad as white supremacy, but not so politically. As James Baldwin put it, "The powerless, by definition, can never be 'racists,' for they can never make the world pay for what they feel or fear."[9] Black supremacy is primarily a powerless *reaction* to white supremacy. It is a last ditch effort of a ravaged Black people, trying to hold on to some sense of self-worth and dignity. Blacks do not have the sociopolitical power to oppress whites in America or anywhere else. The most Blacks do is talk bad, and even that is limited by laws whites enact. In America, whites set the rules for public behavior with little or no consultation with Blacks or other people of color. Just thinking about how long white supremacy has been in place, how much longer it is likely to remain dominant, and how much whites seem to regard it as a part of the natural order of things makes many Blacks seethe with rage.

In contrast to the powerlessness of Black extremists, the white right is a powerful segment of the mainstream white community, and its intention is to make white supremacy the normative value in America and throughout the world. It is very difficult, at least for me, to have a civil conversation with people who deny Black humanity.

West's solidarity with the Black poor undoubtedly influenced him to place the problem of suffering at the center of his philosophy. He is not interested in a theoretical or logical solution to the problem of evil. He does not even ask the age-old theodicy question: if God is all-good and all-powerful, why is there suffering in the world? West's concern is concrete and existential. "How do you really struggle against suffering in a loving way, to leave a legacy in which people would be able to accent their own loving possibility in the midst of so much evil?"[10] This question goes to the heart of West's personal struggle, revealed throughout his work and action in the world.

The evil he is talking about is both social and existential, both aspects feeding off one another. Existential suffering is universal. No one escapes "death, dread, despair, disappointment, and disease." They are mentioned often by West as the "fundamental facts of human existence." He calls Russian writers (like Chekhov, Tolstoy, Dostoyevsky, Turgenev, and others) his intellectual soul mates, because they "explored the fundamental issues of what it means to be human: to wrestle with the problem of evil, to live an intense life in the face of death, to grapple with democratic possibilities and with social justice. To be an intellectual for them means to link the public and the existential issues."[11]

Social evil exacerbates existential suffering in the African-American community. West's essay "Nihilism in Black America" is one of his most insightful and widely read analyses of the interplay of existential *angst* and social evil in the Black community. To be sure, social evil in the inner cities is depressing: runaway "unemployment, infant mortality, incarceration, teenage pregnancy, and violent crime." But "black existential *angst*" is "something else": "the monumental eclipse of hope, the unprecedented collapse of meaning, the incredible disregard for human (especially black) life and property."[12] Although social evil and existential suffering are interconnected, the latter is the most threatening. Nihilism is "a disease of the soul."[13] How do you cope with "a life of horrifying meaninglessness, hopelessness, and (most important) lovelessness?"[14]

West acknowledges that nihilism is not new for Black America. We encountered this threat on the slave ships and the auction blocks, in the cotton fields and every nook and cranny of this land. Wherever we met white authorities in government, churches, schools, and on the job, we also met the threat of meaninglessness. Most Blacks do not even know when the threat is not present.

What is new is not "black existential *angst*" but the breakdown of cultural and civic institutions that shielded Blacks from its most destructive effects. The Black church and other cultural and religious forces gave Blacks a sense of worth as human beings that transcended the white definition of Blacks as beasts. Today these culture institutions are seriously weakened by market values in a world defined by the "culture of consumption." The nonmarket messages of Black cultural and religious institutions cannot compete with the "market moralities and mentalities" bombarding the Black community via television, radio, movies, and other capitalist forces.

For West the nihilistic threat can "never be completely cured" or prevented from returning. But it can be "tamed" or "kept at bay" through what he calls the "politics of conversion," which means that Blacks must "affirm themselves as human beings, no longer viewing their bodies, minds, and souls through white lenses and believing themselves capable of taking control of their own destinies."[15] Love of self and others bestows hope for the future of a degraded people and gives them the courage to make a new world for themselves.

Jack White of *Time* magazine describes West as a "philosopher with a mission."[16] His mission is to love himself through life, bestowing care and compassion wherever and as much as he can so that the "have-nots and have-too-littles" might have a chance to thrive and survive in this terror-stricken world. He used to say to me that he expected to be dead before forty – evidence of the intensity of his own struggle. Thank God brother West is still with us, "doing his thing." For justice's sake, let us hope that he lives to a ripe old age.

Notes

1   See Gayraud S. Wilmore and James H. Cone (eds), *Black Theology: A Documentary History, 1966–1979* (Maryknoll, NY: Orbis Books, 1979), pp. 552–67; and my essay "Black church and Marxism," an occasional publication of the Institute of Democratic Socialism (1980).

2   See the back cover of Cornel West, *Prophetic Fragments* (Grand Rapids, MI: William B. Eerdmans Publishing Company, 1988).

3   See William Julius Wilson, *The Truly Disadvantaged: The Inner City, the Underclass, and Public Policy* (Chicago: University of Chicago Press, 1987).

4   Cornel West, *The Cornel West Reader* (New York: Basic *Civitas* Books, 1999), p. 294.

5   Ibid., pp. 561–2.

6   Cornel West, *Prophetic Reflections: Notes on Race and Power in America* (Monroe, ME: Common Courage Press, 1993), p. 16.

7   See Adam Clayton Powell, *Keep the Faith, Baby!* (New York: Trident Press, 1967).

8   See Cornel West, "The vocation of the intellectual." Typed copy of Inaugural Lecture, Union Theological Seminary, New York, October 13, 1987, p. 2.

9   James Baldwin, *No Name in the Street* (New York: Dial, 1972), pp. 93–4.

10   "The vocation of the intellectual," p. 20.

11   Ibid., p. 555.

12   Cornel West, *Race Matters* (Boston: Beacon, 1993), p. 12.

13   Ibid., p. 18.

14   Ibid., p. 14.

15   Cited in Jack E. White, "Philosopher with a mission." *Time Magazine*, June 7, 1993.

16   Ibid.

6

Religion and the Mirror of God: Historicism, Truth, and Religious Pluralism

George Yancy

Philosophy is filled with metaphors. The trick is to find the best metaphor.

Wilfrid Sellars (personal communication)

We should always feel free to ask whether our metaphors are really helping or not.

Jeffrey Stout

The reader will note that the title of this chapter is reminiscent of Richard Rorty's *Philosophy and the Mirror of Nature*. Rorty's epistemological behaviorism rejects the idea that our epistemic claims depend upon "a theory of representations that stand in privileged relations to reality."[1] In short, he challenges the ocular metaphor that has played such a significant role (from Plato to Descartes) in the history of Western philosophy. Cornel West, deeply sympathetic to aspects of Rorty's epistemological behaviorism and Wilfrid Sellars's psychological nominalism (which involves an antifoundationalist critique of the Myth of the Given), has helped to usher us into our postempiricist moment, with its implications for philosophy of religion, literary theory, moral theory, and the natural/social sciences. Rorty, Sellars, and West emphasize that the process of giving reasons (justification) takes place within a social space and involves issues of social practice.

For West, how is philosophy of religion to be addressed and articulated within an antifoundational historicist framework?[2] What would philosophy of religion look like, for West, within our current post-metanarrative climate? I agree with philosopher Nancy Frankenberry where she observes, "What we do not yet have is a clear idea of the way the insights and methods in this most recent cycle of empiricism might apply to the philosophy of religion."[3]

Although West insightfully draws our attention to the importance of "postmodern thought" on religious discourse and reflection, I am aware that he rejects the appellation "postmodern" *vis-à-vis* his philosophical, religious, and political world-view. It is the nihilistic and conservative tone of postmodernism that he appears to find most problematic. However, many of the critical post-empiricist turns that West accepts as legitimate fall under the discursive umbrella of postmodernism. For example, he accepts that "truth-talk" is local, not ahistorical; apodeictic certainty and incorrigibility are replaced by fallibilism; the Myth of the Given is replaced by epistemological holism and antifoundationalism; the linearity and infallibility of scientific progress and development give way to the significance of contextualism, revisionism, and the possibility of incommensurability; universal rationality-claims are replaced by culturally bounded and historically situated rationality-claims; etc. I have come to think of West as an "affirmative post-modernist" (one who critiques postmodernity and is also open to nondogmatic visionary struggle, hopefulness, and resistance to the absurd dimensions of our postmodern moment), as opposed to a "skeptical postmodernist" (one who adopts a position of deep pessimism, ineluctable despair, hopelessness, and visionlessness, a situation where Neurath's boat is caught within a vortex of an abysmal nihilism).[4] Critiquing what he sees as problematic entailments of the postmodernist views of Quine, Sellars, Goodman, and Rorty, West argues that "their viewpoints leave postmodern American philosophy hanging in limbo, as a philosophically critical yet culturally lifeless rhetoric mirroring a culture (or civilization) permeated by the scientific ethos, regulated by racist, patriarchal, capitalist norms and pervaded by debris of decay."[5]

West is aware, however, of the pervasive impact of their postmodern views. In "The politics of American neo-pragmatism," West writes, "Needless to say, this rudimentary demythologizing of the natural sciences [resulting from the work of Thomas S. Kuhn, Paul Feyerabend, W. V. O. Quine, Wilfrid Sellars, Nelson Goodman, et al.] is of immense importance for literary critics, artists, and religious thinkers."[6] But he is also troubled by their lack of critical attention shown specifically toward philosophy of religion. In "The historicist turn in philosophy of religion," West complains, "Contemporary American philosophy is postanalytic philosophy, with deep debts to pragmatism yet little interest in religious reflection."[7]

Lastly, in the same essay, having praised both Richard Rorty's move from a form of confrontational epistemology (where the knower and known or theory and the world are viewed as involving an antiquated metaphysical problematicity) to a form of social epistemology, and Richard Bernstein's critique of Descartes's either/or disjunction (either epistemological certainty or relativistic nihilisticity) West writes, "Despite their Kuhnian perspectives regarding the social character of rationality, both focus their philosophical concerns almost exclusively on philosophy of science and say nothing about philosophy of religion."[8]

The major task of this chapter is to take seriously, and therefore begin to unpack philosophically, West's historicist philosophy of religion. Within the framework of this philosophical unpacking, it will be shown that West's historicist philosophy eschews the search of Western philosophy for an Archimedean point or metanarrative which transcends idiosyncratic historical processes and historically and culturally constituted epistemic practices. Hence, the truth of the beliefs of a given religious *Weltbild* will be purchased within the very framework of that given religious world-picture. That is, the truth-claims of a particular religion, Christianity in West's case, are forms of discourse specific to a religious community of intelligibility. On this score, there is no metareligion which has access to a prediscursive ontotheological reality. No religion has a mirror, as it were, which reflects a representation (or God-talk) that stands in privileged relation to God. Though slightly altered, it is here that one might ask in a Lyotardian fashion: where, after the metanarratives, can *religious truth* and *legitimacy* reside?

It will also be shown that West calls into question the ontic truth-indicative character of religious beliefs as intended by religious folk. Indeed, on West's view, the ontic truth-indicative character of religious beliefs amounts simply to a given believer's restatement of his or her belief system without the requirement that there exists an extrareligious or metaphysically or religiously realist way of talking about the ontic truth-indicative character of those beliefs. The external question of the "objective truth" of religious beliefs becomes essentially an internal process of examining the various ways that religious discourse functions within a given language-game specific to a given religious community with its own criteria of intelligibility. West's historicist philosophy of religion leaves us, so I will maintain, with a kind of religious paralogy. This, of course, renders problematic the soteriocentricity of many major world religions. Are we to relativize the divine *Arché* to differential frameworks of intelligibility? Indeed, even God might be said *not* to exist beyond the text. Have we not, therefore, moved away from issues of religious truth to issues of utility and contextual pragmatics? Religious truth is no longer an issue of how things are and religious knowledge is not a veridical perception of how things ontotheologically fit together. For West, justification (religious, scientific, etc.) begins and ends in social practices. Concerning questions about the "truth" of Christianity, for example, I will argue that West is left with a Wittgensteinian response, "This is simply what I do." I will argue that West's historicism, and his holism, raises problematic issues in the area of religious pluralism which he does not directly address. For example, within the framework of West's historicist philosophy of religion, how does he conceive of God? Is God a *Ding an Sich* or a religio-communal artifact whose "reality" is relative to a religious discursive field? It will also be shown that despite the fact that West brings to our attention that since the Enlightenment and logical positivism religionists have been on the defensive, his own historicist philosophy of religion actually reinforces a defensive posture on the part of religious believers. Also, through a brief consideration of the implications of a few "postmodern thinkers" (Quine, Goodman, Sellars, Feyer-abend, et al.) *vis-à-vis* religious reflection and discourse, I will show how this defensive posture is possibly further reinforced.

Antifoundational Historicism

West clearly provides us with elements of his historicism, with its antifoundational implications, where he writes:

> My particular version of philosophical historicism is neither the neo-Kantian histori-cism (*à la* Wilhelm Dilthey) which presupposes a positivist conception of the *Naturwissenschaften* nor the Popperian-defined historicism that possesses magic powers of social prediction and projection. Rather the historicism I promote is one which understands transient social practices, contingent descriptions and revisable scientific theories as the subject matter for philosophical reflection.[9]

He also states:

> I hold that historicism should be understood as merely claiming that background prejudices, presuppositions, and prejudgments are requisite for any metaphysical or ontological reflections on the way the world is. This means that those metaphysical or ontological projects which hide and conceal their background conditions are decep-tive and deficient.[10]

Moreover, for West, a "responsible and sophisticated philosophy of religion... must deepen the historicist turn in philosophy by building upon the Quine–Goodman–Sellars contributions."[11] West, unfortunately, does not clearly delineate what would be entailed for philosophy of religion were it to deepen the historicist turn in philosophy by specifically building upon the work of Quine, Goodman, and Sellars.

West, however, does tell us: "The historicist turn in philosophy of religion helps us understand that we are forced to choose, in a rational and critical manner, some set of transient social practices, contingent cultural descriptions and revisable scientific theories by which to live."[12] His brand of historicism, as he makes clear, avoids transcendental objectivism "by rejecting all modes of philosophical reflection which invoke ahistorical quests for certainty and transhistorical searches for foundations – including most realist moves in ontology, foundationalist strat-egies in epistemology, and mentalistic discourses in philosophical psychology."[13] Hence, West's view here is clearly influenced by Nelson Goodman's ontological pluralism and epistemological conventionalism with respect to diverse conven-tional ways of "reality" construction; Wilfrid Sellars's critique of epistemological foundationalism (that is, his rejection that our knowledge-claims are grounded upon particular pre-linguistic *given* elements in experience); and Quine's "eliminative materialist position, namely, the view that there simply are no mental states, but rather neural events. In this way, Quine detranscendentalizes any notion of the subject."[14]

But alongside West's historicism is his allegiance to Christianity: "I follow the biblical injunction to look at the world through the eyes of its victims, and the Christocentric perspective which requires that one sees the world through the lens of the Cross – and thereby see the relative victimizing and relative victimization."[15] He also writes, "The synoptic vision I accept is a particular kind of prophetic Christian perspective which comprehensively grasps and enables opposition to existential anguish, socioeconomic, cultural and political oppression and dogmatic modes of thought and action."[16] For West:

> Prophetic Christianity has a distinctive, though not exclusive, capacity to highlight critical, historical and universal consciousness that yields a vigilant disposition toward prevailing forms of individual and institutional evil, an unceasing suspicion of ossified and petrified forms of dogmatism and a strong propensity to resist various types of cynicism and nihilism.[17]

From what has been developed thus far, it is clear that the prophetic Christian tradition is not based upon ahistorical grounds or decontextualized rational criteria; for West's historicism and pragmatist sentiments inform his view that all cultural descriptions and scientific theories are contingent and are situated within the context of social history and structured by interest-laden constitutive social praxis. Just because there are no ahistorical grounds upon which the prophetic Christian tradition rests, however, this does not mean that there are no criterial reasons for West to accept the prophetic Christian tradition. After all, as was quoted earlier, "we are forced to choose, in a rational and critical manner, some set of transient social practices, contingent cultural descriptions, and revisable scientific theories by which to live."

But what are the epistemological credentials of West's "rational and critical manner" of choosing the prophetic Christian tradition? West argues:

> My acceptance of the prophetic Christian tradition is rational in that it rests upon good reasons. These reasons are good ones not because they result from logical necessity or conform to transcendental criteria. Rather, they are good in that they flow from rational deliberation which perennially scrutinizes my particular tradition in relation to specific problems of dogmatic thought, existential anguish and societal oppression.[18]

There is much here that is problematic. To maintain that something is rational in that it rests upon good reasons only forces us to ask: "But, what are 'good reasons'?" For although West tells us that such reasons are not based upon logical necessity or transcendental criteria, he leaves us without any positive construal of what constitute "good reasons." But even when he finally provides for us the basis upon which a particular set of reasons might be deemed "good," he begins in a very problematic fashion; for "they are good in that they flow from rational deliberation."

Hence, for West, that which is rational is that which is based upon good reasons and good reasons are "good" because they flow from rational deliberation. But, again, what is "rational deliberation"? West, however, leaves us wanting for a clear construal of the various constitutive elements (logical, normative, aesthetic, etc.) of "rational deliberation." But he does tell us, as noted above, that he is interested in that process of rational deliberation "which perennially scrutinizes my particular tradition in relation to specific problems of dogmatic thought, existential anguish and societal oppression." But again, West needs to defend, even if there are no logically necessary grounds or transcendental grounds for such a defense, what he presupposes. He presupposes that it is "good" and "rational" to scrutinize a particular tradition in relationship to dogmatism, existential anguish, and societal oppression. Moreover, West needs to demonstrate why he thinks that the prophetic Christian tradition is a most effective philosophical-religious mode of scrutinizing problems of dogmatism, existential anguish, and societal oppression. And though he says, "I do not believe that this specific version of the prophetic Christian tradition has a monopoly on such insights, capacities and motivations,"[19] he needs to provide us with clear and convincing reasons, though contextual and contingent, as to why he has "never been persuaded that there are better traditions than the prophetic Christian one."[20] Why, for example, is the prophetic Christian tradition more effective at critiquing dogmatic thought, existential anguish, and societal oppression than, let us say, existentialism or atheistic humanism? Or, is it even important that West answers this question?

West does suggest, however, that he would give up his "allegiance to the prophetic Christian tradition if life-denying forces so fully saturated a situation that all possibility, potentiality and alternatives were exhausted."[21] But what would qualify as a situation that was so fully saturated by life-denying forces such that West would give up his allegiance to the prophetic Christian tradition? Would the Atlantic slave trade or Auschwitz or a nuclear holocaust act as sufficient grounds upon which he would relinquish his allegiance to the prophetic Christian tradition? He never clearly delineates the extent to which life-denying forces must obtain before he gives up his allegiance. West's admittance to the conditionality of his continued acceptance of the prophetic Christian tradition is seriously weakened where he contends:

> *despite how tragic and hopeless* present situations and circumstances *appear to be*, there is a God who sits high and looks low, a God who came into this filthy, fallen world in the

form of a common peasant in order to commence a new epoch in which Easter focuses our attention on the decisive victory over our creaturehood, the old creation and this old world, with its history of oppression and exploitation.[22] (Emphasis added)

So, even if West were to encounter a situation that was so fully saturated by life-denying forces, his Christian conviction that there exists a God who loves and protects (to say nothing about what West refers to as our "existential freedom,"[23] which is a divine gift of grace) will provide the necessary framing (hope and salvation) to militate against the perception of the exhaustion of "all possibility, potentiality and alternatives."

But despite West's circularity of argumentation regarding his use of the process of rational deliberation to support his notion of providing good reasons, lack of conceptual specification, and points of inconsistency thus far, what is clear is that his antifoundational historicism rejects any attempt to justify our beliefs on the basis of metaphysical or transcendental grounds. There is no "God's-eye view" from which to survey the nature of reality; for "reality," on West's view, is precisely that which is never given *simpliciter*. Rather, "reality" is a constructed affair inextricably linked to transient social practices. Our epistemic justificatory acts are grounded upon socially negotiated norms of what constitutes reasoning, truth, knowledge, etc.

On this score, rationality becomes a property of our social practices and not "a property of the relation between knower and known or between theory and the world."[24] Hence, for West, knowledge and truth are social products linked to particular knowledge-producing and truth-producing sociohistorical practices that are themselves subject to undergoing radical transformation. For all social practices, coupled with their associated assumptions concerning methodological approaches, aims, etc., are "this-worldly" tethered and thereby are constituted by the dynamics of specific social and historical processes. Therefore, there is no Platonic cave from which we must attempt an escape. Our being-in-history is all that we have. Concerning the source of the grounds for rational persuasion, West writes, "I need neither metaphysical criteria nor transcendental standards to be persuaded, only historically constituted and situated reasons."[25] And it is such historically constituted and situated reasons that are forever linked to some complex narrative or genealogical nexus of historical processes. This is why West's historicism is so partial toward "the demystifying perspectivalism of Nietzsche."[26] But it is here that West needs to provide more than a referential nod to Nietzsche. How much of Nietzschean perspectivism is West willing to accept? For example, is truth always merely an issue of interpretation? Is truth never found or discovered, but only a cultural and historical creation? What are facts? Are there no interpretation-independent facts? Is there a single metanarrative meaning or are there simply multiple narrative meanings? Is truth simply a myth, a chimera? And how does

West's partial acceptance of "the demystifying perspectivalism of Nietzsche" impact his philosophy of religion?

Now given West's historicist framing, what implications will follow for his allegiance to Christianity and the prophetic Christian tradition? We have already seen that West entangles himself within a dire circularity with respect to his defense as to why he accepts the prophetic Christian tradition. But what are the implications of West's historicism for Christianity more generally? For surely, following what has already been established, on West's view, Christianity, as a diversified religious social practice, is not grounded upon a set of *a priori*, incorrigible or apodeictic propositions or "given" states of affairs. As West argues, "to believe that there is a description-free, version-free, theory-free standard which enables us to choose the true descriptions, versions or theories in science and religion is to fall prey to an Archimedean objectivism."[27] As a Christian religionist, given West's reasoning, one moves and has one's being within the context of history, a Christian narrative history which has no particular epistemological privilege that allows for ahistorical justifications of the Christian narrative itself. In short, Christian cognitions do not soar above and beyond the highly socially negotiated interpretive frames of reference that are themselves embedded within the diversified and protean tradition that is Christianity.

This does not mean that Christian critical hermeneutic reflection is not possible. West argues: "Like Gadamer, my version of historicism acknowledges the unavoidable character and central role of tradition and prejudice, yet it takes seriously the notion of sound human judgement relative to the most rationally acceptable theories and descriptions of the day."[28] Nevertheless, West simply states this Gadamerian move; he does not provide us with an example of what constitutes "sound human judgement" as it occurs relative to Christian "theories" and descriptions. But nor has he shown, without dire circularity, that Christianity or the prophetic Christian tradition is one of the most rationally acceptable "theories" or descriptions of the world, self and reality that is available.

Given West's historicism, we are forced to move beyond the notion that religious truth and the existence and nature of God, etc., are based upon the relational logic inherent in the correspondence theory of truth; that is, West's view forces us to be attentive to the various Christian social practices that indeed socially construct what we mean by religious truth, the nature and existence of God, etc.

For West, there is no way that we can *know* that the Christian narrative has the relational or representational force of having "gotten the world right." There is no way to establish externally (that is, outside of Christian social and historical practices) whether one's Christian beliefs correspond to some given metaphysical, transcendent, or ahistorical divine referent. In short, there is no way to stand between one's Christian community of intelligibility and religious ontic reality so as to determine a mimetic fit, as it were. The reader will note that this does not mean that it is *false* that religious ontic reality determines our religious reflections.

Terrence W. Tilley (personal correspondence) made this point clear to me. He reasons that just because all linguistic items are cultural posits does not mean that they do not or cannot refer to or receive meaning from the extralinguistic. As John Dewey might say, religious experiences can be "had" even if it is not clear that they can ever be "known." Tilley goes on to reason, a point he says Wilfrid Sellars made against Richard Rorty once, that although "mirroring reality" cannot be a *measure* of truthful claims, it does not follow from this that "mirroring reality" cannot be a *condition* for such truth-claims. But even if "mirroring reality" is a condition for *religious truth-claims*, the condition, it seems to me, cannot be fulfilled in any epistemologically meaningful way. If we cannot *know* that religious ontic reality determines our religious reflections, then what is the difference between having a situation where religious ontic reality does, as a matter of fact, determine our religious reflections and not being able to show epistemically that this is the case, on the one hand, and having a situation where, as a matter of fact, no religious ontic reality exists at all to determine our religious reflections and not being able to show epistemically that this is the case, on the other hand? In other words, the ontological status of the object, from a strictly epistemological perspective, seems irrelevant.

Although Leon Wieseltier's views on West are based upon a terribly unfair *ad hominem* critique, and completely miss West's allowance for other forms of "transcendence" (*à la* Paul Ricoeur and others), he appears to capture the pulse of the problematic here where he contends:

> The Christian tradition will not be enriched by a faith for which God is not real. Before what, exactly, does the postmodernist bow his head? For the anti-essentialist, what kingdom is at hand? Rorty claims that the abolition of transcendence is necessary for liberalism, but West claims that the abolition of transcendence is necessary for religion. He does not see that his position is a dire contradiction.[29]

So West's historicist philosophy of religion rejects religious discourse understood as referring to or mirroring an extra-Christian communal reality that functions as the transcendent basis from which Christian discourse, values, and descriptions are derived. Hence, religious "truth-talk" spirals back to the various ways in which discourse functions specific to a particular religious language-game (Christian, Hindu, Zoroastrian, etc.). Mason Olds has written:

> there are the language games of ethics, religion, aesthetics, and science; each is a human type of discourse, but none has any transcendental justification or foundation. These are language games invented by humans.... Since no foundation for these games exists outside of language itself, we can say that if you wish to play a particular game, play it in this fashion.[30]

To further develop West's historicism *vis-à-vis* religious reflection and discourse, let us examine his defense of the Christian resurrection-claim. What will be shown is that, for West, acceptance or rejection of the resurrection-claim is not a function of so much or so little empirical evidence; rather, acceptance or rejection of the resurrection-claim appears to be a function of whether one does or does not belong to a particular religious community of intelligibility. That is, evidential-talk is replaced by a candid recitation of the communal beliefs specific to a particular community of which one is a participant-believer.

The Resurrection-Claim: An Antifoundational Historicist and Holist View

The philosophical line of analysis that West specifically brings to bear upon his defense of the resurrection-claim is clearly derived from the work of such philosophers and philosophers of science as Pierre Duhem, W. V. O. Quine, Thomas S. Kuhn, Carl G. Hempel (*qua* reformed empiricist), and others.

In his "A philosophical view of Easter," which is an essay that makes clear use of historicist and holist analyses to support the "truth" of the Christian resurrection-claim and that clearly confines religious "truth-talk" to specific communities of discourse construction, West quickly, and correctly, moves us away from the trappings of sentential reductionism where the resurrection-claim, "Jesus arose from the dead," is "reduced to an equivalent statement consisting solely of observation terms or observables."[31] West argues: "I suggest that just as it is inappropriate to apply the dogma of sentential reductionism and the observational criterion to the most important claims or sentences in scientific descriptions, so it is inappropriate to apply this dogma and criterion to the resurrection-claim."[32] In other words, the logical positivist move to isolate individual sentences and examine their observable consequences as the means for establishing cognitive meaningfulness is rejected. Against this sentential reductionist move, Hempel suggests that cognitive significance "can best be attributed to sentences forming a theoretical system, and perhaps rather to such systems as wholes."[33]

For West, therefore, to raise the issue of the truth-value of the resurrection-claim is really to raise the issue of the truth-value of the entire Christian way of understanding the nature of the self, world, and God of which the resurrection-claim is a central tenet. Hence, how do we know that the Christian *Weltbild*, taken as a whole, is true? After all, one cannot peel back, as it were, the Christian "picture" of the self, world, and God, replete with soteriological, eschatological, doxological, iconographical, and ethical principles, so as to compare it to a description-free state of affairs or ahistorical reality. West maintains: "when we say we '*know*' that a particular scientific or religious description, version or theory of the self, world and God is true, we are actually *identifying ourselves with a particular group of people, community of believers or tradition of social practices*" (emphasis added)[34]

Hence, for West, "knowing" that the resurrection-claim is true suggests an epistemological relation involving "knowledge-that" (between persons and propositional knowledge as embedded within communally shared discourse) as opposed to "knowledge-of" (between persons and some actual state of affairs). To say that one "knows" the resurrection-claim to be true, therefore, is equivalent to an admittance that one plays, though with conviction, a certain religious language game relative to certain aims, goals, values, etc. Perhaps this is why West states, "As a self-avowed Christian, it seems redundant to say that a particular Christian description of the self, world and God is true."[35] As a Christian, it is contradictory to say that Christianity is false. As West says, "The notion of a true religion that does not sustain people through the crises and traumas of life is unintelligible and unacceptable for religious communities."[36] West also adds that "the truth-claims of religious communities, are inseparable from the aims and purposes of those communities, that is, to provide meaning and value in human lives."[37] This is why West finds religious realism, metaphysics, and ontology as practiced in the grand mode problematic. He writes:

> religious realism is an intellectual strategy adopted by those who accept the authority of particular ecclesiastical (or personal) interpretations. The purpose here is to convince one's self and others that their interpretations are true regardless of their role and function in one's life. I reject religious realism because it rests upon a faulty notion of religious "truth."[38]

To choose a particular religious belief system is linked not only to pragmatic aims, but also to the extent to which that religious belief system is "existentially enabling for many self-critical finite and fallible creatures who are condemned to choose traditions under circumstances not of their own choosing."[39] The reader will notice the Sartrean emphasis here placed on the *factical* contextuality and historicity within which we are condemned to choose. West concludes:

> To choose a tradition (a version of it) is more than to be convinced by a set of arguments; it is also to decide to live alongside the slippery edge of life's abyss with the support of the dynamic stories, symbols, interpretations and insights bequeathed by communities that came before.[40]

Given the above, the truth of particular Christian religious beliefs is not determined by an external state of affairs; rather, it is determined by pragmatic aims situated within a particular religious community of intelligibility, one capable of "effectively" addressing one's existential needs. West writes, "I am led to adopt a radical historicist view which renders all 'truth-talk' a contextual affair, always related to human aims and human problems, human groups and human communities."[41] West concludes: "The Christian claim that 'Jesus arose from the dead' or that Jesus is 'the first-born from the dead' is a proclamation of a divine miracle of creation in that God has called back to life a new creature from the old, a new creation from the old, a new history from the old."[42] But from what source does such a "proclamation" derive its authority? From where else but a contingent and historically situated and diverse Christian community of intelligibility; indeed, a diverse Christian community that has no *a priori* hold on us. As West says:

> there is no true description, version or theory of the self, world and God which all must and should acknowledge as inescapably true, but rather particular descriptions, versions or theories put forward by various people, groups, communities and traditions *in order usually to make such views attractive to us*.[43] (Emphasis added)

It is difficult not to conclude that on West's view, Christianity and religious world-views, more generally, are devoid of any ontological explanatory role; that is, religious discourse, like literary theory or poetry, comes replete with its own rules and categories but has nothing to say, in a specifically explanatory way, about extratextual or extrareligious–communal ontic reality. This is not to deny the "explanatory" role of certain religious narratives (cf. the story of Genesis). The point is that the "explanatory" role of the religious narratives is a function of the larger religious traditions within which they are embedded. They do not appear to "explain" anything outside their own narrative framework of intelligibility. But, surely, religious believers are not content to be told that they are to be enthralled simply on the basis of the wonderful and fulfilling meaning disclosure value that religious world-views have to offer. As Philip Clayton maintains, "But Christian explanations can only make sense of the world if believers can believe that they are actually true, that what they claim is the case."[44] That is, for the Christian religionist, God is indeed a "concrete actuality," not just a linguistically constructed notion which evolves out of a religious communal matrix of praxis–meaning–construction. Prayer, for example, is not just a communal/individual locutionary act contributing to the cohesion of the group or ensuring existential consolation; rather, Christian religionists pray to a reality which they believe to exist apart from their communal/individual acts of supplication. But, again, on West's view, Christianity's world-picture, and by implication, Hinduism, Taoism, Islam, and other religious traditions, simply offers a "contingent cultural description" which is linked to "transient social practices." In short, on West's view, we are left with autonomous religious narratives having their own ontologies, truths, categories, etc., without being able to appeal to any transhistorical or transtheoretic criteria for determining which religious narrative accurately represents reality. As Olds writes, "There is no way to determine that one narrative is true and another is false, apart from dialogue within the narrative itself. In other words, *there is no metanarrative by which to check the various narratives.*"[45]

Hence, there is no need to require Christianity or any other religious world-view to justify itself outside of its own discourse practices. Given the incommensurability of religious narratives, the idea of one religious narrative excluding another as a potential contender for truth is placed in critical relief. Given West's historicism, metaphysically realist God-talk is now more like Deweyan "warranted assertability" God-talk. But this removes the intended decontextualized reference involved in the use of God-talk by Christian religionists. When Christians assert that "God exists," they mean more than what West's historicist philosophy of religion will allow. Their assertion is intended to refer to a transcendent Being with such-and-such metaphysical attributes. But for West, the claim that "God exists," as an intended assertorial representational truth-claim, is to be construed as a linguistically constructed contextual affair which is related to human goals, human groups, and human communities. That is, the truth of the claim that "God exists" does not, in any epistemically or ontologically meaningful way, point beyond the grid of the religious discourse specific to a particular religious community. Indeed, there is no transcommunal *justification* that demonstrates that God exists. For West, "the notion of justification is understood to be a way of reminding ourselves and others which particular community or set of we-intentions (e.g., 'we would that . . . ') we identify with."[46] With the Myth of the Given deconstructed, what happens to our realist/metaphysicalist God-talk? West:

> The critiques of the Myth of the Given by Heidegger, Derrida and Wittgenstein share one common theme: the radical finitude and sheer contingency of human existence. Human beings are trapped in either a historical, textual or intersubjective web from which there is no escape. By discarding the Myth of the Given, the quest for certainty and security comes to an end. Philosophy's grand search for the invariable, immutable categories in human experience, expressions and language and theology's bold attempt to establish veridical reference to a transcendent God must surrender and succumb to the ebb and flow of history, the freeplay of infinite substitutions in the confines of texts, and the transient character of intersubjective agreements.[47]

This, of course, places us squarely within the context of religious pluralism. God is no longer conceived as the univocal Transcendental Signified. The notion of *Deus est Veritas* has given way to God as an unstable, intratextual play of signifiers. So how do we determine which religious world-view is "true"? Assuming that "true" here is a function of the extent to which a religious world-view meets one's existential needs and serves certain purposes and interests, then religious truth is reduced to utility. On this score, the notion that certain religious world-views are "better" at providing meaning and value in human lives than others is deeply problematic. For the needs, interests, purposes, and existential crises of a people are specific to their context. Hence, there is no "best" religious world-view, at least on West's view, that transcontextually meets all the needs of all people in various contexts. West concedes this where he writes: "The issue of whether certain religious communities provide the best meaning and value in human lives becomes inescapably circular – precisely because the notion of truth in religious communities is value-laden, i.e., integral to its aims of providing meaning and value."[48] Therefore, Hinduism, Christianity, Buddhism, etc. are particular religious communities that attempt to "preserve regulative self-images and guiding vocabularies," according to West, "that promote various aims and purposes."[49] Each of the above religious world-views involves fluid language games and dynamic systems of symbols; moreover, each comes with its own dynamism of faith and the profound risks involved in the process of sustaining faith and developing and sustaining a particular religious identity. In short, each might be said to adhere to the logical moves inherent in its own language game and to possess idiosyncratic risks involved in various contextually mediated acts of faith. On West's view, however, there is no way of intelligibly talking about a single religious world-view which is *the true* religious world-view with its *ontologically true* language game and its *true* and *authentic* acts of faith. There is no stable divine logos, as it were, which ontologically warrants a single religious world-view.

So how are we to adjudicate between various religious traditions? On West's view we cannot *know* (ahistorically demonstrate) that God is indeed the causal factor constituting the truth of a single or various religious world-views. Indeed, inferring from West's view, the "truth" of a religious world-view (with its conception of the divine) will depend upon its own community of intelligibility and how it meets the pragmatic needs and existential crises of a particular community. But is West willing to admit to a form of polytheism or, as with John Hick, argue that God is a kind of noumenal Real in terms of which various religious communities have their own pragmatic understanding? Assuming the former, how do we reconcile and make sense of multiple divinities across religious traditions? If the latter, how do we render the idea of a *Ding an Sich* (a noumenal Real) religiously and existentially meaningful? Is the notion of God *qua Ding an Sich* religiously and existentially vacuous? Are we not back to an unfortunate form of Kantian transcendentalism with its distinction between phenomena and noumena? And how does a *Ding an Sich* serve the historical and political goals of prophetic deliverance?

The reader will keep in mind here that logical positivism placed the religionist on the defensive, for the positivist was out to show the noncognitive status and hence nonsensicality of metaphysics and religious language. West, however, given his historicism, also places the religionist on the defensive. For although West does not attempt to render religious language and metaphysics cognitively meaningless, the source of the meaningfulness and intelligibility of particular religious narrative ways of understanding the self, God, and the world is not to be found in anything that points beyond the narrative itself. But the religionist will not rest content thinking that what he or she believes about the self, God, and the world does not somehow "accurately represent" nonlinguistic states of affairs. The religiously devout Hindu will not accept the implications of West's historicist and holist philosophical maneuver to assign to the god Shiva an intra-Hindu communal significance only; that is, without any actual ahistorical ontic significance. And the fundamentalist Muslim will deem his pilgrimage to Mecca a holy experience that has a relational ontological significance between the spiritual self-and-Allah. And the Christian, depending upon his or her own biblical interpretive discourse community, will believe that the birth (God made flesh) and resurrection of Jesus was an *actual* event that took place in history, an event grounded upon vertically other-worldly ontological events. Indeed, religious folk believe that the ontological and epistemological status of their religious world-views far exceeds how those world-views existentially function in their lives.

Antifoundational Historicist Philosophy: Religious Metanarrative Truth Well Lost

Let us go on to briefly suggest some of the more general implications of postmodern philosophical thought on religious reflection and discourse. West seems to think that the postmodern demythologizing of the natural sciences is of immense importance to religious thinkers. But we must keep in mind that postmodern philosophers are not necessarily religious apologists. Moreover, just because postmodern philosophy has made a good show of critiquing the analytic and realist presuppositions of much of scientific self-understanding, this does not mean that religionists should not be worried about the larger conclusions drawn from postmodern philosophical presuppositions.

For example, it would appear that many of the postmodern philosophical views of Paul Feyerabend should be eagerly embraced by religionists. After all, for Feyerabend, in the light of Kuhn's thesis of incommensurability, the only things that remain "are aesthetic judgements, judgements of taste, and our own subjective wishes."[50] For Feyerabend, even the Bible might be viewed as an alternative cosmology.[51] But in denying science a privileged voice within the context of the many ontological narratives claiming what is "out there," he does not thereby understand religious narratives as more accurately reflecting some ahistorical reality. Like quarks, which are themselves inextricably linked to historical and socially negotiated conditions of existence, (God) gods are also linked to a projecting sociohistorical mechanism.[52] Feyerabend writes, "as the most fundamental and most highly confirmed theory of present day physics, the quantum theory rejects unconditional projections and makes existence depend on special historically determined circumstances."[53] But such gods "exist" in history; they do not exist outside of the projecting sociohistorical mechanism. Surely, a Christian religionist would find such a postmodernist description (à la Feyerabend) unpalatable to his or her own belief that God is actually transcendentally outside of history as the creator of the world, and can be "known."

But perhaps many religious thinkers who had previously been on the defensive because of the reductionist logic of the verifiability principle of meaning were elated when Quine expressed his objections to the analytic and reductionistic dogmas:

> It is misleading to speak of the empirical content of an individual statement – especially if it is a statement at all remote from the experiential periphery of the field. Furthermore it becomes folly to seek a boundary between synthetic statements, which hold contingently on experience, and analytic statements, which hold come what may. Any statement can be held true come what may, if we make drastic enough adjustments elsewhere in the system. . . . Conversely, by the same token, no statement is immune to revision.[54]

But how many religious thinkers would begin to reassess their elation given the early Quine's suggestion that both physical objects and Homer's gods "enter our conception only as cultural posits."[55] Summarizing Quine's position, Frankenberry writes:

> The point is that epistemologically the "myths" (if we choose to call them that) of physical objects and gods are on the same logical footing. How does the philosopher of science justify such language? How does the scholar of religion justify language about the gods? No a priori norms or principles come to aid here. In neither case can we expect to find justificatory procedures that are anything other than historically evolved conventions. We choose among them according to our various interests and purposes.[56]

It does not take much to infer Quine's position on the monotheism of Christianity or the polytheism of Hinduism. Does the religionist actually prostrate himself or herself before a *cultural posit*? Is his or her own religious self-understanding consistent with such a view?

Nelson Goodman's ontological pluralism and epistemological conventionalism will provide for us many versions of how the world is, but no such versions are based upon knowledge received *sub specie aeternitatis*. For Goodman, "there is no way that is the way the world is."[57] The Christian world-view is believed to be an accurate (true) world-view which is ontologically descriptive of *the way the world is*. But Goodman's notion of a multitude of worlds will not allow for such a limited religious ontological monism. It is not *ontological fit* of theory and world, and the acquiring of *true beliefs* that is involved in the process of world/reality making. Goodman writes, "And knowing or understanding is seen as ranging beyond the acquiring of true beliefs to the discovering and devising of fit of all sorts."[58]

Wilfrid Sellars has described himself as a second generation atheist,[59] and his attack on the Myth of the Given (his antifoundationalism) will certainly cause a great deal of uneasiness for those God-talkers who are very much committed to their belief that God exists and that He allows Himself to be known through revelation; that is, self-authenticating ("given") religious experiences. Sellars, as already noted, once disclosed that philosophy consisted of metaphors. Is it possible that he thought the same applied to religion? Surely, the religionist who ecstatically feels the "presence" of God is not just reacting to the power of a metaphor. Clearly, many religionists will assure us that God is quite literally in their midst during moments of religious ecstasis.

Richard Rorty also places a great deal of emphasis on our use of pictures and metaphors as the determinants of many of our convictions. His epistemological behaviorism problematizes the Platonic drive (a similar drive shared by religionists) to step beyond the limits of our cultural and historical situatedness. He describes this drive as "the impossible attempt to step outside our skins – the traditions, linguistic and other, within which we do our thinking and self-criticism."[60] But it is religious world-views that claim for themselves a nonlocal and nontransient truth-status. However, Rorty argues: "I think that these positions are of interest only insofar as they call on us to do without that notion and that sense, and to experiment with an image of ourselves (i.e., us wet liberals) as local and transient as any other species of animals, yet none the worse for that."[61]

Given the above, many religionists would clearly assume a defensive posture; for the above postmodern implications for religion suggest that religious ways of seeing the world are, broadly construed, simply socially and communally constructed ways of being-in-the-world. We have constructed for ourselves religious systems populated with God/gods, souls, salvation, revelation, sin, angels, etc., that are not reflective of some metanarrative ontic reality, teleological *origins*, foundational *givens*, and ontological *presence*.

However, West's suggestion that postanalytic philosophers (Quine, Goodman, Sellars, Feyerabend, Rorty, et al.) ought to take an interest in religious reflection (rather than principally in science) would at least provide religious thinkers with examples of more sophisticated, postmodern ways of conducting conceptual analyses in the area of philosophy of religion. But there would also be clear and serious postmodern entailments that would tend to reduce religious perspectives to intracommunal utterances, only to have echoed back "divine" responses that we ourselves have constructed relative to our religious social practices. And given West's own historicism, perhaps he would sit well with such entailments. Religious books (the Bible, the Qur'an, the Gita, et al.) would constitute textual discourse possessing affective, metaphorical, moral, and doxological illocutionary force that made no actual reference to an ontic extratextual reality. And even if our religious and theological discourse was somehow informed by an ontic extratextual reality, a so-called divine *Ding an Sich*, it is not clear that such a conception of the divine would serve our deepest religio-existential needs.

It would seem that West's historicist philosophy of religion, which has clear pluralist implications, will not allow for the thematization of religious truth outside of the various religious ways of picturing the self, God, and the world. But then again, and this is a serious philosophical problematic that *he must* resolve, West wants to have his historicism on the one hand, and yet have a religious attitude with metanarrative ontological commitments as well. Describing his own Christian membership identity, West says, "To be a Christian is to have a joyful attitude toward the resurrection-claim, *to stake one's life on it and to rest one's hope upon its promise – the promise of a new heaven and a new earth*"[62] (emphasis added). But as Mason Olds concludes, "To know that God-talk is a part of a language game and to act as if it were an ontic reality is to engage in bad faith, which is contrary to living authentically."[63]

Beyond the question of West's presumed bad faith, however, it is important that he specifically gives greater attention to the nature of the sacred and the divine. Is God a *Ding an Sich*? How useful is such a conception of God to liberation theology? Surely, the liberationist theologian believes in a form of religious realism. God is certainly more than an intertextual semiotic marker that has nominally functional and pragmatic value only within the context of seeking sociopolitical liberation. And to what extent does West's historicist philosophy of religion, given its fluid language games and holism, imply a form of fideism? And assuming that we are living in a post-*presence* philosophical world, a world in which grand metaphysical systems are studied as "anthropologists approach," according to West, "the cosmological schemes of the Hopi Indians," what are we to make of religious experiences? Indeed, in a post-*presence* philosophical world where experience is displaced by a poststructuralist process of linguistification, what do we make of religious and mystical experiences? In a Sellarsian world where self-authenticating experiential episodes are denied, how do we distinguish "genuine" experiences of the divine from experiences that are grounded upon, and induced by, what our religious community, with its socio-ecclesiastical practices and norms, "allows" us to experience? After all, for West, "knowledge claims are secured by the social practices of a community of inquirers, rather than the purely mental activity [or *experiential* content] of an individual subject."[64] Apparently, West is silent on these questions. Moreover, West needs to think through in great detail the religious pluralist implications of his historicist philosophy of religion. On the basis of his historicism and holism, West appears to be open to the proliferation of a multitude of religious world-views with their own specific symbols, ontological assumptions, interests, values, existential crises, social practices, etc. In short, West is committed to the normative status of prophetic Christianity, but logically compelled to admit that for other religionists their religious world-views are equally normative for them. It is here that West is faced with the problem of epistemic parity *vis-à-vis* different religious world-views. Does this lead to a form of religious indifferentism? If there is no way to ascertain which religious tradition is "true" (that is, "true" in a correspondence sense), then does it really matter which religious tradition one embraces? Is it just a matter of Jamesian "live options"? Or is it simply a case of contextual pragmatics and existential utility, saturated with a sense of the hermeneutics of finitude and fear and trembling?

West's Pascalian and Kierkegaardian sensibilities are evident where he maintains:

> Like Kierkegaard, whose reflections on Christian faith were so profound and yet often so frustrating, I do not think it possible to put forward rational defenses of one's faith that verify its veracity or even persuade one's critics. Yet it is possible to convey to others the sense of deep emptiness and pervasive meaninglessness one feels if one is not critically aligned with an enabling tradition. One risks not logical inconsistency, but actual insanity; the issue is not reason or irrationality, but life or death. Of course, the fundamental philosophical question remains whether the Christian gospel is ultimately true. And, as a Christian prophetic pragmatist whose focus is on coping with transient and provisional penultimate matters yet whose hope goes beyond them, I reply in the affirmative, bank all on it, yet am willing to entertain the possibility in low moments that I may be deluded.[65]

But again, for West, what are the actual entailments of such "low moments"? Can they really function as sufficient criteria of falsifiability or lead to a total rejection of the prophetic Christian tradition? Moreover, an "enabling tradition," as West admits, carries no foundationalist epistemic warrant or metaphysical underpinning. It does, however, provide a framework within which one is able to draw strength when often faced with an existential crisis. In other words, from the perspective of the world, self, and God as "gestalted" from within the framework of Christianity, for example, one "tries to promote the valuing of certain insights, illuminations, capacities and abilities in order honestly to confront and effectively to cope with the inevitable vicissitudes and unavoidable limit-situations in life."[66] But how does this view differ from a specifically psychological rendering of religion? An enabling tradition does not, given West's historicism, help to placate the cognitive dissonance and deep anxiety (sustained by the epistemic parity of two or more religious language games) that one feels while attempting to choose between religious traditions with their own unique dynamic narratives, sacred semiotic spaces, and hermeneutic perspectives. Moreover, to appeal to our "fallenness" as an explanatory or narrative way of addressing the difficulties of "knowing" which religious tradition is true has problems of its own; for the notion of "fallenness" is a concept which has a conceptual function which is already part of the Christian framework. Indeed, what is the epistemic status of the narrative detailing our "fallenness"? This places us back within the hermeneutic circle and thus does not alleviate our cognitive dissonance with respect to attempting to decide upon the "truth" of a particular religious tradition. Or shall West pursue the interesting route of Terrence Tilley? Tilley writes:

> The way to resolve the problem of "religious belief " is not to engage in disembodied academic practice of seeking universal or unshakeable foundations or demonstrating that theistic beliefs are rational, but to engage in the embodied and *necessarily shared* practice of seeking to make and live out the wisest religious commitments one can.[67]

But even this prudential approach, despite its many merits and insights, still leaves us to fall back upon our own traditions, values, social practices, and fore-structural understanding of what constitutes a "wise judgment" and "wise commitment." Is it possible that even after a long and honest prudential commitment to a religious tradition that one might discover that one has wagered incorrectly, that one's religious world-view is not a mirror of God, but a mirror reflecting back one's own deepest ontotheological commitments created and sustained from within the matrix of one's own linguistic, cultural, historical, and communal religious and theological practices?

In conclusion, it is my contention that West's historicist philosophy of religion leaves us in a situation of epistemic parity with regard to choosing between religious traditions. Moreover, it is not clear that West offers a way out of this predicament. West would, of course, argue that Christianity deals more effectively, at least for him, with particular social and existential crises than, let us say, Hinduism. In this sense, different religious traditions would be able to meet the needs of different communities of people in light of the reality of differential experiences of pain, loss, angst, and suffering. This simply indicates the disparity of existential crises. This does not, however, resolve the problem of *epistemic parity* with regard to choosing between different religious traditions. This, of course, leaves unaddressed many problems associated with religious pluralism. After all, major religious traditions have different conceptions of the divine. If a single religious tradition has a "true" conception of the divine, how, given West's (antifoundational) historicism, can this be *known*? From the perspective of a hermeneutics of finitude, West could argue that we are all limited and finite creatures and therefore cannot possibly grasp the true meaning and nature of the divine. He could then maintain that all religious traditions in some sense possess "true," though partial and limited, conceptions of the divine. But given West's framework, how do we demonstrate the "truth" that each conception is indeed a partial and limited view? Again, on West's view, this cannot be *known*. Are we not back to God as a mysterious *Ding an Sich*? Why should we worship a divine *Ding an Sich*, about which nothing can be known, as opposed to worshipping nothing at all? Indeed, how do we avoid an *atheological* humanism? And what do we do when two or more religious traditions hold truth-claims about the divine that contradict each other? Clearly, not all of the various conceptions of the divine can be true. But is it possible that each is false? These are questions that West should attempt to address within the framework of his historicism.

In the end, I would argue, West might be described as a crypto-fideist, particularly given his Wittgensteinian and Kierkegaardian sensibilities. Once the Myth of the Given has been deconstructed and religion as a mirror of God has been shattered, and, of course, all of our epistemic acts of knowing are acknowledged as activities embedded within our social practices, are we not, according to West's view, forever bounded by our cultural and historical *facticity*, condemned to bear witness to mere cultural idols, existential fissures, and our own deepest ontotheological projections? Now that we live in a postmetaphysical moment (that is, where we openly admit that our metaphysical speculations are grounded within social practices and are relative to specific traditions), are we not committed to spin our religious narratives without "deeper" metaphysical comfort? And though some form of "metaphysical" speculation is inescapable, as West admits,[68] this will not resolve the problems of religious pluralism; for his conception of metaphysics is too ontotheologically deflationary. We are not brought any closer to "knowing" what exists beyond, as it were, our own specific religious traditions. Lastly, what awaits on the other side of religious metaphysical demystification is perhaps too thin for many religionists to accept.

Acknowledgments

I would like to thank philosophers Andrew J. Dell'Olio, Wilhelm Wurzer, and Fred Evans for their helpful comments on this chapter, especially Dell'Olio and Evans for their close textual reading.

Notes

1   Nancy Frankenberry, *Religion and Radical Empiricism* (New York: State University of New York Press, 1987), p. 75.
2   The reader will note that not all historicists are necessarily antifoundationalists. West's antifoundationalism, however, seems to follow from his historicism.
3   Frankenberry, *Religion and Radical Empiricism*, p. 77.
4   Pauline Marie Rosenau's *Post-Modernism and the Social Sciences: Insights, Inroads and Intrusions* (Princeton, NJ: Princeton University Press, 1992) does a fine job of elaborating upon these two forms of postmodernism.

5   Cornel West, "Nietzche's prefiguration of postmodern American philosophy." In Cornel West (ed.), *The Cornel West Reader* (New York: Basic *Civitas* Books, 1999), p. 210.

6   Cornel West, "The politics of American neo-pragmatism." In John Rajchman and Cornel West (eds), *Post-Analytic Philosophy* (New York: Columbia University Press, 1985), p. 265.

7   Cornel West, *Keeping Faith: Philosophy and Race in America* (New York: Routledge, 1993), p. 126.

8   Ibid., p. 127.

9   Ibid., pp. 130–1.

10 Cornel West, *Prophetic Fragments* (Grand Rapids, MI: William B. Eerdmans Publishing Company, 1988), p. 267.

11 *Keeping Faith*, p. 130.

12 Ibid., p. 134.

13 Ibid., p. 131.

14 *The Cornel West Reader*, p. 206.

15 *Keeping Faith*, p. 133.

16 Ibid.

17 *The Cornel West Reader*, p. 14.

18 *Keeping Faith*, p. 134.

19 Ibid., pp. 133–4.

20 Ibid., p. 134.

21 Ibid.

22 Cornel West, "A philosophical view of Easter." *Dialog: A Journal of Theology*, 19(1), 1980, p. 24.

23 Cornel West, *Prophesy Deliverance! An Afro-American Revolutionary Christianity* (Philadelphia: The Westminster Press, 1982), p. 18.

24 David R. Hiley, *Philosophy in Question: Essays on a Pyrrhonian Theme* (Chicago: University of Chicago Press, 1988), p. 124.

25 *Keeping Faith*, p. 134.

26 Ibid., p. 131.

27 "A philosophical view of Easter," p. 23.

28 *Keeping Faith*, p. 131.

29 Leon Wieseltier, "The unreal world of Cornel West: all and nothing at all." *The New Republic*, March, 1995, p. 34.

30 Mason Olds, "God-talk or no God-talk – is there a difference?" *Religious Humanism*, 27(4), 1993, p. 179.

31 "A philosophical view of Easter," p. 22.

32 Ibid.

33 Carl G. Hempel, "The concept of cognitive significance: a reconsideration." *Proceedings of the American Academy of Arts and Sciences*, 80, 1951, p. 74.

34 "A philosophical view of Easter," p. 23.

35 Ibid.

36 *Prophetic Fragments*, p. 269.

37 Ibid.

38   Ibid.

39   *The Cornel West Reader*, p. 14.

40   Ibid.

41   "A philosophical view of Easter," p. 23.

42   Ibid., p. 24.

43   Ibid., p. 23.

44   Philip Clayton, *Explanation from Physics to Theology: An Essay in Rationality and Religion* (New Haven, CT: Yale University Press, 1989), p. 176.

45   Olds, "God-talk or no God-talk," p. 188.

46   Cornel West, *The Ethical Dimensions of Marxist Thought* (New York: Monthly Review Press, 1991), p. 3.

47   Cornel West, "Schleiermacher's hermeneutics and the myth of the given." *Union Seminary Quarterly Review*, 34(2), 1979, p. 82.

48   *Prophetic Fragments*, p. 269.

49   Ibid., p. 268.

50   Clayton, *Explanation from Physics to Theology*, p. 45.

51   Paul Feyerabend, *Against Method: Outline of an Anarchistic Theory of Knowledge* (London: NLB, 1975), p. 47n1.

52   Paul Feyerabend, "Realism and the historicity of knowledge." *Journal of Philosophy*, 86(8), 1989, pp. 398, 400, 402, 404, 406.

53   Ibid., p. 402.

54   Willard Van Orman Quine, "Two dogmas of empiricism." In *From a Logical Point of View* (New York: Harper and Row, 1963), p. 43.

55   Ibid., p. 44.

56   Frankenberry, *Religion and Radical Empiricism*, p. 73.

57   Nelson Goodman, "The way the world is." In *Problems and Projects* (New York: Bobbs-Merrill, 1972), p. 31.

58   Nelson Goodman, *Ways of Worldmaking* (Indianapolis: Hackett, 1978), p. 138.

59   Wilfrid Sellars, "Autobiographical reflections." In Hector-Neri Castaneda (ed.), *Action, Knowledge and Reality: Critical Studies in Honor of Wilfrid Sellars* (Indianapolis: Bobbs-Merrill, 1975), p. 281.

60   Richard Rorty, *Consequences of Pragmatism* (Minneapolis: University of Minnesota Press, 1982), p. xix.

61   Richard Rorty, "Putnam and the relativist menace." *Journal of Philosophy*, 90(9), 1993, p. 461.

62   "A philosophical view of Easter," p. 24.

63   Olds, "God-talk or no God-talk," p. 189.

64   *Prophesy Deliverance!*, p. 21.

65   *The Cornel West Reader*, p. 171.

66   "A philosophical view of Easter," p. 22.

67   Terrence W. Tilley, *The Wisdom of Religious Commitment* (Washington, DC: Georgetown University Press, 1995), p. 152.

68   Maintaining that metaphysical and ontological reflections should continue, West agrees with Max Weber's contention that we are "finite human animals suspended in webs of significance we ourselves spin" (see *Prophetic Fragments*, p. 267). West also argues that

"acceptable forms of metaphysical reflections are those of synoptic narratives and overarching vocabularies that provide enhancing self-images and enabling coping techniques for living" (see *Prophetic Fragments*, pp. 269–70). And in defending a version of John Dewey's redescription of nature and experience, West allows for "metaphorical versions of what one thinks the way the world is in light of the best available theories. I find nothing wrong with this kind of intellectual activity as long as one acknowledges the needs and interests it satisfies" (see *The American Evasion of Philosophy*, p. 96). In other words, West supports a form of "metaphysical" reflection which is tempered by both a pragmatist framework and a thick historicist emphasis on situationality and contextuality.

7

Is Cornel West also Among the Theologians? The Shadow of the Divine in the Religious Thought of Cornel West

Victor Anderson

For those familiar with responses by American theologians to John Dewey's *A Common Faith*,[1] the title of this chapter is an adaptation from the article written in the 1930s by Henry Nelson Wieman and critical reviews of that article by Edwin Ewart Aubrey and John Dewey. In "John Dewey's common faith," Wieman offered a highly sympathetic and appreciative review of Dewey's book.[2] He extolled the book as a naturalistic yet theistic interpretation of human possibilities for creative exchange through the union of the actual and ideal, symbolized in the name, God. Aubrey challenged Wieman's interpretation of Dewey's book. And in "Is John Dewey a theist?," Aubrey questioned the very association of Dewey and theism.[3] For Aubrey, Dewey's integrating power that binds the actual and ideal is not God but human imaginative intelligence. Dewey himself would stand between Aubrey and Wieman. In agreement with Aubrey, he says that Wieman had "read his own position into his interpretation of mine." However, Dewey experienced no joy in correcting the theologian, who, when compared to his many theological critics, sympathetically treated his work.

I have evoked this historical note in order to situate a certain disclaimer that I want to make at the start. Remembering Wieman, I have the deepest appreciation for and sympathy with the vision, critiques, and moral possibilities that Cornel West articulates in his religious thought. Hence, the immediate temptation that poses a challenge for me is to read my own views into West's, forging complete commensuration between his views and my pragmatic theology.[4] Therefore, like Aubrey and Dewey himself, I do not wish to distort West's religious thought by making West, the Christian social critic, into my kind of academic theologian. I am fully aware that West rejects such a professional identification. However, I provide an interpretation and reading of West, particularly on the metaphysical aspect of pragmatic historicism. West suggests this metaphysical possibility, but it remains a shadowy possibility not developed in his religious thought. The question of metaphysics in religious thought invites a conversation with West and academic theology that has not been of engaged concern in his writings on religion and religious thought.

West's estimation of academic theology as a discipline is not very favorable. However, this is a mitigated judgment. Several descriptions characterize his estimation. One, he sees the theological discipline as suffering from an intellectual crisis. Two, he sees much that goes by the name academic theology as insufficiently public in relevance. On both points, West stands in good company with the American theologian Van A. Harvey, who has genuine interests in religious questions, the history of theology in the West, and models of religious social leadership. Yet, like West, Harvey finds much of academic theology ridden with crises. Both thinkers construe the crisis of academic theology as a crisis of marginalization. I want to focus on Harvey's description of this crisis because it has crystallized the suspicions of many social critics about the intellectual status of academic theology.[5] It certainly stands in the background of West's estimation of academic theology.

Harvey argues persuasively that academic theology has become irrelevant to most intellectuals. He sees the secularism of contemporary social life in the United States as so publicly entrenched and pervasive that the explanations and norms of traditional Western theology are completely incommensurable with the pluralism of our culture. Harvey credits the intellectual marginalization of academic theology to historical factors of scientific secularization and naturalism that dominated many of the state and land grant universities and colleges in the late nineteenth and early twentieth centuries. He especially targets the increased professionalization and specialization of theology in America's divinity schools and seminaries as culprits that rendered academic theology practically irrelevant. Conceiving their projects in technical and academic terms, rather than appealing to the laity, theologians confine themselves to their own circle of other academics. Moreover, many seminary and divinity students who are not headed for careers in the academy find much of academic theology irrelevant and unpractical, as do many members of the clergy. Because of the daily operations and demands of church life and pastoral care, many of the clergy are not likely to turn to much of contemporary constructive, academic theology for help or consolation, not even for continuing education.[6]

According to Harvey, the respectability of academic theology is as much called into question in the academy as it is questionable in the larger culture and in the church. He thinks that the intellectual marginalization of theology is the fault of academic theologians themselves, who are moved intellectually by every narcissistic turn and fad infiltrating higher learning. To many in the academy, academic theology has undermined its own intellectual relevance as it has been shaped by "The slightest breezes that have stirred the trees of the groves of academe."[7] What can be made of a discipline's integrity that fragments between a "theology of the death of God," a "theology of play," a "theology of hope," a "theology of liberation," a "theology of polytheism," a "theology of deconstruction," and even redundantly, a "theology of God," says Harvey.[8]

Of course, Harvey's criticisms are satirical. However, he makes a salient point about the state of academic theology and its intellectual significance. As a discipline, it appears that much of academic theology has lost its metaphysical center and seems lost for a substitute subject matter and distinctive barring. Rather than an innovation in American scholarship, academic theology appears parasitic on progressive, and sometimes, I think, not so progressive projects in the humanities and social sciences. It seems to provide little intellectual, moral, and religious leadership among the various faculties of the arts and sciences; rather, theologians in university-based schools are often treated with suspicion by other faculties, or bear the brunt of their clerical caricaturing.

For church and social leaders, many of whom have studied theology in American divinity schools and seminaries, the constructive interests of many academic theologians are alienating. For after deconstructing metaphysical and ontological canons of received doctrines and interpretations of God, Creation, the ordering of human relations, Christ, and the place of the Church in the world, many students, pastors, religious seekers, and social leaders find our contemporary constructive theologies spiritually, practically, and publicly bankrupt. Having deconstructed its Western theological metaphysical canon, many inside and outside the academy find academic theologians producing little that is preachable or teachable within local churches and community forums. And the secular news media can hardly recognize in the languages of academic theologians anything worth translating into sound bites for public consumption. American academic theology seems to provide few valuable critical resources for helping the churches and society to transcend America's persistent social crises and contestations.

Cornel West shares much of this description of academic theology, although in a mitigated manner. In an important essay, "The crisis of theological education," West suggests that "our seminaries and divinity schools are not only simply in intellectual disarray and existential disorientation; our very conception of what they should be doing are in shambles."[9] In that essay, West also ties the marginalization of academic theology in our present context to:

> the demystifying of European cultural hegemony, the deconstruction of European philosophical edifices, and the decolonization of the third world [which] has left theology with hardly an autonomous subject matter (hence a temptation to be

excessively frivolous and meretricious in its enactments) and with little intellectually respectable resources upon which to build.[10]

With Harvey, West also suggests that academic theologians have consequently tried to assure their discipline by attaching themselves to other disciplines from which they can garner intellectual legitimacy. In the end, the intellectual justifications and legitimacy of academic theology stand or fall with the logical justifications and legitimacy of the disciplines with which theology couples itself. Although the essay cited above was published in 1988, there is little evidence in *The Cornel West Reader* that West's perception on the state of academic theology has sufficiently changed.[11] My suspicion is that these perceptions might also account for the lack of West's critical engagement with academic theologians in his critical writings on religion and religious thought.

Lurking behind West's estranged relation to academic theology, I think, is the problem of metaphysics in theology, or, at least, West's suspicions about the metaphysical aspect of theology. "In dispensing with metaphysics in religious thought," West credits the historicist turn in contemporary philosophy as the fundamental intellectual movement that has all but exploded any residue of the prior metaphysical and epistemological tenets that have sustained academic theology, especially in the modern age.[12] In this regard, "A historicist turn has occurred in contemporary philosophy which has not yet awakened some theologians from their dogmatic slumber," says West.[13] He suggests that the new historicism, what William Dean describes as "pragmatic historicism,"[14] has had a profound negative effect on the traditional epistemic structures of both religious philosophy and theology.

A number of practices are typified by pragmatic historicism. One, it proposes that there are no extrinsic or "objectively neutral" basis, grounds, or foundation for adjudicating competitive theories, interpretations, and descriptions of the world and human realities. Two, the historicist turn makes finitude and fallibility operative conditions that are co-present in all descriptions and interpretations, including theological ones. Three, pragmatic historicism is less a doctrine or a method and more a disposition that the credible intellectual or scholar brings pursuant to his or her project. It is a disposition that brings to consciousness prejudices, presuppositions, and prejudgments attending every metaphysical or ontological depiction of the way things are. Four, where all intellectual judgments are conditioned by these background conditions, for West "metaphysics and ontology in the grand mode or in the old sense are anachronistic, antiquated, and most importantly, unwarranted."[15] All metaphysical and ontological judgments are relative to particular traditions, theories, and social locations and practices.

Of course, West's preference for and commitment to pragmatic historicism need to be seen in contrast to the tradition of metaphysical philosophy and religious realism he wants to dispense with and which he sees as particularly operational in much of academic theology. For West, the preoccupation of many contemporary theologians with "method" betrays a certain failure of nerve, on the part of theologians, to embrace the historicist turn. Too many suspend the historicist recognition that there are no grounding strategies – based on transcendental conditions, appeals to which can provide theology with universal and necessary postulates – that will render theological judgments non-arbitrary and cognitively successful. Preoccupations with such methodological concerns fall under West's critique of "metaphysics" or "religious realism" in theology. Religious realism is for West "an intellectual strategy adopted by those who accept the authority of particular ecclesiastical (or personal) interpretations. The purpose here is to convince one's self and others that these interpretations are true regardless of their role and function in one's life."[16] "I reject religious realism because it rests upon a faulty notion of religious 'truth'," says West.[17]

To be sure, there is a complex relation between interpretation and truth that mitigates West's critique of metaphysics in religious thought. As defined by West, religious realism is worth rejecting (if, in fact, his descriptions of such strategies do the work he ascribes to them). For West, judgments of truth in religious thought are not likely to be settled by theologians appealing to a really real beyond the apparent, or by the search for a religious *a priori* in the general order of things or human consciousness. Truth in theology is not a question of epistemic justification. Rather, I take it that, for West, theological descriptions are as true as they make sense of human life, sustaining human beings against the historical, social, cultural, and, yes, individual crises that circumscribe the ordinary world of human existence.

As I read West, truth in theology is judged in terms of the existential satisfaction it provides. Theological claims are fitting responses of discrete religious communities and their theologians' attempt to make sense of the world and human life and the effectiveness of their norms and interpretation to sustain persons against fatedness. On this point, West says, "The notion of a true religion that does not sustain people through the crises and traumas of life is unintelligible and unacceptable for religious communities."[18] The reasonableness of theological descriptions depends on their adequacy for interpreting or describing the way things are and can be. There is no other credible sense in which one can speak of truth in theology. To put the matter in the language of William James, theological judgments and interpretations are as true as they are "truthful" to the aims, purposes, existential realities, and human values that keep life socially and morally livable.

On these criteria, West certainly does not think that every religious description or theology equally meets this test of adequacy. While maintaining the necessity of relativity in all matters of cognitive judgments, claims to validity, and determination of value, the principle of relativity is balanced in West's religious thinking. He is not intellectually committed to the principle of absolute relativism, the charge that is most targeted toward many who embrace his kind of pragmatic historicism. West is quite clear that the rejection of using reality as a principle of arbitration brings historicists under the charge of being vulgar relativists who "are portrayed as either disbelieving in sense-independent objects or claiming that there are no rational standards to distinguish better and worse interpretations."[19] West's talk of relativity, social location, and value-laden descriptions ought not to be reduced to the claim that there is no world to take hold of, that there is no Reality as such, or that there is no non-human environs that meet human beings as they enter the world. Rather, it is to reject "value-neutral and theory-free notions of Reality as standards for philosophical arbitration," says West.[20] I take it that this judgment is equally extended to theology.

Although West has a strong aversion toward the norm of a priority in prior metaphysical philosophy and theology, I think it is important to note that his judgment does not foreclose on all metaphysical and ontological strategies in philosophy and theology. "The Age of Metaphysics is over, yet inescapable metaphysical reflections will and must go on," says West.[21] Later, he concludes, "I suggest that acceptable forms of metaphysical reflections are those of synoptic narratives and overarching vocabularies that provide enhancing self-images and enabling coping techniques for living."[22] These passages suggest a metaphysical aspect to pragmatic historicism and a metaphysical intentionality in religious thought. However, having said this, West himself is not very open or substantive about what might be meant by these possibilities. They remain veiled possibilities in his religious thought.

From what West says, I take him to suggest that descriptions, which take into themselves the widest ranges of perception and make use of a plenitude of languages to provide a sense of the whole, hold a certain legitimacy in both philosophy and theology. This is what I call the "shadow of the divine" in West's religious thought. However, this metaphysical suggestion comes very close to being vitiated by West. He finds it difficult to make a strong claim for metaphysical thinking in relation to postmodern challenges and tendencies that focalize the particular of the particulars, proliferate into apparently incommensurable narratives spawned by contemporary preoccupations with difference, and characterize a moral culture ridden with moral fragments and rabid individualism. Notwithstanding these postmodern challenges, West nevertheless suggests that there remains an existential need for metaphysical thinking in religious thought. This is especially the case where nihilism and fatalism threaten individual lives and shared communal life is threatened by what Karl Barth once referred to as "The Shadow of Nothingness," the threat of non-being, or the sense of radical evil. In other words, I take it that for West academic theology is as legitimate as its metaphysical possibilities, interpretations, and descriptions land, connect, support, and enable people to cope with and transcend the existential miseries that tragically define the human condition.

Immanence is foregrounded in West's religious thought. Categories of immediacy, urgency, crisis, and immanent engagement in the human situation frame much of his religious thought. Yet, given the priority of these categories in his thinking, one puzzles over West's talk of metaphysical necessity in religious thought. What are we to make of the category of transcendence in his religious thinking? George Yancy puts this question to West. Yancy asks, "In his controversial essay in the *New Republic*, Leon Wieseltier claims that you maintain that the abolition of transcendence is necessary for religion and that you don't realize the dire contradiction that you've created. What is your response?"[23] West responds: "I've never rejected transcendence per se.... Certainly anybody like myself who talks about struggle, who comes out of a Christian tradition, which includes some kind of overcoming – to use the Hegelian term, *Aufhebung*, which is a kind of transcendence per se, would never really want to call into question transcendence per se."[24] Still, it is not very clear what West means by transcendence here. The category appears a recessive and minimally conceived possibility.[25] This then leads Yancy to ask, "Staying with the concept of transcendence, what does a 'Westian,' as it were, conception of God look like?"[26]

It is interesting that Yancy himself identifies a certain natural or apparent connection between transcendence and the idea of God, which on my account amounts to a maximalist conception of transcendence. However, this maximal connection is not immediately apparent from West's statements on transcendence. The possibility of "overcoming," minimally conceived, does not lead naturally into the idea of God. However, Yancy's question opens a line of clarification in West's thought that is worth citing at length:

> West: Well I don't think that we have such a thing as a "Westian" anything, really. There are certain lenses through which I look at the world, but, for me, any God-talk is so inextricably linked to talk about so many other things that it would have to do with the nature of the stories and narratives where God is invoked as an agent in order to provide illuminations about what it means to be human. And so I tend to side with those in the Christian tradition that put a high premium in Christ. So I'm a kind of Christocentric thinker in that regard and therefore, following Karl Barth, the greatest Christocentric thinker of the twentieth century, I think that our concrete images of God are best rendered in the various narratives told about Christ as loving, struggling, sacrificing, suffering and overcoming. And in that regard, I probably would want to send somebody to certain Barthian texts or make certain links to James Cone, who, of course, was a very close student of Karl Barth.[27]

Particularly worth commenting on in this passage is the association that West makes with Karl Barth, whose conception of transcendence is extremely maximal, while West's own conception of transcendence is minimal. It is a comparison of points of view, which on a number of levels appear quite incompatible. One, talk of God is for West not fundamentally a commitment to "ontotheology" or to a radically transcendent metaphysical/ontological subject who commands absolute loyalty. But this is exactly who God is in Barth's theology. God is the absolute, transcendent subject who meets all humanity, regardless of their particular narratives or stories, as the creator. And God's command, for Barth, ontologically structures all human ethical responses. Two, West holds a strong identification between talk of God and human meaning. The correlation is so strong in West's religious thought that conceptions of God appear to be self-referential human self-descriptions. This is an interpretative move more reminiscent of Ludwig Feuerbach than Barth.[28] That is, such "asymptotic" movement between God-talk and human meaning appears quite at odds with Barth's theological castigation against the human tendency toward overcoming the ontological divide between God and humanity. For Barth, God's YES and NO mark the transcendental boundary between the creator who commands and the creature that obeys.[29]

There is perhaps more agreement between Barth and West on Christology or the meaning of Christ in history. Yet, even here, the two thinkers do not appear to be saying the same things. In my judgment, West rightly sees Christ as the center and norm of Christian faith and action. The centrality is tautological and historical. At one level, the centrality of Christ is a logical marker of Christian identity, i.e. a Christian is one who follows Christ. Were Christ not the center or norm of Christian faith, it is difficult to say in what sense one can be said to be a Christian. That is what I mean by the centrality of Christ being tautological. However, the centrality is of historical significance. For most Christians, the Christ of history is the one whom we have to deal with in belief, faith, action, and loyalty.

In West's substantive description of the centrality of Christ in his religious thought, it is not so much the Christ of the Church (high Christology), or Barth's exalted and transcendent subject that frames his understanding of what it means to be human and Christian. The stories and narratives of the Gospels that display the person and work of Jesus command West's attention and compel his loyalty, affection, and actions. Again, the critical principle through which Christ is centered in West's religious social criticism is the lens of radical immanence. As West takes up the centrality of Christ in his own account of Christian identity, the radical transcendence that marked Barth's Christocentrism appears to have receded into the background, if it is present at all. Barth centralized the ir-repeatability of the Christ-event on the Cross, the exaltation of Christ, not only in the resurrection narrative or Easter narrative but also in the post-resurrection stories, and the ontological reconciliation between God and humanity which was fulfilled through Christ's mediatorial loyalty to the command of God. In the comparison of West and Barth on Christology, a major difference turns on West's minimalist conception of transcendence in religious thought. West, without a Christology, retrieves Christ. And the maximalist conception of transcendence that Barth ascribes to both God and Christ appears as a shadow of the divine in West's religious thought.

The minimalist conception of transcendence in West's religious thought invites a certain conceptual problem for West's religious critique of culture. It tends to identify Christian faith and radical democracy under an ethical reductivism. I want to tease out this problem in reference to the German-American theologian Paul Tillich. Tillich stated the problem paradoxically. He said, "the paradox of the churches is the fact that they participate, on the one hand, in the ambiguities of life in general and of the religious life in particular and, on the other hand, in the unambiguous life of the Spiritual Community."[30] The churches are entailed in a "secular history with all the disintegrating, destructive, and tragic-demonic elements, which make historical life as ambiguous as all other life processes," says Tillich.[31] As a spiritual community, the churches are differentiated from other human organizations by theological doctrines and religious functions that are not transferable to other organizations without a real loss to their religious identities.[32] Tillich's point of view is dialectical enough, but it is also triadic in structure. It postulates a third, mediatorial subject between the churches and the ambiguities of life, the world and the existential realities of the human condition.

Like Barth's, Tillich's conception of transcendence is maximal. It is his critical principle for balancing the paradoxical relations between Christian critiques of culture and the cultural critiques of Christianity. As a critical principle in religious criticism, Tillich's judgment squares with West's pragmatic historicism, tracking the paradoxical relation of the Christian engagement with culture as being in the world, participating in the world, and yet distanced from the world in its demonic tendencies toward totality and closure. Christian faith embraces the world and culture. It also maintains a prophetic relation to these realities, calling human communities to reach beyond the limits of the world and their immediate familiar relations. It summons Christians to embrace a larger whole, to enlarge their vision of human possibilities, and, at the same time, to be aware of the limits that meet them at every turn. Tillich defined such commitments as a radical commitment to protest "the tragic-demonic self-elevation of religion and liberate religion from itself for the other functions of the human spirit, at the same time, liberating these functions from their self-seclusion against the manifestations of the ultimate".[33] In other words, Tillich's maximalist conception of transcendence provides a third lens that resists any easy equivocation of Christian faith with cultural expectations and resists the identification of Christian norms with radical democracy.

At moments, West himself seems to approach Tillich in embracing a paradoxical disposition between immanence and transcendence in his religious thought. But unlike Tillich's (and for that matter other theologians who have informed West's Christian perspective – Barth and Reinhold Niebuhr), West's minimalist conception of transcendence comes very close to reducing transcendence into immanence and Christian faith into radical democracy. On West's account, transcendence in religious thought seems to be a creative transformative practice that affirms the ideals of individuality and democracy as a distinctive human possibility. It arises from digging deep in the depths of human particularities and social specificities in order to construct new kinds of connections, affinities and communities across "empire, race, gender and sexual orientation, or the damaging dogmas about the homogeneous character of communities of color."[34] At one point, West appears to identify these modes of human transcendence as Christian norms. "The Christian norms of individuality and democracy are inseparable from systematic social analysis which attempts to keep track of those major social logics which presently undermine these norms," says West.[35] Here, the principles of individuality and democracy are defined as Christian norms. However, it is not clear from what West says about these principles or from any particular Christian story or narrative what makes these norms especially "Christian." What is clear is that the near identification of Christian faith with radical democracy is sustained not by rejecting transcendence as a critical principle but by providing a minimalist conception of it.

West might rightly see behind my question – what makes radical democracy particularly Christian? – and my use of both Barth and Tillich, an attempt to normalize a maximal conception of transcendence in Christian social criticism. That between our various Christian interpretations, stories, narratives, and Christians' encounters with social misery and joy, limits and openings, coercive powers and moral freedom is a *tertium quid*, a metaphysical subject mediating the interstices of Christian faith and radical democracy and rendering problematic their identification. West is likely to identify this hankering for a third something in the experience of Christian living and the world as the metaphysical fallacy of religious realism. With good reasons, he rejects religious realism, what I call the metaphysical aspect of theology, as a dangerously distracting propensity in religious thought. That is, it has dangerous potential for distracting Christians from the real burdens of social and political life, turning their critical gaze from the human condition and the need for human answers, while compelling their loyalties toward a radically transcendent subject in whose hands all is well and good. I think that for West such a preoccupation with metaphysical thinking in academic theology is not likely to move theology from its intellectual marginalization in American culture.

I share many of West's worries about metaphysical thinking in religious thought. I agree with him that being a Christian is a certain way of viewing the world.[36] Indeed, the stories, narratives, and Christian texts (including epistles, creeds and confessions, and doctrines) that inform this perspective involve great selectivity. And this selectivity betrays individual Christians' preferences for certain kinds of texts. The preferences are based on how these sources of religious insight square with one's sense of what is real, what matters, and what one loves. With West, I also think that being a Christian is to "look at the world both through the eyes of its victims and through the Christocentric perspective that requires Christians to see the world through the lens of the cross".[37] However, I perhaps differ from West on this point. The difference is not radical, but it is substantive.

West fixes his critical perspective on the Cross and Easter. Mine is a Christian perspective that views the Cross as only a liminal symbol on the way toward the resurrection narratives. However, the resurrection narratives do not consummate the existential meaning of the Cross and human suffering. For even resurrection narratives of hope, triumph, and transcendence over death and the threat of nonbeing are not total. Like the cross, they occupy a liminal space in the Christian story. To evoke William James again, each narrative points to the *more*. These narratives reach beyond themselves toward an ever-expanding vision of expectation and openness narrated in the Ascension narrative and narratives of Christian expansion. And even these narratives are not total, but they dispose Christian reflection to attend to the exalted Christ in the proclamation narratives and letters. As I read it, the Christian story pushes toward a maximal conception of transcendence.

What work does such a conception provide? I think that it better informs certain critical dispositions that West himself wants to normalize. It resists any identification of the meaning of Christian faith to an ethical essence that would then allow the critic to judge the relative worth of one's particular Christian practice in terms of whether it squares with the Christian norms of radical democracy. From my account, based on Josiah Royce, each story or narrative taken singularly opens up only a relative or fragmentary insight into the meaning of Christian faith. However, taken together the fragments open Christian thought to an ever-enlarging vision of the *more* in the way of human experience and the world. For Karl Barth (not only one of the greatest Christocentric thinkers of the twentieth century but also one of the more radical theocentric thinkers of his time), Christ's ultimate loyalty was not to himself, nor to his family. His radical loyalty was not even to the eradication of sickness and death or the liberation of the disinherited. Christ had a maximal conception of transcendence that directed his absolute loyalty not to an ethical ideal of the Kingdom of God: his absolute devotion was to God – not the idea of God.

I think that the distinctive contribution of theology to Christian social criticism is the manner in which transcendence is developed as a critical principle of cultural criticism. However, the metaphysical aspect of theology need not be construed as incompatible with West's interests in pragmatic historicism. In this regard, Richard Niebuhr understood that there is no talk of Christian faith that is not historical through and through. Theology is a particular point of view, and this point of view is informed by the historical contingencies of faith communities and their intentions to conceptually take hold of God. In Niebuhr's thought, God is the metaphysical-ontological subject whose being and value are not reducible to the inferences or extrinsic valuations of any particular faith, person, or political vision. God's being and value, Niebuhr proposed, are intrinsic to the subject itself.

Therefore, theology, at its best, discloses the human recognition of and responses to God, the perceived Other, whose value is revealed in human experience and appreciated in faith, devotion, and loyalty. In religious realism, as Niebuhr construes it, God is taken hold of as a tertiary being orienting Christians' loyalties to Christ (who was himself devoted to God as the supreme good) and culture (mediating institutions oriented toward the fulfillment of basic human needs and goods).

West is right when he argues that religious realism admits a metaphysical subject into academic theology. However, this metaphysical possibility does not mean that historical Christian principles provide absolute and final answers to our pressing social and public problems. Religious realists are deeply aware of the great pluralisms that shape our cultural life, especially among Christians themselves. Nevertheless, it provides a regulative yet relativizing principle that acknowledges the fragmentary character of all Christian interpretations and descriptions. In Niebuhr's words, religious realism "transcends the wisdom of all [Christ's] interpreters yet employs their partial insights and their necessary conflicts."[38] However, holding such a conviction is relative to one's already valuing such a maximal conception of transcendence.

It may be the case that theology is, foremost, invested in maximal conceptions of transcendence. But on West's own terms, there may be existential necessity and warrant for such a preoccupation. For while a Christian is one who belongs to a religious community for whom Jesus Christ is of supreme value for how one understands the self and the world, no person – not even Christ – is reducible to an ethical essence or to axiomatic propositions. It is impossible to say anything theologically and morally about this person that is not relative to the particular standpoint of the church, history, or the culture of the one who undertakes to describe him, says Niebuhr.[39] The conception of transcendence under which Christ is taken hold of is also a religious point of view that is historical. In the end, however, Christian faith transcends the stories and narratives that inform it. It seeks the lover in the story, the sufferer in the narrated experience of the Cross, and the companion who directs the believer's loyalties. It orients Christian theological reflection toward a third subject who transcends the theologian's own historical faith, theology, social loyalties, and ethical commitments to radical democracy.

To conclude, West and I have no dispute over the tasks, purposes, and ends of religious cultural and social criticism, namely to promote the increase of genuine emancipatory practices consistent with the ends of democratic fulfillment and transcendence. Our philosophical disagreement has much to do with how we come to terms substantively with the idea and reality of transcendence in Christian social criticism. West's is a Christian vision of and commitment to radical democracy and its principles of individuality and democratic participation. Both the vision and the commitment are framed between the limits of human finitude and human capacity for self-transcendence. Christ is the ethical model that legitimates West's vision, and it appears that for West the "essence" of the Christian life is an ethical disposition toward humility of expectations, hope against the threat of nihilism and fatedness, and active engagement in the political life in pursuit of social transformation.

Mine is a maximal vision of transcendence that makes me suspicious of identifying Christian faith with the norms of radical democracy. It recognizes the primacy of the active life as a fitting response to Christ's life and works. Yet my maximal conception of transcendence pushes Christian faith itself beyond Christian ethical consciousness to a relational theology that seeks union with God. From such a point of view, Christ is not reducible in meaning and significance to a set of ethical mandates. Christ is the one whose life of active devotion to God compels my commitment to radical transcendence as a critical principle of social criticism. What difference does this difference make? Perhaps there is no real difference in how West or I pursue the ends of Christian social criticism. The difference may be in how we interpret the world, take hold of its meaning, possibilities, limits, and moments of transcendence. The difference may simply be in the adequacy of our different Christian points of view to enlarge our visions of the *more* in human experience, human possibilities, and the world.

Is Cornel West among the theologians? Not really, if, as I maintain, the metaphysical aspect of theology is and ought to remain a primary preoccupation of theological construction. However, his openness to metaphysical necessity in religious thought makes him a welcomed conversation partner with theology in the ongoing task of envisioning better ways to enlarge our vision of the world and human fulfillment. From a maximal conception of transcendence, such a metaphysical possibility may keep Christian social criticism critically open to the unfolding future of God in the world, and from a minimalist conception of transcendence, pragmatic religious thought may remain open to the shadow of the divine.

Notes

1   John Dewey, *A Common Faith* (New Haven, CT: Yale University Press, 1934).
2   Henry Nelson Wieman, "John Dewey's common faith." *The Christian Century*, 51(46), November 14, 1934, pp. 1450–2.
3   Edwin Ewart Aubrey, Henry Nelson Wieman, and John Dewey, "Is John Dewey a theist?" *The Christian Century*, 51(49), December 5, 1934, pp. 1550–3.
4   Victor Anderson, *Pragmatic Theology: Negotiating the Intersection of an American Philosophy of Religion and Public Theology* (Albany: State University of New York Press, 1998).

5   Van A. Harvey, "On the intellectual marginalization of American theology." In
    Michael J. Lacey (ed.), *Religion and Twentieth-Century American Intellectual Life* (Cam-
    bridge: Cambridge University Press, 1989).
6   Ibid., p. 191.
7   Ibid., p. 173.
8   Ibid.
9   Cornel West, "The crisis of theological education." In *Prophetic Fragments* (Grand
    Rapids, MI: Eerdmans Publishing Company, 1988), p. 273.
10 Ibid., p. 274.
11 This particular essay is not republished in West's newly published anthology, *The
    Cornel West Reader* (New York: Basic *Civitas* Books, 1999).
12 Cornel West, "Dispensing with metaphysics in religious thought." In *Prophetic Frag-
    ments*, pp. 267–72.
13 Ibid., p. 267.
14 See William Dean, *History Making History: The New Historicism in American Religious
    Thought* (Albany: State University of New York Press, 1988).
15 Prophetic Fragments, p. 267.
16 Ibid., p. 269.
17 Ibid.
18 Ibid.
19 Ibid.
20 Ibid.
21 Ibid., p. 267.
22 Ibid., pp. 269–70.
23 Cornel West and George Yancy, "On my intellectual vocation." In *The Cornel West
    Reader*, p. 27.
24 Ibid., p. 28.
25 I have employed a distinction devised by Jerome Stone to differentiate a possible way
    of bridging the intellectual gap between theology and secularism. Where the one is
    defined by a commitment to theism (maximal conception of transcendence), the other
    totalizes human capacities for self-transcendence. The minimalist conception of trans-
    cendence admits an openness to the more in our experience of the world and human
    life without committing one to talk of God and opening human thought to realms of
    possibilities not accredited to human capacities. See Jerome A. Stone, *The Minimalist
    Vision of Transcendence: A Naturalistic Philosophy of Religion* (Albany: State University of
    New York Press, 1992).
26 The Cornel West Reader, p. 28.
27 Ibid.
28 See chapter 2, "The true or anthropological essence of religion." In Ludwig Feuer-
    bach, *The Essence of Christianity*, trans. George Eliot (New York: Harper Torchbooks,
    1957), pp. 33–43.
29 Karl Barth, "Ethics as a task of the doctrine of reconciliation." In *The Christian Life:
    Karl Barth, Church Dogmatics volume IV, part 4*, trans. Geoffrey W. Bromily (Grand
    Rapids, MI: Eerdmans Publishing Company, 1981), pp. 3–46.

30 Paul Tillich, *Systematic Theology in Three Volumes, volume 3* (Chicago: University of Chicago Press, 1967), p.165.

31 Ibid.

32 Ibid.

33 Tillich, p. 245.

34 West, "The new cultural politics of difference." In *Keeping Faith: Philosophy and Race in America* (New York: Routledge, 1993), p. 26.

35 West, "Critical theory and Christian faith." In *Prophetic Fragments*, p. 121.

36 See West, "A philosophical view of Easter." In *The Cornel West Reader*, pp. 415–20.

37 West, "Critical theory and Christian faith," p. 113.

38 H. Richard Niebuhr, *Christ and Culture* (New York: Harper and Row, 1951), p. 2.

39 Ibid., p. 14.

8

Cornel West's Improvisational Philosophy of Religion

M. Shawn Copeland

America [is a] hermeneutical situation.   Charles H. Long

You must become a blues singer – only you find the rhythm and catch it good and structure it as you go along – then the song is you.   Romare Bearden

Nobody can heal the spiritual disorder of an "age." A philosopher can do no more than work himself free from the rubble of idols which, under the name of an "age," threatens to cripple and bury him; and he can hope that the example of his effort will be of help to others who find themselves in the same situation and experience the same desire to gain their humanity under God.   Eric Voeglin

I

For nearly twenty years, Cornel West has shouldered the discipline of philosophy – the work, the effort, the questioning, the intellectual appropriation, the sustained and constant exertion. Indeed, he has embodied the burdens of philosophy in his very body, his very being. A Black man philosophizing, in the face of white racist supremacy, his experience discloses just how "serious...even...dangerous" an affair philosophy is.[1] His project calls for a renascence of philosophizing in the tradition of John Dewey, who "saw knowledge as basically a criticism of life, believed that neither philosophy nor poetry [nor music, for that matter] could avoid politics and social issues, and emphasized humanistic values grounded in experience."[2] And whether that tradition may be tainted with anti-Platonism,[3]

West's concerns are redolent of that far, far older tradition of philosophy which insists that the most important problem of philosophy is the problem of the right way, the most choiceworthy way, to live.

West's admirers find his "moral argument and prophetic vision" invigorating and capacious.[4] More importantly, these men and women never hesitate to argue with him, to correct him. For instance, womanist theologian Delores Williams in her razor-sharp reading of West's politics of conversion, which is centered in a love ethic,[5] points out his naivete. Because Black women, Williams declares, have been exploited by demands of love, they are to be suspicious of any ethic of *unqualified* love of others.[6] Still, as controversial as West's work and the range and style of that work are, even the most strenuous critics concede that he is "one of the most creative and insightful thinkers in American intellectual life."[7]

II

What is it that a theologian finds of interest in the work of Cornel West? With his blend of progressive (Gramscian) Marxism, prophetic Christianity anchored in African-American experience, and neopragmatism, West presents theologians with a historical and philosophical critique of the intellectual, religious, psychological, and moral terrain of America. He tells us the most cauterizing and, therefore, potentially most healing truth about ourselves and our country: ours is a house built on race, and we have colluded in and profited from its construction. Thus, for West and for us, race matters are as "urgent a question of power and morality" as they were for James Madison and Thomas Jefferson. More importantly, race matters are for too many Americans "everyday matter[s] of life and death."[8] West's work importunes theologians to rigorous reflection on the religious and cultural, human and social (that is, political, economic, technological) experiment that is America. For theologians, this means critically understanding that "the connection between salvation and liberty has always been centered in a political context,"[9] grappling with "the failure of our [country's] success,"[10] and providing an analysis of the nature of Christian faith and life that decisively repudiates all forms of disempowering and debasing white supremacist hegemony.

It is true that theology is but a finite and limited perspective on problems that can only have a transcendent or divine solution. Yet it is equally true that theological reflection possesses a relevance to the realization of America as an instance of a common human good. Theology can animate, reinforce, and correct individual and communal responses in the cultural and social domains – pointing out some of the ways in which judgments and decisions, institutions and systems are disordered and deformed or intelligent and valuable. At the same time, theology is bound to relate any and all efforts toward realization of a common human good to the dangerous memory of the life-death-resurrection of Jesus of

Nazareth. If Jesus' prophetic praxis reveals the passion of an eschatological imagination in the midst of a concrete human set-up, the cross shows us its radical risk, the resurrection its impertinent and transcendent hope.

For those of us theologians who are committed to critical transformation of the cultural and social orders that constitute America, the humanity and realities of poor, oppressed, despised human beings – particularly children, women, and men of color – must move to the foreground. Then, new questions can orient our reflection on the ultimate meaning of human existence. What does the fact that most of humanity is oppressed mean for salvation in history? Where is the Triune God in a history awash in the blood, bones, and tears of its victims? What might it mean for poor, despised women and men of color to grasp themselves as subjects? How are marginalized, despised human persons to construct an identity for themselves in a society that prefers to behave as if they do not exist? What can the practice of rationality and autonomy (reason and freedom) mean in the face of irrationality and alienation? How can human persons flourish; that is, live lives of integrity or authenticity? What set of concrete conditions generate a common human good that can support the flourishing of all human persons?

Under the rubric of an *improvisational philosophy of religion*, West's work assures theologians that we are not alone in our work. He stands shoulder-to-shoulder with us in our rethinking Christian theological and religious praxis from the side of the victims of history. Theology has the responsibility "to influence the cultural context, to translate the word of God and . . . project it into new mentalities and new situations."[11] But it can have no influence if theologians are biased, if they cultivate a studied and arrogant ignorance of their histories and social and cultural contexts.[12]

With his sensitivity to the impact of logical positivism on the very possibility of truth-claims, to the relativizing of moral vocabularies, and to the "near collapse" of philosophy of religion, West makes a crucial intervention in our mediation of religion in America.[13] This intervention calls for a "rapprochement" between philosophical historicism and "the moral vision, social analysis and political engagement" represented by liberation perspectives.[14] Such a rapprochement would not only reclaim the intellectual and moral integrity of philosophy in America, but also provide deeper and more substantive ground for the social and cultural analyses offered by liberation thinkers and theologians. As a philosopher of religion, West enacts this rapprochement through a prophetic criticism that is anti-imperialist, democratic, humane, and compassionate; that contests all "illegitimate authority and arbitrary uses of power"; that takes African-American experience seriously;[15] that holds the ordinary lives of everyday women and men in esteem; and that advocates a style of living which cherishes "curiosity, wonder, contingency, adventure, danger, and improvisation."[16]

West's project, then, is large, urgent, and modern. He puts forward a radical critique of the meanings, values, and institutions of the social order; an interrogation and affirmation of the adventure, the wonder, the sheer joy of human living that opens up to the moans of "despair, dread, disappointment, and death"; and a demand for a religiously inspired political prescription for praxis.[17] Standing with us before the cross of Christ, West plays out this philosophy in dialectical engagement with pragmatism, an analysis of society and culture by means of a Gramscian appropriation of socialist insights, a broad critical reading of theology and the existential condition of Black humanity under the hegemony of white racist supremacy. West stands with us as a philosopher who understands himself as "first and foremost a blues man in the world of ideas – a jazz man in the life of the mind."[18] To read West is not only a pleasure, but a demanding and disturbing pleasure. To read West is to encounter the work of a "most inventive, most innovative jazz musician of the mind." His improvisations fire off solos, riffs, and breaks which seek out ways ("the way") to "cope with disjuncture and change but also [provide] a basic survival technique that is commensurate with and suitable to the rootlessness and the discontinuity so characteristic of human existence in the contemporary world."[19] Here is an improvisational philosophy of religion – blues transcendent.

III

There is a jazz cadence in American culture. That rhythm rises from massive Black human suffering, from the splintering of Black flesh and bone, from the spilling of Black blood. Theologians who would be wise in their mediation of the Christian soteriological message within the dialectic of meanings and values that constitute American culture will need to grasp the complexity of the emergence and unfolding of those meanings and values. In this endeavor, *Prophesy Deliverance! An Afro-American Revolutionary Christianity*[20] sets a benchmark in grappling with the American experiment. Even as *Prophesy Deliverance!* dialectically engages the conflicting meanings and values of European America and African America, it recontextualizes familiar tropes of immigration and exile, wilderness and progress, and uncovers their convergence and obstinacy in a master narrative of dispossession, rupture, violent erotics, and exploitation.

   Prophesy Deliverance! is West's first sustained attempt to give an account of the American experiment and its relation to the Enlightenment, to the emergence and decline of modernity. Like historian of religions Charles Long, whose judgment stands as the first epigraph to this chapter, West reads the relation of the Enlightenment to the Black experience in such a way as to anticipate some postmodern and postcolonial concerns. Long uncovered not only the Enlightenment's other and enervating side, but its paradoxical and absolutizing character as well. Long writes:

In some sense all modern colonized peoples are products of this period, for within the heteronomous context of the Enlightenment the basis for modern racist theory, capitalism, humanitarianism and Christianity may be located. The Enlightenment, true to its name and symbolic reference, attempted to overcome the opaqueness of the concrete forms of human life and nature. Its analytical methods dissected reality for the sake of knowledge and relegated the sheer depths of the real to the arena of unknowability. It is this seeing through rather than "standing before" and "coming to terms with," which is the hallmark of this cultural orientation.[21]

In *Prophesy Deliverance!*, West unpacks that cultural orientation, unmasks the collusion of Enlightenment philosophers – Hume and Jefferson, Montesquieu and Voltaire, and Immanuel Kant – in this endeavor, thus laying bare the failure of criticality in the age of criticality, and delineates a genealogy of modern racism. In short, to borrow a phrase from Enrique Dussel, West provides an account of the "invention of America."[22]

The first chapter of *Prophesy Deliverance!* distinguishes four stages in the invention of America. In a first stage, Europeans in America show themselves, at once, as children of the Enlightenment and colonial desire, but stereotyped as provincial and local. From their energy and will-to-power, they derive identity. Africans, involuntarily situated in America, were denuded of their religiocultural heritages and accorded a kind of "talking animal" status. In the face of effective and intentional exclusion and enslavement, Africans dared the value of human life and the meaningfulness of human existence.[23]

The poignant search for an American culture, the rise of industrialized capitalism, and the brashness of the bourgeoisie activated a second stage. Romance, novelty, innovation, and freedom serve as agents of cultural and social transformation. On the underside of this stage, Africans wrestled with the power of religious experience: they found themselves again and the divine in the hidden God of slave Christianity, created culture through religious self-mediation, and retrieved and purified Jefferson's notion of democratized and equalized status of all persons before God.[24]

The moral consequences of the previous two stages coalesce in a third stage "either–or dilemma [for] industrial provincial American culture."[25] White literary artists, critics, and philosophers confronted the choice either to create an indigenous idiom in literature, music, and art or to become European. But the test of that indigenization was acknowledging the unheard, unseen, *invisible* Black presence in America. Perhaps, only Mark Twain came close. Black petit bourgeois artists and intellectuals continued to pursue access to the legal, political, and economic institutions of American life through nonviolent reform. W. E. B. Du Bois and Booker T. Washington clashed over a choice of means, but the end was Black inclusion in America life: either through economic self-help or through activist engagement in the social and political spheres. But, on both sides of the color line, redistribution of wealth, exploitative capitalist practices, inhumane modes of production, and American imperialism in Puerto Rico and the Philippines went unquestioned.[26]

In the stirrings of postmodernism, this dilemma evaporated and gave rise to a fourth stage. But, rather than resolve the predicament, postmodernism extended the crises: philosophy relinquished its regulative control over science and permitted attacks against the subject, while the spiritual state of Europe evoked the notion of "*Die Langeweile der Welt*, the boredom of the world, Hegel's symbol for the spiritual state of a society to whom its gods have died."[27] For the Black working poor and the underclass, the stakes under postmodernity were and remain high: the heavy and dirty work of the nation completed at their expense, these men and women now find their labor and their bodies disposable. They are powerless politically, crippled economically, and stalled socially. With their families and personal relationships devastated by abuse, brutality, violence, and drugs, these women and men face the Absurd; that is, a form of nihilism – loss of hope and absence of meaning.

Still, the invention of America, an age of boredom, and a people's descent into hell do not simply happen. By taking a genealogical approach, West locates, excavates, and examines fields of discourse as well as discursive institutions, formations, and practices; proposes new and critical narratives of emergence, of breakdown or collapse, of transformation. With regard to the idea of white supremacy, this approach does not so much intend *to explain* the rise of modern racism as it offers "a theoretical inquiry into a particular neglected variable, i.e., the discursive factor, within a larger explanatory model."[28] This approach obviates those reductionist arguments that attempt to account for the emergence of white racist supremacy "in terms of the psychological needs of white individuals and groups or the political and economic interests of a ruling class."[29] Rather, West exposes those powers within modern discourse that gave rise to racism: "powers to produce and prohibit, develop and delimit, forms of rationality, scientificity, and objectivity which set perimeters and draw boundaries for the intelligibility, availability, and legitimacy of certain ideas."[30] These powers are located within those controlling metaphors, notions, categories, and norms that have shaped the predominant conceptions of truth and knowledge in modern Western civilization – that is, within the structure of modern discourse. This structure is further proscribed by Cartesian subjective idealism, the scientific revolution, and the classical revival.

The classical revival achieves what West terms a "normative gaze," namely an ideal aesthetic standard by which to categorize and compare observations.[31] The arrogation of the classificatory procedures of natural history to the "normative gaze" stands as a first stage in the emergence of the idea of white supremacy as an object of discourse. A second stage is located in the rise of phrenology and physiognomy. The criteria for these disciplines were classical aesthetic and cultural ideals: the "normative gaze" was derived from a distortion of Greek ideals of beauty. The consequence: the delimitation of the "structure of modern discourse" and the restriction of Black equality are given intellectual legitimacy and moral support. In this way, the very idea of white supremacy becomes intelligible.

But if white supremacy is intelligible, is it necessary or inevitable? On the one hand, "there is no iron necessity at work in the complex configuration of metaphors, notions, categories, and norms that produce and promote this idea." On the other hand, adverting to that complex configuration accents the cultural and aesthetic impact, the consequent evil impact of white supremacy on the everyday life of Black people.[32] White racist supremacy is neither necessary nor inevitable, but the result of human agency, of deliberation, of biased choice, of biased action. West concludes with a shocking, even insulting and infuriating, image:

> The idea of white supremacy is a major bowel unleashed by the structure of modern discourse, a significant secretion generated from the creative fusion of scientific investigation, Cartesian philosophy, and classical aesthetic and cultural norms. Needless to say, the odor of this bowel and the fumes of this secretion continue to pollute the air of our postmodern times.[33]

Aesthetic sensibilities may shudder, minds may reel, but the point is made: the stench of white racist supremacy and its practice attaches to us all. But we need not live in moral refuse. With this genealogical examination, West has paved the way for theology's most serious consideration of race, culture, and cultural formation.

IV

What is it that a *Black theologian* finds of interest in the work of Cornel West? Even as *Prophesy Deliverance!* disclosed a pattern in which the genealogy of white racist supremacy became evident, it also continued a second dialectical engagement by bringing together the insights of Black theologians and Black Marxist thinkers.[34] Rephrasing Marx's eleventh thesis on Feuerbach, West wrote, "the primary aim of this encounter is to change the world, not each other's faith; to put both groups on the offensive for structural social change."[35] So, rather than linger over the sharp and the subtle polarities of Christian and Marxist positions, West concentrated on a fundamental commonality of prophetic Christianity and progressive Marxism: "commitment to the negation of what is and the transformation of prevailing realities in light of the norms of individuality and democracy."[36]

From this trajectory, West undertook an inquiry into Black theology from the perspective of Marxist social analysis. From this standpoint, Black theology is read as critique. West's inquiry aimed to provide a new conception of Black theology of liberation in which the positive content of the earlier stages – critique of slavery, of institutional racism, of white North American theology, of capitalism – would be sublated into a fifth critique of capitalist civilization.

The earliest conceptions of Black theology had thematized three basic claims: that God sides with and acts on behalf of the poor and oppressed; that religion possesses subversive as well as opiative potential in the struggle for liberation; and that white racism is at the core of an exploitative capitalist society.[37] But there were shortcomings. Despite concern for the concrete social situation of Black people, early formulations of Black theology lacked a systematic analysis of that situation and so failed to delineate the relations between racism, sexism, class exploitation, and imperialism. A second shortcoming was the absence of a comprehensive social vision or program to bring about political and economic liberation. Finally, West stated, Black theology tended "to downplay existential issues such as death, disease, dread, despair, and disappointment" which are related to, yet not identical with, suffering caused by oppressive structures.[38] However, these limitations, West argued, could be overcome in a critique of capitalist civilization.

This fifth critique would examine those meanings, values, structures, foundations, and roles that have been shaped and formed by imperialist domination, class exploitation, racial oppression, and gender suppression. To undertake this analysis means that Black theology deliberately hands over its praxis to the service of the poor and the marginalized in American society; interrogates civil or political religions in remembrance of the crucified Christ; scrutinizes religious, cultural, social, and moral values in American society; resists confinement to any restricted theoretical or praxial domain; unmasks all theories and theologies that either covertly or pseudo-innocently support anti-Semitism, sexism, racism, homophobia, imperialism, or colonialism; and contests any reduction of knowledge, of objectivity, of reality, of truth, of meaning.

V

In *Prophesy Deliverance!*, West reconstructs and interprets traditions of Black activism and counter discourse to white racist supremacy. Asserting that "culture is more fundamental than politics in regard to Afro-American self-understanding,"[39] West poses four ideal types of African-American reactions and responses to white supremacy in modern and postmodern America. These types are: the exceptionalist, assimilationist, marginalist, and humanist; they can be read as traditions of discourse and activism. Each aims to develop an internally rational and intelligible account of the African experience of America; each aims to meet the two basic challenges which continually confront African-Americans – self-image and self-determination. The humanist tradition, in West's judgment, is most attuned to

African-American critical thought, to African-American philosophical, cultural and political praxis, and, we might add, theology.

The humanist tradition of reaction and response "provides a springboard" in facing the issue of self-identity and connects the political struggle of African-Americans to progressive elements in American society.[40] Moreover, the humanist tradition welcomes the "*organic* intellectual traditions [of African-American life]: *the black Christian tradition of preaching and the black musical tradition of performance.*"[41] Both of these traditions, West continues:

> though undoubtedly linked to the life of the mind, are oral, improvisational, and histrionic. Both traditions are rooted in black life and possess precisely what the literate forms of black intellectual activity lack: institutional matrices over time and space within which there are accepted rules of procedure, criteria for judgment, canons for assessing performance, models of past achievement and present emulation and an acknowledged succession and accumulation of superb accomplishments.[42]

These organic intellectual traditions are compatible with the humanist tradition and promote individuality.

This individuality is not to be confused with the acquisitive, alienated anomie of modernity. Rather, this individuality embraces *existenz* – that is, being oneself – but that self is formed in recognition of the significance of the social dimensions of life, including the authority of the group and tradition. This notion of individuality is empowered by an authentic (that is, neither romanticizing nor rejecting) appropriation of the African-American past and by democratic control (that is, egalitarian, consensual, and critical) over the everyday institutions that regulate the lives of everyday people. For West, the premier model of the humanist tradition (the model of the organic Black intellectual) is novelist and essayist Ralph Ellison. It is Ellison who has appropriated the African-American aesthetic with the most intellectual seriousness and wrestled most creatively, heroically, with the existential demands of Black life.

From its inception, Black theology has given serious attention to the Black Christian tradition of preaching, but not nearly enough to the Black musical tradition of performance. So it is important to note that the individuality promoted by the humanist tradition is, in fact, the individuality of the blues musician, the jazz musician. The musician is steeped in a discipline, a desire, and an excellence. In the blues or jazz musician, individuality is sensitive to structure, idiom, and rhythm; disciplined, yet transgressing boundaries in creativity; hungry for "dialogue or conversation or even argument . . . with peers, with other[s, with] the world at large, with the form itself."[43]

The blues and jazz are, at once, the simple, yet most profoundly complex, fruit of Black folk's social suffering and spiritual strivings. The blues "did not just happen. . . . There is a history to the birth and form of our music. There is every element of life in it – religion, romance, tragedy, faith, hope and primitive abandon – brought together and paid for at a tremendous price."[44] The blues are also that precious gift given by Black folk to any man or woman who finds himself or herself "utterly miserable, physically exhausted, totally humiliated . . . overwhelmed by feelings of helplessness, [and] dare [not] complain or talk back, because [his or her] fate" rests in the hands of implacable power.[45]

> My burden's so heavy, I can't hardly see,
> Seems like everybody is down on me,
> An' that's all right, I don't worry, oh, there will be a better day.

But to be compelled to sing the blues is to transcend the blues:

> I'm goin' down to the river, sit down and begin to cry,
> If the blues overtake me, I'll drink that old river dry.[46]

To transcend the blues is to experience, to endure, to candidly acknowledge, to soberly accept adversity as an inescapable condition of human existence.[47] "The blues," Ellison wrote, "is an impulse to keep the painful details and episodes of a brutal experience alive in one's aching consciousness, to finger its jagged grain, and to transcend it, not by the consolation of philosophy but by squeezing from it a near-tragic, near-comic lyricism."[48] Thus, the blues are neither a set of abstract ideas nor propositional truths; "they are the essential ingredients that define the *essence* of the black experience. . . . [T]he blues [are] a *state of mind in relation to the Truth of the black experience.*"[49]

In a trenchant essay, "Christian theological mediocrity," West charged that American theologians and religious scholars have tended to rely on European sources, but these have proved insufficient in dealing with problems of race, gender, and war in the postmodern situation.[50] The discovery of sources to meet the crises of our time is a problem for all American theologians. But, in reminding African-American theologians of those organic intellectual traditions, West points us toward the rich deep well of Black life, culture, history, and struggle. Here are resources for critical reflection, moral and ethical analysis, metaphysical and ontological judgments. Here the theological vocation invites us to a discipline, a desire, an independence, a virtuosity, an excellence. Theology like the blues, like jazz, will flow from our attention, reverence, and devotion to the Black life-world.

Notes

1   Alexandre Koyré, *Discovering Plato*, trans. Leonora Cohen Rosenfield (New York: Columbia University Press, 1968), p. 69; see Cornel West, *The Cornel West Reader* (New York: Basic *Civitas* Books, 1999), pp. 5–6; West, "Identity: a matter of life and death." In *Beyond Eurocentrism and Multiculturalism. Volume 2, Prophetic Reflections: Notes on Race and Power in America* (Monroe, ME: Common Courage Press, 1993), pp. 163–8; West, *Race Matters* (Boston: Beacon Press, 1993).

2   John Patrick Diggins, *The Promise of Pragmatism: Modernism and the Crisis of Knowledge and Authority* (Chicago: University of Chicago Press, 1994), pp. 382–3.

3   Richard Rorty, "Pragmatism and philosophy." In Kenneth Baynes, James Bohman, and Thomas McCarthy (eds), *After Philosophy: End or Transformation?* (Cambridge, MA: MIT Press, 1987), p. 31.

4   Sanford Pinkser, "What's love, and candor, got to do with it? A review of *Race Matters*, by Cornel West." *Virginia Quarterly Review*, 70 (Winter), 1994, p. 175.

5   West, *Race Matters*, pp. 11–20.

6   Delores S. Williams, "A review of *Race Matters*, by Cornel West." *Theology Today*, 51 (April), 1994, p. 160.

7   Mark A. Sanders, "Responding to contemporary crisis. Review of *Race Matters*, by Cornel West." *Callaloo*, 17 (Spring), 1994, p. 645; see also Russell Jacoby, "Pragmatists and politics. Review of *The American Evasion of Philosophy: A Genealogy of Pragmatism*, by Cornel West." *Dissent*, 37 (Summer), 1990, pp. 403–5; Nancy Bancroft, "Review of *The Ethical Dimensions of Marxist Thought*, by Cornel West." *Journal of Religion*, 72 (October), 1992, pp. 618–19; Glenn Lourry, "Preaching to the converted. Review of *Race Matters*, by Cornel West." *The Wilson Quarterly*, 17 (Summer), 1993, pp. 80–3.

8   West, *Race Matters*, p. xi; see Madison, *Federalist Papers*, pp. 51, 54; Jefferson, *Notes on the State of Virginia*, Query 14.

9   Gustavo Gutierrez, "Response." In Gustavo Gutierrez and Richard Shaull, *Liberation and Change* (Atlanta: John Knox Press, 1977), p. 181.

10 Richard Shaull, "The death and resurrection of the American dream." In Gustavo Gutierrez and Richard Shaull, *Liberation and Change* (Atlanta: John Knox Press, 1977), pp. 97–119, especially p. 105.

11 Bernard Lonergan, "Theology in its new context." In William F. J. Ryan and Bernard J. Tyrrell (eds), *A Second Collection by Bernard J. F. Lonergan, SJ* (Philadelphia: Westminster Press, 1974), p. 62.

12 Here, I use the term "bias" in a technical way that corresponds to Lonergan's usage, see his *Insight: A Study of Human Understanding* (London: Longmans, Green and Company, 1957), pp. 218–42. Bias is to be distinguished from conventional or common-sense reference to particular or inordinate preference or tendency and from psychological connotations such as inclination or temperament. Bias denotes a more or less conscious refusal or exclusion of insight (false consciousness and intentionality). Bias is ideology: it distorts and inhibits conscious performance in everyday living by blinding our understanding.

13   Cornel West, *Keeping Faith: Philosophy and Race in America* (New York: Routledge, 1993), p. 128.
14   Ibid., p. 129.
15   Cornel West, *Prophesy Deliverance! An Afro-American Revolutionary Christianity* (Philadelphia: Westminster Press, 1982), p. 9.
16   West, *Keeping Faith: Philosophy and Race in America*, p. xi.
17   West, "The making of an American radical democrat of African descent." In *The Cornel West Reader*, p. 14.
18   Ibid., p. xv.
19   Albert Murray, "Improvisation and the creative process." In Robert G. O'Meally (ed.), *The Jazz Cadence of American Culture* (New York: Columbia University Press, 1998), p. 113.
20   See West, *Prophesy Deliverance!*
21   Charles H. Long, "Structural similarities and dissimilarities in black and African theologies." *Journal of Religious Thought*, 33 (Fall/Winter), 1975, p. 19.
22   See also, Enrique Dussel, *The Invention of the Americas, Eclipse of "the Other" and the Myth of Modernity* (New York: Continuum, 1995).
23   West, *Prophesy Deliverance!*, p. 31.
24   Ibid., p. 35.
25   Ibid., p. 39.
26   Ibid., pp. 38–9.
27   Eric Voegelin, "On Hegel – a study in sorcery." *Studium Generale*, 24 (1971), p. 335.
28   West, *Prophesy Deliverance!*, p. 65.
29   Ibid., p. 49.
30   Ibid.
31   Ibid., p. 54.
32   Ibid., pp. 64–5.
33   Ibid., p. 65.
34   West, "Black theology and Marxist thought." In Gayraud S. Wilmore and James H. Cone (eds), *Black Theology: A Documentary History, 1966–1977* (Maryknoll, NY: Orbis Books, 1979), pp. 552–67; and West, "Black theology in socialist thought." *The Witness*, 63(4), 1980, pp. 16–19.
35   West, *Prophesy Deliverance!*, p. 107; see Karl Marx, "Theses on Feuerbach." In *On Religion* (Moscow: Progress Publishers, 1975), p. 63.
36   Ibid., p. 101.
37   Ibid., p. 106.
38   Ibid.
39   Ibid., p. 71.
40   Ibid., p. 91.
41   West, "The dilemma of the black intellectual." In *The Cornel West Reader* (New York: Basic Civitas Books, 1999), p. 306.
42   Ibid., p. 306.
43   Murray, "Improvisation and the creative process," p. 113.
44   Ollie Stewart, "What price jazz?" *The Chicago Defender*, April 7, 1934, p. 12, cited in Jon Michael Spencer, *Blues and Evil* (Knoxville: University of Tennessee Press, 1993), p. xxvi.

45 Alan Lomax, *The Land Where the Blues Began* (New York: Bantam Doubleday Dell Publishing Group, Inc., 1993), p. 274.
46 Ibid., p. 5.
47 Albert Murray, *The Hero and the Blues* (New York: Random House, 1995, orig. 1973), pp. 106–7.
48 Ralph Ellison, "Richard Wright's blues." In *Shadow and Act* (New York: Random House, 1972), pp. 78–9.
49 James H. Cone, *The Spirituals and the Blues: An Interpretation* (Maryknoll, NY: Orbis Books, 1991, orig. 1972), p. 102.
50 West, "Christian theological mediocrity." In *Prophetic Fragments* (Grand Rapids, MI: William B. Eerdmans Publishing, 1988; Trenton, NJ: Africa World Press, Inc., 1989), p. 195.

9

Existential Aptness and Epistemological Correctness: West and the Identity of the "Lord"

Josiah Ulysses Young III

"Existential aptness and epistemological correctness" refers to a sermon I heard Cornel West deliver in 1979 or 1980 at Union Theological Seminary, where he used to teach and I used to be a student. He preached on the story of Jesus and the rich man (Matthew 19:16–34 or perhaps Mark 10:17–25). The rich man asks, "Good Teacher, what must I do to inherit eternal life?" Jesus responds by reiterating portions of the Law. The rich man assures him that he had long honored his parents, told the truth, etc. "And Jesus looking upon him loved him, and said to him, 'You lack one thing; go sell what you have and give it to the poor... and come, follow me.'" Unable to endure the "non-identity" such a call proffered, the rich man's "countenance fell, and he went away sorrowful; for he had great possessions." Jesus had his disciples take note – "it is easier for a camel to go through the eye of a needle than for a rich man to enter the kingdom of God." West's interpretation of that parabolic line was that the rich man was not only "epistemologically incorrect, but also existentially inept."

His quip brings to mind something James Baldwin penned in his Freudian-like essay, *The Devil Finds Work*. For Baldwin, "the identity of the Lord" is "either a private agony or an abstract question." And Baldwin goes on to assert that "unless one can conceive of (and endure) an abstract life, there can be no abstract questions. A question is a threat, the door which slams shut, or swings open: on another threat."[1] As theologian Jürgen Moltmann puts it, "it is not a matter of indifference whether doors open and opportunities offer themselves, just as it is not a matter of indifference whether [we] go through the door," especially if liberation is on the other side.[2]

West preached that the rich man had slammed the door. In his *Prophesy Deliverance! An Afro-American Revolutionary Christianity*, West is among those who open the door. In that text, West argues that a "revolutionary Christian perspective" complements both the Afro-American humanist tradition, *à la* Ralph Ellison, and progressive Marxist thought. The three values uphold individuals' rights to self-expression (existential aptness), which are inextricable from democratic structures championed by Marxist praxis (epistemological correctness). As envisioned by West's humanistic Black consciousness, personal liberty and justice-for-all define Christian hope, socialist ethics, and the Lord's identity.[3]

A course I took from West broadened for me his homily's implications and showcased the thinker behind *Prophesy Deliverance!* The name of that course escapes me, but Ludwig Feuerbach and to a lesser extent Sigmund Freud, two of the philosophers I encountered there, help one ponder the identity of the Lord. Emmanuel Levinas, upon whom I have stumbled only recently, is also helpful. I would thus like to do two things for the remainder of this chapter: (a) employ those philosophers and insights from West's *Prophesy Deliverance!* and *Race Matters* in light of the question, what is "the identity of the Lord?"; and (b) apply my discussion to Rwanda's *l'agonie* because of my passion for Africa.

I

Ludwig Feuerbach, who rejected theism and embraced a humane atheism, observed that "Faith has within it a malignant principle."[4] To quote Feuerbach further, "faith necessarily passes into hatred, hatred into persecution, where the power of faith meets with no contradiction, where it does not find itself in collusion with a power foreign to faith, the power of love, of humanity, of the sense of justice."[5] Faith abusively denies humanity (the Thou). Heaven undermines earthly life. For Feuerbach, then, the "hope" for a life after death is a regression – is born from a denial of the body and its organic ties to other bodies, the earth, water, and other cosmic relations. Abstracted from the earth, "heaven" undermines nature and hastens the demise of its pinnacle through a basic disregard of the *common good*. In sum, theistic alienation results in dehumanization.

There is an affinity between Feuerbach and West, for West would hold that a certain theism accounts for the "countless calamities perpetrated by Christian churches."[6] In such churches, the identity of the Lord *is an abstract question* – an apotheosis of values alienated from the neighbor and the earth. West's revolutionary Christianity, however, ponders the Lord's identity as a *private agony* born from suffering "the realm of history [as] the realm of the pitiful and the tragic." Here, one *decides* to embrace an a-theistic hope "that every individual regardless of class, country, caste, race, or sex should have the opportunity to fulfill his or her potentialities."[7] For West, therefore, the Lord signifies a "transcendent God before whom all persons are equal." This God "endows the well-being and ultimate salvation of each with equal value and significance." According to West, who hardly embraces Feuerbach's "anthropotheism," this negation of the malignancy of faith is "the Christian principle of the self-realization of individuality within community." Christians often caricature this principle as:

> simply the salvation of *individual* souls in heaven, an otherworldly community. But such a truncated understanding of the core of the Christian gospel accents its otherworldly dimension at the expense of its this-worldly possibilities. The fuller prophetic Christian tradition must insist upon both this-worldly and otherworldly salvation as the proper loci of Christianity.[8]

Although some may argue that the resurrection *from* the dead means that salvation is *never other* worldly but the hope for *this* world as the unity of heaven and earth, West's observation about "this-worldly and otherworldly salvation" must not be taken as some use for abstract questions.[9] "A transcendent God before whom all persons are equal" is a human God, a humane Lord – otherwise West would have no basis to claim that "existential freedom is an effect of the divine gift of grace which promises to sustain persons through and finally deliver them from the bondage to death, disease, and despair."[10] Were the Lord an abstract question, were "He" but a theistic deity who personifies what Feuerbach deems as a "malignant principle," "He" would have no concern for extinction, affliction and hopelessness.

For the sake of the "divine *Ego*," however – itself inextricable from what West calls the "'political unconscious' of American society: the sanctity of private property and the virtue of capital accumulation"[11] – such a humane God has been marginalized by "post-industrial cosmopolitan American culture."[12] The role that "post-industrial cosmopolitan American culture" has played in Africa is particularly illustrative.

Adam Hochschild's *King Leopold's Ghost* points out that Joseph Désir Mobutu, Leopold's heir to the Congo, was in large measure funded by the United States: "For its heavy investment, the Unites States and its allies got a regime that was reliably anti-Communist and a secure staging area for CIA and French military operations." In this African context, a humane God is marginalized in that powerful, political, socioeconomic forces have no regard for the African poor. That Reagan welcomed Mobutu, a notorious tyrant and human rights violator, "at the White House several times, praising him as [a] 'voice of good sense and good will'" is shameful.[13] Equally shameful is the fact that conservatives, including the Christian Right and Black conservatives, found that the "policies of the Reagan and Bush administrations" were "morally acceptable and politically advantageous."[14] Moltmann argues that such morality serves a Lord for whom a certain pre-millenarianism is "politicized through 'the moral majority'... who... have linked this apocalyptic fundamentalism with the political right in the USA, and with the preparation for a nuclear Armageddon."[15] If one can say that what West has called America's political unconscious is at work in such "apocalyptic fundamentalism," if the "divine *Ego*" is at work here, then the future is in great jeopardy.

As Freud notes in *Beyond the Pleasure Principle* – and here I take a certain liberty with his text – "the Lord" as the product of "the political unconscious of American society" would thus mean "there is no difference in principle between an instinct turning from an object to the ego and its turning from the ego to the object... the turning round of the instinct upon the subject's own ego" is but "a return to an earlier phase of the instinct's history, a regression."[16] As I see it, "instinct" here signifies Feuerbach's sense that theism, a form of political self-apotheosis, is world-denying sterility, while "regression" signifies West's claim that "the United States has seized Western cultural leadership in a declining and decadent age."[17]

For West, America's regression indicates that humankind hardly arrived at its divinity in the twentieth century, but, rather, entered into its angst-ridden, postmodern epoch. As West put it, "postmodernism is an accentuation and acceleration of the major developments and processes in European modernism. It is a deepening of the decline of modernism, with little sense of what is to follow, if anything at all."[18] A correlation can thus be drawn between "our white Christian civilization" (Freud) and its postmodern crisis, which West thinks "reflects fear of the future." His point is well taken.[19] The genuineness of the threat of a nuclear Armageddon evinces the truth of Sigmund Freud's observation that we act like wolves toward the Other – "*Homo homini lupus.*" The *imago Dei*, then, does not mean "men are... gentle creatures who want to be loved, and who at the most can defend themselves if they are attacked." Rather, "men" are driven by "a powerful share of aggressiveness," which leads to sadistic (and masochistic) behavior – rape, theft, calumny, torture, murder.[20]

Given our postmodern crisis, "the Lord" can be said to mean that "man," who had displaced his cultural ideals in his gods, has today so actualized those ideals that "he has almost become a god himself." As Freud further states, "Man has, as it were, become a kind of prosthetic God." Technological genius may be said to constitute the resplendency of "all his auxiliary organs; but those organs have not grown on to him and they still give him much trouble at times."[21] Gleaming space probes really mean that the "Fathers" "would have no difficulty exterminating one another to the last man."[22] For Freud, the egoism Feuerbach deems as "political vindictiveness" had become all too *aggressive*: The "narcissism of minor differences" gave rise to a malignant principle from which Freud himself had to flee.[23]

This malignant principle has been foundational to the United States. Here, the "narcissism of minor differences" is in fact quite major when the Black body is an issue. The very prospect of Black–white intimacy is deemed as an aberrant venture. West tackles that problem in arguing that white America's fear of the Black body has produced myths of "distorted, dehumanized creatures whose bodies – color of skin, shape of nose and lips, type of hair, size of hips – are already distinguished from the white norm of beauty."[24] According to West, "Two hundred and forty-four years of slavery and nearly a century of institutionalized terrorism in the form of segregation, lynchings, and second-class citizenship were aimed at precisely this devaluation of black people."[25] West dubs the expression of this narcissistic drive as "white supremacist ideology," in which God-ness is the antithesis of Blackness. To fear God is thus to acquiesce in a hegemony in which Blacks are over determined as aberrant beings.

According to West, this fear of the Lord (God) is even a factor in Black churches in which sanctified mores – no blues, no unsaved dancing – are a function of the myth that the Black body is "brazen."[26] If such a myth is latent in Black churches where the icon of choice is the Aryan Jesus, and if that Lord is a ramification of "white supremacist ideology," a species of theism, then West calls us to an a-theistic praxis in which the identity of the Lord is a "private agony": "Only by living against the grain can we keep alive the possibility that the visceral feelings about black bodies fed by racist myths and promoted by market-driven quests for stimulation do not forever render us... fearful of each other's humanity."[27]

II

Rwanda, the context of what is perhaps the most horrific holocaust of recent times, exemplifies both the export of "the narcissism of minor differences" and the aversion to the Black body. The journalist Fergal Keane makes the point that up to one million people were murdered. Apparently, the Western world forgot its post-Second World War cry – never again! – because:

> it is easy to see a black body in almost abstract terms, as part of the huge smudge of eternally miserable blackness that has loomed in and out of the public mind through the decades: Biafra in the sixties; Uganda in the seventies; Ethiopia in the eighties; and now Rwanda in the nineties. We are fed a diet of starving children, of stacked corpses and battalions of refugees, and in the end we find ourselves despising the continent of Africa because it haunts and shames us.[28]

The conflict between the two ethnic groups, the Tutsi and the Hutu, who are no longer as different from one another as they, perhaps, once were, is at the heart of the Rwandan crisis. The Tutsi, who reportedly migrated to Rwanda from East Africa, were, it is held, tall, so-called fine-featured "Hamitic" people, while the

Hutu were so-called "Negroid" in appearance. At one time, the Germans and Belgians propped up the Tutsi, calling them "Europeans under a black skin," and so confirmed "everything the turn of the century liked to believe: the inequality of 'races' . . . cultural diffusion and the biological basis of social phenomena."[29] While ethnic tension antedated colonial rule, the Europeans invented the "forms under which" the Blacks "were supposed to relate to each other in order to fit in with the ideological fantasies and practical needs of the European"[30] (*Homo homini lupus*).

Here we have a disturbing take on the ramifications of West's sense of "capitalist civilization," Feuerbach's God of the patriarchs, and Freud's pessimistic view that "Fate is looked upon in the strictly religious sense of being nothing else than an expression of the Divine Will."[31] Rwanda's dysfunction is attributed to cultural underdevelopment, a view that "nosily" denies the fact that Rwanda is a European (*qua* "patriarchal") invention. As V. Y. Mudimbe put it, "The father's auto-biography" is "a kind of history. His word is accorded a permanence that follows us from place and across the years. It becomes the memory of the world. . . . [But] 'what if my father was wrong?' "[32] The insight Mudimbe affords is precisely this: Africa's skyscrapers, results of the "professionalization of science" (and slave-like labor), reflect Europe's image, but so do famine and corruption and holocausts.[33] I do not shift the blame for the holocaust from Hutu shoulders to the Western world. Still, the West has a terrible complicity in the matter, which is repressed through the tacit and not so tacit appeal to providence – "a normative gaze" that is no more than an apologetic for Africa's misery.

West's sermon and *remarkable* teaching at Union, both of which concern the identity of the Lord, are unforgettable. His witness was a highlight of my seminary experience. I am *still* learning from some of the philosophers he introduced me to so many years ago. Figures such as Feuerbach (and Freud) are compelling for me precisely because the connection between anthropology – in its conscious (and unconscious) modes – and the identity of the Lord is *perilously* close. A Lord with murder in his eyes springs from this closeness, this malignancy of faith.

I think West's sermon on the rich man was inspired by the healthiness of faith – faith in a poor man who may redeem the rich man. West suggests – and the scripture (Mark 10:27) says as much – that we not condemn the rich man, for most of us resemble him. Rather, in recognizing ourselves in him, humane Christians realize with West that:

> contradiction and transformation are at the heart of the Christian gospel. The former always presupposes what presently is; the latter, the prevailing realities. For Christians, this "what is" and these "prevailing realities" are products of fallen, finite creatures, products that bear the stamp of imperfection. *This dialectic of imperfect products and transformative practice, of prevailing realities and negation, of human depravity and human dignity, of what is and the not-yet constitutes the Christian dialectic of human nature and human history.*[34]

So how do we (imperfectly) constitute the not-yet?

We see the Lord and "eternal life" in the nakedness of the Other's face.[35] That indeed, it seems to me, complements the point of *Prophesy Deliverance!*: existential aptness concerns the interiority, the intentions, that animate the question, "Good Teacher, what must I do to inherit eternal life?" Eternal life is solipsistic (and no *life* at all) if wrenched from the Other's naked face: "the face of the poor, the stranger, the widow, and the orphan, and, at the same time, of the master called to invest and justify my freedom."[36] In short, the indigent master is the Lord, in the face of whom *we* live or die – eternity (infinity) is won or lost depending on whether we see with Levinas that:

> [an] idea of the Infinite would be a thought disengaged from consciousness, not according to the negative concept of the unconscious, but according to the thought that is perhaps most profoundly thought; that of dis-inter-estedness which is a relationship without hold on a being, which is not an anticipation of being – rather, a pure patience. As de-ference in passivity, it would be beyond all that which is assumed; it would be a de-ference that is irreversible like time. That is, it is patience or length of time in its dia-chrony, where tomorrow is never reached today. Prior to every activity of consciousness, more ancient than consciousness, would this not be the deepest thinking of the new?[37]

"Good Teacher, what must I do to inherit eternal life?": "dis-inter-estedness which is a relationship without hold on a being" is surely apt. West put it this way in his humane take on the identity of the Lord:

> [He] is the Truth, a reality which can only be existentially appropriated (not intellectually grasped) by fallen human beings caught in ever-changing finite descriptions. . . . This means that any "true" Christian description makes the reality of Jesus Christ available, that it encourages the putting of oneself on the line in the negation of what is and the transformation of prevailing realities, of going to the edge of life's abyss and finding out whether the reality of Jesus Christ – though understood through one's finite Christian description – yields life sustenance, self-formation, self-maturation, and social amelioration.[38]

While a seminary professor, West noted the patience involved in such spirituality as follows: "only the praxis of imperfect human beings renders it [life with the Other] desirable and realizable."[39] Epistemological correctness, then, is surely born from great humility – the profoundest, future-bound respect for the lives of Others one can muster. Get that wrong and we – especially the wretched of the earth – will all suffer the consequences of existential (wolfish) ineptness. Any *imago Dei* who desires eternal life but is afraid of the future – itself dependent on radical sharing – is likely mystified by "thematization, and the impatience of grasping."[40] For West (and me too) this *impatience* "is an urgent question of power and morality; for others, it is an everyday matter of life and death" – a private agony.[41]

Notes

1   James Baldwin, *The Devil Finds Work* (New York: Laurel/Doubleday Dell, 1976), p. 18.
2   Jürgen Moltmann, *The Church in the Power of the Spirit* (Minneapolis: Fortress Press, 1993), pp. 190–1.
3   Cornel West, *Prophesy Deliverance! An Afro-American Revolutionary Christianity* (Philadelphia: The Westminster Press, 1982), p. 146.
4   Ludwig Feuerbach, *The Essence of Christianity* (New York: Prometheus Books, 1989), p. 321.
5   Ibid., p. 260.
6   Ibid., p. 16.
7   Ibid.
8   West, *Prophesy Deliverance!*, p. 16.
9   I am indebted to Jürgen Moltmann for this view that salvation is always this-worldly and that the resurrection from – and *of* – the dead is inextricable from the renewal of *this* world. See Moltmann's *God in Creation* (Minneapolis: Fortress Press, 1993); and his *The Coming of God: Christian Eschatology* (Minneapolis: Fortress Press, 1996).
10   West, *Prophesy Deliverance!*, p. 18.
11   Ibid., p. 132.
12   Ibid., pp. 43–4.
13   Adam Hochschild, *King Leopold's Ghost: A Story of Greed, Terror, and Heroism in Colonial Africa* (New York: Houghton Mifflin, 1999), p. 303.
14   West, *Race Matters* (Boston: Beacon Press, 1993), p. 55.
15   Moltmann, *The Coming of God*, p. 159.
16   Sigmund Freud, *Beyond the Pleasure Principle* (New York: W. W. Norton, 1989), p. 66.
17   West, *Prophesy Deliverance!*, p. 43.
18   Ibid., p. 42.
19   Ibid., p. 41.
20   Freud, *Civilization and Its Discontents* (New York: W. W. Norton, 1989), pp. 68–9.
21   Ibid., p. 44.
22   Ibid., p. 112.
23   Ibid., pp. 72–3. According to Freud the "narcissism of minor differences" means that the enmity that gives rise to racial cleansing is emergent from distinctions that are so blown out of proportion as to become a religious principle.
24   West, *Race Matters*, p. 83.
25   Ibid., p. 85.
26   Ibid., pp. 87–8.
27   Ibid., p. 91.
28   Fergal Keane, *Season of Blood* (New York: Penguin, 1996), pp. 29–30. See as well Philip Gourivitch, *We Wish to Inform You that Tomorrow We Will Be Killed with Our*

Families: Stories from Rwanda (New York: Farrar Straus and Giroux, 1998). Gourivitch writes that the "low-tech," murder-by-machete holocaust was swift: "of an original population of about seven and a half million, at least eight hundred thousand were killed in just a hundred days. Rwandans often speak of a million deaths, and they may be right. The dead of Rwanda accumulated at nearly three times the rate of Jewish dead during the Holocaust. It was the most efficient mass killing since the atomic bombings of Hiroshima and Nagasaki" (p. 3).

29   Gérard Prunier, *The Rwanda Crisis: History of a Genocide* (New York: Columbia University Press, 1997), p. 347.

30   Ibid., p. 348.

31   Freud, *Civilizations and Its Discontents*, p. 88.

32   V. Y. Mudimbe, *The Idea of Africa* (Bloomington: Indiana University Press, 1994), p. 192.

33   To quote Crawford Young, "The silent revenge of the colonial state was surreptitiously to embed in its post-independence successor the corrosive personality of Bula Matari." *Bula Matari* means "Breaks Stones" ("he who crushes rocks") and signifies the intimidation – the high-tech gun and dynamite – Africans faced on account of capitalists such as Henry Morton Stanley, "an American [*sic*] in Leopoldian livery." See Crawford Young, *The African Colonial State in Comparative Perspective* (New Haven, CT: Yale University Press, 1994), pp. 1–2 and 242.

34   West, *Prophesy Deliverance!*, p. 17.

35   As Levinas put it – for he calls to mind West's sermon and the philosophy of religion he taught me – "atheism . . . means positively, that our relation with the Metaphysical is an ethical behavior and not theology, not a thematization, be it a knowledge by analogy, of the attributes of God. God rises to . . . supreme and ultimate presence as correlative to the justice rendered to men" and women. See Emmanuel Levinas, *Totality and Infinity* (Pittsburgh: Duquesne University Press, 1998), p. 78.

36   Ibid., p. 251.

37   Levinas, *Of God Who Comes to Mind* (Stanford, CA: Stanford University Press), p. xiii.

38   West, *Prophesy Deliverance!*, p. 98.

39   Ibid., p. 19.

40   Levinas, p. xiii.

41   West, *Race Matters*, p. xi.

Part III
Political Philosophy

10

Cornel West on Gender and Family: Some Admiring and Critical Comments

Iris M. Young

Cornel West has always been an engaged intellectual. He believes that intellectual work should be pragmatic in a broad and partisan sense, which is to say, guided by problems that masses of people face who are on the disadvantaged side of relations of domination and oppression. Not only should the work be engaged in the struggles for greater justice, but in order to do that work well the intellectual himself or herself has to be involved in civic and political organizations where people with different occupations and ways of life make the institutional base for these struggles. West has contributed to organizations in this way more than most intellectuals.

West's many writings range from very theoretical to politically programmatic, with a significant amount of cultural analysis in between. Most of these writings are politically engaged, and often make strong judgments about American politics which invite dispute. In this chapter I want first to review the general social-theoretical framework that West has developed, *genealogical materialist prophetic pragmatism*. Then I will discuss some of West's more popular and political writing, particularly as it concerns men, women, and feminism. I will take a look at the hard hitting feminism that West expresses in his book, *Race Matters*, and argue that his more recent book, *The War Against Parents*, is seriously in tension with these earlier analyses. I suggest that in his eagerness to offer solutions to America's persisting sources of suffering and cynicism, West has wrongly distanced himself from the subtlety of genealogical materialist prophetic pragmatism.

Western Theory

Several of the essays in *Keeping Faith* articulate theoretical frameworks and politically engaged orientations West recommends for progressive intellectuals. This
framework has evolved as "genealogical materialist prophetic pragmatism." A
genealogical materialist analysis applies some of the methods of Foucault to analyze
the emergence, development, and sustenance of discourses that help produce and
legitimate oppressive social structures, particularly racism. Like Foucauldian analysis, this analysis is genealogical in that it explores how these discourses operate in
the everyday lives, self-conceptions, and interactions of people; such microsocial
analysis makes the method materialist in that it seeks to explain inequality and
domination and their reproduction. Unlike Foucauldian analysis, however, this
method retains from traditional Marxism a macro level of analysis; we cannot give
a full account of relations of oppression and domination without conceptualizing
large-scale social *structures* that constrain the lives of some categories of people at
the same time that they privilege others. The method of genealogical materialism,
then, analyzes discourses as having material effects because they play out in people's
actions and interactions, which, together with the effects of market exchanges and
the sedimentation of material social environments, produce and reproduce structures.

West's first major book, *Prophesy Deliverance!*, brilliantly used this genealogical
materialist method. Chapter 2 of that book locates a major source of modern
racism in the collaboration of procedures of scientific investigation, Cartesian ideas
of transparent self-reflection abstracted from the body, and the modern appropriation of classically Greek ideas of beauty and the primacy of vision. The logics of
modern science and aesthetics merge in modern biological and anthropological
discourses which both bring humans under the scientific observational gaze to be
classified hierarchically and assign different aesthetic and moral values to humans
classified into distinct classes in the hierarchy. Such logics of classificatory and
aesthetic hierarchy continue to pervade both academic discourse and popular
culture, still providing fertile soil for racist thinking.

Prophesy Deliverance! also traces the complex genealogy of prophetic African-
American Marxist response to the discourses and structures of racism as entwined
with the operations of capitalism in America. It offers a Marxism that remains
rooted in specific material analysis of relations of ownership and labor, both wage
and non-wage labor, but without a general theory of necessary stages of
history. There and in his later work, moreover, West insists that a materialist social
theory must be tied to an explicitly *moral* philosophy of equality and human
dignity.

To genealogical materialism West adds both a Christian spirit of prophesy, a
form of radical social criticism that invokes transcendent aspirations and values of

redemption, and pragmatism, an anti-metaphysical, anti-epistemological approach to philosophy that uses tools of scientific inquiry, conceptual analysis and moral theory for the sake of proposing ways to improve economy and society.

One of the essays in *Keeping Faith*, "Theory, pragmatism and politics," characterizes prophetic pragmatism as a stance of reflective critique with practical and political intent. The engaged intellectual scrutinizes both academic and popular received wisdom, and subjects them to processes of demythologization and demystification. Demythologization is "a *mapping* activity that reconstructs and redescribes forms of signification for the purposes of situating them in the dynamic flow of social practices."[1] That is, this critical process takes ideas and knowledge claims which appear to have their grounding only in other ideas or constituted evidence, and reconnects them to the social circumstances that motivate their generation and in the context of which they have significance. Demystification, on the other hand, "is a *theoretical* activity that attempts to give explanations that account for the role and function of specific social practices."[2]

The American Evasion of Philosophy most completely articulates this notion of prophetic pragmatism. Pragmatism offers to this theoretical mix, for West, an "unashamedly moral emphasis and...unequivocally ameliorative impulse."[3] West thinks that we live in an era of pessimism and cynicism, and that recent academic trends such as postmodernism, which are important for gaining critical insight, contribute to this pessimism and sense of paralysis about positive change. The spirit of pragmatism offers a more optimistic way of conceiving possibilities for social transformation toward greater social justice.

West admits that *American Evasion* offers a highly selective interpretation of American pragmatism which not only includes figures standardly associated with pragmatism, such as Emerson, Dewey, and Rorty, but also others not so often put in this tradition, such as W. E. B. Du Bois and Roberto Unger. He explains how this tradition of inquiry refuses the classical philosophical questions of epistemology and metaphysics. Classical philosophy from the Greeks through the moderns launches what Dewey called a quest for certainty, a project that seeks the foundations of knowledge in formal science and general laws. That project effectively detaches itself from the context of problematic action from which the desire for knowledge arises. Pragmatism criticizes such detachment and reinterprets logical and epistemological insights in light of historical and social hierarchies and projects. American pragmatism pulls the project of knowledge back down to earth and weds it to ideas of moral value and social improvement.

West gives his own genealogy of this American pragmatist tradition in light of late twentieth-century intellectual concerns with postmodernism, multiculturalism, and the continued imperative to criticize American economic and international power. Thus he constructs an account of certain twentieth-century American intellectuals as in this pragmatic tradition – Sidney Hook, C. Wright Mills, Reinhold Niebuhr, W. E. B. Du Bois, and Lionel Trilling. Each in his own way engages in social criticism concerned with economic structures and at the same time concerned with art and culture.

These, then, are the ingredients of genealogical materialist prophetic pragmatism: an account of social structures which exposes the irrationalities of capitalist economic processes and some insight into possibilities for creating a more just set of economic relations; a method of genealogy, where the supposed expert knowledges of the present can be shown as historically embedded in power relations; a Christian spirit of prophetic social criticism and redemption; and a pragmatic evasion of questions about epistemological or metaphysical foundations. It is a wonderful recipe, from which valuable social criticism can be made.

The Theory Applied to Race Matters

West brings the theoretical insights of this sophisticated academic discourse to bear on understanding and evaluating American society and possibilities for emancipation in his book *Race Matters*. African-Americans in particular ought to follow the example of W. E. B. Du Bois and speak truth to power, in order to strip white supremacy of any discursive authority, yet express an open and reconciliatory spirit with white Americans engaged in the project of historical reinterpretation and forging a collective future. In the course of this project, social critics should avoid certain dichotomies that have come to frame discussion of race matters in American politics, such as liberal–conservative or structure–behavior.

For the most part, contemporary Americans, both those labeled liberals and those labeled conservative, "fail to see that the presence and predicaments of black people are neither additions to nor defections from American life, but rather *constituent elements of that life*."[4] Political and policy polarization on race matters tends to construct relations between white Americans, Black Americans, Latino Americans, and so on as zero sum trade-offs. More government private investment in central cities means less for suburbs, university affirmative action policies targeting people of color means fewer opportunities for whites, and so on. Both so-called liberals and conservatives should better recognize that the fates of white Americans are tightly interwoven with those of African-American and other racialized minorities, in a way that puts such zero sum thinking into question. Racial and class competition ultimately makes us all worse off.

Liberals and conservatives also often tend to polarize around a false dichotomy of social structure versus individual behavior to account for the poverty, crime, family fragility, low skills, and so on, which disproportionately describe the situation of many African-Americans. Conservatives tend to lay responsibility for such lack of well-being in the hands of individual persons and their families. Liberals, on the other hand, tend to argue that such appeals to personal responsibility or culture of poverty blame the victims. The circumstances that keep some people poor, unskilled, antisocial, and lacking in hope must be traced to structures of institutionalized racism and economic structures of competition and profit seeking; for example, capitalist consumer forces that are structural-cultural and have masculinist elements that conservatives will not examine. Major mass media and advertisers use sexual and military imagery in order to titillate consumers. West applies his understanding of cultural materialist politics to an analysis that transcends the dichotomy. In keeping with prophetic pragmatism and left-wing romanticism, in *Race Matters* West reflects on the role of despair in perpetuating oppression, and looks for hope as a means to liberatory social movement.

West is one of the few African-American male political intellectuals to bring analysis of sexism and heterosexism directly into his account of the contemporary African-American condition. Especially in *Race Matters*, he expresses an uncompromising feminism that condemns the judgments and behavior of some African-Americans as well as of white society. Part of the responsibility for the limited hope and material suffering some Blacks in America feel should be laid at the door of Black misogyny and homophobia. These are inevitably structured by the dominance of white society, but their effects cannot be reduced to racism.

West believes that there is not enough discussion among either Blacks or whites of both myths and realities of Black sexuality. (In *Race Matters* West often writes as though in America there are only two racial groups, Black and white. He is not alone in such oversimplification, but it is unfortunate, one might argue, especially when the subject is sexuality.)

Patriarchal racist structures give African-Americans of both sexes and all sexual orientations a very limited set of styles and performances for sexual expression. Social forces tend to propel them toward one or the other pole of a sexual dichotomy structured by racism, where neither pole is acceptable and freeing. On the one hand, they can adopt "cool" styles of sexual assertiveness in dress, speech, manner, and action, which allow a certain playful self-expression and power. Whether adopted in a male or female mode, however, such styles reinforce racist stereotypes of aggressive Black male and female sexuality that position Black sexuality as outlaw and trigger white fears. The best way to avoid such outlaw positioning, on the other hand, is to conform to white bourgeois norms of "respectability" that inhibit sexual expression altogether.

At either pole Black homosexuality is not an option, and Black women's sexuality is dominated and distorted. West is most critical, however, of the structures of "cool" machismo sexuality. Nihilism and cynicism of American society in the 1990s, West believes, are due to a significant extent to the shallow stimulation and promises of gratification offered in popular media and consumer culture. Today that culture magnifies the coolness of Black machismo styles, to the extent that not only Black youth but white, Latino, and Asian youth are influenced by these styles and behaviors, and often imitate them. Such Black machismo styles are "fast," "sharp," and glorify violence in ways that capitalist marketers find effective in selling goods.

Black machismo has complex effects as situated in terms of racist, sexist, and heterosexist structures. Either there is an utter homophobic silence about the existence of homosexual practice among Black men, or homosexuality becomes the butt of male power jokes among Blacks. Black female homosexuality suffers less notice only because it is more invisible and even more taboo a subject of discussion. The stance of Black machismo links images of sexiness for Black men to violence. Such symbolic and practical linkage between sexuality and violence in certain Black masculine styles has material consequences not only for women and men perceived to be gay, but also for straight Black machismo men who challenge one another to be real men.

Black heterosexual women try to express and assert themselves under the cloud of patriarchal power. Efforts by African-American political organizations and ambitious individuals too often rely on these patriarchal meanings and structures to forge Black unity in the confrontation with white supremacy. West strongly argues that what he refers to as "racial reasoning" among African-Americans often has sexist and heterosexist aspects. Racial reasoning tends to consider all Blacks as good and all whites as not to be trusted, and demands loyalty from Blacks to other Blacks simply on grounds of their Blackness. This "closing ranks" mentality fosters a unifying essentialism that allows male heterosexual perspectives of Blackness to dominate. "The idea of black people closing ranks against hostile white Americans reinforces black male power exercised over black women (e.g., to protect, regulate, subordinate, and hence usually, though not always, to use and abuse women), in order to preserve black social order under circumstances of white literal attack and symbolic assault."[5]

West offers two quite disparate examples of such racial reasoning which he claims have these sexist implications. During the time when he was under scrutiny by the US Senate, Clarence Thomas invoked his Blackness both against the white judiciary committee and in order to rally African-American sentiment as support. His speeches during his confirmation hearings denigrated certain women, in the obvious person of Anita Hill, but also in the person of his sister Emma Mae, whom he denounced as a welfare queen in order to prove himself a good Black conservative.

West here recalls the support of Louis Farrakhan's Nation of Islam for Clarence Thomas as another symptom of the racial reasoning with sexist and conservative implications. Despite the Nation of Islam's opposition to Republican Party programs and its own radical economic strategies, their Black nationalist and Black male-centered claims to Black authenticity reinforce Black cultural conservatism.[6]

Political Programs

Recently, West has issued a series of co-authored books on the state of American society and politics, which include specific programs for remedying exclusion and social pathologies. I will discuss two of these, one briefly, the other more extensively. While this recent work is admirable in its commitment to social and economic equality and its radical pragmatics, I will suggest that it has become more economistic in its focus than it would seem that West's earlier theoretical work recommends. Particularly in one of these books, moreover, West expresses positions about gender and family relations that I regard as antifeminist, and which seem to me seriously at odds with his own earlier feminist commitments.

In *The Future of American Progressivism*, West joins pens with one of those who, in *American Evasion*, he characterized as a left romantic – Roberto Unger. This small book analyzes the state of neoliberalist capitalism and class inequality in America, and how it condemns too many to dead end lives. Unger's stamp appears in the approach to social change that the book expresses: most critics of injustice who call for policy-guided change assume a dichotomy in approach. Incrementalists think that realistic change can only happen one legal reform at a time, and revolutionaries think that the only way to make real change is to bring the whole economic system down and build a new one. West and Unger reject both approaches, and argue instead that radical reform can realistically be put in place with a package of synergistically related policies. I agree with this general approach. I cannot envision what fostering general social and economic revolution means for action, but I can envision how a determinate set of policy initiatives working together can have transformative effects. At the same time, this approach attends to the fact that isolated reforms sometimes only displace rather than remove problems.

The main purpose of the book, then, is to offer such a policy package to the American left. West and Unger call for replacing a national income tax with a value-added tax, as well as the implementation of a social inheritance program. A social inheritance is a way of equalizing starting life chances by giving everyone a fund that they might use for training or investing in a business. Accepting that wage labor is the primary way to organize work and get a livelihood in the twenty-first century, and also accepting that job status will be ever more flexible and mobile, they call for greater social support for education and training throughout life. Recognizing that children of all races and sexes are the most vulnerable, they propose child targeted food, medical, and dental support, as well as publicly subsidized pre-school and after-school care. Perhaps their most radical proposal is that access to productive resources should be democratized through means such as public–private venture-capital funds. Besides such measures at economic reform, they call for supporting associational activity, creating more civic spaces where

Americans of different races and classes meet and discuss social problems, and campaign finance reform.

One can easily complain that West and Unger's program for the renewal of American progressivism is very thin on policy specifics and tactics for achieving them. As I read this book, however, their intent is to start discussion along those lines, rather than end it. Unfortunately, I see little sign that progressives have been discussing their ideas, although there may be discussion groups I do not know about. My main problem with their program is not that it is sketchy or utopian, but that in the end it focuses on such a narrow set of issues and remedies. Despite their verbal gestures acknowledging how racist, sexist, and heterosexist structures intersect with economic class, they do not offer a description of the workings of privilege and disadvantage in America that integrates these different structural axes. To do so they would need to analyze more completely how popular culture and advertising use images of sexuality, pleasure, violence, and coolness to foster profits. Moreover, while the book does set the widening gap between haves and have nots in America in the context of changes in global capitalism, more needs to be said about this connection. Changes in work and the division of labor of the past two decades are monumental and touch most people in the world, with very specific consequences for economic status and opportunities for women, racial minorities, and immigrants. Specific policy proposals need to be set in the global economic pressures as well. Especially in light of the visionary ideology critique of West's earlier work, the policy recommendations offered in this book are disappointingly tame, only slightly more radical than the mainstream of the Democratic Party.

In *The War Against Parents*, co-authored with economist Sylvia Ann Hewlett, West turns his attention to the effects on parents and children of these economic changes, as well as government retreat from economic regulation and social wage support. While Hewlett and West's analysis lays a great deal of emphasis on economic issues such as wage structures and cost of living, this book also has a great deal to say about values, popular culture, and organizations' responses to cynicism. Unfortunately, from a feminist point of view, what they say on these issues verges dangerously on the reactionary. Despite their repeated protestations to the contrary, their stance is antifeminist, and looks for remedies for pressures on parents in a nostalgic idea of family. In light of the hard-hitting analysis of patriarchal structures I summarized as central to *Race Matters*, this nostalgia is surprising.

Hewlett and West make the case that many parents labor under nearly impossible stresses in trying to make the lives of their children safe, healthy, nurturing of intellectual development, and happy. Needing two paychecks in a household to keep its members out of poverty, and with many jobs becoming more insecure and poorly paid, parents have too little time and too much to worry about. Neither government nor private employers do very much to ease parental burdens, and even less to offer support for what is arguably the most important responsibility people can have: helping a child achieve flourishing adulthood. Hewlett and West are responding to a right-wing family values rhetoric that holds individual parents personally responsible for the fact that too many children are not at all flourishing. Their diagnoses of the current situation of parents is on the mark. It is about time that the answer came back that social policy needs to support parents' work.

The nostalgia appears when Hewlett and West contrast the current situation of parents with their situation in the 1950s. Back in those good old days there were two pillars of family strength that have since toppled. First, the US federal government had a wide array of programs and policies that helped families dwell in economic security. West and Hewlett single out the GI Bill and various supports for affordable housing for special praise. They barely acknowledge that these housing supports and the suburban development they made possible had devastating implications for racial segregation, the effects of which we are still living out. Nor do they seem terribly bothered by how post-war housing construction isolated many women working in their homes.

The second 1950s pillar of family strength, they claim, was a general cultural commitment to marriage and family life that was reinforced in popular media by positive images of wise fathers and careful mothers. While they mention that these idyllic family values lay within a patriarchal context whose norms "became increasingly unacceptable to progressive sensibilities," they seem to think the patriarchal context can be separated from the particular orderliness this image of family provides. They fail to attend, moreover, to the fact that underlying this order was an unfair gender division of labor whose basic structure has not changed and whose consequences to women today can be argued as more onerous.

Consonant with their dual account of the supports for the once-upon-a-time strong family, Hewlett and West name two culprits responsible for its wounding: government withdrawal of support for families, and 1960s permissive individualism, including feminism. They argue persuasively that the erosion of government-funded programs for progressive tax policy, housing, urban development, education, college loans, and many other programs have left many families more vulnerable than before to the stresses of dislocation, insecurity and poverty. Here they are completely right that a society in which all families can live well requires positive government support of the quality of life. I think they somewhat overstate the role of government cutbacks as causes of greater vulnerability of many families, however, and do not emphasize enough the global restructuring of production and labor that have pulled millions of women into the workforce, reduced opportunities and wages for many men, and closed off the possibility of middle-class life for most young people who do not go to college. More responsibility should be laid at the door of private enterprise.

Even more troubling, however, Hewlett and West claim that the social movements of the 1960s are responsible for a breakdown in family life, because these movements have only cared about individual freedom, choice, and self-realization at the expense of community cohesion. As a consequence, they claim, contemporary progressives are no friends of families:

> Scratch the surface and you will find at least some folks on the left who don't particularly like marriage or children. In their view, the enormous quantity of other-directed energy absorbed by families gets in the way of freedom of choice, and ultimately self-realization. This is particularly true for women, which is why radical feminists tend to see motherhood as a plot to derail equal rights and lure women back into subservient, submissive roles within the family.[7]

Hewlett and West rely on a stereotype of the man-hating feminist to buttress their claim that the women's movement is a primary cause of family breakdown:

> Ideas that women don't need men, women can do whatever they want without men, men are responsible for all the evil in the world, children need only a loving mother, and men only teach children how to be patriarchal and militaristic have become standard fare on the cutting edge of the women's movement.[8]

Such statements are embarrassing. But worse, Hewlett and West fail to acknowledge the most important feminist efforts to revalue family life. As I pointed out above, a feminist critique of the idyllic 1950s family claims that it was founded on an unfair sexual division of labor. It is feminist analysis that has brought to consciousness the fundamental importance of care work to thriving lives, not to mention the number of hours a week needed for housework. The worlds of warfare, policies, and production have been fueled by the vast energies of privatized women doing mostly unnoticed and little-valued work. One of the central feminist demands, which still has hardly been heard, let alone acted on, is that this work should be more noticed and valued and that *men should do their fair share*. Hewlett and West do want at least the work of parenting to be more noticed, and they do want men to do more of it. But they fail to reflect on the fact that those who have studied these issues consistently seem to find that husbands, even husbands of working wives, do much less domestic and care work than their wives. If there is a battle of the sexes today, this is one of its major terrains, and no doubt it is often a source of tension in families. The world of paid work, moreover, continues to operate as though all workers have someone else at home to take care of children, aged parents, and delivery people. Hewlett and West recognize this as a problem for families to the extent that they call for more flextime and paid days off for family responsibilities. They do not sufficiently analyze how this continued gender division of labor is a major source of family stress, partly accounting for parental separation or low family income.

To remedy the sorry conditions under which many children grow, Hewlett and West recommend a wide array of mostly government funded programs. I support nearly all their recommendations, such as generous child allowances, more subsidized child care, and child-targeted funding for health, nutrition, and education. In many ways their program calls for nothing more radical than what has long been assumed as normal government support for parents and children in France.

Another aspect of their recommended cure for family distress is more disturbing, however. Men and women should get recommitted to marriage, for the sake of children. Children ought to be raised by their biological parents. Children need precisely two parents, a father and a mother. Fathers are generally less motivated to commit themselves to the welfare of children, however, if they are not genetically related to them. It is important, moreover, that they can be sure that the children of their wives are genetically theirs, and not some other men's. Marriage is important, moreover, because in it women exercise a civilizing influence on men, who otherwise tend to be irresponsible, selfish, and violent. Statements like these are offensive coming from anyone today, but coming from supposed progressives, they are frightening! Privileging marriage and genetic ties of parenting in this way is heterosexist and insulting to adoptive parents, and wrongfully supports continued stigmatization of single mothers. It also fails to bring received social consensus under question, as the method of genealogical materialism would seem to recommend.

Hewlett and West gesture in the direction of the freedom of men and women to love others of the same sex. Their entire discussion of parenting, however, rings as though being gay and being a parent are mutually exclusive. This assumption appears starkly when they report that the parents they surveyed for the most part do not care one way or the other about gay rights, including gay marriage. This makes it sound like none of their parents are gay or lesbian, and if that were true, they did not pick a very representative sample of parents! Of course, some parents are gay or lesbian, and many parent together with same sex partners. The children of gay and lesbian parents do no worse or better in life than the children of heterosexual parents. To hold strongly that all children ought to be parented by one man and one woman condemns these parents and their children to continued stigma.

The same rhetoric condemns families headed by one parent, most often a woman, to continued stigma. There is no question that parenting children alone is often more difficult than in partnership with other adults. Families headed by women are more likely to be poor than others, because the job opportunities and wages available to these women continue to be structured by devaluation of women's work. Lack of benefits, poor transportation access, work hours, and responsibilities that do not accommodate the needs of parents with sole responsibility for their children all contribute to serious stresses on these families. As with others in American policy discussion who vilify single-parent families, the only concrete remedy Hewlett and West offer for this alleged pathology is to make divorce more difficult. Wouldn't raising women's wages and structuring work hours, transportation, cooperative living arrangements, and day care in such a way that all parents could have more supporting relationships with other adults in their parenting and were better able to combine working outside the home with working in it be a much deeper and more effective way of dealing with the stresses of single parenting? Why should policy turn to the restrictions on liberty that stricter divorce regulation implies when there may be better alternatives?

Hewlett and West's biologism is quite far-fetched. They claim that step-children are worse off than biological children, and for this reason biological parents have a responsibility not to divorce. They claim that men are more motivated to be committed to the well-being of children if they can be sure the children are genetically "theirs." If this latter claim is true (and I doubt it), this does not recommend the male character. It appeals to an "ownership" of children attitude which is not good for children and it gives men an excuse to control the behavior of the women with whom they are in relationships. This biologism, moreover, is an insult to the millions of loving families where the children are adopted. Indeed, Hewlett and West later in their discussion apparently contradict their position by arguing that the severing of legal ties of children to biological parents should be made easier so that more children can be adopted.

Hewlett and West rightly worry that contemporary culture and political discourse offer boys and men few models of citizen and parental responsibility, and often ignore and obscure the plight especially of young men without a trade or college education in today's labor market. In response to male anomie they applaud the efforts of two organizations whose mission is to persuade men to be committed to families: the Promise Keepers and the Nation of Islam. In both cases they laud the spirituality of these groups and their ability to motivate many men to commit themselves to be responsible "leaders" of their families, without attending to the dangerous nostalgia fueling the image of families of both groups. Of course it is true that neither group recommends that men who lead their families should do so with the iron fist of domination. They believe that the harmonious family is one founded on mutual love. These nurturers of family values nevertheless promote in men a notion of entitlement: in return for committing themselves to caring for children and sacrificing their time to earn a living for their families, these men are entitled to control a woman's sexuality, to be adorned with the civilizing trappings of domesticity, and looked to as the family leaders. This all works fine as long as men believe that they are getting what they are entitled to. If they believe that their wife is cheating on them, however, or the domestic care is not to their liking, or their wife disagrees with them about what the family should do, the men with this sense of entitlement are liable to retreat from their commitment, or worse, become violent. One wonders where West has taken his analysis of the realities and dangers of machismo.

What has happened to the critical and creative stance of genealogical materialist prophetic pragmatism? While he retains a serious social democratic commitment to public support for the needs of poor and working people, in these recent political works, it seems to me that West shows a dulled imagination for cultural critique and envisioning creative alternatives to contemporary resignation and cynicism. Especially when thinking about issues of family and children, we need more of the demythologizing and demystification that West's earlier work theorizes. Rather than revoicing myths of a harmonious nuclear family now gone, or reinforcing popular attachments to biological reductionism, genealogical materialism would show how these recurring ideas are linked to individualism and private property. Rather than ignoring with popular culture the continued effects of a gender division of labor in the family, a prophetic pragmatism would put workplace accommodation to family needs at the center of its demands. Genealogical materialist analysis of families has traced the history of the normalization of patriarchal family relations in bolstering both class inequality and racism, and has analyzed how the resurgence of nostalgic family discourse is successfully reinscribing the positioning of lower income people, especially lower income people of color, as morally inferior to the more upstanding and professionalized middle class. A prophetic pragmatism should imagine not only ways that state policy should support health care, education, affordable housing, and accessible transportation, but also how workplace and civic life might facilitate everyday personal support and cooperation among wide networks of adults and children, rather than put all the burden on a tiny nuclear family.

Notes

1 Cornel West, "Theory, pragmatism and politics." In *Keeping Faith: Philosophy and Race in America* (New York: Routledge, 1993), p. 89.
2 Ibid.
3 Cornel West, *The American Evasion of Philosophy: A Genealogy of Pragmatism* (Madison: University of Wisconsin Press, 1989), p. 4.
4 Cornel West, *Race Matters* (Boston: Beacon Press, 1993), p. 3.
5 Ibid., p. 24.
6 Ibid., p. 27.
7 Sylvia Ann Hewlett and Cornel West, *The War Against Parents* (New York: Houghton Mifflin Company, 1998), p. 95.
8 Ibid., p. 161.

11

Prophetic Pragmatism as Political Philosophy

Charles W. Mills

Cornel West is the most prominent Black intellectual in the United States, and, *a fortiori*, the most prominent Black philosopher (though it is a label he is somewhat ambivalent about, and he is not in fact in a philosophy department).[1] The author, co-author, or interlocutor of fifteen books, the co-editor of another six, the subject of cover stories in national news magazines and interviews on national television, one of the few Black intellectuals with a national bestseller,[2] averaging a demanding three talks a week for the past twenty years, he is a public figure who has received both extravagant praise and no less extravagant condemnation.[3] The breadth of subjects covered in his work and the range of references are dizzying – West is the grand eclectic, the great synthesizer, the man to go to for the Big Picture. In this chapter, I will focus narrowly on the question of West's political philosophy. If all Black intellectuals have perforce had, or been taken to have, some political commitments, West's famous hybrid formulation of *prophetic pragmatism* is apparently a distinctive and original position that fits awkwardly in a standard taxonomy of liberal or conservative, Marxist or Black nationalist. Thus it is worth examining as a contribution to the ongoing debate about how we should understand Black oppression, and what are the appropriate measures to alleviate or end it. I will try to elucidate and analyze the various components of West's political philosophy, their sources, the possible tensions between them, and some of the strengths and potential problems of his viewpoint. Obviously, given limitations of space, this chapter can be no more than an initial step toward the task.

Political Philosophy

The natural place to start is with a characterization of political philosophy itself. In the analytic tradition, it is standard to distinguish between normative issues (social justice: how material goods, rights, and political power should be distributed) and descriptive issues (sociopolitical structures: how material goods, rights, and political power actually are distributed).[4] A subdisciplinary division of labor is then assumed, in which political *philosophy* is supposed to be restricted to the former, while inquiry into sociopolitical structures is relegated to political *theory/science*. But obviously this farming out of the work is to a certain extent arbitrary, stipulative, and even those who draw the line in the conventional way often concede that factual matters are unavoidably relevant to the normative debate.[5] Writers with left or radical sympathies, such as "critical theorists," make the stronger case that theorizing about the way things are (human nature, social structure, political origins) should be formally recognized as an integral part of political philosophy. Thus Iris Marion Young argues for "critical theory" as "a normative reflection that is historically and socially contextualized.... [G]ood normative theorizing cannot avoid social and political description and explanation."[6] For in the absence of a self-conscious examination of the sociopolitical facts, what will be shaping normative inquiry is often a "common sense" that is actually highly questionable, embedding classist, racist, and sexist presuppositions about the social world. So these claims need to be brought into explicit focus, identified as theoretically loaded, and subjected to critical scrutiny.

I suggest, then, that we think of political philosophy in this comprehensive sense as including both the factual (though generally at a higher level of abstraction than political science) and the evaluative. We could also include the strategic, in the sense that the point of political philosophy is to intervene in the world. So there are three elements. First, there is the mapping of the sociopolitical terrain, empirical and theoretical: a particular understanding of the polity, what its crucial components and central political actors are, and in general how it works. Then there is a set of value-commitments, judgments about what is right and wrong, just and unjust, that will determine overall normative assessments of the present situation and an outline of what should be striven for. And, finally, there will be operationalizing prescriptions about what practically should be done to bring about the desired political end. In sum: here is what it looks like; here is how and why it is good or bad; and here is what we should do about it. And our expectation in general, obviously, is that the elements of the theorist's political philosophy will be defensible and be integrated with one another, that the facts will match up with what we know of the world, that the values will be morally attractive, and that the strategy makes sense in the light of the factual and normative picture offered.

Now before we turn to an examination of West's prophetic pragmatism against this background, there are some preliminary problems to be dealt with, problems that might in fact derail the whole enterprise. I have been writing as if it were obvious that prophetic pragmatism is West's political philosophy. But at places West denies what it would be natural to infer, i.e. that prophetic pragmatism should become the guide to a transformative political movement. Thus, in the closing chapter of *The American Evasion of Philosophy*, he writes:

> Prophetic pragmatism purports to be not only an oppositional cultural criticism but also a material force for individuality and democracy. By "material force" I simply mean a practice that has some potency and effect or makes a difference in the world. There is − and should be − no such thing as a prophetic pragmatist movement.[7]

This injunction is puzzling, since surely the whole point of articulating a synthesis which is represented as the culmination of the pragmatist tradition, and which one wants to be a "material force," is so it can inspire a movement of political change. Moreover, this passage comes after a discussion of Antonio Gramsci, whose "metaphilosophical perspectives" West claims prophetic pragmatism "closely resemble[s] and, in some ways, [converges] with."[8] But Gramsci's conception of Marxism as the "philosophy of praxis" was intended precisely as an intervention in the "contradictory consciousness" of the Italian working class, so that Marxism could become a material political force which would combat, and ultimately overthrow, ruling bloc hegemony. We would have found it strange for Gramsci to have wound up the *Prison Notebooks* by declaring (except perhaps for the purpose of misleading the fascist censors) that there should be "no such thing" as a Marxist movement.[9] So it raises the question of whether I am mistaken in thinking of prophetic pragmatism as West's political philosophy. What kind of political philosophy is it that is *not* intended to guide a political movement?

And there is a second problem. Not only may prophetic pragmatism not be West's *political* philosophy; it turns out that it may not even be *West's* philosophy. On the introductory page of the "American pragmatism" section (part III) of the *Cornel West Reader*, West makes the following statement:

> My own conception of prophetic pragmatism is what emerged when I dipped this tradition [pragmatism] into the furnace of black suffering and resistance in America. Yet prophetic pragmatism is not my philosophy or particular vision of the world. Rather, it is a fecund discursive space in which I can put forward many views and viewpoints. It is the philosophical space occupied by my Chekhovian Christian perspective.[10]

I confess that I do not know what to make of this. West's tendency toward abstraction at crucial points, which hostile commentators have found "evasive" in the straightforwardly pejorative sense, is singularly unhelpful here. What is a "fecund discursive space"? If it is a space in which many different viewpoints can be put forward, then what is distinctively prophetic or pragmatist about it? And what, if any, are the political implications (within this "space") of Chekhovian Christianity? It might be argued that I am assigning too much weight to what is, after all, only an introductory paragraph. But the *Reader* is West's compilation of those pieces which "best represent the crucial moments of an evolving whole," in which he aims "to lay bare the basic structure of my intellectual work and life."[11] West is looking back on twenty years' work, selecting what he sees as the essays most illustrative of his evolving beliefs, and putting them into an overall pattern. So it is hard not to take this statement as some kind of retrospective judgment on the whole prophetic pragmatist project. And as such, it seems to be something of a distancing, but one that does not bill itself as such. (He is *not* saying, "As a result of criticisms of prophetic pragmatism, I now realize ... " He seems to be saying, "Who, me? A prophetic pragmatist?")

At any rate, I am going to proceed, *pace* West, on the assumptions both that prophetic pragmatism is a political philosophy, and that it is, or was for a long time, West's political philosophy. If it is not, then it is what seems to come closest, and in any case it is of interest in its own right.

Sources of Prophetic Pragmatism

Let us turn then to the various components of prophetic pragmatism. It should be noted to begin with that there are several obstacles to getting clear on West's position. West has written so much, in so many places, on so many subjects, invoking so many sources, and making so many qualifications, that it is difficult to pin him down. Moreover, his position has evolved over time – he has, after all, been writing for twenty years now.

First, there is the sheer volume of his work – fifteen books, including the *Reader*. Of course, not all of these are of equal importance for understanding his politics, since some do not deal directly with political matters at all; for example, *Jews and Blacks* (Black–Jewish relations), *The War Against Parents* (the contemporary American family), and *The Future of the Race* (W. E. B. Du Bois's "talented tenth" thesis).[12] One also needs to distinguish between the more scholarly and the more self-consciously popular works, the latter being shorter, aimed at a mass audience, with no footnotes and with few or no academic sources cited (for example, *Race Matters*, *The Future of American Progressivism*).[13] *Breaking Bread* is a set of dialogues with bell hooks; *Restoring Hope* is a set of interviews by West of various well known Americans.[14] So I see the most important books for reconstructing his political philosophy as *Prophesy Deliverance!* (1982), *Prophetic Fragments* (1988), *The American Evasion of Philosophy* (1989), *The Ethical Dimensions of Marxist Thought* (1991), *Prophetic Thought in Postmodern Times* (1993), *Prophetic Reflections* (1993), and *Keeping Faith* (1993).[15]

Even this reduced number would be a lot to assimilate (especially given the blizzard of references to be ploughed through within them). But a further problem is that only *Prophesy Deliverance!*, *American Evasion*, and *Ethical Dimensions* (based on his dissertation) offer a sustained, book-length argument. The others are collections of essays, book reviews, speeches, brief notes, interviews, and other episodic pieces, sometimes as short as a page or two ("fragments"), and covering a wide variety of topics. Moreover, in developing his position, West draws numerous distinctions and enters various qualifications about the bodies of thought he is canvassing. Finally, he is critical of particular aspects of the theories he is utilizing, so that his appropriation of them is often hedged in various ways. All in all, then, his position is a highly complicated and nuanced one that is easy to misrepresent, which, despite my efforts, I will doubtless be doing to a certain extent at least.

Let me sketch the contours of the wood before examining the trees. The natural reading – though even this turns out to be less clear on closer inspection – is to see prophetic pragmatism as an attempted synthesis of Christianity and pragmatism, with Marxist influence (though not equal standing) coming through liberation theology, and informed throughout by the Black experience. Thus Robert Gooding-Williams speaks of West's effort "to combine in a single narrative his Christian, socialist, black freedom fighting and pragmatist allegiances."[16] Lewis Gordon comments on "his trinity of Christ, Marx, and Dewey."[17] It is an interesting trio, who would doubtless have much to say to each other over the dinner table. But their respective prominence is not equal – it could hardly be, considering the tensions between the three thinkers – or constant over time. As a believer, West necessarily has to distance himself from a full-blooded Marxism, in a way that he does not have to do for pragmatism and Christianity. (He refers to his "critical acceptance of certain elements of Marxist analysis."[18]) So Marxism was always a subordinate rather than an equal component. Yet, as just noted above, the pragmatic element itself seems to have diminished somewhat by the time of writing, and he has in fact also had various criticisms of pragmatism all along. So it is really only Christ who emerges unscathed and undiminished at the end of the day. Of his many hats (and if all of us have multiple identifiers, West is a veritable hat rack), West chooses in the *Reader* introduction to wear that of the "Chekhovian Christian," and the Russian writer also earns pride of place in the two epigraphs, and the names in the dedication ("above all") of the book.

First, the pragmatism. Traditionally, pragmatism has been viewed, in the words of John Stuhr's recent anthology on the subject, as "classical American philosophy," the distinctive contribution of the United States to Western philosophy. But the label covers a wide variety of thinkers, with significant differences among them, so that even apart from the partially "anti-philosophical" character of pragmatism, it can be difficult to characterize it accurately. Stuhr lists seven "defining characteristics and commitments": (a) the rejection of modern philosophy (as a purely theoretical quest for eternal truths); (b) fallibilism (as antidogmatism); (c) pluralism (about reality and human values); (d) radical empiricism; (e) the continuity of science and philosophy; (f) meliorism; and (g) the centrality of community and the social.[19] Stuhr's selection of central theorists includes Ralph Waldo Emerson (as a precursor, in the prologue), and then, in the heyday of American pragmatism, Charles Sanders Peirce, William James, Josiah Royce, George Santayana, John Dewey, and George Herbert Mead. (A subsequent section adds the figures of Jane Addams, Borden Parker Browne, Alain Locke, and John Herman Randall, Jr.)

It will be obvious that, at least on Stuhr's account, there is little explicit political commitment here; pragmatism is not a political philosophy like, say, liberalism, conservatism, or Marxism, but a certain methodological outlook. West's own characterization of pragmatism in *American Evasion* is that its "common denominator" is "a future-oriented instrumentalism that tries to deploy thought as a weapon to enable more effective action," and its "basic impulse" is "a plebeian radicalism that fuels an antipatrician rebelliousness for the moral aim of enriching individuals and expanding democracy." So its "distinctive appeal" is "its unashamedly moral emphasis and its unequivocally ameliorative impulse."[20] For him, the "three principal slogans of [American pragmatism's] banner" are "voluntarism, fallibilism and experimentalism."[21] But unlike Stuhr, West sees pragmatism as "unique as a philosophical tradition in the modern world in its preoccupation or near obsession with the meaning and value of democracy."[22] (One wonders whether Dewey is being inflated to stand for the pragmatist tradition as a whole, and in one interview West does in fact say, "For me [pragmatism] is principally Dewey," whom he sees as "the giant of this tradition.")[23] Nor does West endorse the centrality of science. In his first book, *Prophesy Deliverance!*, he sees the "veneration of scientific method and the practices of the scientific community" as a "major shortcoming" of pragmatism, and recommends, instead, emphasis on "the political dimensions of knowledge."[24] On the metatheoretical question, he suggests that "three theses are basic: (1) antirealism in ontology...; (2) antifoundationalism in epistemology...; and, (3) detranscendentalizing of the subject."[25]

West concedes, of course, that the "rebelliousness" he finds in pragmatism has been historically restricted by the actual ethnocentrism, racism, and sexism of its proponents.[26] But he sees the philosophy as having the resources to overcome the limitations of its practitioners.

In *American Evasion*, whatever his later disclaimers, he writes explicitly that: "My own conception of prophetic pragmatism...serves as the culmination of the American pragmatist tradition," and that he has promoted American pragmatism "as both a persuasive philosophical perspective and an indigenous source of left politics." The idea is to provide "an interpretation of a progressive tradition that can inspire and instruct contemporary efforts to remake and reform American society and culture."[27] So this certainly makes it sound as if prophetic pragmatism is a philosophy (admittedly in the qualified sense pragmatists prefer), is a political philosophy, and is his own political philosophy. His own more restricted focus is on Emerson, Peirce, James, Dewey, and then the mid-twentieth century figures of Sidney Hook, C. Wright Mills, W. E. B. Du Bois, Reinhold Niebuhr, Lionel Trilling, and finally such contemporaries as W. V. O. Quine and Richard Rorty. (Du Bois, Black America's most accomplished intellectual, is enlisted by West as an unheralded pragmatist, a claim vigorously contested by Robert Gooding-Williams in his critical review of West's book.[28]) West's own *prophetic* pragmatism seeks to combine the pragmatist tradition with Black liberation theology.

So that brings us to the second, "prophetic" part. On an earlier impressionistic skimming of the book, I had assumed – as I believe most people would have – that a pragmatism prefixed by "prophetic" had to be intrinsically religious in character. But on reading the text more carefully than I had originally done, I realized that this was not the case. If the political component of prophetic pragmatism is fairly loosely attached to the label, the religious component turns out to be even more so – in fact, to be fully detachable. West writes that the "prophetic" denomination:

> harks back to the Jewish and Christian tradition of prophets who brought urgent and compassionate critique to bear on the evils of their day. The mark of the prophet is to speak the truth in love with courage – come what may. Prophetic pragmatism proceeds from this impulse. It neither requires a religious foundation nor entails a religious perspective, yet prophetic pragmatism is compatible with certain religious outlooks.[29]

Now this seems to me to be an astonishing concession, though one would certainly not think so from the casual tone in which it is said. The distinctive and interesting feature of prophetic pragmatism had, I thought, been the synthesis with religion. Now it turns out that there is no such synthesis – or only in *West's* particular version. So one experiences a frustrating sense of a position evaporating through one's fingers even as one tries to get a handle on it. What *is* prophetic pragmatism?

One interpretive solution might be to distinguish "thin" and "thick" senses of prophetic pragmatism, the first (theologically neutral kind) having universalist aspirations, the latter (religiously committed kind) being just West's particular version of the position. (He does say, for example, "My own version of prophetic pragmatism is situated within the Christian tradition."[30]) But this move runs into problems of its own, for both thin and thick senses.

Consider the latter first. In the layperson's use of the term *philosophy* – the sense in which someone will say, "Well, that's my philosophy of life" (to be stoic, or hedonistic, or to never give a sucker an even break) – one can characterize an idiosyncratic personal outlook as a "philosophy." But it would be strange to represent a political philosophy this way. A political philosophy as I have characterized it is offering descriptions of the social world, passing normative judgments about it, and urging us to action, all implicitly or explicitly in the name of its putative superiority to other descriptions, normative judgments, and prescriptions. It is not supposed to be a matter of individual taste – I like chocolate ice cream, but you may well prefer vanilla – but a theory being put forward with claims on our belief. So if West's is a thick version of a personal kind, tailored to his individual predilections, but with no expectation that others will follow, or that if they do they will have any rational basis for doing so, this is a political philosophy of a very peculiar sort. Thus for me it raises again the worry that I am trying to force prophetic pragmatism into a role it was never meant to play. (However, would West not then be engaged in a performative contradiction in trying to win people over to the plausibility of his view, as his many books are presumably intended to do?)

What of the more minimal version that is explicitly projected as rising to the level of generality? Can it be maintained that there *is* enough content in a "thin" prophetic pragmatism (independent of a religious foundation) that it can be a political philosophy on its own? The problem here should be obvious. Apart from the dubious stipulation of "in love" (see quote above), prophetic pragmatism in this more minimalist sense would just seem to amount to standing up for your principles, speaking truth to power, if needs be in a dramatic let-the-heavens-fall kind of way. Not only does this have no necessary connection with religion, it has no necessary connection with *any* political position, unless one wants to erect antiopportunism, or courageous and loving antiopportunism, into a politics. One can be a secular humanist, a committed anticlerical, a militant atheist attacking organized religion in a "prophetic" way, speaking truth to the organized power of the church, and still be a prophetic pragmatist. Or one can be a liberal, a conservative, a Marxist, bringing "urgent and compassionate critique" to bear on such evils as, respectively, the unconstrained market, the constrained market, the market *qua* market, and still be a prophetic pragmatist. But this is obviously to dilute the semantic content of "prophecy" so far as to include virtually everything. A political philosophy – indeed a theory in general – cannot merely *include*, it has to *exclude*. Certain claims and positions have to be incompatible with it, or one is merely uttering vacuities.

I conclude, then, that for prophetic pragmatism to be an interesting and viable contender, it must be taken in the religious sense. So we move on to the second component: liberation theology. Originally most closely associated with Latin America, the term was devised by progressive Catholic priests who argued that the Christian gospel actually required solidarity with the poor, the peasants, and the workers, as against the big landowners, the death squads, and the military (an eminently reasonable position, remarkable only for what it reveals about the history of Latin Catholicism that it was necessary for somebody to *say* this, and be deemed radical for doing so). But as Black theologians in the United States and elsewhere pointed out, long before this appropriation, the Bible had been re-read as a revolutionary text by captured Africans. Historically, Christianity has provided the most influential intellectual framework for Black struggles in the New World, with the slaves reinterpreting the Bible to represent themselves as Israelites in captivity under Pharaoh's hand. Christianity has been the source of a worldview, a theory of history, moral judgments, spiritual inspiration, and hope in the face of overwhelming odds.

As noted above, it is the Christian theme that is the most consistent note in West's career, and he is critical of the organized left for its secularism.[31] His first book, *Prophesy Deliverance!*, was subtitled *An Afro-American Revolutionary Christianity*, and his present incarnation, as mentioned, is as a Chekhovian Christian. So other things may change, but the Christianity remains constant. In *Prophesy Deliverance!*, West characterizes the Black prophetic Christian tradition as:

> guided by a profound conception of human nature and human history, a persuasive picture of what one is as a person, what one should hope for, and how one ought to act. It also proposes the two fundamental moral norms of individuality and democracy as the center of Afro-American thought.[32]

Elsewhere he talks about three crucial Christian values: "the notion of the *imago dei*," the "subversive" universalism and egalitarianism implied by the concept that we are all made in the image of God; the "fallenness" that points toward "radical democratic values" to prevent institutional corruption; and the "kingdom-talk" that empowers one in the face of evil.[33] So Christianity is a source of moral values, of meaning, and of "combative spirituality."[34] For the Black community, belief in God has helped people "to deal with the absurdity of being Black in America, for many of us it is a question of God and sanity, or God and suicide."[35]

What Christianity does *not* do, however, is provide a social theory, even if it does offer a certain "conception of human nature and human history." West says explicitly that "the descriptive dimension of political discernment rests upon sophisticated systemic social analyses," not the Christian gospel. The latter provides the "normative dimension," but "there is no such thing as 'Christian' social analysis."[36] He is also critical of those pragmatists, particularly Rorty, who deprecate the need for social theory. So even if he does not use the term "political philosophy," or carve things up conceptually as I have done, West is committed to agreeing that the descriptive/explanatory dimension of sociopolitical analysis is crucial to political philosophy.

Enter, then, Marxism. The role of this third member of the trinity is to provide (in necessarily qualified and modified form) the systemic analysis of the workings of the polity to be found neither in pragmatism nor in Christianity. But if there are different strains within the pragmatist tradition, and ongoing internecine battles about the meaning of the Christian gospel, there are also, of course, myriad Marxisms. One could differentiate Second International from Third International Marxism, Western from "Eastern" Marxism, First World from Third World Marxism, existentialist/humanist from structuralist Marxism, Hegelian Marxism from analytic Marxism, Black from "white" Marxism, and so forth.

West develops a taxonomy of what he sees as the "six major streams in the Marxist tradition": the "revisionist" Marxism of Eduard Bernstein, which holds "that socialism can arise through legislation and bourgeois electoral politics"; the orthodox "Leninist stream," which advocates "the need of a vanguard party composed of professional revolutionaries"; Stalinist Marxism; Trotskyist Marxism; the "councilist" stream associated with Rosa Luxemburg, Anton Pannekoek, and Karl Korsch, which repudiates Leninist elitism for "the self-organization and self-guidance of the working class movement"; and finally the "Gramscian stream," which "combines the Leninist and Councilist viewpoints." For West, the Stalinist, Leninist, and Trotskyist streams are all "regressive, or right-wing, Marxism," while the others are in different degrees progressive.[37] In later works, he identifies himself specifically as a "neo-Gramscian," or a "neo-Gramscian pragmatist." Gramsci's famous phrase for Marxism was the "philosophy of praxis," so there is a happy convergence here with West's pragmatist sympathies. Whatever their other differences, however, all six of the streams have in common "commitment to the dialectical method for understanding social reality, viewing class struggle as a central dynamic of the historical process, and affirming socialism as a desirable social arrangement."[38]

However, West is critical of many aspects of Marxism, even as social analysis, so that his overall judgment is that it is "an indispensable – though by itself inadequate – intellectual weapon in the struggle for individuality and democracy."[39] Among Marxism's many weak spots or blindnesses are its undeveloped discussion of ethics, its incomprehension of culture, its insensitivity to nonclass identities such as those of women and people of color, its lack of a fine-grained conception of power comparable to Foucault's "microphysics," its "exaggeration of human possibility," and its pretensions to scientificity which "can lead in positivistic directions."[40] So Marxism has to be supplemented by other bodies of theory. One of the reasons why West favors a Gramscian Marxism is because of Gramsci's more historicist view of Marxist theory, and his attempt to understand culture and language within a Marxist framework.

So these are the three components. At the start, I suggested that we could regard a political philosophy as having descriptive, normative, and operational dimensions. We can now see the rough division of labor between West's components and these dimensions. The descriptive sociopolitical side is to be handled by a modified Marxism in conjunction with other bodies of theory. The normative dimension is to be provided by pragmatism (in the general sense of being a pro-democracy, pro-individualism outlook) and, at a deeper spiritual level, by Christianity. (West *does* think there is an ethical dimension to Marxist thought, but it is underdeveloped by comparison with the analyses of the other two.) Finally, all three have some input on the strategic question, since prophetic Christianity, pragmatism, and Marxism are all oriented toward changing the world, though obviously (and here, to anticipate, is one source of tension) in very different ways.

Strengths of Prophetic Pragmatism

Prophetic pragmatism as a political philosophy constitutes a challenging attempt to synthesize different traditions. Let me begin by pointing out some of its strengths.

(1)   Obviously, whether at the start of the twenty-first century, in the wake of the global collapse of the socialist ideal, one sees the incorporation of *any* kind of Marxism, even modified and criticized, as a political virtue, will depend entirely on one's already-existing sympathies. There is no room to make a case here to the nonconverted – the question is how convincing West's moves will seem to those few still on the left.

For most of the twentieth century, the American left had to labor under the burden of what has sometimes been called "American exceptionalism." Why in this most modern of nations, with no feudal past worth speaking of, has there been no effective radical labor movement and national social-democratic party comparable to those in Western Europe? It is often pointed out that there is a long tradition in American political culture of nativism, fear of the foreigner (this despite the fact that the country is a nation of immigrants). Left-wing ideas have been seen as the result of "alien" influences. The very name of HUAC, the House Committee on Un-American Activities, is testimony to this. Part of the achievement of the right is that "America" has been so defined that taking a certain political position automatically puts you against the *nation*, makes you an anti-patriot, a betrayer of what America stands for. You are not an American with somewhat variant political views, to be debated openly on their merits and demerits; you are an un-American with views that are anathema, which we know *a priori* to be wrong.

So one of the achievements of West's synthesis, if it worked, would be a strategy for "Americanizing," domesticating, left-wing theory. He points out "the reluctance of American Marxism as a whole to take seriously indigenous American radicalism."[41] By attempting to show the convergence between pragmatism and Marxism, West hopes to radicalize the former and make respectable the latter. By merging socialism with this most authentically indigenous of philosophies, socialist ideas could be wrapped in the American flag rather than, as at present, being seen as an incendiary for the American flag. The American traditions of activism, meliorism, and democracy would be harnessed to a left agenda. In the judgment of one reviewer, "He salvages left-wing theory – in a practical, democratic, and cultural form – from the dust-heap of irrelevance."[42]

(2)   If nationalism and patriotism have been successfully fused with conservatism by the right, the merger with Christianity is even older. God is represented not as the crucified revolutionary "who sides with the oppressed and the exploited,"[43] but as the biggest property-owner of all, the Lockean landlord of the Universe, someone taking personal offense at left-wing sympathies. So to be on the political left has meant being un-Christian as well as un-American. In the United States, this has been a particularly onerous handicap since a higher percentage of the population are religious believers than in any other Western industrialized nation. And Marxist socialism has, of course, been not merely irreligious but usually actively antireligious, both because of Marx's famous critique of religion and because the church has been seen as lined up on the opposite side of the barricades. But as West emphasizes, religion has been among the most powerful intellectual influences on humans, providing them with a world-view, a set of moral guides, and a source of spiritual strength. If one could mobilize this set of resources on one's side rather than have them hostilely arrayed against one, it would obviously be a great advance. West argues that "any radical movement without a Christian counterpart in American society is doomed."[44] His attempt (more clearly in evidence in the earlier writings) to show a convergence between certain positions of Marxism and radical Christianity would then be a boon for progressives. Moreover, this is arguably of especial importance for mobilizing the Black American population, since religion has been far more potent and influential than any secular world-view.

(3)   The emphasis on morality is also welcome as a corrective to the deficiencies of Marxism. As mentioned, there are many different interpretations of Marxism, but certainly on the level of the practice of "official" Marxism in the form of actual communist parties, it has too often been the case that moral considerations have been sneered at. An instrumentalist view of morality, sometimes a kind of unqualified super-consequentialism in which the right is whatever serves to bring about/ maintain socialism (or what is represented as such), has usually been the practice.[45] This is not to say that there have not been many principled and moral leftists, but that often they have been overruled by the dictates of the party. Nor is it, of course, to deny for a moment that opportunism, expediency, and ruthlessness can be found

on the right also, or in respectable mainstream liberals. But if, in Oscar Wilde's classic line, hypocrisy is the homage that vice pays to virtue, then a theory which in its official incarnations has not even recognized virtue will not even generate the benefits that accrue from hypocrisy. So what one wants is a normative critique of capitalism that builds on, but goes beyond, the historical advances of liberalism, and that can win over the politically disengaged. And one also wants a revolutionary ethic that will constrain an "anything-goes" political practice, and guide the creation of a new society. With the collapse of the Eastern Bloc, and the revelations of the horrific body count of "actually existing socialism," the consequences of disdain for normal moral considerations should be disastrously obvious.

(4)   Finally, West is also to be applauded for bringing race and the Black experience into political theory. (He is not, of course, alone in this, but he is one of the most high-profile figures doing so.) As argued at the beginning, it is a mistake to think that political philosophy can be purely normative, since factual claims at different levels of abstraction necessarily guide moral judgments. Our assumptions about what the sociopolitical facts are will point us toward, or away from, issues of structural injustice that tend to become invisible precisely because they are so embedded in the social order. And race is one of those structures that has been inadequately dealt with both in mainstream liberal and in radical Marxist theory.

As Rogers Smith has shown in his recent work, *Civic Ideals*, the consensus in mainstream American political theory for the past century and a half has made race marginal to conceptualizing the country's history. In the work of Alexis de Tocqueville, Gunnar Myrdal, and Louis Hartz, one finds a view of American political culture in which racism is an "anomaly."[46] So at the conceptual level of an overarching intellectual framework – how we should understand the polity, what it essentially *is* – race is marginalized or ignored altogether. The USA is seen as basically an egalitarian liberal democracy, with a few (when they are acknowledged) racist "deviations." Racism is located in the individualistic framework of prejudice and bigotry, not in a framework of structural advantage and subordination. But though Marxism favors structural accounts, there are problems with orthodox Marxist theory also, which has too often been class-reductionistic in its analysis of race. West's essays on elucidating the origins and logic of white supremacy, and his critique of American Marxism for its inadequacies on race, are therefore valuable contributions to our overall understanding of the American polity and European domination in general.

So those are some of the strengths of prophetic pragmatism. Let me now turn to what I see as some of its problems.

Problems of Prophetic Pragmatism

(1)   The first obvious problem is in the fact of the attempted synthesis itself: the question of how well, if at all, the various components hang together. Ideally, a political philosophy should be an integrated body of thought, with no internal inconsistencies. But this is difficult enough to achieve when one set of related ideas is being developed; the problems are greatly compounded when different sources are being brought together. It is not necessarily, or not always, a matter of straightforward contradiction, since bodies of political theory are not usually set out as axioms with strict logical entailments following in nice clean lines. Things are generally a lot fuzzier than that, and there is a certain slack afforded by possible divergences of interpretation and strategies of highlighting certain elements at the cost of others. Nonetheless, every theory has certain minimal commitments – if it did not, it would not be a theory – and at the very least, tensions may arise between rival assumptions. The danger will then be that rather than producing an inspired synthesis that remedies weaknesses in X by borrowing from the strengths of Y, one creates an eclectic hybrid whose conflicting commitments render it incapable of doing the work of either. Or, alternatively, one so modifies X or Y that it becomes questionable whether what remains still merits the theoretical designation. Or one vacillates between alternative frameworks in an inconsistent and self-defeating way.

Consider the issue of materialism, for example. Most commentators have seen Marx as an ontological materialist,[47] someone committed to the view that all that exists is material entities, so that there are no souls, no minds independent of the thinking brain, and no God. At the fundamental ontological level, then, Marxism and Christianity are indeed in necessary opposition: the former committed to a thoroughgoing naturalistic, scientific understanding of the world, the latter to a dualistic, theocentric one in which the claims of modern science are deemed to be restricted in their scope and validity. (If West is correct that pragmatism is ontologically antirealist, then this also is incompatible with Marxism.) Religious believers attracted to Marxist theory, such as liberation theologians, have therefore standardly solved the problem by dropping the ontology. The politicoeconomic analysis is assumed to be detachable from the metaphysics, and one accepts, or at least takes seriously, the historical materialism (claims about the dominance of patterns of socioeconomic causality in determining large-scale historical events), while rejecting the ontological materialism.

But West's own move is somewhat different. He has a "radical historicist" interpretation of Marxism which "calls into question the very notion of ontology" and "puts an end to ontological inquiries."[48] He claims that, for Marx, "the very notion of an 'ontology' itself is a Platonic remnant whose justification requires philosophic (i.e., objectivism/relativism, necessity/contingency, etc.) moves similar to those of Plato."[49] Now this seems quite wrong to me. I believe the traditional interpretation is the correct one, and that though Marx was disdainful of what he termed "philosophy," he did indeed have an ontology, and that it was a materialist one. Short of a lengthy detour into textual exegesis, this claim can obviously not be vindicated here.[50] But what I want to point out is that West's synthesis is achieved here through eviscerating Marxism of what many would see as one of its defining features.

However, the alternative route of finessing the problem through simply rejecting the ontology outright still remains (i.e. not denying that Marxism *is* materialist, or that this issue is somehow transcended, but simply disagreeing with the claim). So let us turn to "materialism" in what could be called the historical or sociological sense. (The ontological and historical/sociological positions are logically distinct, since one could be an ontological materialist, holding that ideas are brain events, and a historical idealist, holding that the battle of ideas determines the course of history. Marx and Engels's negative judgment on Feuerbach's materialism – that "As far as Feuerbach is a materialist he does not deal with history, and as far as he considers history he is not a materialist," but a theorist, rather, who "[relapses] into idealism" – illustrates both their awareness of the distinction, and, I would claim, their endorsement of both senses.[51]) Again, to invoke the standard interpretation, Marxism is seen as claiming that in social theory, *political economy* is crucial. So what is involved is a thesis of causal asymmetry: society is a complex whole, but it is not the case that all social causality is of equal importance in determining the overall shape of things, the long-term, macrohistorical patterns. One does not have to endorse crude base-and-superstructure formulations, but without some theoretical commitment to explanatory materialism in sociopolitical theory, it is dubious that what remains can really count as "Marxism" any more.

Now West's synthesis draws not merely on the "big three" upon which we have focused (Marxism, pragmatism, Christianity), but also on other competing social theories to remedy Marxism's deficiencies. So the already-existing potential in the original combination for intertheoretical inconsistencies is even further increased. His analysis of Black oppression, for example, is what he terms a "genealogical materialist analysis," which calls not merely upon Marxism, but also neo-Freudianism and Foucauldian poststructuralism. The resulting conception, for West, is both "more radically historical than is envisioned by the Marxist tradition," and "more materialist than that of the Marxist tradition, to the extent that the privileged material mode of production is not necessarily located in the economic sphere":

> Instead, decisive material modes of production at a given moment may be located in the cultural, political or even the psychic sphere. Since these spheres are interlocked and interlinked, each always has some weight in an adequate social and historical explanation. My view neither promotes a post-Marxist idealism (for it locates

acceptable genealogical accounts in material social practices), nor supports an explanatory nihilism (in that it posits some contingent yet weighted set of material social
practices as decisive factors to explain a given genealogical configuration, that is, set of
events).[52]

But it seems to me that this is merely verbal conjuring. If location in the "psychic
sphere" can count as "decisive" determination by a "material mode of
production," and *not* "idealism," then "materialism" has been evacuated of all
content. You can call this various things, and it may even be right, but it is
ludicrous to still be calling it historical materialism.

Moreover, there is a tension between a historical-materialist explanatory framework and the frameworks implicit in Christianity and pragmatism. Christianity
may have no social theory as such, but insofar as it has a "conception of human
nature and human history" (see above), it is at least minimally committed to what
could be characterized as a naive individualism, for which personal choice, moral
character, and im/moral motivation are explanatorily crucial. And pragmatism, as
West describes it (at least for Royce and Dewey), is explicitly voluntaristic,
"putting a premium on human will, human power and human action."[53]

But while human causality *is* ultimately central for Marxism, human action takes
place in an arena dominated by the congelations of *past* human causality, so that
classes, institutions, and social structures are the real engines of the social process.
Accordingly, Marxism is famous for its *anti*-voluntaristic understanding of the
social order, its repeated emphasis – for example, throughout *The German Ideology*
– that it is by no means a matter of mere "will," since people "act, produce
materially, and . . . work under definite material limits, presuppositions and conditions independent of their will."[54] So moral motivation and free-floating wills do
not make the world go round. The danger is, then, that in shuttling back and forth
between Christian/pragmatist and Marxist frameworks, one may end up giving to
God what is due to Caesar. A vocabulary of class domination, material interests,
shifts in patterns of capital accumulation, etc. is obviously radically different from a
moralized Christian vocabulary of conversion and the appeal to moral considerations independent of (or actually in opposition to) vested material interests, or a
pragmatist vocabulary of will. So there is at least a potential tension here in the
different views of the social dynamic presupposed by prophetic pragmatism's
different components.

A good illustration of the kinds of difficulties involved is the controversy stirred
by West's claims in *Race Matters*, and in his public lectures around the same time,
about Black "nihilism." West stated in *Race Matters* that "the most basic issue
now facing black America" is "*the nihilistic threat to its very existence*," nihilism being
"a disease of the soul," which requires a "politics of conversion" at whose center is
"a love ethic."[55] The idea of a "love ethic" had been introduced in earlier writings
in connection with Martin Luther King, Jr's study of Gandhi's philosophy:

The love ethic of Jesus Christ was a moral and practical method – a way of life and way of struggle in which oppressed people could fight for freedom without inflicting violence on the oppressor.... In this sense, the application of the love ethic of Jesus Christ in the social sphere requires not only tremendous moral discipline and fortitude, but also *profound trust* in the redemptive power of love and in the salvific plan of God.[56]

For King, however, it was part of a program of nonviolent protest. In West's appropriation, by contrast, the political program seems to have vanished and it is just a matter of individualized redemption. Thus the effect – in a popular book that has sold 400,000 copies – is to cede theoretical ground to the right.

Stephen Steinberg argues that West's conceptualization of the issue obviates the need for "expensive new programs of social reconstruction," thereby tacitly underwriting a conservative agenda:

One cannot fault West for trying to bridge the chasm between religion and politics. However, he has not placed himself in the tradition of Martin Luther King, Jr., who invoked religious symbols and appealed to spiritual values in order to mobilize popular support behind a political movement. King did not believe that a love ethic could ever serve as an antidote to spiritual breakdown. The only remedy was a political transformation that eliminated the conditions that eat away at the human spirit. West, on the other hand, offers no political framework for his so-called politics of conversion. Indeed, he explicitly divorces nihilism from political economy.[57]

Less harshly, but somewhat similarly, David Theo Goldberg argues that West's analysis in *Race Matters* critiques the "egoistic individualism" of the liberal model by appealing to a "background communitarianism," and frames racist exclusion in terms of "hate," so that the corresponding solution turns out to be "self-love and love of others": "These two framing ideas – communitarianism and a call for love – draw West away from a more radical focus on political economy and the continuing legacy of racist discourse." The overall result is that his "radical critical voice [is] muted," as he "seems moved to adopt a set of terms widely circulating in the public domain even as he has critically rejected the presuppositions on which they are based."[58] In sum, the uneasy relationship between West's divergent frameworks pulls him here into a position dubiously defensible as a product of any viable intellectual synthesis between them.

Many other examples could be cited, though space prohibits any detailed exploration of them. A commitment to science and the empirical method is common to both pragmatism and Marxism (with a greater emphasis on theory for the latter), and Stuhr sees this as important enough to be listed as a "defining characteristic and commitment" of pragmatism in general. But West's poststructuralist sympathies block a consistent extension of a scientific methodology to the social world. Thus he endorses Rorty's version of pragmatism, which repudiates the Enlightenment quest, and denies the need for evidentiary norms for religious beliefs. Yet at the same time, West is critical of Rorty for his cavalier attitude toward social theory, and insists on the importance of theory for political trans-formation. But if the shape of the world doesn't really matter, why should theorizing it be important? Normatively, he seeks to redeem official Marxism's somewhat arid and instrumentalist moral consciousness with the values of individ-uality and democracy from the Christian and pragmatist traditions. But he also flirts with Foucauldian and Nietzschean conceptions which are notorious for undermining the normative foundations of any positive humanistic account of moral values. Isn't this trying to have things both ways? Metatheoretically, he claims to find common, converging historicist assumptions in both the descriptive and moral realm for pragmatism, Marxism, and Christianity. But the most import-ant body of Christian normative thought is natural law theory, which is famous for being objectivist, and both Christianity and Marxism would be dubious about his watering down of the significance of the truth-claims in factual judgments about the world. If prophetic pragmatism is essentially about speaking truth to power, if that is where it gets its rhetorical impact, then doesn't the whole enterprise become somewhat bathetic if "truth" is diluted down to the "needs" and "interests" of particular communities?[59] Existentially, the categories of the "absurd" and the "tragic" loom increasingly large in his work, and part of the motive for assuming the "Chekhovian Christian" identity is that it helps him deal with these problems. But from a left point of view, "absurdity" is one face of Marxist "contradiction," the blocking of socially desirable and technologically achievable alternatives not by cosmic jest but by class restrictions on social possibility, while "tragedy" often misnames as fated what should be seen as the blameworthy causality of the socially powerful.[60] Many things *are* genuinely outside our control in any system, of course (materialism implies this also), but the danger is that a theocentric framework may lead us to mislocate the line demarcating the naturally ordained from the socially determined.

It may be that it is possible to reconcile all these conflicting commitments, but certainly it is no easy task. West is a high-wire artist juggling numerous theoretical balls, and while one watches in awe, one is also conscious of the long fall to the ground below.

(2)   But let us now turn to the more substantive issue of the political content of prophetic pragmatism. The point of locating oneself in the pragmatist tradition is in part to Americanize left-wing voices not usually seen as politically legitimate, and to make the issue of race a mainstream political concern. To this end, as we saw above, West designates Du Bois as a pragmatist. Robert Gooding-Williams, however, denies that this identification is plausible, and sees West's failure to make the case as having "substantive implications" for the whole project:

The figure of Du Bois bears the full weight of West's effort to link the progressive
feminist, racial and third world preoccupations of prophetic pragmatism to what
otherwise appears to be the received history of the pragmatist tradition. Subtract Du
Bois from this history...and that narrative will have little if anything to say to
progressive feminist, anti-white-supremacist and third world social movements....
Since, however, Du Bois's voice cannot be unequivocally or even plausibly interpreted as that of a pragmatist, and so should be eliminated from West's narrative,
West's representation of his voice as a repetition of Du Bois' voice, contrary to his
intention, is best read as marking a huge rift between his history of American
pragmatism and the politics essential to prophetic pragmatism.[61]

And in fact Gooding-Williams concludes that since West's twin intentions to map
the genealogy of American pragmatism and to represent himself and his own work
as the "most recent stage" of that tradition "stand or fall together," in the end they
"fall together."[62]

Now I do not myself know this literature well enough to adjudicate the
dispute.[63] But assume, for the sake of argument, that Gooding-Williams is right
about Du Bois having been misappropriated by West. From the fact that
(white) American pragmatism has not historically been much interested in issues
of racial subordination, it would not follow that it is impossible to develop a
Black pragmatism. After all, the same could be said about liberalism and Marxism.
In general, one needs to differentiate between the writings of particular theorists in
a tradition and the conceptual resources of the tradition itself; the latter should not
be collapsed into the former. Subordinated groups routinely try, with
differing degrees of success, to adapt existing bodies of political theory to address
their own concerns. Think of liberal feminism and Marxist feminism, and, corres-
pondingly, of Black liberalism and the attempts to develop a distinctively Black
Marxism.[64] Sometimes the central assumptions of the theory are intrinsically sexist
and racist, or at least incompatible with adequately theorizing gender and racial
subordination. But sometimes the silences or sexist/racist pronouncements are
traceable to the sexist/racist socialization of the theorists themselves, and the
theory is salvageable. So, *pace* Audre Lorde, sometimes it *is* possible to use the
master's tools to dismantle the master's house. Admittedly, it would be easier if one
could invoke Du Bois as a forefather. But there is the pioneering African-
American philosopher Alain Locke (mentioned, interestingly, neither by West
nor Gooding-Williams, though scholars such as Leonard Harris have seen him as
emphatically pragmatist, if a "radical pragmatist,"[65] and he is included in the Stuhr
collection). So the "huge rift" need not be unbridgeable. Note – with respect to
gender issues – that Jane Addams is excerpted by Stuhr as a feminist pragmatist, and
there is also the contemporary work of Charlene Haddock Siegfried.[66]

So this obstacle, even if it exists, is by no means insuperable. Let us move to the
politics. On the religious question, I suggested above that it was illuminating to

distinguish "thin" and "thick" senses of prophetic pragmatism, and I argued that the thin version was too emaciated to count as a substantive position. A parallel distinction can be drawn with respect to sociopolitical content. The "thick" sense would incorporate what I designated at the start as the descriptive aspect (what West terms "social theory") of a political philosophy. But West often uses the term "prophetic pragmatism" in what I would see as a "thin" sense that abstracts away from such commitments. Thus in a characterization reaching truly stratospheric heights, he writes:

> The distinctive hallmarks of a prophetic pragmatist are a universal consciousness that promotes an all-embracing democratic and libertarian moral vision, a historical consciousness that acknowledges human finitude and conditionedness, and a critical consciousness which encourages relentless critique and self-criticism for the aims of social change and personal humility.[67]

But who today is *not* going to claim they are committed to democracy and liberty? Obviously these values and ideals are now pretty well accepted by all sides of the political spectrum, except perhaps outright fascists. The real struggle will be over the content of these values – these are, to use W. B. Gallie's old phrase, "essentially contested" concepts. Libertarians in the Nozickian sense will certainly insist that they are committed to liberty, but so will many Marxists. The crucial question is whether it is negative or positive freedom that is at stake, whether economic constraints are seen as unfairly limiting freedom or not, and so forth. Similarly, in the grim Third World arenas where the Cold War was actually battled out, Western-backed counter-insurgency forces fought under the banner of freedom and democracy, as did the self-described liberation movements they were combating. So the hard questions are all avoided by this formulation, and one gets the political equivalent of an endorsement of Mom and apple pie.

The idea of a "historical consciousness" is equally unhelpful, since this is the very notion often embraced by conservatives who oppose it to the "abstract rationality" of the left, which they see as failing to take account of the shaping role of historical conditions ("human finitude and conditionedness") that preclude radically changing the human condition. Think of Edmund Burke and Michael Oakeshott, for example. Moreover, it raises the obvious question of *whose* history, since, as the "textbook wars" have shown, this issue is contested also. James Loewen's *Lies My Teacher Told Me* is subtitled *Everything Your American History Textbook Got Wrong*, and shows in devastating detail the systemic omissions and misrepresentations in texts used around the country.[68] Students raised on such orthodox accounts will have a historical consciousness quite radically divergent from those who accept the oppositional narratives of progressives like Loewen. "Relentless critique" can obviously be done from all quarters of the political spectrum, including enfilades from the right-wing think-tank or talk-show host, while an emphasis on personal humility is often found, for example, in religious conservatism, whose judgment is that as God's fallen creatures we should be waiting for posthumous rather than temporal deliverance. And of course one can be agitating for a "social change" that is a turning *back* of the clock to the good old days sanctified by historical precedent, as in right-wing communitarianism.

The problems of such an abstract formulation should be manifest. Why is West drawn to such high-flying characterizations? It could be that he wants a formulation that will recruit as many people as possible. Thus, in a sentence that has attracted the critical attention of a number of commentators (Martha Minow, Robert Gooding-Williams), he writes at one point that "it is possible to be a prophetic pragmatist and belong to different political movements, e.g., feminist, Chicano, black, socialist, left-liberal ones."[69] The apparent implication is that prophetic pragmatism rules out very little. (It might seem to rule out *non*-progressive movements, but – depending on what one means by "progressive" – even this is questionable, since there are obviously Black and Chicano activists who see themselves as part of the struggle against racism, but who are politically conservative.) So the danger is that prophetic pragmatism is being articulated at a level of abstraction so high that it can encompass pretty well anything. This slimmed down version has a normative commitment and a meliorist stance, deriving from Christianity and pragmatism, but in the absence of theoretically engaged sociopolitical descriptions it can point in virtually any direction. As Gooding-Williams comments, following Minow:

> it is hard to see how West could produce anything *but* mere campaign slogans without being more specific about what messages he wants to communicate to which particular political movements. Were he to become more specific, however, it is not clear that he could speak effectively to some of the constituencies he wants to court without alienating others. As West well knows, the politics of race, class, and gender often contradict each other.[70]

The basic point, then, is that what West seems to think of as a strength is actually a weakness. A political philosophy that can be endorsed by everyone, or nearly everyone, is not a political philosophy but a platitude. Hard decisions have to be made, arguments have to be given, rival analyses of the social order have to be decided between, different historical accounts have to be adjudicated. These questions cannot be sidestepped if a political philosophy is to give real guidance on the question of what is to be done. In the thin sense, prophetic pragmatism is simply a noncontender. Nearly everyone can agree with it at the abstract level, but the minute one has to descend to concrete questions of operationalization, the fighting will start.

So that leaves the thick sense, where the social theory *is* part of the package. In this sense, prophetic pragmatism's political content is based on a Marxism modified by the criticisms of the "new social movements" of the 1960s and 1970s. Thus in his "Reply" to critics of *American Evasion*, he writes that "The politics of prophetic pragmatism proceeds from a class-based analysis – with crucial racial, gender and sexual orientational dimensions."[71] And elsewhere, he writes, "my social-analytical perspective is post-Marxist without being anti-Marxist or pre-Marxist; that is, it incorporates elements from Weberian, racial, feminist, gay, lesbian and ecological modes of social analysis and cultural criticism."[72] So in this sense, West's views are familiar to anyone active on the US left in the past few decades. Without seeking, or believing that there can be, a "unified field theory" of oppression, he thinks some form of socialism is a prerequisite, or at least a major advance, for ending other forms of oppression, though they have their own sources and will need to be struggled against independently.

There are two basic lines of critique here, depending on where you stand politically. For those similarly located on the political spectrum, West's view is, of course, laudable, a position to which all progressives will give at least lip service (i.e. that they should be sensitive to issues of race, gender, sexual orientation, etc.). But it raises the question of how much work the eponymous "prophetic" and "pragmatist" components are actually doing in the combination. If the thin sense is not in itself substantive enough to count as a political philosophy, the thick sense is basically driven by contemporary radical theory, so that there is the danger of the other components seeming superfluous.[73] This is not to say that West himself has not done interesting and valuable work in what he calls "social theory"; for example, his "genealogical" analyses of racism and white supremacy. But the point is that this work is not integrally connected to either the pragmatism or the Christianity.

The idea of a synthesis carries the connotations of a fusion and transformation into something new, with the constituent elements radically changed. Perhaps the most famous synthesis in political theory is Marxism itself, which some commentators have seen as combining British political economy, French socialism, and German philosophy. Here, by contrast, what one really has is a somewhat uneasy and forced linkage of different elements. (Lewis Gordon comments that the combination is "more de jure than de facto.")[74] That the connection is not organic is illustrated by the ease with which the elements can be detached: by West's own characterization, as we saw above, religion is not necessary to it. Moreover, both the normative component and the practical orientation, which were supposed to be the distinctive contributions of pragmatism and Christianity, can if necessary be internally generated, or borrowed from elsewhere, indeed with better credentials. Marxism needs no external inspiration for its activist engagement with the world. And it is neither in pragmatism nor in Christianity but in contemporary *liberalism* – the Rawls and post-Rawls literature – that the different senses of "democracy," "freedom," and the ideals of individual autonomy and flourishing have been worked out in the detailed ways that can be drawn upon by Black theorists seeking a normative standpoint for a critique of the present nominally post-Jim Crow, but still racial, social order.[75]

Admittedly, though, as discussed above, the pragmatist and religious components can help to remove the "un-American" and "antireligious" stigma of radicalism, and to attract people who would be turned off by orthodox left theory. And normatively religion will provide an alternative spiritual foundation for those for whom classic humanist values are inadequate. But this brings us to the other line of critique. From the perspective of mainstream America, where, with the rightward shift over the past decades in the political center of gravity, even "liberal" has long since become a term of odium, the socialist component will be enough to doom prophetic pragmatism to irrelevance.

West's attempt to indigenize Marxism through pragmatism and to depict Christ as a revolutionary may have been able to accomplish something with respect to the "alien ideology" and "Godless atheism" charges. But in the postcommunist world of the past decade, the more fundamental criticism that has emerged – the final vindication of the Austrian school – is that socialism in the Marxist sense just *does not work* economically. Even if you can go to church, and there is no Gulag, you can't even get toilet paper, much less VCRs. So in a sense, one could conclude that quite apart from all the problems I have indicated, the time for (socialist) prophetic pragmatism may simply be past. The revival – though this is the wrong word for something never really alive in the first place – in some distant future of the socialist project in the United States will need, as a minimum prerequisite, to make persuasive the idea that this system can deliver the goods, and neither Christianity nor pragmatism can help much with that. With the end of the Cold War and the collapse of the Eastern Bloc, lefties are seen less as subversive bearers of an alien ideology than as outright crazies. West's recent work has veered away from political issues, and it is noteworthy that in his short 1998 collaboration with Roberto Unger, *The Future of American Progressivism*, the language throughout is of "reform," "piecemeal reconstruction," and the need for the "democratizing of the market economy in America."[76] The 2000 West so prominent in the mainstream Bill Bradley Democratic campaign is not the 1980s' West who was endorsing revolutionary class struggle. The past two decades have been painful for all of us still harboring socialist dreams.

(3)   I want to close by talking specifically about race, which is, after all, what we started with, and the problem we expect to be of primary concern in a Black intellectual's political philosophy. If socialism is not on the agenda, then what are the chances for the next best thing, a nonwhite supremacist, perhaps social-democratic, capitalism?

In addressing this issue, West's treatment of race is, I suggest, in crucial respects inadequate. I had not previously gone systematically through the West *oeuvre*, but I had automatically assumed (to report again on my unscholarly proneness to jump to conclusions) that it was full of analyses of race. But in fact it is not. There is remarkably little, especially considering how much West has written, and given his high public profile as a, or the, Black intellectual talking about race. There is no book-length academic treatment, and in the collections there are actually few substantial essays specifically on the subject – by my (surprised) count, no more than three.[77] West *refers* to race all the time, but rarely analyzes it in depth. He would agree, of course, that race has been central to American, and indeed recent Western, history. But it seems to me that the implications of this for his political philosophy have not been worked out, in terms of identifying the obstacles to progressive change. Goldberg comments on *Race Matters* that in the essays in this book West is "virtually silent about the central matter of racialized power."[78] I think this critique is of more general application. In his eagerness to distance himself from a narrow Black nationalism, and a vulgar Marxism, West fails, I would argue, to see, or at least to theorize, how central *racial power* and *white racial group interests* are to the functioning and reproduction of the polity. To the extent that, at crucial points, prophetic pragmatism rests its hopes for change on a moral determinism, or a self-proclaimed hybrid materialism that does not recognize the centrality of white racial interests, it is likely to be disappointed.

West often uses the term "white supremacy." But the sense he means is basically discursive, in keeping with the discursive turn in sociopolitical theory. A Black nationalist theoretical framework would put white racial domination, and white group interests, front and center. But Black nationalism tends to be separatist, sometimes predicated on biologistic or other mystified transhistorical assumptions of white iniquity, and in general not compatible with West's Christian cosmopolitanism.[79] A Marxist theoretical framework would make historicized material group interests central. But Marxist accounts of racism tend to be inadequate and class-reductionist, and in any case West is scornful of an old-fashioned materialism.[80] So the result is that in the ostensibly more-materialist-than-thou analysis offered by West's own "genealogical materialism," no mention at all is made of material group interests of a racial kind. On the material level, one could say, race does *not* "matter" for West! Instead, the theoretical emphases are on "the cultural traditions of civilizations," and the "three white-supremacist logics" of racialized Christianity, science, and the psychosexual. West does refer briefly to the "macrostructural" level, but this is a theoretical promissory note unredeemed in any of his other work.[81] So there is little or no discussion of the racial state and the racialization of the economy. He critiques past Marxist attempts to understand race, but his own proposed theory does not see the extent to which, in the necessary New World rethinking of Marxism, racial group interests attain a materiality of their own, so that white domination needs to be conceptualized systemically as a structure of power with its own material socio-economic "base."

Recent work in the (largely) white academy in political science, history, sociology, and legal theory is beginning to make respectable what for Black oppositional thinkers, academic and non-academic, has always been old news: that race and racism have been central to US history, and have foundationally shaped the political economy. Rogers Smith's massively documented *Civic Ideals* definitively discredits the orthodox Tocqueville/Myrdal/Hartz thesis that racism is an "anomaly" in US political culture.[82] Desmond King's and Anthony Marx's work demonstrates that where Black Americans are concerned, the federal government has not been weak and neutral, but strong and biased, with full citizenship historically denied to Blacks, and the "nation" constituted as white.[83] Matthew Frye Jacobson's history of whiteness shows that while American whiteness has evolved over time, it has always limited democracy, while David Roediger's work in labor history demystifies the myth of white wage-laborers concerned solely about class interests rather than their racial interests and the additional wages of whiteness.[84] Melvin Oliver and Thomas Shapiro track the processes by which wealth is accumulated to reveal the huge material advantage that being white in America has historically given one.[85] And in critical race theory, numerous theorists – Derrick Bell, A. Leon Higginbotham, Ian F. Haney Lopez, Cheryl Harris – have mapped the imbrication of the law with racial subordination and racial advantage, showing how "whiteness" is legally constituted, *de jure* and *de facto*, as "property."[86]

Now it seems to me that the complementary task such work suggests for the political philosopher seeking to conceptualize race is to take white supremacy as a global theoretical object: a political system, with ramifications for the workings of the state, the legal realm, and the economy, as well as culture and moral psychology, that tends to reproduce itself in significant measure because of vested material interests.[87] The realist tradition in political theory (which includes, but should not be reduced to, the materialism of Marxism, since it also encompasses such respectable fields as postwar pluralism) does not see moral motivation as playing the crucial role in major social change. Rather, *group interests* are the important thing. So a political movement to get rid of racism and white supremacy (not the same thing, since differential white advantage can survive racism's demise) needs to confront the obstacle of white perceptions of their racial interests, and to understand the ways in which white supremacy shapes moral conceptions and feelings of entitlement.

The recent research of two political scientists, Donald Kinder and Lynn Sanders, shows that of all the myriad groups in the United States, out of all the multiple identities that subject people to "various crosscutting pressures," it is race that emerges as "a single profound line of cleavage." Whereas "among postindustrial democratic societies, the United States tends to finish near the bottom on measures of class polarization," there is a racial divide in opinion on public policy that is without parallel:

> Political differences such as these are simply without peer: differences by class or gender or religion or any other social characteristic are diminutive by comparison. The racial divide is as apparent among ordinary citizens as it is among elites. It is not a mask for class differences: it is rooted in race itself, in differences of history.[88]

And they conclude that the single most important factor in the determination of these attitudes is whites' and Blacks' perceptions of their collective group interests, of group advantage and disadvantage.[89] "Group interests matter...through the threats blacks appear to pose to whites' collective well-being."[90]

Race is not just another group interest for whites, but in a sense the most important one, the one that tends to trump others when conflicts arise. A realist political project has to confront this fact, and, if socialism is no longer on the agenda, devise a strategy for making materially attractive to some section of the white population what has never existed in the United States: a nonwhite supremacist capitalism. The kind of moral appeal upon which West falls back at crucial moments will be of little help here. In the first place, realist assumptions (and isn't a "genealogical materialist" account supposed to be realist?) should make us skeptical that moral agitation on its own will be sufficient to overcome significant vested material interests in white privilege. And in the second place, moral values and moral consciousness will themselves be shaped and remolded by white supremacy. West cites the "prophetic" example of Martin Luther King, Jr's "American jeremiads...[calling] America back to its founding ideals of democracy, freedom and equality,"[91] and he claims that King's "all-embracing moral vision facilitated alliances and coalitions across racial, gender, class, and religious lines."[92] But as we saw above, even apart from race, there are standard left–right controversies about how these values should be interpreted. And once one takes white supremacy seriously as a global system, it should be obvious that the ideals will themselves be racially inflected, whether simply by being restricted in the scope of the populations to whom they are to apply (as at the founding), or through being operationalized by different rules by whites and Blacks. Kinder and Sanders, for example, have documented how differently Blacks and whites interpret such norms of the American Creed as "equality" and "individualism."[93] And the furore around the nomination of Lani Guinier demonstrated what hostility will be evoked by any suggestions to increase the fairness of representative democracy, and end the current white winner-take-all pattern (for example, through such "remedial voting tools" as cumulative voting and supermajority voting) that leaves Black group interests unmet.[94]

In sum, many whites will continue, consciously or unconsciously, to be influenced by what could be called – after Pierre van den Berghe's famous phrase to describe the United States, "*Herrenvolk* democracy"[95] – a "*Herrenvolk* ethics," a sense of "white right" that shapes their feelings of entitlement and moral fairness.[96] Far from seeing the dismantling of their differential racial advantage as a moral duty they have to recognize (even if they are reluctant to comply with it), they will actually view such measures as an unjust *encroachment* on their rights. Morally motivated racial reform would therefore have to achieve not merely the task, difficult enough in itself, of overcoming material interests by moral exhortation, but – even worse – that of overcoming the *combination* of material group interests and the conviction of moral entitlement.

Moreover, this realist analysis is not merely hypothetical and *a priori*. Philip Klinkner and Rogers Smith's recent book, *The Unsteady March*, makes a strong empirical case that significant racial progress in US history has been confined narrowly to three periods – the Revolutionary War, the Civil War, and the Cold War – and has depended on a peculiar combination of circumstances: war crisis, a strong domestic movement for change, and the willingness of white elites to back the movement for conjunctural reasons.[97] None of these applies in the present situation, and in fact the authors see us as in many ways going backward, repeating the post-Reconstruction regression of a century ago. Yet this is being done today precisely under a moral banner, in the name of national ideals of "color-blind" justice, individualism, equality, antidiscrimination, etc. Thus their analysis underlines the vainness of hoping for a redemptive moral transformation that is not linked to countervailing material interests. Any political philosophy seeking racial equality for Blacks and other people of color needs to face and grapple with this reality.

Conclusion

Cornel West's prophetic pragmatism is an original and stimulating contribution to political theory in general and to Black political theory in particular. Through both his writings and his public appearances, West has performed an admirable service in advancing national awareness about race, and preaching for a more democratic and inclusive America. But for the reasons I have indicated, prophetic pragmatism itself – at least in its present form – seems to me to be problematic as a solution to continuing Black oppression in the twenty-first century. In its thin version, it is too abstract and all-encompassing to really be counted as a political philosophy. And in its thick version, even purged of socialist commitments, it would need to be enhanced by a theorization of race that pays greater attention to old-fashioned material interests. One hopes that West, as our most prominent Black thinker, will put his considerable ability to the task of devising an analysis adequate to understanding and undermining the continuing reality of white racial privilege, by finding a vision that can activate alternative identities and mobilize other possible group interests for a transformative political project.

Notes

1   See his interview with George Yancy in Yancy (ed.), *African-American Philosophers: 17 Conversations* (New York: Routledge, 1998), pp. 32–48. Reprinted as "On my intellectual vocation." In Cornel West, *The Cornel West Reader* (New York: Basic *Civitas* Books: 1999), pp. 19–33. The *Reader* is a compilation of representative work on various subjects from West's previous twenty years' writings. Where pieces are reprinted in the *Reader*, I give both citations.

2   West's *Race Matters* (Boston: Beacon Press, 1993) was on the *New York Times* bestseller list, and according to West had sold nearly 400,000 copies by 1999: West, *Reader*, p. 514.

3   Among the harshest assessments are (from the right) Leon Wieseltier's polemic "All and nothing at all: the unreal world of Cornel West." *The New Republic*, March 6, 1995, pp. 31–6; and (from the left) Adolph Reed's notorious "What are the drums saying, Booker? The current crisis of the black intellectual." *Village Voice*, 40(15), 1995, pp. 31–6. Reed's piece – the fallout from which is still being felt – was not focused on West in particular, but was a general broadside against the "new black public intellectuals": West, Henry Louis Gates, Jr, bell hooks, Michael Dyson, Robin Kelley. The debate was continued over 1995/6 in the pages of *New Politics*, with the main protagonists being Reed and Manning Marable (West himself did not reply).

4   See, for example, Robert E. Goodin and Philip Pettit (eds), *A Companion to Contemporary Political Philosophy* (Malden, MA: Blackwell, 1993), pp. 1–4; and Jonathan Wolff, *An Introduction to Political Philosophy* (New York: Oxford University Press, 1996), pp. 1–5.

5   Thus Goodin and Pettit, while endorsing the conventional subdisciplinary partitioning, go on to include in their *Companion* sections on history, sociology, economics, and legal studies, as well as political science.

6   Iris Marion Young, *Justice and the Politics of Difference* (Princeton, NJ: Princeton University Press, 1990), p. 5.

7   Cornel West, *The American Evasion of Philosophy: A Genealogy of Pragmatism* (Madison: University of Wisconsin Press, 1989), p. 232.

8   Ibid., pp. 230–2.

9   Antonio Gramsci, *Selections from the Prison Notebooks*, ed. and trans. Quintin Hoare and Geoffrey Nowell Smith (New York: International Publishers, 1971).

10   West, *Reader*, p. 141.

11   Ibid., p. xiii.

12   Michael Lerner and Cornel West, *Jews and Blacks: A Dialogue on Race, Religion, and Culture in America* (New York: Plume, 1996); Sylvia Ann Hewlett and Cornel West, *The War Against Parents: What We Can Do for America's Beleaguered Moms and Dads* (New York: Houghton Mifflin, 1998); Henry Louis Gates, Jr and Cornel West, *The*

Future of the Race (New York: Vintage Books, 1996). Note, though, that Iris Young finds a reactionary gender politics in *The War Against Parents* (see her chapter in this book).

13   West, *Race Matters*; Roberto Mangabeira Unger and Cornel West, *The Future of American Progressivism: An Initiative for Political and Economic Reform* (Boston: Beacon Press, 1998).

14   bell hooks and Cornel West, *Breaking Bread: Insurgent Black Intellectual Life* (Boston: South End Press, 1991); Cornel West, *Restoring Hope: Conversations on the Future of Black America*, ed. Kelvin Shawn Sealey (Boston: Beacon Press, 1997).

15   Cornel West, *Prophesy Deliverance! An Afro-American Revolutionary Christianity* (Philadelphia: Westminster Press, 1982); West, *Prophetic Fragments* (Grand Rapids, MI and Trenton, NJ: William B. Eerdmans Publishing Company and Africa World Press, 1988); West, *American Evasion*; West, *The Ethical Dimensions of Marxist Thought* (New York: Monthly Review Press, 1991); West, *Beyond Eurocentrism and Multiculturalism, volume 1: Prophetic Thought in Postmodern Times* (Monroe, ME: Common Courage Press, 1993); West, *Beyond Eurocentrism and Multiculturalism, volume 2: Prophetic Reflections* (Monroe, ME: Common Courage Press, 1993); West, *Keeping Faith: Philosophy and Race in America* (New York: Routledge, 1993).

16   Robert Gooding-Williams, "Evading narrative myth, evading prophetic pragmatism: Cornel West's *The American Evasion of Philosophy*." *The Massachusetts Review*, 32(4), 1991/2, pp. 532–3.

17   Lewis R. Gordon, "Black intellectuals and academic activism: Cornel West's 'Dilemmas of the black intellectual.'" In Gordon, *Her Majesty's Other Children: Sketches of Racism from a Neocolonial Age* (Lanham, MD: Rowman & Littlefield, 1997), p. 195.

18   West, *American Evasion*, p. 7.

19   John J. Stuhr (ed.), *Pragmatism and Classical American Philosophy: Essential Readings and Interpretive Essays*, 2nd edn (New York: Oxford University Press, 2000), pp. 1–9.

20   West, *American Evasion*, pp. 4–5.

21   West, "Pragmatism and the sense of the tragic." *Reader*, p. 175. See also the related essay, "Pragmatism and the tragic." *Prophetic Thought*, pp. 31–50.

22   West, "Beyond Eurocentrism and multiculturalism." *Prophetic Reflections*, p. 140.

23   West, "The political intellectual: interview by Anders Stephanson." *Prophetic Reflections*, p. 81; *Reader*, p. 278; West, *American Evasion*, p. 71.

24   West, *Prophesy Deliverance!*, p. 21.

25   West, "The political intellectual," p. 81; *Reader*, p. 278.

26   West, *American Evasion*, p. 5.

27   Ibid., p. 7.

28   Gooding-Williams, "Evading narrative myth."

29   West, *American Evasion*, p. 233.

30   Ibid., p. 232.

31   West, "Religion and the left." *Prophetic Fragments*, pp. 13–21; *Reader*, pp. 372–9.

32   West, *Prophesy Deliverance!*, p. 16.

33   West, "South Africa and our struggle." *Prophetic Reflections*, pp. 184–5.

34   West, "A world of ideas: interview by Bill Moyers." *Prophetic Reflections*, p. 109; *Reader*, p. 298.

35   hooks and West, *Breaking Bread*, p. 8.

36   West, "Critical theory and Christian faith." *Prophetic Fragments*, pp. 112–13. Cf. "South Africa and our struggle," pp. 183–7.

37   West, "Afro-American revolutionary Christianity." *Prophesy Deliverance!*, pp. 134–7.

38   Ibid., p. 134.

39   West, *Ethical Dimensions*, p. xxiv; *Reader*, p. 11.

40   See, for example, West, "On the influence of Lukacs: interview by Eva L. Corredor." *Prophetic Reflections*, pp. 61, 64 (reprinted in the *Reader* as "The indispensability yet insufficiency of Marxist theory," pp. 214–30); West, "Beyond Eurocentrism and multiculturalism," pp. 139–40; West, *Prophesy Deliverance!*, pp. 99–101.

41   West, *Prophesy Deliverance!*, p. 140.

42   Martha Minow, "Cornel West delivers." *Reconstruction*, 1(2), 1990, p. 62.

43   West, "A world of ideas." *Prophetic Reflections*, p. 106; *Reader*, p. 297.

44   West, *Prophesy Deliverance!*, p. 140.

45   See, for example, Steven Lukes, *Marxism and Morality* (New York: Oxford University Press, 1987).

46   Rogers M. Smith, *Civic Ideals: Conflicting Visions of Citizenship in US History* (New Haven, CT: Yale University Press, 1997).

47   See, for example, John Mepham and David-Hillel Ruben (eds), *Issues in Marxist Philosophy, volume 2: Materialism* (Brighton: Harvester Press, 1979).

48   West, "On Georg Lukacs." *Keeping Faith*, pp. 155–6.

49   West, *Ethical Dimensions*, p. 166. West cites Marx's "Theses on Feuerbach" as evidence for his radical historicist interpretation (pp. 63–9). For a contrary materialist and realist reading of the "Theses," see Wal Suchting, "Marx's *Theses on Feuerbach*: a new translation and notes towards a commentary." In Mepham and Ruben, *Materialism*, pp. 5–34.

50   However, I can't resist the following familiar point of objection. Engels was clearly an ontological materialist, and explicitly represented Marxism as ontologically materialist in the popularizing books and pamphlets he wrote late in his life. If Marx were in disagreement on this issue, wouldn't he, as Engels's literary partner for four decades, have gently conveyed this fact to him at some earlier stage?

51   Marx and Engels, *German Ideology*, p. 41. For a discussion of different senses of "materialism" in Marx, see my "Is it immaterial that there's a 'material' in 'historical materialism'?" *Inquiry*, 32(3), 1989, pp. 323–42, and " 'Ideology in Marx and Engels' revisited and revised." *The Philosophical Forum*, 23(4), 1992, pp. 301–28.

52   West, "Race and social theory." *Keeping Faith*, pp. 265–6; *Reader*, p. 262.

53   West, "Pragmatism and the tragic." *Prophetic Thought*, pp. 37–9.

54   Marx and Engels, *German Ideology*, p. 36.

55   West, *Race Matters*, pp. 19, 29.

56   West, "Martin Luther King, Jr: prophetic Christian as organic intellectual." *Prophetic Fragments*, p. 10; *Reader*, p. 432.

57   Stephen Steinberg, "The liberal retreat from race during the post-Civil Rights era." In Wahneema Lubiano (ed.), *The House that Race Built: Black Americans, US Terrain* (New York: Pantheon Books, 1997), pp. 37–9.

58   David Theo Goldberg, "Whither West? The making of a public intellectual." In
     Goldberg, *Racial Subjects: Writing on Race in America* (New York: Routledge, 1997),
     pp. 123–6.
59   See Wieseltier, "All and nothing at all." In his unremitting critique of West, this is one
     of the few points with which I am in agreement.
60   Cf. Elizabeth Spelman's critique that West's invocation of the "language of tragedy"
     runs the risk of "exonerating white America": Spelman, "Theodicy, tragedy and
     prophesy: comments on Cornel West's *The American Evasion of Philosophy*." *American
     Philosophical Association Newsletter on Philosophy and the Black Experience*, 90(3), 1991,
     pp. 19–23.
61   Gooding-Williams, "Evading narrative myth," pp. 530–1.
62   Ibid., p. 518.
63   For West's reply, see Cornel West, "Response." *American Philosophical Association
     Newsletter on Philosophy and the Black Experience*, 90(3), 1991, pp. 26–8.
64   See Cedric J. Robinson, *Black Marxism: The Making of the Black Radical Tradition*
     (Chapel Hill: University of North Carolina Press, 2000).
65   See Leonard Harris (ed.), *The Philosophy of Alain Locke: Harlem Renaissance and Beyond*
     (Philadelphia: Temple University Press, 1989). Harris characterizes Locke's philosophy
     as "radical pragmatism" (p. 17). See also the Locke selection, edited by Harris, in Stuhr,
     Pragmatism, pp. 667–88.
66   Charlene Haddock Siegfried, *Pragmatism and Feminism: Reweaving the Social Fabric*
     (Chicago: University of Chicago Press, 1996).
67   West, *American Evasion*, p. 232.
68   James W. Loewen, *Lies My Teacher Told Me: Everything Your American History Textbook
     Got Wrong* (New York: Touchstone, 1996).
69   West, *American Evasion*, p. 232.
70   Gooding-Williams, "Evading narrative myth," p. 533.
71   West, "Reply," p. 28.
72   Cornel West, "The historicist turn in philosophy of religion." *Keeping Faith*, p. 133;
     Reader, p. 370.
73   Cf. Gooding-Williams, "Evading narrative myth," pp. 536–7.
74   Gordon, "Black intellectuals," pp. 195–6.
75   See, for example, David Cochran's case for the use of "autonomy" as an overarching,
     respectable liberal value to advance the cause of black equality in the present period:
     Cochran, *The Color of Freedom: Race and Contemporary American Liberalism* (Albany, NY:
     SUNY Press, 1999).
76   West and Unger, *Future of American Progressivism*.
77   Obviously many of his other essays deal in part with race, since they are talking about
     the black experience, but what I mean here is systematic academic investigations of the
     subject (as against the popular pieces in *Race Matters*). By that criterion, the only real
     candidates are: "A genealogy of modern racism." *Prophesy Deliverance!*, pp. 47–65;
     "Toward a socialist theory of racism." *Prophetic Fragments*, pp. 97–108; and "Race
     and social theory." *Keeping Faith*, pp. 251–70.
78   Goldberg, "Whither West?", p. 125.
79   West, *Ethical Dimensions*, pp. xviii–xix; *Reader*, p. 6.

80 West, "Race and social theory." *Keeping Faith*, pp. 257–65; *Reader*, pp. 256–61.

81 Ibid., *Keeping Faith*, pp. 265–70; *Reader*, pp. 261–5.

82 Smith, *Civic Ideals*.

83 Desmond King, *Separate and Unequal: Black Americans and the US Federal Government* (Oxford: Clarendon Press, 1995); Anthony W. Marx, *Making Race and Nation: A Comparison of the United States, South Africa, and Brazil* (New York: Cambridge University Press, 1998).

84 Matthew Frye Jacobson, *Whiteness of a Different Color: European Immigrants and the Alchemy of Race* (Cambridge, MA: Harvard University Press, 1998); David R. Roediger, *The Wages of Whiteness: Race and the Making of the American Working Class* (New York: Verso, 1991) and *Towards the Abolition of Whiteness* (New York: Verso, 1994).

85 Melvin L. Oliver and Thomas M. Shapiro, *Black Wealth/White Wealth: A New Perspective on Racial Inequality* (New York: Routledge, 1995).

86 Richard Delgado (ed.), *Critical Race Theory: The Cutting Edge* (Philadelphia: Temple University Press, 1995); Kimberle Crenshaw, Neil Gotanda, Gary Peller, and Kendall Thomas (eds), *Critical Race Theory: The Key Writings that Formed the Movement* (New York: The New Press, 1995).

87 For my own attempts in this direction, see Charles W. Mills, *The Racial Contract* (Ithaca, NY: Cornell University Press, 1997), and *Blackness Visible: Essays on Philosophy and Race* (Ithaca, NY: Cornell University Press, 1998).

88 Donald R. Kinder and Lynn M. Sanders, *Divided by Color: Racial Politics and Democratic Ideals* (Chicago: University of Chicago Press, 1996), pp. 34, 90, 287.

89 Ibid., pp. 261–89.

90 Ibid., p. 85.

91 Cornel West, "Martin Luther King, Jr." *Prophetic Fragments*, p. 11; *Reader*, p. 433.

92 West, *American Evasion*, p. 235.

93 Kinder and Sanders, *Divided by Color*, pp. 128–60.

94 See Lani Guinier, *The Tyranny of the Majority: Fundamental Fairness in Representative Democracy* (New York: The Free Press, 1994).

95 Pierre L. van den Berghe, *Race and Racism: A Comparative Perspective*, 2nd edn (New York: Wiley, 1978).

96 See Mills, "White right: the idea of a *Herrenvolk* ethics." *Blackness Visible*, pp. 139–66.

97 Philip A. Klinkner and Rogers M. Smith, *The Unsteady March: The Rise and Decline of Racial Equality in America* (Chicago: University of Chicago Press, 1999).

12

"Radical Historicism," Antiphilosophy, and Marxism

John P. Pittman

All our dignity consists in thought.... Let us then strive to think well; that is the basic principle of morality.   Blaise Pascal

Cornel West has for many years now done yeoman service for progressive causes, using his pulpit as "public intellectual" to hammer away at the legacies and realities of oppression and institutionalized inhumanity. West has also always articulated his philosophical account of his own political and intellectual commitments in lively dialogue with Marxism. The single most sustained piece he has written to date on the theme of Marxist philosophy was the dissertation he wrote for the PhD in philosophy at Princeton University in 1980. That text, originally entitled "Ethics, historicism, and Marxist tradition," was published in 1991, with only very minor changes, by Monthly Review Press under the title *The Ethical Dimensions of Marxist Thought* (hereafter cited as EDMT).[1] The 1991 edition sported a substantial new introduction in which West situated the writing of the dissertation within the flow of his developing political views and practices, both before and since his days as a graduate student at Princeton.

In the dissertation, West counterposes what he characterizes as Marx's adoption of "radical historicism" to the three leading philosophical attempts in the Marxist tradition to provide an ethical theory for Marxism: Engels's, Kautsky's, and Lukács's. He characterizes these three, respectively, as the "teleological," the "naturalist," and the "ontological" alternatives. In each case, he argues, the alternatives are not fully successful because they are advanced from positions within the problematic of objectivism and relativism that is distinctive of the Cartesian (and

Platonic) inheritance of the Western philosophical tradition. In short, West claims that these Marxists are insufficiently radical because they remain within the philosophical project which Marx abandoned. It is worth noting that these alternatives seem to be accorded increasing levels of respect and attention, and this respect correlates to the degree to which the respective alternative acknowledges the relative autonomy of human agency and is further removed from a mechanistic or reductive account of historical development. Alternatively, these three attempts at a Marxist ethics can be seen as three philosophical readings or construals of Marxism. Engels presents a straightforwardly precritical teleology; Kautsky a naturalism (mis)informed by a crude account of Kantian epistemology; and, Lukács a Hegelian dialectical ontology of the "identical subject-object." But ultimately these are all foils for a Marx configured by West as sharing an agenda with a post-philosophical neopragmatism.

I will try to show the difficulties with West's post-philosophical presentation of Marx after his own image. First, I argue that West takes considerable liberties with Marx, so much so as to raise questions about the integrity of the "radical historicism" West argues is Marx's own view. I will then take up the distinction between philosophy and theory that West makes a decisive feature of his presentation of Marx's own turn into a radical historicist. While West makes this distinction into a rigid dichotomy, I will argue that the approach he adopts in EDMT does not make the case he wants to of banishing what he identifies as philosophical considerations from the theoretical project he identifies with the post-1845 Marx. Third, I will suggest some basis for characterizing West's own version of radical historicism, a position I claim involves substantial philosophical elements of its own. Finally, I will consider some of the things West has written since the dissertation to examine to what extent his attitude toward Marxism has shifted since the basic line laid out in the dissertation.

I

It is worth pausing first to notice the organization of EDMT. In the introduction, West presents a "wholesale critical inventory" of himself and his "communities of struggle" (p. xv). Chapter 1 is an account of radical historicism. The second and third chapters trace Marx's early intellectual development, beginning with his letter to his father of 1837 through to his "adoption of radical historicism" in the *Theses on Feuerbach* and *The German Ideology* in 1847. There are three chapters dealing with the ethical writings of Engels, Kautsky, and Lukács, respectively, and finally a conclusion. In each of the main chapters, West pursues his argument by marshalling extensive quotations from the writings of Marx, Engels, Kautsky, and Lukács. I will focus my remarks on West's explication of what he takes to be the young Marx's "radical historicist" move, and the consequences of it, in the first three chapters of the dissertation.

The first chapter, which begins the text of the dissertation proper, spells out what West means by radical historicism. West's introduction of radical historicism is in a discussion of the traditionally conceived philosophical dispute between objectivism – West calls it "hard objectivism" – and relativism. Against objectivist assertions that "there must be necessary grounds, universal foundations, for moral principles" (p. 4) – the relativist affirms the context-dependence and consequent diversity of moral principles and standards. The various shadings of relativism differ in part according to how seriously they take the consequences of this affirmation to be. But what they share is this way of framing the problem, in terms which are derived from the objectivist positions. The relativists are fighting on enemy turf, as it were. West takes radical historicism to involve an abandonment of the objectivist framework altogether. It should be noted that although West introduces "radical historicism" in the context of a discussion of moral philosophy, in subsequent chapters he makes clear the applicability of this conception to critical trends in epistemology and the philosophy of science as well. And this very inclusiveness of the conception points to a basic ambiguity in West's use of the term – which sometimes seems to figure as one philosophical position contesting with and in opposition to others in the context of standard subdisciplinary academic formations, at other times as an alternative to philosophy altogether, a radically antiphilosophical intellectual orientation beyond the discipline itself. We will return to this point later.

What I want to draw attention to here is the peculiarity of juxtaposing this first, "conceptual chapter," as it were, to the two historically specific chapters that follow it. This chapter cites only one source, an article on moral relativism by one of West's mentors at Princeton, Gilbert Harman. It should be said – West doesn't say it – that the conception of "radical historicism" and the conceptions related to it that West discusses in that first chapter and throughout the work are all conceptions drawn from the "metaphilosophical" discourse of the second half of the twentieth century. These terms are then grafted onto a historically specific account of the development, in the second quarter of the nineteenth century, of Marx's youthful intellect. One will not find these terms and conceptions in Marx, or in the other Young Hegelians, or in Hegel. In saying this, I am not claiming that the issues pointed to by these conceptions were not implicit in the philosophical discussions in which the young Marx was engaged, or that it is a mistake to characterize Marx's development as having, in some respects, an antiphilosophical force. But there is something strangely aprioristic about the organization of the body of EDMT.

To a very limited extent, West compensates anecdotally for this structure in the introduction to the Monthly Review edition, written a decade later. In that introduction, entitled "The making of an American democratic socialist of African descent," West does acknowledge the decisive role of one of his professors in particular – Richard Rorty – on his intellectual development, especially when he was at Princeton. But even here West does not supply the full background relevant to the story. It is worth recalling that the mid-seventies, when the dissertation was written, was a period of extensive discussion of the metaphilosophical issue of "foundationalism" by its proponents and critics. This was a wide-ranging discussion, centering in the areas of epistemology and the philosophy of science, and focused on modern philosophy's obsession, since Descartes, with grounding all knowledge on absolutely certain foundations. Rorty was one of those arguing that the foundationalist project had collapsed and should be abandoned. His arguments derived in large part from consideration of recent developments in Anglo-American analytic philosophy, focusing especially on the work of Sellars, Quine, and Davidson. These writers had been challenging the supremacy of the positivist philosophical positions associated with transplanted Central European philosophers of science; this attack created an opening for "pluralism" generally and a neopragmatism in particular. Rorty took advantage of this opening, subsequently aligning his arguments with more global trends in twentieth-century thought, and with the names of Dewey, Heidegger, and Wittgenstein in particular. And although Rorty did not put it this way, it could well be argued that the significant impetus to and backdrop of these intellectual developments came from the unraveling of the "American century" made manifest in the rice paddies of Vietnam and the social movements that swept, in the late fifties, the sixties, and the seventies, through the campuses and streets outside the hallways of academe. Foundationalism had, since Descartes, given a central role to natural and especially physical science, closely identifying humanity's interests with the unbridled development and expansion of technology. In the sixties and seventies, it was beginning to become clear to large numbers of people how imperfect an instrumentality - technology is.[2]

By contrast, the philosophical situation facing the young Marx was fundamentally different in crucial respects. The disintegration of the Hegelian orthodoxy was already under way when Marx arrived upon the scene in Berlin in the early 1840s. An intellectual struggle over the interpretation of and to claim the mantle of the master's legacy between the left- and right-wing Hegelians was being fought out against the backdrop of political reaction and the consolidation of the post-revolutionary status quo in Europe.[3] The broader philosophic debate revolved around the interpretation of the Hegelian dialectic and its implications for the political and social agenda in post-Napoleonic Germany. Among the Young Hegelians more particularly, the issue was how to rework the philosophic – read Hegelian – inheritance into a critical weapon to advance the anti-absolutist and emancipatory agenda of 1789. Two of the most important themes taken up in the writing of the young Marx are the need to go beyond the Young Hegelian obsession with the criticism of religion and the problem of the backwardness of

Germany relative to (Western) European conditions. For Marx, these became wedded in a concern with the analysis of actual social conditions, an analysis he increasingly identified with the writings of French and British social theorists. The basic issue for Marx and Engels was not foundationalism as such; their concern was to open up the Left-Hegelian discourse to wider currents of European thought and turn it away from arid post-Hegelian interpretive disputes and toward the actual ongoing European class struggles from which the "German ideology" kept them sealed off.

What West does in EMDT, then, is to conflate these two substantially different historical moments and corresponding antiphilosophical movements by reading the one over or into the text of the other.[4] This might be taken, on one hand, as a political gesture of reinscribing the force of a political radicalism onto a contemporary movement of thought that is, otherwise, of less radical import and aspiration: an attempt to appropriate, in the name of a democratic socialism, the intellectual energies of proto-Marxism for neopragmatist post-philosophy. Less charitably, it might be seen as itself a symptom of Princeton-style analytic philosophy's indifference to the adequate representation of the historical actuality of philosophy's situatedness, a kind of disingenuous display of philosophy's presumed autonomy from history itself. For this style of philosophical theorizing, of course, philosophy is spelled with a capital "P," and refers to an ideality that knows no historical determination. One antiphilosophical movement must be in principle commensurate with any other. (It goes without saying that such a perspective amounts to a sell-out of the program of historicism from the get-go.) Or, to be even more blunt, this might be taken as an enactment of the colonization of the past by the concerns of an ahistorically conceived present effected by the collapsing of that past into the post-historical moment of neopragmatism's antiphilosophical and indeed antitheoretic new intellectual order. Indeed, while West works hard in EDMT to distinguish philosophic from theoretic terms and discourse – arguing that Marx correctly rejected the former in favor of an exclusive attention to the latter – he has come more recently to criticize and complain publicly about neopragmatism's – that is, Rorty's – wholesale rejection of both in favor of barely intelligible liberal pieties as a surrogate for either.[5] And, after all, EDMT is a dissertation, written, as West points out, in his mid-twenties, and, it should be added, fairly early in the neopragmatist breakout.[6] And it is perhaps fitting that it is in his doctoral dissertation that West should look to the philosophical canon for a figure to personify his own critical post-philosophical position; and that it is Marx who should be so personified. But such a political gesture should not be confused for a historically situated and nuanced account of the complexities of the intellectual situation attending the birth of Marxism.

II

West's account of what he calls Marx's "radical historicism" depends on the distinction he draws between philosophy and theory. This distinction takes on the character of an absolute dichotomy in West's account. The dichotomy is marked by the use of terms that suggest a fateful either–or with regard to moral discourse, though sometimes West presents it in less than absolute terms. "Instead of philosophic notions such as status, validity, objectivity, the radical historicist approach prefers theoretic notions such as role, function, description, and explanation" (p. 2). Although West is careful to frame the difference here as one of preference (that is, of degree) – to indicate the possibility of Marxist concern for questions of the justification and validity of moral claims – he elsewhere reads these kinds of questions altogether out of Marxist moral discourse. "The task of ethics," for the radical historicist, "is not *philosophic*, it is not to put forward irrefutable justifications of particular moral viewpoints . . . the [theoretic] task is to discover ways in which to develop a larger consensus and community . . . without the idea of a last philosophic court of appeal in the background" (p. 3).

The basis of this dichotomy, or at least the historicist's basis for grasping the theoretic side as opposed to the philosophic one, is that "The radical historicist approach to ethics . . . rejects the vision of philosophy as the quest for philosophical certainty, the search for philosophic foundations" (p. 12). West describes this as the basic "metaphilosophical move" Marx and all radical historicists make. It is by invoking this "move" that West summarizes Marx's turning his back on philosophy, emblematized in the famous eleventh of Marx's *Theses on Feuerbach* of 1845. In characterizing this whole development of Marx's thought as a "metaphilosophical move," West is implicitly reinscribing this development within the context of academic philosophic discourse. For "move" is a term of art in the rhetoric of that very discourse to refer to a moment in an argumentative strategy intent upon the attack on or defense of a contested philosophical claim or position. Similarly, "metaphilosophy" is a term referring to that subdisciplinary formation concerned with philosophical discourse concerning philosophy itself.[7] By characterizing Marx's turn from post-Hegelian criticism to critical-constructive historical theory as a "metaphilosophical move," West suggests that the new theoretical approach is, and should be, articulable within the confines of philosophical discourse itself. And much of what West does in the text is to provide a broadly philosophic account of what that "move" entails.

The dichotomy underpinning West's account is absolute in one sense, but not in another: the same distinctions that previously had been identified as philosophic, are, in other contexts, identified with the pursuit of theoretic aims by Marx:

> Marx rejects the fundamental philosophic distinctions of reality/appearance, object-
> ivism/relativism, essential/accidental in order to discard the aim of providing philo-
> sophic criteria, grounds, and foundations for reality, objectivity, or essentiality. These
> distinctions may be employed for theoretic aims, i.e., under-a-description, but they
> then are to be understood in a completely different way, having a different status and
> viewed as an instance of a dynamic human social practice. (p. 80)

Notice that West here could have characterized this as a revision and reconception
of philosophic discourse, but instead brings these distinctions under the sway of
"theoretic aims," contrasted radically with the philosophic aims construed as
foundationalist, by definition, it seems. The reality/appearance distinction is particularly relevant to the form of historicism Marx (and Engels) develops beginning
in *The German Ideology*, and becomes a crucial distinction employed in the critique
of political economy as well. As we shall see, West attempts to reconceive the work
this distinction does in Marx's "theory," as he insists on calling it.

West, in trying to articulate this border country between philosophy and theory,
distinguishes between Marx's radical historicism and his "materialist theory" of
history. It is between these two that the border lies, as the following passage
suggests:

> Marx's materialist conception of history is supported by his radical historicist view-
> point. . . . The materialist theory holds that a certain kind of social practices serves as
> the ground of history; and the radical historicist perspective claims that these dynamic
> social practices are revisable human conventions which cannot serve as immutable,
> invariable grounds, criteria or foundations for philosophic validity or objectivity.
> Marx . . . attempt[s] to replace philosophic grounds with dynamic and social prac-
> tices, . . . to replace philosophic concerns with historical, explanatory (i.e., theoretic)
> aims. . . . Marx's materialist conception of history, aided by his radical historicist
> perspective, leaves philosophy no space to exist. (p. 87)

Perhaps the most plausible way to read this passage is by assimilating Marx's
"radical historicist viewpoint" to the precincts of philosophy, and his "materialist
conception of history" to the realm of theory. But the last clause undermines such
an interpretation, as well as the very spatial terms in which it is conceived. For the
change effected is such as to leave "philosophy no space" at all. This way of putting
it suggests that philosophical discourse has, since Marx's "move," the "status" of a
superseded stage in a developmental process, one with a "logic" of its own, as
it were. Of course, here we are in danger of redeploying the kind of
"metanarrative," replete with its own version of rational necessity, that would
consign the whole project to the discredited lineage of those bad, grand philosophical systems. Not so "radical" historicism, after all!

Leaving aside for now this play of metaphors in and beyond West's text, I want
to pick up on another notable feature of the account given in the passage, as well as

elsewhere in the dissertation. West's specification here of "revisable human conventions" as a core conception of the radical historicist perspective seems to me to undermine his claim, at the very beginning of the passage, of a logical or conceptual continuity between that perspective and Marx's materialist conception of history. Indeed, on the very first page of EDMT, West connects the radical historicist project with the notion of "the contingent, community-specific agreements people make" in relation to moral norms and goals (p. 1). This bears out the seriousness with which we are to treat West's own radical historicist commitment to the conventional character of moral – and indeed generally of social – phenomena. But the materialist conception that Marx elaborates can only with significant distortion be identified with such a "radical conventionalist" account of social and moral phenomena. This way of characterizing moral phenomena is in keeping with West's own democratic socialist agenda, but hardly chimes with the agenda Marx spells out in his own writing about morality after 1845.

West goes on from there to elaborate the theme of the ideological function of "the illusory idea of philosophy's autonomy" which underpins philosophy in bourgeois society (p. 90). This conception results in "a radical distinction between moral practices and moral ideals": moral ideals are to be understood in terms of their "ideological role and function," while moral practices are to be seen as historically situated in a particular social, political, and cultural context. To the degree that Marx uses moral ideals in his own writing, it is only because it is historically necessary to do so. "When Marx claims that 'communists do not preach morality at all' he does not mean that communists do not employ moral language. Rather he means that this employment is unavoidable but never a sufficient means for social change" (p. 91). On the contrary, "it is crucial not to confuse changing people's moral ideals – sometimes a result of employing moral language – with changing societal circumstances, or even patterns of moral practices." West sees the "fundamental problem in ethics for Marx" as:

> the discrepancy between the rhetoric of universal interests and the reality of particular class interests within the limits circumscribed by particular systems of production and the boundaries of the concomitant social and political institutions and cultural ways of life. The problem can be solved only when the rhetoric/reality discrepancy is overcome. (p. 92)

This is possible, West claims, only with the abolition of private property and the development of a classless society. Thus the overcoming of the rhetoric/reality discrepancy is a practical matter:

> which will ultimately render ideology useless and permit the realization of the coincidence and transparency, i.e., publicity, of particular class interests and universal

societal interests. Therefore, to employ moral language without understanding the rhetoric/reality discrepancy in history and hence to preclude any practical way of overcoming this discrepancy is, in essence, to engage in rhetoric, to fall prey to ideology, and ultimately to impede the practical overcoming of this discrepancy. (p. 93)

Notice that the contrast here is not between the actuality of particular class interests and the absolute unreality of universal interests, but between the rhetoric of universal interests and the reality of particular interests which that rhetoric conceals. Indeed, he refers in the passage above to the eventual "coincidence" of particular class interests and universal societal interests. This raises a question about West's account of a Marxist ethics. This refers to the character – dare I say "status"? (identified by West as a "philosophic" notion) – of the conception of a "classless society" in which the "coincidence" of particular and universal interests becomes possible. How are we to evaluate this conception, which seems to be or to involve a moral ideal all its own? What would a "theoretic" analysis of this conception look like, and how would it be achieved?

But if the notion of an achieved classless society serves as a fulcrum for the entire project of a post-philosophical ethics along Marxist lines, then how much of an improvement is this over more traditional, "foundationalist" philosophical ethics? An achieved communism would represent the transcendence of what West calls the rhetoric/reality discrepancy in which particular class needs are masked in universal moral terms. This is where West's account of Marx's ethics ends up, as it were. But it is worth contrasting West's insistence on rejecting the idea of a "last philosophic court of appeals" with his indulgence of the "good utopia" of the "end-of-prehistory" conceptual scenario that fills out Marx's account of the resolution of the discrepancy between moral ideals and moral practices. The problem this prospect presents for West's post-philosophical construal of Marxist ethics is that of an achieved final, and therefore "ahistorical", standpoint beyond particular class interests, a standpoint from which no further self-critical "enlargement" of the field of moral discourse is possible. Here all demystification must cease, and so the theoretic function of moral inquiry is exhausted. If, as it appears from the foregoing, this prospect of achieved classlessness is foundational for this conception of Marxist ethics, then this conception is not, it turns out, "post-philosophical" in the requisite way after all. If not, then this Marxist ethics becomes a merely meliorist Enlightenment account of an indefinitely extended series of incremental improvements – a conception indistinguishable from a liberal humanism which, as much as any philosophical foundationalism, is a prime candidate for Marx to have "radically" gotten beyond.

West addresses these questions explicitly in the last section of his account of "Marx's adoption of radical historicism." In his discussion of the science/ideology distinction that is crucial to the self-understanding of Marx's political-economic writings, West poses the question: "How does Marx understand the status of his own critique of political economy?" (p. 95). The underlying distinction here "between appearance and reality" is characterized as a "theoretic rather than philosophic" one, because Marx is "concerned with the concrete problems that promote" the discrepancy between "what people perceive about societies" and what they don't. This concern on Marx's part is connected with a motivation to criticize and transform existing reality. West ultimately fleshes out the "theoretic" appearance/reality distinction by recourse to three notions identified with the terms "dialectic," "demystification," and "self-criticism." The first is Marx's "dialectical approach," exemplified by a citation of Marx's own characterization of dialectic in the introduction to the first volume of *Capital*. Central to that characterization is the assertion that the dialectic "includes in its comprehension and affirmative recognition of the existing state of things, at the same time also, the recognition of the negation of that state, of its inevitable breaking up" (p. 96). It is worth noting first of all that this passage is accompanied in Marx's text by homage to Hegel, whom Marx credits with being "the first to present [the dialectic's] general form of working in a comprehensive and conscious manner."[8] The second point to note here is Marx's invocation of the "inevitability" of the break-up of the existing order. Here we should recall West's caveat that Marx's employment of "necessity" as a category of analysis qualifies as theoretic rather than philosophic in kind. But the account is of a "method" (Marx's term) or "approach" (West's), a term which seems to slip through the dichotomy West is employing between philosophic and theoretic discourse, particularly given the context of West's recourse to it here: he is attempting to account for the "status" of Marx's discourse as scientific – that is to say, theoretic. But the appeal to Marx's "approach" here to account for or explicate the character of his analyses as "theoretic" seems to verge on circularity: what, it may be asked, makes this approach a "theoretic" rather than a "philosophic" one in the first place? (Indeed, this claim of Marx's is on a sufficiently high level of generality as to suggest the philosophic.) This circularity is illustrated in West's observation, shortly before the quote from *Capital*, that "Marx's radical historicist viewpoint leads him to acknowledge and accent the dynamic character of reality." Why is this not a "philosophic" viewpoint, insofar as it seems to involve a characterization of "reality" in general?

West summarizes Marx's dialectical approach shortly after the *Capital* quote as insisting "that there is something deeply wrong with any theorist who defends a state of affairs either by rendering it difficult to call this state of affairs into question or by refusing to acknowledge that this state of affairs is being called into question." He then attributes to Marx the belief that "this lack of genuinely critical posture holds for bourgeois economists principally because the very nature of capitalist society itself is deceptive" (p. 96). Now West fleshes out this notion that capitalism is inherently deceptive by quoting from Marx's famous discussion of the commodity-form in chapter 1 of *Capital*. But of course this raises questions about how the phenomenal appearances thrown off by a social formation can be inherently deceptive. West does not address such questions in EDMT, but it would surely be part of a clarification of Marxist theory to substantiate and elaborate such a possibility. And such an investigation would be substantially a philosophic one, insofar as in addressing its object – the systematic deceptiveness of a social formation – it would clarify concepts central to any thinking about social reality. The fact that one is concerned with "concrete problems" does not in itself insure against the eruption of philosophical problems in the course of inquiry – unless, of course, one has narrowed all philosophy down to the issue debated by post-positivist epistemology-centered Anglo-American academics in the second half of the twentieth century. What, after all, is a more "concrete problem" than that of the nature of the commodity in conditions of capitalist production, about which Marx claims, in the passage from the discussion of the commodity-form West quotes, that the analysis of a commodity "shows that it is, in reality, a very queer thing, abounding in metaphysical subtleties" (p. 96).

The systematically deceptive character of capitalist production leads to the second move West makes – an invocation of the "hermeneutics of suspicion," a phrase or conception derived from Paul Ricoeur, and identified by West as "a dialectical approach whose aim is primarily that of demystification" (p. 97). Demystification is connected by West to Marx's ability to "grasp retrospectively why [the pioneers of political economy] perceived what they did and why they may have been mystified" in other respects. But of course demystification and the appeal to the deceptiveness of appearances – and to what the political economists missed – implies an appeal to reality of just the kind that West wants to disallow as being unhealthily philosophical. In his discussion of Lukács's account of Marxism, West pinpoints Lukács's project as that of discovering a "new foundation" for social inquiry, "the 'dialectics' inherent in the nature of social and historical reality" (p. 161). Because West takes this to be a substitution of one kind of foundationalism for another, he criticizes Lukács's project, claiming that it "still clings to the realist, objectivist dream – that of appealing to a reality which allows us to adjudicate between competing theories about reality" (p. 165). It seems as if West comes perilously close here to a "philosophical" tangle of his own: for how can one demystify, uncovering the deceptiveness of capitalism, without "appealing to a reality" which allows adjudication between competing theories? (Marx, for one, seemed to have no qualms about appealing to reality, when he wrote, in a letter to Engels: "It is only by replacing conflicting dogmas by the conflicting facts and real antagonisms which form their hidden background that political economy can be transformed into a positive science."[9]) Why, then, does adjudication have to be from a neutral, theory-independent perspective?

West in effect acknowledges that it does not: he appeals, finally, to the idea of the "self-criticism of [a scientific] discipline," in this case the discipline being political economy. Self-criticism was the moment of Marx's "advantage over Smith and Ricardo," of his "defense of this theory against the bourgeois economists of his day" (p. 97). This "self-criticism of the discipline," results in an "augmenting or enlarging of the conversation among political economists, coupled with an augmenting or enlarging of the awareness of concrete problems or impending crises." And it is this, says West, that "signifies that this theory is 'scientific' and 'objective' and not mere ideology" (p. 98). West claims that because of his political commitment, Marx "calls into question crucial assumptions of political economy." This results in an "enlargement" in the sense that what had been taken for granted, and so not itself a topic of investigation, now becomes itself a question, an object of conversation. The political commitment involved is, of course, Marx's "political concern for the exploited working class," developed early in his career as a newspaper editor in the Rhineland, before he left Germany for Paris in 1843. West traces this political commitment and gives it a decisive role in Marx's intellectual development, particularly his "working through" the conundrums of philosophy and emergence on the other side as a post-philosophical revolutionary intellectual. So, in effect, Marx is able to effect an "enlargement" of the "conversation" of political economy because of the "enlarged" sympathies he brings to his critical intellectual activity to begin with. It thus seems that West grounds the "objectivity" of Marx's approach in his initial adoption of a commitment to the political project of emancipating the oppressed, a moment that might be traced, textually, to his declaration, in 1843, that "the criticism of religion ends with the doctrine that man is the highest being for man, hence with the categorical imperative to overthrow all those conditions in which man is a degraded, enslaved, neglected, contemptible being" (p. 41).

I want to call attention to the universality of that declaration, a universality belied only by the gendered noun which is its subject. This universality suggests two points regarding Marx's "moral project," if you will, and West's characterization of it. First, implicit in what West says about Marxism elsewhere, and since the dissertation, is a critical distance from the cultural falsity, you might say, of the very universality Marx puts, here, at the heart of his concerns and those of Marxism. And it is not simply that the universality of Marx's concern comes to be focused, famously and for the first time in that very piece of writing, on the "dissolution of society as a particular class" that is the "proletariat" (p. 42). Rather, as West, to his great credit, tirelessly insists, Marxist thought "is an indispensable tradition for freedom fighters... despite its blindnesses and inadequacies – especially in regard to racism, patriarchy, and homophobia" (p. xiv). West's critical distance – also a historical distance – is rooted in an "enlargement" of the community of concern to which he addresses himself. What is this, however, but a more rigorous insistence on the universality that is at the heart of Marx's original declaration? It is indeed remarkable to notice the force of this insistence in defining West's moral project. West himself grounds his project in the introduction to EDMT to his embrace of "distinctive Christian conceptions of what it is to be human," which include "the prophetic Christian identification and solidarity with the downtrodden and disinherited, the degraded and dispossessed" (p. xxviii). That introduction has as its focus both West's retrospective contextualizing of the dissertation project it introduces and a "wholesale critical inventory" of the engagements and identities that make up West's own subject position. Both of these concerns reflect West's ambition to capture the "radical historical conditionedness of human existence" in his writing. But this intellectual activity of situating himself and his work can also be seen as a kind of self-justification, in the sense he gives the word "justification" in the radical historicist approach. For West, "the notion of justification is understood to be a way of reminding ourselves and others which particular community or set of we-intentions (e.g., 'we would that...') we identify with" (p. 3).

It is striking that West's "particular community" is precisely one that is constituted by the insistence of the demand of universalism, of a Marxist-inflected Christian provenance. And there seems more to the "reminder" than the particularist reflexiveness of finger-pointing. For West's practice of historical situating is most aggressively Marxist, with the broadest category of historical conditionedness being consistently the "capitalist mode of production." Whether one chooses to characterize that as a "theoretic" or a "philosophic" conception may be just a semantic quibble. But the justification of the use of that conception cannot simply be a matter of reminding oneself which community one identifies with, nor of rehearsing some "historical record" to make sure one's gotten one's facts all right. The use of that conception, and of all the others that are called forth in its train, demands a continual effort to clarify, articulate, and specify their scope, applicability, and interconnection. That reflective, critical effort to see how "things in the broadest possible sense of the term hang together in the broadest possible sense of the term,"[10] is most honestly situated in acknowledgment of its filiation with philosophy in the broadest sense of the term.

III

Perhaps it has become clear by now how much slippage there is in West's employment of the philosophic/theoretic dichotomy, and how persistently what can only be described as philosophical questions seem to resist West's attempts to outrun them. While suggesting at one point that radical historicism leaves behind all concern with issues of validity and objectivity, West spends considerable effort to construct – whether successfully or not – a reformed, post-philosophical account of the validity and objectivity of the claims of Marx's political economy. While writing at one point of the "virtual disappearance of philosophy" (p. 76) given Marx's "metaphilosophical move" away from foundationalism and the quest for certainly, elsewhere West writes instead of "Marx's farewell to the old vision of philosophy and ethics" (p. 69), Generally, however, West presses the more radical of these two interpretive positions. But there is sufficient waffling to make it unclear which is the preferred view. So, for example, in the first chapter, in which he distinguishes between moral relativism and radical historicism, West maintains that "For the radical historicist, the task of ethics is not philosophic...[but] theoretic." Then, on the following page, he claims that the radical historicist "assumes a different conception of philosophy" than does the moral relativist, who is still captive to the old quest-for-certainty model (p. 4).

In the middle of the third chapter, on Marx's adoption of radical historicism, there is a passage in which West seems to suggest how he can have it both ways. This is, appropriately enough, in West's discussion of the decisive eleventh thesis on Feuerbach. After spelling out what he takes this thesis to signify in the context of Marx's work, West steps back to make a more general comment on radical historicism. He invokes four names as exemplars of this view: Pascal, Kierkegaard, Marx, and Wittgenstein. Then he draws a contrast between "the philosophically inclined radical historicist, like Wittgenstein," and the "theoretically inclined radical historicist, like Marx" (p. 69). While the former is concerned to "change the dominant conception of philosophy," the latter chooses to "leave the confines of philosophic discourse...and plunge eagerly into full-fledged theory construction." Notice, however, that after identifying four exemplary radical historicists, he hangs the distinction between the "philosophically inclined" and the "theoretically inclined" on the last two of these figures. What about Pascal and Kierkegaard? While neither one of them make it into the index (neither does Wittgenstein), they do resurface in the lengthy autobiographical inventory in the introduction to the Monthly Review edition. There West recalls anticipating, arriving at Princeton for graduate work in philosophy, "the undermining of [his] Christian faith" by the analytic philosophers there. But it turned out that "nobody cared about religious faith....So I kept my Pascal, Kierkegaard, Montaigne, Thurman, and Unamuno close to my heart" (pp. xix–xx). And, indeed, Pascal and Kierkegaard have been there, close to West's heart, all along.[11] Anyone perusing the recently released hand-picked collection in The Cornel West Reader will find their names popping up with considerable frequency: West doesn't write about them, but they do come up quite a bit in interviews. And it is quite appropriate that they are figures, for West, of Christian faith, indeed, of his Christian faith.[12] They could be characterized, as a pair, as "radical fideists," with more justice perhaps, than West's characterization of them as radical historicists in the dissertation. And, it would be tempting to say, they cannot fairly be grouped with Wittgenstein as philosophically minded, or with Marx as theoretically minded. They were, it is true, radically dissident from "the dominant tradition in the West" (p. 68). But that hardly seems sufficient to qualify them as radical historicists. Unless, of course, radical historicism does not involve substantively

more than such dissidence *per se*. This may, in fact, be West's bottom line, but he
consistently figures this dissidence in terms of antifoundationalism and the rejection of the search for certainty. Search for an objectivist certainty by philosophical
means, that is. And this does seem to be a commonality of the four thinkers listed.
It all depends, however, on what philosophical means you mean. A careful
examination of Marx's political-economic writings would uncover a very substantial philosophical core to the discourse which Marx presents there as
"scientific." The word as he used it has an unfamiliar, nineteenth-century German
significance, not far removed from Hegel, that involves reason that could only be
described as philosophic. To think that makes it unscientific is to accede to the
criteria of logical positivist provenance. The only theoretical basis for denying the
philosophical character of much of the *Capital* writings would be the adoption of a
narrow conception of philosophy, one focused exclusively on foundationalist
epistemology. But there may be other motivations as well. In his discussion of
Kautsky in EDMT, West comes down to speculation about where "Kautsky's
heart" is. We know that West's heart has been close to Pascal and Kierkegaard, two
"radical fideists" who, more than perhaps any other writers in the Western
philosophical canon, worked to articulate a subjectivist conception of certainty
grounded in Christian faith. And it is on that account, if any, that they might be
counted as dissidents from that tradition. Their dissidence is not from the determinations West specifies in focusing his attack on the foundationalist search for
certainty. For isn't it here rather a matter of what one takes to be foundational –
and of dissidence from the exclusively rationalist or scientistic description of what
that foundation is to be? Whether it is the Pascalian "reasons of the heart" or the
Kierkegaardian "leap of faith," the point of these "radical historicisms" is not only
to "make room for faith," but thereby to open the insular systematicity of
philosophical discourse to a "radical" and "existential" situatedness of the thinking
and feeling individual. But this involves a disconnection of such faith – a shielding
of it – from both the philosophical, representing the (from this standpoint mistaken) attempt to fully rationalize the foundations of religious faith, and the
theoretical, representing the (equally reductive and mistaken) attempt to have
done with religious faith altogether and provide a secular ground for the kind of
situated practical orientation an engaged historicism demands. For both of these
would threaten the required radical contingency such faith demands.

So, if we were to ask, given West's own formulation, is West himself a
"theoretically inclined" or a "philosophically inclined" radical historicist, what
response should we give? He characterizes himself, in the introduction, as a
"cultural critic with philosophical training who works out of the Christian
tradition," and this suggests a theoretical rather than a philosophical inclination.
But the context of this self-characterization is a section devoted to both West's
"prophetic vocation," his own shunning the role of "a theologian who focuses on
the sytematic coherency or epistemic validity of Christian claims" (p. xxix), as well

as to the "irreconcilable differences between Marxists of whatever sort and Christians of whatever sort" (p. xxvii). The differences are that "Christian insights speak on existential and visceral levels neglected by the Marxist tradition"; "Marxist thought is not and cannot serve as a religion," since it "does not purport to be an existential wisdom – of how to live one's life day by day." So it seems to me more accurate to characterize West as an "existentially inclined" radical historicist, in the sense that he wants to open a radical fissure in the texture of any systematic discourse on the historical situatedness of practical reflection. And it is this inclination that determines his distance from Marxist historical materialism, since his "conception of Christian faith is deeply, though not absolutely, historical," embracing, as it does, "depths of despair, layers of dread, encounters with the sheer absurdity of the human condition, and ungrounded leaps of faith alien to the Marxist tradition" (p. xxvii). Could it be that historical materialism is more "radically historicist" than radical historicism itself is prepared to be?

This question might deserve an answer in the affirmative if there were a philosophically active – but not philosophically articulated – conception of history lurking underneath the notion of radical historicism and its attendant philosophy/theory distinction. In the introduction to EDMT West says that his "basic claim is that Marx's turn toward history resembles the anti-foundationalist arguments of the American pragmatists," even though Marx continues to make "social explanatory claims" of a kind the pragmatists did not. Two pages later West identifies those social explanatory claims in describing the "twin pillars of Marxist social theory: historically specific accounts of structures such as modes of production, state apparatuses and bureaucracies, and socially detailed analyses of how such structures shape and are shaped by historical agents" (p. xxiii). West identifies these in the dissertation with "historical materialism," saving radical historicism to refer to the more abstract "metaphilosophical move" that is, in one sense, internal to philosophical discourse, consisting as it does of antifoundationalist arguments and the rejection of the philosophical agenda of "hard objectivism." This has the advantage of allowing West to gather all his philosophical heroes under one umbrella term, and a "radical" one at that. It has the double disadvantage, as I have already suggested, of robbing the account of these thinkers of much of their specificity, as well as reproducing the "old" philosophy's abstract and contextless alienation of thought from reality. In that way radical historicism remains firmly the reactive but ahistorical child of the ages-old tradition.

There may be some political point to this dislocation of Marx's purported radical historicism from his "materialist conception of history": while embracing the more abstract radical historicism, West can nonetheless distance himself from the specific shape of historical materialism as a "metanarrative," while draping his favored intellectual projects in the mantle of a conceptual radicalism relatively without content because "metaphilosophical." This slippage is effected in part through an equivocation on the sense of "history" and "historical" as employed in the passages quoted in the second and third sentences of this paragraph. The phrase "Marx's turn toward history" depends for its sense on the "reality" of a preexistent – or pretheorized – referent that shows on its face a determinate content – a content suggesting a fullness of assurance that we have here escaped the empty abstractness of the merely philosophical. Yet in characterizing the two "pillars" – and what more "foundationalist" image could be had? – of social theory, "historical" seems to have the sense, in its first use, of an "under-a-description" place-holder indifferent as between different possible (conceptual) determinations of that description – and hence allowing the radical flexibility or openness of revisionist redescriptions. Its second use in that passage, in "historical agents," reverts to an already given, conceptually determined "history" seemingly independent of whichever "historically specific accounts" one is intent on giving. This second sense points to a philosophical conception of history distinct from historical materialism, one which figures crucially in West's account of his own philosophical interests as:

> motivated primarily by the radical historical conditionedness of human existence and the ways in which possibilities and potentialities are created, seized, and missed by individuals and communities within this ever changing conditionedness, including our inescapable death, illness, and disappointment. (p. xvii)

This conception of history is "philosophical" in appealing to an absolute characterization of an inescapable reality, one captured equally well in Pascal's bitter summary of the lineaments of an all-too-human life: "The last act is bloody, however fine the rest of the play. They throw earth over your head and it is finished forever."[13]

IV

This account of West's relation to Marxism might end there, but for a sense that much that he has written since EDMT is of significance for evaluating his continuing engagement with Marxism. At this point, I can only address one intervention that brings out most clearly West's further elaboration of what I have identified as a central difference of his project from Marxism – his assimilation of Marx to a thin version of the possibilities and prospects for social theory. The context is West's critical appraisal of "Fredric Jameson's American Marxism."[14] West criticizes Jameson for giving Marxism – albeit the reconstructed hermeneutical Marxism of Jameson's works – the function of "transcending" in thought the duality of "good and evil" among others. This particular contestation comes in the course of a discussion and critical elaboration of Jameson's reading of Hegel and of Nietzsche in what may be one of Jameson's most polemically Marxist texts – *The Political Unconscious*.[15] Jameson takes Hegel to have "gone beyond" the Kantian formulation of morality, with its foundation in the categorical imperative, and Nietzsche to have attempted an overcoming of the opposition between master and slave moralities through the life-affirming figure of the eternal recurrence. A substantive issue in this dispute concerns the radical intellectual's stance toward morality. While West stresses the political necessity of invoking moral discourse, Jameson is concerned to demystify any appeal to ethical identities, or "we-intentions," as a basis for political practice. Jameson consequently employs Nietzsche's account of moralities to foreground the deeper "historical con-ditionedness" of any "we-intentions." West responds with a reading of Nietzsche that assimilates Nietzsche's project to that of constructing a new social ethic, one in effect articulating the possibilities of a new social movement historically distinct from that of a modernizing bourgeoisie. My sense is that this is an "overly socialized" account of Nietzsche's textual productions, one that bends over back-ward to recoup a Nietzsche useful for a socialist project from the dominance of poststructuralist appropriations of his legacy. This leads West to underestimate Nietzsche's hostility to any collective politics, and certainly to the socialist and democratic ethos that he identified as the latest historical fruit of a slave revolt in morality – a revolt motivated by *ressentiment*. But what is noteworthy in West's response to Jameson's reading of Nietzsche is West's diagnosis of the malady at the root of what he takes to be Jameson's misreading of Nietzsche.

West sees Jameson's formulations as insufficiently "cured" of the poststructuralist attempt to conceptually transcend binary oppositions. According to West:

> Jameson reads Hegel through poststructuralist lenses in which "the double bind of the merely ethical" is a philosophical problem that demands categorical transcendence, rather than through Marxist lenses in which [it] is an ideological activity to unmask and transform by collective praxis. (p. 184)

In this connection West writes, contrasting his Marx with Jameson's:

> What is distinctive about the Marxist project is that it neither resurrects, attacks nor attempts to "go beyond" metaphysical, epistemological and ethical discourses.... Marx ignores, sidesteps and avoids discussions of metaphysical, epistemological and ethical issues not because he shuns his inescapable imprisonment in binary oppos-itions...but rather because, for him, the bourgeois forms of discourse on such issues are "dead," rendered defunct by his particular moment in the historical process. (pp. 186–7)

The difference here between West and Jameson seems to revolve around the question whether radical thought needs to constantly engage the "double binds" of "metaphysical, epistemological, and ethical discourses" or can be rid of them once and for all, because they have been "rendered defunct." West puts this in terms of the distinction between what he takes to be Jameson's aim of "categorical transcendence" and his own view that Marx "ignores, sidesteps, and avoids" such issues altogether. The difference between these two is vague; West continues pegging the outmoded or "defunct" formulations of issues as "philosophical," to which he opposes an activist stress on the collective action to overcome real conditions. But that contrast, though rhetorically charged, is, I think, unhelpful. The contrast should be that between philosophy and theory, though, as we have seen, that distinction on closer inspection is not as neat as it appears and obscures as much as it reveals. That this is what West has in mind is indicated by passages like this:

> Marx's rejection [of bourgeois ethics] is based on giving up the Kantian dream of ideal resolutions of moral conflicts, giving up the Hegelian dream of philosophical reconciliation of the real and the ideal, and surrendering the poststructuralist dream of philosophical transcendence of metaphysical, epistemological and ethical double binds. The Marxist concern is with practically overcoming historical class conflicts.... The Marxist aim is to discern an evolving and developing *Sittlichkeit* in the womb of capitalist society, a *Sittlichkeit* whose negative ideal is to resist all forms of reification and exploitation, and whose positive ideals are social freedom and class equality. (p. 185)

This passage reveals several things about the basis from which West's criticism of Jameson proceeds. The last sentence of the passage identifies the theoretic task using a Hegelian category transplanted into a Marxist obstetric metaphor.[16] It perhaps need not be said that this way of writing takes these categories and (mixed) metaphors for granted, using them as though their content were assured in advance, and despite what has happened since. This assurance may be related to the assertion that "the bourgeois forms of discourse on such issues are 'dead,'" but crucially it is these categories that are to fix for us the shape of "things to come." West's neopragmatic grounding of moral discourse in the reiteration of "we-intentions" is visible in his specification of the content of the *Sittlichkeit* to be discerned: moral discourse, for West, seems to have little cognitive function, serving only as a kind of strategic underwriting of the requirements of social mobilization. Finally, that "class equality" should figure as a Marxist ideal suggests some distance between West's "we-intentions" and Marx's use of the concept of class.

West, in concluding his account of Jameson, suggests that Jameson's works are "too theoretical" (p. 190). Here West's ambivalence to conceptually dense and articulated theory – shall we call it "philosophy"? – theory as such, and his neopragmatist reluctance to assign any cognitive function to philosophy, become evident in his criticism of Jameson. For one way of thinking of West's response to Jameson is that the latter makes critical demands on philosophy, whose usefulness for radical politics survives the activist rejection of an ahistorical foundationalist paradigm. It seems clear that Jameson puts stock in the possibility of a creative dialectical philosophical project, while West's intended trajectory is to leave philosophy, both as a disciplinary figment of academic organization and as a living option for critical theoretical activity, behind. This may be related to the fact that West's uses of Marxism always seem to be distanced, eclectic, taking up what formulations he likes, without concern for anything like the integrity or the development of Marxist thinking as such. This makes sense given West's deeply pragmatic intellectual sensibility – I mean a kind of scavenging and practically oriented disposition to draw upon theoretical traditions as resources for one's own purposes without felt constraint to renew those resources as such.

I cannot resist bringing all this back to the Pascalian–Kierkegaardian moment of what I have called West's "existentially inclined radical historicism" – that is, the one for which neither the theoretic nor the philosophic modes of intellectual articulation suffice. This intellectual stance is related to West's prophetic calling, representing, as it does, the mode of response of bearing witness, in an act of existential identification, with those who are suffering. This existential inclination might account for a refusal to take too much to a purely intellectually or conceptually articulated response to personally experienced quandaries or intellectual problems, a refusal motivated by a profound desire to keep himself open to the experience of these problems as existentially freighted absolutes. This should be contrasted, however, with Marx's labor in the British Museum, where his escape from the Hegelian philosophy of his youth propelled him in search of the means for uncovering the reality of the social contradictions of capital. That labor involved the sustained confrontation of conceptual contradictions with their social bases, a process that demanded a continued activity of critical thought trained upon the materials of social reality, an activity fully in keeping with the most vital tendencies of a long tradition of dialectical philosophy.

Notes

1   *The Ethical Dimensions of Marxist Thought* (New York: Monthly Review, 1991). Hereafter cited as EDMT. Page references are given in parentheses in the body of the text.
2   It is worth pointing out here that though Rorty, and to some extent West, provide a pragmatist reading of the unravelling of foundationalism, the story has other variants than the American one. Indeed, the explosion of what might be called French Nietzscheanism in the 1960s, and the opening up of Marxist discourse following the publication of Marx's early writings in the late 1950s, are also part of the story of foundationalism's late twentieth-century undoing.
3   It was only a few years before Marx's birth that his father Heinrich Marx felt compelled to convert to Protestantism to ensure his career in the provincial civil service.

4   Indeed, the evasion of historical specificity is even more elaborate than that, given the structure of EDMT summarized above. After positing a young Marx who speaks the language of contemporary analytic moral philosophy, that text goes on to present the views of the young Marx as providing the solution, in advance, to the problems confronted by representatives of three succeeding generations of European Marxist social philosophers!

5   See especially his afterword to the anthology *Post-Analytic Philosophy*, entitled "The politics of American neo-pragmatism," pp. 259–75.

6   Recall that Rorty's major repudiation of the analytic establishment, *Philosophy and the Mirror of Nature*, only appeared in 1979.

7   Indeed, this subdisciplinary formation is of extremely recent vintage, most likely postdating what West elsewhere describes as "the age of Europe" (1492–1945).

8   *Capital, volume 1* (New York: International Publishers, 1967), p. 20.

9   The letter is dated October 10, 1858, *Marx–Engels Selected Correspondence* (Moscow: Progress Publishers, 1975), p. 200.

10 This is Sellars's characterization, found in *Science, Perception, and Reality* (London: Routledge & Kegan Paul, 1963), p. 1.

11 The original version of the dissertation had four epigraphs: one quote each from Pascal, Kierkegaard, Marx, and Wittgenstein. Each of these is a disparaging comment on the reality of philosophers' practice.

12 I cannot help but point out the contrast here between two secular Central European "crypto-Jews" and two militantly antisecular Protestant "enthusiasts."

13 *Pensées* (Harmondsworth, England: Penguin, 1966), p. 82.

14 "Fredric Jameson's American Marxism," in *Keeping Faith* (New York: Routledge, 1993), pp. 165–91. Page references to this article are listed in parentheses in the text.

15 *The Political Unconscious: Narrative as a Socially Symbolic Act* (Ithaca, NY: Cornell University Press, 1981).

16 G. A. Cohen has recently emphasized the importance of such metaphors in Marxism.

13

Cornel West and Afro-Nihilism: A Reconsideration

Floyd W. Hayes III

Only recently has this nihilistic threat – and its ugly inhumane outlook and actions – surfaced in the larger American society. And its appearance surely reveals one of the many instances of cultural decay in a declining empire.

Cornel West, "Nihilism in Black America"

American life . . . is nihilistic to its core.　　　　　William Barrett, *Irrational Man*

Cornel West is commonly acknowledged as one of America's foremost public intellectuals. He speaks and writes with passionate grace, analytical power, and intellectual brilliance so captivatingly that he always demands attention. I have read much of what he has written, I have seen several of his public lectures, and I have watched his numerous television interviews. Whether reading or listening to West, I often find myself awed by the breadth and depth of his reading and thinking and by the eloquence of his presentation. His ability to integrate seemingly unrelated ideas and perspectives is awesome. For example, listen to West talk about connections between John Coltrane and Anton Chekhov![1] West, like only a few others, may very well come to join the pantheon of Black intellectuals headed by W. E. B. Du Bois. Yet West often is difficult to fathom, and some of his ideas are troubling. Because of his intellectually dexterous style, perhaps West is the figure of the enigmatic Black public intellectual in the evolving postmodern age of cultural and political complexity, ambiguity, and chaos.

As a Black American thinker, who pragmatically embraces usable philosophical fragments from existential, Marxist, Christian, social Democratic, and blues-jazz systems of knowing and feeling, West seeks to balance his philosophical concerns between the tragic sense of life and the more joyful dimension of living. Among his broad intellectual and policy interests, West focuses much attention on the issues of human suffering and redemptive resistance, particularly Black suffering and resistance in the face of anti-Black racial oppression, economic exploitation, and cultural domination. He challenges the absurd existence of white supremacy and its attendant forms of degradation. Indeed, he appears to speak on behalf of the disinherited and the disenfranchised masses of Americans. However, the more I read and think about West, the more I find myself struggling to understand his perspective. Perhaps this is as it should be when grappling with the work of a postmodern intellectual – one whose philosophical outlook on the world is pragmatic and antifoundational.

Nowhere is my concern about West's perspective more disquieting than with respect to his essay "Nihilism in Black America."[2] In this piece, West articulates what he considers the most serious crisis facing African America today: "*the nihilistic threat to its very existence*."[3] The way in which West designs his analysis of the nihilistic threat suggests that the problem is internally induced by African-American despair and dread. But what precipitates this existential predicament? In passing, West mentions that American civilization is nihilistic, when he says: "Only recently has this nihilistic threat – and its ugly inhumane outlook and actions – surfaced in the larger American society. And its appearance surely reveals one of the many instances of cultural decay in a declining empire."[4] Moreover, he clearly charges American capitalism and white supremacy with causing Afro-nihilism. Why doesn't West probe deeply into the ramifications of these lines of thought? Additionally, West offers a unique conception of nihilism. "Nihilism is to be understood here not as a philosophic doctrine that there are no rational grounds for legitimate standards or authority; it is, far more, the lived experience of coping with a life of horrifying meaninglessness, hopelessness, and (most important) love-lessness."[5] Why is West so selective in his definition of nihilism? These questions trouble me. Surely there can be no radical, or even revolutionary, vision and practice emanating from the manner in which West constructs the Black predicament in this essay.

My intent here is to reflect critically on West's challenging and often confusing essay, paying particular attention to deep-seated contradictions and dilemmas emerging from his perspective and ideological leanings. Following a careful exegesis of his argument, I want to suggest a radical alternative regarding the development and meaning of Afro-nihilism. Going beyond West's conception of nihilism, I want to argue that Afro-nihilism represents not simply consciousness of the absurdity of racist/capitalist oppression in America, as West seems to suggest. With the assistance of Nietzsche, Max Scheler, and Albert Camus, I assert that nihilism induced by white supremacy and capitalist exploitation gives rise to *ressentiment* within impoverished and disinherited African-American individuals and involves not merely a culture of criminality, as West seems to argue, but their outrage and rebellion against American social injustice. Afro-nihilism and its attendant *ressentiment* represent the death of faith in the promise of American democracy. They exemplify a fundamental disbelief in America's values, which the dominant culture itself has devalued. Nihilistic and decadent to its core, American civilization is caught in the throes of moral chaos, social anarchy, and self-annihilation. America is beyond redemption, for it represents a culture of death and destruction.

Afro-Nihilism as Blaming the Victim

In analyzing the causes of social problems and setting forth prescriptions for curing them, liberals tend to locate origins in the social structure and suggest changes in the social structure as the solution. Conservative social analysts generally point to problems within the individual and argue for changes in individual values, attitudes, and behavior. Correctly exposing the limitations or weaknesses of both these perspectives, West argues that what is needed is an investigative strategy that privileges culture and penetrates existential and subjective realities because of "the profound sense of psychological depression, personal worthlessness, and social despair so widespread in black America."[6]

By this, West means an interrogation of Afro-nihilism as a threat to Black American existence. "In fact, the major enemy of black survival in America has been and is neither oppression nor exploitation but rather the nihilistic threat – that is, loss of hope and absence of meaning."[7] Seeming to absolve white supremacy and capitalist exploitation from the causes of the African-American predicament, West locates the problem within Black individuals. This sounds like the conservative strategy of blaming the victim. Yet West also asserts, in passing, that anti-Black racism and a market-oriented mentality victimize Black people, suggesting that these twin evils give rise to Afro-nihilism. How confusing! How is one to make sense of West's contradictory claims?

West's characterization of the nihilistic threat to the dominant culture and to African America is problematic. He views the larger society's nihilism as recent, but sees Afro-nihilism as historic. This perception prevents him from identifying the dominant culture's nihilism or its racist capitalism as the external cause of Afro-nihilism. Apparently, then, Afro-nihilism becomes a self-generated phenomenon. Moreover, West's narrow notion of Afro-nihilism as a culture of criminality affords him the opportunity to talk about cultural strategies, structures, and traditions Black folk historically employed in order to resist the horrors of nihilism. Largely because of the selective manner in which he defines Afro-nihilism, West imagines that contemporary impoverished African-Americans no longer have the cultural armor to fight off the nihilistic threat. Rather, they have succumbed to antisocial impulses and behavior. Hence, West's theory of Afro-nihilism amounts to the conservative culture of poverty thesis that blames impoverished Black folk for their own predicament and for being unable to rid themselves of it.[8] He asserts that "it must be recognized that the nihilistic threat contributes to criminal behavior. It is a threat that feeds on poverty and shattered cultural institutions and grows more powerful as the armors to ward against it are weakened."[9]

What must be done in order to beat back the nihilistic threat to African-American survival, according to West? Sounding very much like the Black neo-conservative economist Glen Loury,[10] West once again places the burden on African-Americans. He calls for a collective and accountable structure of Black leadership that possesses the attributes of moral integrity, character, and democratic statesmanship. Moreover, he burdens this new leadership dynamic with the job of promoting a *politics of conversion*, which has at its core an ethic of love – self-love and the love of others. According to West, this is the kind of cultural politics that can restore a sense of human dignity, personal worth, and self-affirming hope to impoverished and depressed African-American individuals. Advanced by collective leadership, the *politics of conversion* works most effectively at the local level and within grassroots democratic organizations, according to West.

What is troubling about West's essay is that he completely lets the dominant culture off the hook. Much like the Black neoconservatives, who try to deny the central importance of white supremacy and capitalist exploitation, West requires nothing from ruling-class whites. Is the *politics of conversion* supposed to change their vicious and brutish hearts, minds, and conduct? Will the *politics of conversion* terminate or promote the termination of white supremacy and overthrow capitalism? Will it liberate Black Americans? Will it endow them with the power to struggle against the evils of white supremacy, economic exploitation, and cultural domination? Why does West assert the love ethic when, indeed, the dominant culture has devalued this and other higher values? Why doesn't West ask and answer these kinds of questions? I am terribly disturbed about his analysis of the African-American predicament and his suggestions for its amelioration.

What is required is an alternative conception of Afro-nihilism – its causes and consequences – that captures the meaning of the Black existential situation at the dawn of the new millennium. It necessarily entails a critique of West's constrained idea of nihilism. In what follows I attempt a reconsideration of Afro-nihilism.

Nihilism, *Ressentiment,* and Rebellion

I will undertake the development of an alternative and more expansive conception of nihilism – one that goes beyond West's perspective – by means of a theory of *ressentiment*. For nihilism and *ressentiment* do, in fact, constitute dominant themes in American civilization today. For West, nihilism is associated with despair, dread, and the tragic sense of human existence. It represents a form of human consciousness characterized by meaninglessness, hopelessness, and lovelessness. West rejects nihilism as a critique of rational foundationalism, preferring to conceive of this phenomenon as a more subjective or psychological dynamic in the lived experiences of tormented individuals. Additionally, for West, nihilism is bad and its adherents are criminals. In short, Afro-nihilists are low-life underclass individuals who need to be transformed by a *politics of conversion*. Does West's conception of Afro-nihilism provide a sense of agency to those individuals and communities victimized by the dominant culture? Whose interests does West's perspective support – those of the dominant culture or those of the oppressed and impoverished Black masses? Does his conception of nihilism provide a positive alternative for those Black people who are the victims of white supremacy and economic exploitation? Assuredly, not!

In the face of political, societal, and cultural decadence, nihilism also can represent a fundamental skepticism about the meaning of existing reality. In the words of Albert Camus, "A nihilist is not one who believes in nothing, but one who does not believe in what exists."[11] Feeling betrayed by the present state of affairs, the nihilist rejects as absurd the values and laws articulated by society's dominant culture, which itself devalues its own values and breaks its own laws. The nihilist becomes a rebel.

According to Nietzsche, *ressentiment* emerges out of the crucible of nihilism, which marks the deep pathology in modern Western culture and experience. Nietzsche uses the French word "*ressentiment*," according to Manfred Frings, because its meaning contains "a strong peculiar nuance of a lingering hate."[12] As a matter of fact, there is no German word for "*ressentiment*," and in German the French word is employed in common speech.[13] Nietzsche's account of nihilism pursues a diversity of interconnections among political experience, culture, and subjectivity, and it turns out to be a tale about how culture can refract oppression and perpetuate domination. Nietzsche's argument in *On the Genealogy of Morals* suggests that experiences of meaninglessness – with their attendant bad conscience and *ressentiment* – can be explained as psychological vestiges of political tyranny. Nietzsche's genealogical narrative traces "slave morality" or *ressentiment* back to original slaves, the most politically dominated and culturally dispossessed classes of ancient civilizations. From this representation one can conclude that *ressentiment* will manifest itself wherever political oppression is joined with cultural marginalization. In essence, *ressentiment* entails not only a consciousness of one's wretchedness, but also a personal outrage and outward demonstration against social injustice.[14]

Nietzsche asserts that *ressentiment* is a corrosive and contemptible impulse that contaminates anyone who experiences it. In a decadent and meaningless world, *ressentiment* masks a self-imposed helplessness (in contrast to the actual hopelessness of the real slave) and a consequent submissiveness. Even the person consumed by *ressentiment* may condemn the world. Nietzsche conceives of *ressentiment* as a destructive impulse that disables the mighty (as "bad conscience") and also incapacitates the weak. In Nietzsche's view, then, *ressentiment* is a basic dimension of human emotions in modern Western culture.

Inherent in the experience of *ressentiment* is the question of power, domination, repression, and revenge.[15] Following yet differing from Nietzsche, Max Scheler[16] understands *ressentiment* as a self-poisoning, but not a self-pitying, mental attitude that begins with a consciousness of powerlessness. Therefore, *ressentiment* is reactive rather than proactive. It is long-lasting and caused by the systematic repression of certain emotions. For Scheler, *ressentiment* is characterized by an assortment of sentiments, including revenge, hatred, malice, envy, jealously, and spite.

The hunger for revenge, Scheler argues, is the fundamental cause of *ressentiment*. This restless desire, which should be distinguished from active and aggressive sentiments, is a response to a prior attack or injury. Yet, according to Scheler, the attitude of revenge is not quite the same as the impulse of retaliation or self-defense, even when this reaction is associated with anger, fury, or indignation. What marks revenge, anger, and rage as the key determinants of *ressentiment* is that these impulses are restrained and repressed. The consciousness that an immediate reaction would result in defeat postpones these impulses. Hence, a recognition of one's helplessness or weakness in the face of the powerful accompanies the attitude of *ressentiment*.

Scheler points out that although revenge is *ressentiment*'s main ingredient, there is a progression of attendant impulses: envy, malice, and rancor. All of these sentiments, he says, come close to *ressentiment*, but they are not its synonym. The desire for revenge, and its related attitudes, vanishes, for instance, when one exacts vengeance, when the offender has been disciplined or has disciplined himself, or when one truly forgives the offender. Similarly, we cease being envious when the envied possession becomes ours. In contrast, *ressentiment* is an attitude that is much more encompassing and long-lasting than revenge, envy, hatred, or rage. As Scheler observes, "Revenge tends to be transformed into *ressentiment* the more it is directed against lasting situations which are felt to be 'injurious' but beyond one's control – in other words, the more the injury is experienced as a destiny."[17] Finally, *ressentiment* signals outrage at a social order that may articulate such lofty values as freedom, justice, equality, but that does not practice them. Scheler declares:

> *Ressentiment* must therefore be strongest in a society like ours, where approximately equal rights (political and otherwise) or formal social equality, publicly recognized, go hand in hand with wide factual differences in power, property, and education. While each has the "right" to compare himself with everyone else, he cannot do so in fact.

Quite independently of the characters and experiences of individuals, a potent charge of *ressentiment* is here accumulated by the very *structure of society*.[18]

Ultimately, Nietzsche hoped for an age free of *ressentiment*, or at least an age in which some Overmen and *ressentiment*-free thinkers would come into existence. To be sure, their time has not come. Rather, what seems to be occurring is a progressive expansion and intensification of *ressentiment*, subverting the hopefulness of Western culture's Enlightenment form of modernism. The emerging era appears increasingly to be distinguished not by a civilized pessimism but by a cold-blooded cynicism and a renewed nihilism.[19]

White Supremacy, Capitalist Exploitation, and *Ressentiment*

What is disturbing is that West overlooks the significance of African-Americans' terrorized and tortured lives during and after enslavement. West is too brilliant not to recognize that Black people's long-suffering experience at the hands of white Americans has produced a complex of reactions. Criminality is not the sole result of historic impoverishment.

As historic victims of racist oppression, Black people have had to struggle with the long nightmare of living desperate lives as outsiders within the crucible of Western civilization. In the particular case of the United States of America, the native African-American experience is unique, for its origins are characterized not by immigration but by chattel slavery – dislocation from Africa, relocation to America, and then isolation on slave plantations. Moreover, no war of independence liberated African-Americans, thereby creating their own sovereign nation-state. Neither has the nation mourned the death of millions of captured and enslaved Africans. Rather, the dominant culture continues to deny the significance and lasting political, cultural, and economic effects of Black enslavement and genocide. In the face of such horrifying and cruel conduct, the larger society possesses no sense of evil.[20] The result is that African-Americans have remained largely marginalized, ambiguously and simultaneously excluded from and included in the American political community.

In view of the above remarks, it might be useful to acknowledge that the argument here is not an appeal to transcendental or ideal *ressentiment*; rather, it is ordinary or general *ressentiment* that I examine in this chapter. *Ressentiment* is not a necessary or universal response to racist oppression. *Ressentiment* is not essential to Black identity. I do examine a complex of responses by African-Americans to white supremacy and capitalist exploitation.

For African-Americans, racial oppression is both a historical and a contemporary phenomenon. One can trace its genealogy back to the period of the Atlantic slave trade and chattel slavery when slave traders and slave owners sought to dehumanize captured Africans. Herein lies the original cause of the long nightmare of African-American *ressentiment*. Slave traders and slave owners based the entire filthy enterprise of enslavement on the premise that Black people were subhuman property, to be used, but not respected. As Orlando Patterson[21] has written, enslavement constituted for captured Africans a form of "social death."

In his classic study, *The Peculiar Institution: Slavery in the Ante-Bellum South* (1956), Kenneth Stampp recounts the psychological and physical violence slave owners employed to create the perfect slave. Stampp collected material for this discussion primarily from the manuals and other documents slave owners prepared on the system of managing and training slaves.[22] In order to dehumanize enslaved Africans, slave owners encouraged each other to impose on their slaves rigid discipline, demand from slaves unconditional submission, impress upon their slaves a sense of innate inferiority, develop in their slaves a paralyzing fear of white people, train their slaves to adopt the slave owners' value system, and instill in their slaves a sense of complete helplessness and dependence. Hence, slave owners developed a system designed to dehumanize, degrade, and depersonalize enslaved Africans. The psychological roots of African-American *ressentiment* grew in the soil of chattel slavery.

Grounded in the economic imperative of capitalist profit making, the system of chattel slavery in America represented a new era of human degradation reinforced by the ideology and practice of white supremacy and Black inferiority. Slave owners came to define African slaves and their American descendants as sub-human. Yet enslavement produced slaves with a variety of personality types. As historian John Blassingame points out in *The Slave Community: Plantation Life in the Antebellum South*, the command power of the slave owner largely shaped the personality development of the slave. A so-called benevolent slave owner might have good-natured, industrious, and trustworthy slaves. In contrast, the large majority of chattel slaves faced a daily existence of their owners' unrelenting and savage brutality: constant beatings, rape, cruelty, overwork, insufficient food, indecent living conditions, family and community destabilization, no formal education, and no health care. Therefore, the broad mass of chattel slaves – whether they became submissive, depressed, indifferent, or belligerent – despised, hated, and resented their slave owners. As Blassingame reports, "Often the slaves had to mask their feelings in their relations with their masters because of their attitudes toward whites. Most slaves hated and were suspicious of all whites."[23] Here is the source of Afro-*ressentiment*.

In the context of the United States of America, the dehumanizing system of chattel slavery and the vicious ideology of white supremacy that buttressed it have become deeply embedded in the nation's cultural and institutional beliefs and practices. After the Civil War, racial apartheid supplanted chattel slavery.

Significantly, a veritable culture of racism came to distinguish the American social order, notwithstanding the overthrow of the system of legal segregation.[24] Today, large sectors of white America exhibit a particularly virulent form of white supremacy. They may acknowledge disenchantment with powerful images of anti-Black racism, like the Ku Klux Klan. However, much of white America cynically refuses to see the systematic, historic, and *present* quotidian incidents of more subtle forms of racist culture – the refusal to rent or sell houses to Blacks in certain neighborhoods, persistent and increasing police murder of Black people, the legal system's decadent economy of Black incarceration, the use of various kinds of racially charged language in political and academic work, or the racial ceiling in matters of employment. As Lewis Gordon argues in his book *Bad Faith and Antiblack Racism*,[25] a particularly virulent dimension of anti–Black racism is its denial as ordinary lived experience. Such a denial is an act of bad faith or lying to oneself.[26] As legal scholar Derrick Bell declares, "Racism lies at the center, not the periphery; in the permanent, not in the fleeting; in the real lives of black and white people, not in the sentimental caverns of the mind."[27] Anti-Black racism is absolutely evil, and it is America's longest hatred.

America's culture of racism defines, delimits, and disfigures all aspects of Black social existence. The systematic practice of racist oppression dramatizes the being of Black people, constructing them as representations of absolute negativity. For instance, many white intellectual and cultural elites frame African-Americans as the criminal, ugly, lazy, weak, useless, undesirable, or unwanted segments of American civil society.[28] The absurdity of racial oppression forces Black people to experience life as a series of negations; they become the depersonalized markers of American society's problems: reverse racists, the underclass, the poor, welfare queens, gang bangers, or teenage mothers.[29]

However, what cannot be denied or overlooked is that postindustrial-managerial urban America has become a wasteland. It is a terrain where the prospect of a future has become increasingly questionable or even threatening for disinherited African-Americans, who continue to experience the process of dehumanization first introduced in the Colonial Era, and characterized by enslavement, segregation, racism, and capitalist exploitation. Entrapped by poverty and powerlessness, members of the urban dispossessed remain alienated from America's mainstream, while their institutions are under attack and their children are betrayed in public schools where the fundamental tools of knowledge have been discarded, academic motivation subverted, and positive character building perverted.[30] Embittered and angry, an expanding class of disenfranchised urban dwellers struggles to exist in a nation where inner-city unemployment is extraordinarily high and where this population's right to reproduce and survive in an age of advanced science, technology, and knowledge is a matter of growing concern.

University of North Carolina economist William A. Darity, Jr[31] argues persuasively that the African-American urban dispossessed may become even more endangered in the evolving postindustrial-managerial society than the traditionally poor were in the declining industrial-capitalist social order. Looking at the long-term trajectory of the postindustrial-managerial society, he theorizes that the new social order may very well spell the doom of disenfranchised urban African America. For it may become subject to the evolving social order's theory and practice of population management – the Law of the Progressive Elimination of Undesirable Population.[32]

According to Darity, endangered sectors of the population defined by the professional-managerial elite as culturally, mentally, physically, racially, and behaviorally undesirable – obviously, a population more inclusive than African-Americans – might become the victims of various managerial strategies of population control and extermination in the new knowledge-intensive and techno-scientific age. These might include such policy measures as mandatory abortions for unmarried girls, sterilization of welfare mothers, and a designated "optimum population." Additionally, undesirable or excessive members of the population might serve, wittingly or unwittingly, as guinea pigs for scientific experimentation and research, including genetic engineering, environmental modification, psychochemical drugs, and general physiological technology. In Darity's words, "The unlimited development of science, therefore, means unlimited potential for removing the managerial society's 'undesirables' forever."[33] As examples of what the future might hold, Darity points out that in the overwhelmingly African-American city of Washington, DC, the number of abortions annually exceeds the number of live births, and more than 25 percent of Native American Indian women in the childbearing years have been sterilized. If we add to this equation the growing plague of AIDS, the very survival of dispossessed urban African-Americans and other "undesirables" seems to be at stake in the developing postindustrial-managerial order.

Why doesn't West examine the historic legacy of African-American enslavement, capitalist exploitation, white supremacy, racist segregation, and contemporary urban impoverishment as sources of Afro-nihilism? Anyone taking the time to read him knows immediately that West is well informed about American history and contemporary developments. By ignoring these complex forces as catalysts for Black rage and anger, that is to say *ressentiment*, West produces an incomplete analysis that misreads the genealogy and character of Afro-nihilism and blames impoverished African-Americans for their own absurd and unjustified predicament. His neoconservative perspective allows him to be satisfied with an assessment of Afro-nihilism solely as criminal behavior, the perpetrators of which require transformation by way of a *politics of conversion*. This is unsettling.

Afro-Nihilism, *Ressentiment,* and Rebellion:
A Radical Alternative

West opens his essay with a long quotation from one of writer Richard Wright's works, *12 Million Black Voices*.[34] I am not quite sure why West used this piece, except that it is a nonfiction account of urban Black America. In it, Wright speaks about the possibility of Black death, but he also refers to the remembrance and importance of things past in America. But West forgets the past. He seems only interested in dealing with a Black culture of criminality and death. Perhaps West might more fruitfully have begun his essay with a quotation from or reference to Wright's novel, *Native Son*.[35] However, that would have forced West to take his analysis in a different and more complex direction. It would have required a different conception of Afro-nihilism, one more akin to a theory of *ressentiment* and Black rebellion. For in the words of Nietzsche, "The driving force is: *ressentiment*, the popular uprising, the revolt of the underprivileged."[36]

It so happens, then, that the long-standing and ever-present impulse of *ressentiment* gives way to rebellion. At times, the feelings of hatred, anger, and revenge are unleashed against the oppressor, transforming individuals experiencing *ressentiment* into persons who decide to embody a sense of freedom by resisting the injustice of a racist culture. I want to examine briefly Wright's perspective in *Native Son* because he has much to say about Afro-nihilism and *ressentiment*.

Richard Wright understood the significance of nihilism as an asset in the expression of Black culture. In contrast to West's constricted perspective that nihilism in some way denotes the death of meaning, Wright draws some significance from a definite nihilistic attitude that is hostile to anti-Black racist oppression.[37] Wright's powerful and shocking novel of ideas is instructive regarding the subject of Afro-nihilism and *ressentiment* in his representation of Bigger Thomas, the story's nihilist-rebel. Thomas is a young Black man caught in the corrosive clutches of urban Chicago's poverty, despair, and anger. White supremacy is an ever-present reality, circumscribing every aspect of his existence in such a way that he loathes both himself and others. He is a man of profound *ressentiment*, for he both fears and hates white people. Because of circumstances beyond his control, Thomas accidentally kills a white female. He later deliberately kills his Black girlfriend. Although he attempts to escape, Thomas is caught and tried in court for raping and murdering the white woman. Ironically, he is not remorseful for his crimes; rather, he expresses hatred for the dead white woman and indifference toward the Black girlfriend he murdered.

Wright skillfully constructs this situation in such a fashion as to transform Thomas from a man of *ressentiment* into a man of rebellion. In a long defense statement, Thomas's attorney points out the issue of *ressentiment* and its violent consequences:

Kill him and swell the tide of pent-up lava that will someday break loose, not in a single, blundering, accidental, individual crime, but in a wild cataract of emotion that will brook no control. The all-important thing for this Court to remember in deciding this boy's fate is that, though his crime was accidental, the emotions that broke loose were *already* there; the thing to remember is that this boy's way of life was a way of guilt; that his crime existed long before the murder of Mary Dalton; that the accidental nature of his crime took the guise of a sudden and violent rent in the veil behind which he lived, a rent which allowed his feelings of resentment and estrangement to leap forth and find objective and concrete form.[38]

The lawyer suggests that Thomas's *ressentiment* emerges from and reflects the Black individual's outrage about the lack of justice for Black people in America. Attendant attitudes, such as anger, rage, revenge, and spite, emerge out of the contradiction between the theory and practice of freedom and justice. Racial oppression, economic exploitation, cultural domination in a theoretically democratic society can result in intense Afro-nihilism, *ressentiment*, and rebellion. Thomas's lawyer later states:

Every time he comes in contact with us, he kills! It is a physiological and psycho-logical reaction, embedded in his being. Every thought he thinks is potential murder. Excluded from, and unassimilated in our society, yet longing to gratify impulses akin to our own but denied the objects and channels evolved through long centuries for their socialized expression, every sunrise and sunset make him guilty of subversive actions. Every movement of his body is an unconscious protest. Every desire, every dream, no matter how intimate or personal, is a plot or a conspiracy. Every hope is a plan for insurrection. Every glance of the eye is a threat. *His very existence is a crime against the state!*[39]

Thomas's violence represents the dialectic between the violence of the op-pressor and the counterviolence of the oppressed. Thomas's violence is as brutal as his perception of the marginalized, oppressive, and alienating character of his life. His predicament transforms him from passive victim to active rebel. And at the novel's end, Thomas takes responsibility for his violent actions, which allows him to experience a sense of freedom. He says to his lawyer:

I don't know. Maybe this sounds crazy. Maybe they going to burn me in the electric chair for feeling this way. But I ain't worried none about them women I killed. For a little while I was free. I was doing something. It was wrong, but I was feeling all right. Maybe God'll get me for it. If he do, all right. But I ain't worried. I killed 'em 'cause I was scared and mad. But I been scared and mad all my life and after I killed that first woman, I wasn't scared no more for a little while.[40]

Significantly, the spirit of rebellion exists in a society where a theoretical equality masks great factual inequalities. Wright's novel of ideas demonstrates why there is the ever-present possibility of revolt, and even anarchy, in American society. The Constitution and other sacred political texts, which set forth America's highest political values of freedom, justice, and equality, are the very heart and soul of the American social order. Failure to practice these political values results in corresponding problems of Afro-nihilism, *ressentiment*, and rebellion. When Black and other oppressed people of color lash out in forms of hostile insurgency – as, for example, in the violent 1992 uprising in Los Angeles following the exoneration of several white cops who brutally beat Rodney King – it evidences public outrage against structures of racist injustice. What West overlooks in his analysis of Afro-nihilism is that the practice of rebellion overtakes the attitude of *ressentiment* when justice is denied.

Conclusion

In this chapter, I have sought to examine critically Cornel West's argument with respect to Afro-nihilism. Although West suggests, in passing, that Afro-nihilism reflects the larger society's nihilistic threat, he does not pursue this line of analysis to its logical conclusion. Rather, he claims that the nihilistic threat to Black America emerges within the internal dynamics of African-American cultural life. Additionally, West's narrow notion of nihilism only allows him to understand Afro-nihilism as criminal behavior. I have challenged both claims, arguing that Afro-nihilism is a reaction to the dominant culture's nihilism. Moreover, I have argued that an alternative view of Afro-nihilism connects it with the impulse of *ressentiment* and the act of rebellion in a society that professes justice but practices injustice. Constrained over time, the attitude of *ressentiment* is both consequence and cause of African-American outrage about racist oppression, economic exploitation, and cultural domination. Chattel slavery and segregation characterized America's past; a deeply rooted culture of racism distinguishes its present. A great melancholy of human existence is that the past cannot be altered. However, the future can be refashioned, but only if reconstituted communities of people so desire. Presently, prospects for societal renewal in America are remote.

Significantly, the nihilistic threat to the larger American society is not recent, as West claims. On the contrary, American cultural and political life always has been thoroughly nihilistic. The nation's dominant culture always has devalued its highest moral and political values. A runaway market mentality and a consumerist culture have killed a belief in the Protestant Ethic. The dominant culture in America preaches to the mass public and to the world the values of freedom, justice, equality, and even the sanctity of human life. Yet, at home and abroad, Americans constantly have devalued and inverted those values by employing powerful systems of oppression, injustice, inequality, and mass destruction *since the establishment of the American polity*. White Americans increasingly engage in domestic terrorism. Importantly, their children increasingly commit mass murders in suburban schools throughout America. The nihilistic threat to American culture is substantial, and it is expanding.

At the beginning of the new millennium, American society is engulfed in a rising tide of social pessimism and cultural nihilism; it is a cancer of the spirit. Suspicion is mounting. Trust is declining. There is a growing sense of despair about the modern culture of progress that America is supposed to embody. An increasing proportion of Americans are skeptical about whether the institutions of progress are viable and beneficial: political leadership, public bureaucracies, business corporations, public schools, universities, political parties, religious organizations, the legal system, the mass media, and even the family. Popular discontent is becoming more comprehensive, penetrating, and corrosive.

What do these facts signify? They represent the cultural decay and disarray of a declining American empire. Plagued by an intensification of white supremacy, social anarchy, and moral nihilism, American civilization is culturally exhausted and headed for self-annihilation. Its racist culture renders the nation beyond redemption. America has no sense of evil. Where do we go from here, Martin Luther King, Jr once asked? Certainly not to the beloved community for which King hoped. An awareness of moral chaos and cultural death increasingly haunts the soul of American civilization. When all the current reasons – moral, aesthetic, religious, social, political, and so on – no longer guide the people's lives, how can they sustain life without succumbing to nothingness?

Acknowledgments

For their helpful comments on this chapter, I thank Deidre Crumbley, Rick Hill, Samuel Hay, N. Jeri Jackson, Mack Jones, and Carl Fpight. And a special thanks to my old friend Robert Chee-mooke.

Notes

1   Cornel West. "Chekhov, Coltrane and democracy." In Cornel West (ed.), *The Cornel West Reader* (New York: Basic *Civitas* Books, 1999).
2   Cornel West, *Race Matters* (Boston: Beacon Press, 1993).
3   Ibid., p. 12.
4   Ibid., p. 18.
5   Ibid., p. 14.
6   Ibid., p. 13.
7   Ibid., p. 15.

8 For example, see E. Banfield's *The Unheavenly City*, 2nd edn (Boston: Little, Brown, 1970). Also see T. Sowell's works *Race and Economics* (New York: David McKay, 1975) and *Ethnic America: A History* (New York: Basic Books, 1981).

9 West, *Race Matters*, p. 16.

10 See Glen C. Loury, *One by One from the Inside Out: Essays and Reviews on Race and Responsibility in America* (New York: The Free Press, 1995).

11 Albert Camus, *The Rebel: An Essay on Man in Revolt* (New York: Vintage Books, 1984), p. 69.

12 Manfred S. Frings, "Introduction." In *Ressentiment*, trans. L. B. Coser and W. W. Holdheim (Milwaukee: Marquette University Press, 1994), p. 5.

13 See ibid.

14 See R. C. Solomon, "Nietzsche, postmodernism, and resentment: a genealogical hypothesis." In C. Koelb (ed.), *Nietzsche as Postmodernist: Essays Pro and Con* (Albany: State University of New York Press, 1990) and "One hundred years of *Ressentiment*: Nietzsche's *Genealogy of Morals*." In R. Schacht (ed.), *Nietzsche, Genealogy, and Morality: Essays on Nietzsche's On the Genealogy of Morals* (Berkeley: University of California Press, 1994).

15 See M. Warren, *Nietzsche and Political Thought* (Cambridge, MA: MIT Press, 1988).

16 See M. Scheler, *Ressentiment*, trans. L. B. Coser and W. W. Holdheim (Milwaukee: Marquette University Press, 1994). I am grateful to my longstanding friend and philosopher Robert CheeMooke for bringing this book to my attention.

17 Ibid., p. 33.

18 Ibid.

19 See Solomon, "Nietzsche, postmodernism, and resentment."

20 See A. Delbanco, *The Death of Satan: How Americans Have Lost the Sense of Evil* (New York: Farrar, Strauss and Giroux, 1995).

21 See O. Patterson, *Slavery and Social Death: A Comparative Study* (Cambridge, MA: Harvard University Press, 1982).

22 See especially chapter 4, entitled "To make them stand in fear."

23 John Blassingame, *The Slave Community: Plantation Life in the Antebellum South* (New York: Oxford University Press, 1972), p. 209.

24 See D. T. Goldberg, *Racist Culture: Philosophy and the Politics of Meaning* (Cambridge, MA: Blackwell Publishers, 1993).

25 See Lewis Gordon, *Bad Faith and Antiblack Racism* (Atlantic Highlands, NJ: Humanities Press, 1995).

26 See also Lewis Gordon, *Fanon and the Crisis of European Man: An Essay on Philosophy and the Human Sciences* (New York: Routledge, 1995), and Jean-Paul Sartre, *Being and Nothingness: A Phenomenological Essay on Ontology* (New York: Washington Square Press, 1956).

27 Derrick Bell, *Faces at the Bottom of the Well: The Permanence of Racism* (New York: Basic Books, 1992), p. 198.

28 See M. Edelman, *Constructing the Political Spectacle* (Chicago: University of Chicago Press, 1998).

29 See N. Glazer, *Affirmative Discrimination: Ethnic Inequality and Public Policy* (New York: Basic Books, 1975), L. Mead, *Beyond Entitlements: The Social Obligations of Citizenship*

(New York: The Free Press, 1986), *The New Politics of Poverty: The Nonworking Poor in America* (New York: Basic Books, 1992), C. Murray. *Losing Ground: American Social Policy, 1950–1980* (New York: Basic Books, 1984), and C. A. Valentine, *Culture and Poverty: Critique and Counter-Proposal* (Chicago: The University of Chicago Press, 1968).

30 See J. R. C. Mazique, "Betrayal in the schools." In F. W. Hayes, III (ed.), *A Turbulent Voyage: Readings in African American Studies* (San Diego, CA: Collegiate Press, 1992).

31 See W. A. Darity, "The managerial class and surplus population." *Society*, 22 (November/December), 1983, pp. 54–62.

32 See W. A. Darity and S. L. Myers, Jr, *The Black Underclass: Critical Essays on Race and Unwantedness* (New York: Garland Publishing, 1994).

33 Darity, "The managerial class and surplus population," p. 61.

34 Richard Wright, *12 Million Black Voices* (New York: Viking Press, 1941).

35 Richard Wright, *Native Son* (New York: Harper & Brothers, 1940).

36 F. Nietzsche, *The Will to Power* (New York: Vintage Books, 1968), p. 108.

37 See N. De Genova, "Gangster rap and nihilism in black America: some questions of life and death." *Social Text*, 43 (Fall), 1995, pp. 89–103.

38 Wright, *Native Son*, pp. 330–1.

39 Ibid., pp. 335–6.

40 Ibid., p. 300.

14

On Cornel West on W. E. B. Du Bois

Lucius T. Outlaw, Jr

If all of my writings but one had to disappear, this essay is the one piece I hope would survive. Its fundamental point of the full-fledged humanity of black people continuous with that of others and Du Bois's lifelong effort to convince the West of this basic truth are at the core of my work and life. Needless to say, this essay is my first and only sustained encounter with the greatest of all black intellectuals – Du Bois.

As with any great figure, to grapple with Du Bois is to wrestle with who we are, why we are what we are and what we are to do about it.   Cornel West

I

There are a number of serious challenges to be faced when endeavoring to produce a critical writing about a person. Among these, there is the matter of the scale of the writing – a chapter, in this case – relative to the full life, not yet ended, of the person who is the subject-figure of the writing: the full sweep and complexity of his or her beliefs and convictions, actions and involvements, articulations and intentions, to say nothing of desires, hopes, and fears. As a quite engaged – one might say even *hyperactive* – very public "public intellectual" and scholar and teacher, Cornel West is a particularly busy activist and prolific scholar. No full, adequate account and critical assessment of his unfinished life and works can be provided within the scope of a single chapter.

How, then, to produce an essay account and an assessment of a hyperactive focal figure with a substantial and still growing legacy of writings, speeches, lectures, and ongoing engagements that can be judged fairly, by the writer and readers, as having veracity? On what terms, since such accounts and assessments are inherently interpretive ventures on the part of the producer? By terms set forth by the focal figure himself or herself? According to standards the subject did not or does not acknowledge and affirm explicitly but "should have" because they were in play appropriately in the organizational, professional, institutional, and/or broader enveloping and conditioning social contexts in which he or she was involved, thus making it reasonable to hold him or her accountable by those standards?

To my mind, it is important that, first and foremost, as much as possible, the endeavor to give an account and assessment of a person be of the nature of an *immanent critique*: that is, be governed by relevant norms to which the subject figure has committed herself or himself and that as critic one verify both the norms and the commitment. However, it is also important that the account-giver and critic take the substantial risks of reconstructing, if need be, of recapitulating relevant norms prevailing in the lifeworld contexts of the focal figure in order to hold him or her accountable on context-relevant prevailing terms and thereby to avoid, as best one can, producing a distorted and anachronistic account. Of course, lifeworld situations are seldom, if ever, so socioculturally and historically homogenous and monodimensional as to be without normative complexity and conflict. Settling, then, on the "relevant" norms is another venture in interpretation. All the more reason, then, why the critic is compelled to take due diachronic and synchronic account of complex social world(s) in which the focal figure was or is situated in recovering and recapitulating prevailing norms while giving due diligence to the formation of the interpretive framework and agenda in terms of which the account and assessment will be made. Unavoidably, one will be "taking a stand," as it were, in endeavoring to hold the subject figure accountable, with or without guidance from the figure herself or himself.

Still, in my judgment it is imperative that the account-giving critic not judge the focal figure by standards and agendas to which he or she had no occasion, as best determined, to consider whether to agree or not agree, implicitly or explicitly, to be bound because these norms were not available as real options. Certainly, I think, it would not be appropriate to judge him or her as having failed to comply with either norms and/or agendas of the present, those of the critic especially, with which he or she could not reasonably be expected to comply because the norms and/or agendas are artifacts of present conditions in which the focal figure did not live and which are substantially different from those in which he or she did live. Yet this interpretive stance is not to preclude asking important "what if" questions such as "Would so-and-so's convictions, actions, strategies, etc., of yesterday be appropriate in circumstances of today?" For questions such as this allow us to test the potential continuing viability of the orientations and efforts, the legacies, of predecessors.

There is less danger of my producing a historically anachronistic assessment of Cornel West since we are contemporaries, soul-mates to a large extent, and professional cohorts as well as close personal friends – which, of course, makes for other difficulties in producing an account and assessment that has veracity. Other challenges remain and are substantial. How to resolve them while offering a critical essay worth the reading?

By taking my guidance from Brother Corn' West himself and focusing on one of his writings in particular, "Black Strivings in a Twilight Civilization,"[1] an essay in which Corn' takes on W. E. B. Du Bois and one which he has singled out in a most poignant way: "If all of my writings but one had to disappear, this essay is the one piece I hope would survive" (prefatory note to "Black Strivings . . ." in *Reader*, p. 87). For the limited expanse and purposes of this chapter, I find this a most compelling criterion by which to select from the corpus of Corn's prodigious writings one piece to devote my attention to in endeavoring to understand and assess some of his efforts and contributions. The focal figure has identified a single work he would have survive among all he has written, and, apparently, those he expects to write. Furthermore, there is no need to worry about determining the author's intention in producing the piece, for Corn' makes this explicit: "Its fundamental point of the full-fledged humanity of black people continuous with that of others and Du Bois's lifelong effort to convince the West of this basic truth are at the core of my work and life" (prefatory note, *Reader*, p. 87). Of course, there is a need to be concerned about the extent to which authors – any people – can be assured of the degree to which they have a clear, firm, and undistorted grasp of themselves and their intentions, and of the degree to which, in offering any autobiographical representation, one is fully honest in one's disclosures about oneself. Critical caution, if not quite skepticism, is called for.

This is especially so when, as in the case of "Black Strivings in a Twilight Civilization," the writing project involves, among other things, the author's positioning himself against a person he regards as a "great figure," W. E. B. Du Bois: "this essay is my first and only sustained encounter with the greatest of all black intellectuals – Du Bois" (prefatory note, *Reader*, p. 87). Of particular note, however, Corn' makes it clear, in the prefatory note as well as in the essay, that he endeavors not only to take the measure of Du Bois in critical fashion, but to measure *himself* against Du Bois: "As with any great figure, to grapple with Du Bois is to wrestle with who we are, why we are what we are and what we are to do about it" (*Reader*, p. 89; *Future*, p. 57). These statements are not to be taken lightly.

Indeed, they have guided me in setting the focus of the limited agenda of this chapter: concentration on a particular writing by Cornel West in an endeavor to enrich my sense of and appreciation for him by taking critical stock of his assessment of W. E. B. Du Bois, and of his own sense of himself as someone who stands on the shoulders of Du Bois and seeks to take up his mission as an engaged scholar and public intellectual. Neither the occasion of this chapter, nor the circumstances of its writing, however, permit me to take on the full task of following Corn' closely in his characterization and critique of Du Bois's assessment and proposals regarding the enhancement of the lives and efforts of Black folk, and of assessing Corn's attempt to essay "the souls of black folk" – that is, to take stock of Black life in the USA and to set forth prospects and strategies for the betterment of Black life – on terms that, in my judgment, he believes best the efforts of Du Bois. Such a full account and assessment would require an essay of substantial scope. Here I will limit my focus to the sections of "Black Strivings..." that are primarily concerned with Du Bois, and even then I will not be able to take up all that is of significance in this very rich, provocative, and challenging essay in which Corn' marshals a cosmopolitan host of intellectual resources in striving to set, and hit, what he takes to be the highest mark for a proper public intellectual. Nonetheless, in pursuit of my limited agenda, I expect to learn more about Cornel West, a friend and colleague of great public notoriety and academic accomplishment by whom I am often inspired, frequently challenged, and from whom I continue to learn. And if Corn' is right about the consequences of grappling with notable figures, then I can expect that this essaying effort on my part will result in my learning more about myself. Hopefully, you, reader, will learn something of value about both of us that will make your investment in reading this chapter worthwhile.

II

I read "Black Strivings in a Twilight Civilization," by his own estimation, as Corn' West's most noteworthy offering of a critical generalized account of the efforts – the *strivings* – of Black folks in late twentieth-century conditions constitutive of the United States of America, a nation-state and civilizational project that, in his judgment, is in its "twilight," an offering he is confident will contribute to the enhancement of Black life. It is, however, an accounting and offering that he models after similar efforts by Du Bois:

> For those of us interested in the relation of white supremacy to modernity... the scholarly and literary works of Du Bois are indispensable. For those of us obsessed with alleviating black social misery, the political texts of Du Bois are insightful and inspiring. In this sense, Du Bois is the brook of fire through which we all must pass in order to gain access to the intellectual and political weaponry needed to sustain the radical democratic tradition in our time (*Reader*, p. 88; *Future*, p. 55).

However, of particular importance, "Black Strivings..." is not only an effort by Corn' West which he measures against similar efforts by Du Bois, but, as I read the essay, is an unmistakable effort to best Du Bois in providing the "intellectual and political weaponry" for engaging in the work of sustaining a tradition of "radical democracy" (which he is convinced is *the* necessary, if not quite sufficient, resource for envisioning and realizing for Black folk, to the fullest extent possible, individual and shared life of the very best humanity can produce and enjoy, and for *all* other peoples and persons as well).

The essay opens with "W. E. B. Du Bois is the towering black scholar of the twentieth century." Why? Because "The scope of his interests, the depth of his insights and the sheer majesty of his prolific writings bespeak a level of genius unequaled among modern black intellectuals" (*Reader*, p. 88; *Future*, p. 55). The second paragraph ends with Corn' positioning Du Bois's works as "the brook of fire" to be passed through if one would explore the relation of white supremacy to modernity and be concerned with alleviating Black social misery. But, in opening the third paragraph, Cornel declares, "Yet even this great titan of black emancipation falls short of the mark" (*Reader*, p. 88; *Future*, p. 55). In three paragraphs Cornel summarizes his having taken the measure of Du Bois and found him inadequate in providing what he (Cornel) thinks is called for in terms of "intellectual and political weaponry," his high regard for this "great figure" notwithstanding. From this point on, the essay, to my mind, is devoted not just to making the case for Du Bois's missing the mark, but to Corn's effort to both define and hit it, thus surpassing Du Bois.

How is it that Du Bois "falls short of the mark"? On what terms does Corn' take the measure of Du Bois? Well, first, Du Bois is "*the* towering *black* scholar" whose level of genius is "unequaled among modern *black* intellectuals" (*Reader*, p. 88; *Future*, p. 55; emphasis added). Du Bois is a "towering" figure of genius among *Black* scholars and intellectuals, though "we all," Corn' declares – apparently without regard for the raciality, ethnicity, or other factors of personal and social identities of those he refers to – must pass through "the brook of fire" of engaging seriously Du Bois's political texts if we are interested in matters of modernity and white supremacy and in mitigating Black social misery. As I read "Black Strivings...," for Corn' there are at least two categories of accomplishment in terms of which Du Bois is measured: one constituted by the efforts of Black intellectuals who explore Black life and do so particularly well; another constituted by the efforts of intellectuals, the most exemplary of whom for Corn' are not Black, though their not being Black is decidedly *not* a determining factor for him, since there will be stellar Black figures in this group as well. Rather, they are persons whom Corn' regards as having set the standard for plumbing existential depths not reached – and unreachable – by Du Bois because, in Corn's estimation, he suffered from two important and especially crippling shortcomings: "philosophic inadequacy and personal inability." "The grand example of Du Bois remains problematic owing to his inadequate interpretation of the human condition and his inability to immerse himself fully in the rich cultural currents of black everyday life" (*Reader*, pp. 88–9; *Future*, pp. 55–6). More pointedly, "My fundamental problem with Du Bois is his inadequate grasp of the tragicomic sense of life – a refusal candidly to confront the sheer absurdity of the human condition" (*Reader*, p. 89; *Future*, p. 57). For Corn', a most important mark to be hit is how one responds to "the problem of evil – to undeserved harm, unjustified suffering and unmerited pain" (*Reader*, p. 89; *Future*, p. 56). By these standards, Du Bois, in Corn's judgment, is short of the mark.

What Corn' does not provide, however, are clearly articulated, well argued for criteria for an "adequate" interpretation of "the human condition," nor does he endeavor to make a case for the viability of the notion "the human condition" in contrast to perhaps more appropriate and viable interpretations of the life conditions and prospects of a particular individual or a particular racial or ethnic grouping of humans who are simultaneously similar amidst their differences, different amidst their similarities. The troubling normative weightiness of the notion of "the human condition" for Corn's critique of Du Bois will become clearer as we proceed and take note of the examples he offers of intellectuals whom he judges as having hit the mark.

What is also needed from Corn', and not provided, is a persuasive argument, if not quite a justification, in support of his evaluative characterization of "the human condition" as a matter of "sheer absurdity." How did this sense of life become the normative interpretation of the condition of life for all humans? Why are Du Bois, and other intellectuals, not allowed to offer a different characterization of life? I am not convinced by what Corn' provides in the way of evidence and persuasive argument in support of his judgment that "ordinary" Black folk, generally and to a large extent, did and do regard life, their lives, as "sheer absurdity," namely, his interpretation of the "structures of meaning and feeling" created by Black folk struggling to fashion viable lives in the USA and manifested, particularly, in music and religious experiences and practices that give form and shape to the core of Black cultural life. It is Corn' who believes "the human condition" to be a matter of "sheer absurdity," not Du Bois – nor a great many "ordinary" Black folk, in my experience, though this might well be an appropriate summary characterization of the most weighty sense of their existence for many other Black folk. Is it appropriate to seek a single, overarching interpretation of the meaning of life for all Black folk? Or will such an effort run aground of the heterogeneity of Black life in the USA? I think so.

Corn' works hard to make the case for Du Bois's alleged inability by setting out what he takes to be the conditionings structuring Du Bois's limitations and inabilities: his being "a child of his age . . . shaped by the prevailing presuppositions and prejudices of modern Euro-American civilization" (*Reader*, p. 88; *Future*, p. 55). More pointedly, Du Bois was "a black New England Victorian seduced by the Enlightenment ethos and enchanted with the American dream," who, consequently, came to have an orienting "perspective" determined by "three basic foundations": "*an Enlightenment worldview* that promoted *Victorian strategies* in order to realize an *American optimism*" (*Reader*, p. 89; *Future*, p. 57; original emphasis). Corn' regards Du Bois's "Enlightenment worldview" as having given rise to an orientation that Corn' terms "a mild elitism": Du Bois's call for a "talented tenth" among Black folks to provide the leadership needed to save the "race," Black folks in the USA in particular, as a historically, sociologically, and culturally distinct and flourishing *people*. This orientation prevented Du Bois, in Corn's estimation, from learning fundamental lessons about life from those Corn' refers to – but does not identify fully enough – as "ordinary" Black people, though the commentary Corn' presents on the way to this conclusion does not suffice as a well reasoned interpretation supported by biographical evidence. He even goes as far as to charge Du Bois with having "underestimated the capacity of everyday people to 'know' about life" (*Reader*, p. 90; *Future*, p. 58).

Here Corn's articulation of his judgment of Du Bois is problematic, at the very least ambiguous. Du Bois certainly wrote and spoke of what he took to be the prevailing induced *ignorance* of many Black folk – that is, his judgment of their *lack of knowledge* "of life and its wider meaning" (Du Bois's words from *The Souls of Black Folk*, quoted by Corn' on p. 90 of *Reader*, p. 58 of *Future*). It is also the case that Du Bois distinguished ignorance and backwardness, induced conditions he thought *suffered by* many Black folk at the turn of the century, from "civilized" living involving qualities and conditions of life which he aspired to and advocated for Black folk. But it is not true to claim, as Corn' does, that Du Bois estimated "ordinary" Black folk as not having the *capacity* to know about life's meanings and be able to teach him about the same, and thus not having the capacity to be "as wise, insightful and 'advanced' as he," a recognition and admission, Corn' claims, that Du Bois "could not do" (*Reader*, p. 90; *Future*, p. 58).

Corn's characterization and assessment of Du Bois do not square with what I come to in this regard after returning to Du Bois's *The Souls of Black Folk*. Consider "Of the Meaning of Progress" in *Souls*, the essay devoted to recounting his summer experiences living among and teaching Black folk "in the hills of Tennessee" during his years as a student at Fisk.[2] Note what Du Bois writes of Josie, "a thin, homely girl of twenty, with a dark-brown face and thick, hard hair" (*Souls*, p. 63), and of her family:

> She seemed to be the centre of the family: always busy at service, or at home or berry-picking; a little nervous and inclined to scold, like her mother, yet faithful, too, like her father. She had about her a certain fineness, the shadow of an unconscious moral heroism that would willingly give all of life to make life broader, deeper, and fuller for her and hers. I saw much of this family afterwards, and grew to love them for their honest efforts to be decent and comfortable, and for their knowledge of their own ignorance. There was with them no affectation. (*Souls*, p. 64)

And of his experiences overall:

> For two summers I lived in this little world; it was dull and humdrum ... I have called my tiny community a world, and so its isolation made it; and yet there was among us but a half-awakened common consciousness, sprung from common joy and grief, at

burial, birth, or wedding; from a common hardship in poverty, poor land, and low wages; and, above all, from the sight of the Veil that hung between us and Opportunity. All this caused us to think some thoughts together; but these, when ripe for speech, were spoken in various languages. . . . The mass of those to whom slavery was a dim recollection of childhood found the world a puzzling thing: it asked little of them, and they answered with little, and yet it ridiculed their offering. Such a paradox they could not understand, and therefore sank into listless indifference, or shiftlessness, or reckless bravado. There were, however, some – such as Josie, Jim, and Ben – to whom War, Hell, and Slavery were but childhood tales, whose young appetites had been whetted to an edge by school and story and half-awakened thought. Ill could they be content, born without and beyond the World. And their weak wings beat against their barriers – barriers of caste, of youth, of life; at last, in dangerous moments, against everything that opposed even a whim. (*Souls*, pp. 69–70)

And concluding his reminiscence of his return to the world in the hills years later, finding Josie dead and much else changed, Du Bois asked: "How shall man measure Progress here where the dark-faced Josie lies? How many heartfuls [*sic*] of sorrow shall balance a bushel of wheat? How hard a thing is life to the lowly, and yet how human and real! And all this life and love and strife and failure – is it the twilight of nightfall or the flush of some faint-dawning day?" (*Souls*, p. 75).

Where is Du Bois's underestimation of the capacity of "lowly" people to know about life? Devaluations – even outright denials – of the capacities of Black folk *because of* their supposed raciality were foundational to white supremacy. Du Bois's efforts in scientific research, scholarship, and teaching were devoted to establishing the pernicious untruths at the core of these denials as a foundation for liberating Black and white folks from all involved in and resulting from their formulation and propagation. So, too, his advocacies and activist engagements. Du Bois could utterly detest what he regarded as the ignorance and backwardness of many among "ordinary" Black folk without detesting "ordinary" Black folk whom he believed to be worthy humans with capacity and potential denied to them by the architects and proponents of white racial supremacy. Cornel knows and appreciates all of this about Du Bois, indicated by his identifying his own work and life with what he characterizes as "Du Bois's lifelong effort to convince the West of this basic truth," namely, "of the basic full-fledged humanity of black people continuous with that of others" (prefatory note to "Black Strivings . . .," *Reader*, p. 87). Dear to Du Bois, a principal source of his abiding motivation, though this motivation waxed and waned under vexing conditions across a very long life, was his convinced belief in the *capacity* of Black folk for "progressive" development into a "civilized" people. Cornel provides no evidence in support of his odd claim that Du Bois underestimated the capacity of Black folk. I think there is none to provide. Rather, *The Souls of Black Folk* provides evidence to the contrary.

What of his claim that Du Bois, given his Black New England, Enlightenment, and Victorian sensibilities, was unable to "immerse himself in black everyday life," which "precluded his access to the distinctive black tragicomic sense and black encounter with the absurd" (*Reader*, p. 90; *Future*, pp. 57–8)? Well, I think it appropriate to argue that Du Bois's sensibilities, his sense of himself especially, were such that he was opposed to fully immersing himself in the everyday life of "ordinary" Black folk if one has in mind such persons as those in the hills of Tennessee about whom he wrote, or those he surveyed in Philadelphia's Eleventh Ward and wrote about in *The Philadelphia Negro*, and if by "immersion" one has in mind living life as such folk lived it and on their terms, with their understandings and expectations, their ambitions. No, indeed. But if one means living among these persons so as to *understand* scientifically the conditioned nature of their lives so as to be best able to account and provide remedies for the impediments to civilized and civilizing, flourishing existence, then Du Bois certainly went about immersion on a quest for such understanding – and not just of scientific facticity, though there is no question that Du Bois was also a convinced positivist – even of the very constitutive and distinguishing *souls* of Black folk, whether they lived in the back woods of Tennessee, the Eleventh Ward of Philadelphia, or the agriculture-based political and social systems of the South (such as Farmville, Virginia, a site researched by Du Bois) from which Black folk migrated to cities such as Philadelphia.

Du Bois sought to *understand* Black folk in the variety of their conditioned and conditioning lives, conceived as constituting various "levels," "high" and "low"; he was not intent on living as they lived *on their terms*, "immersing" himself in their lives in that way. For him there were better possibilities of living to be realized, and some persons better able than others to pursue and realize those possibilities for enhanced, civilized living which made them responsible for serving those further and furthest down by leading the way in identifying and realizing those possibilities. If that makes Du Bois even a "mild" elitist and thus suspect, I need from Corn' a persuasive argument against this "elitism." None is provided. And this leads me to conclude that Corn' is invoking "elitism" as a much misused term which, rather than accurately representing Du Bois, reveals more about his own felt need, perhaps, as a very public intellectual, to avoid the charge of being an "elitist" by establishing and maintaining "organic" solidarity with "ordinary" Black folk. Furthermore, I am unaware of Cornel having immersed himself in the lives of "ordinary" Black folk and thus of living a life in stark contrast, in this regard, to how Du Bois lived. Since leaving home for college, Corn', to my knowledge, has yet to live either a home-life or institutional work-life among Black folk as Du Bois did.

Nonetheless, Corn proceeds apace to take the measure of Du Bois and find him short of the mark by examining his "Victorian strategies," i.e. "the ways in which his Enlightenment worldview can be translated into action" (*Reader*, p. 93; *Future*, p. 64). The central tenet of Du Bois's strategies, in Corn's judgment, is the former's notion of leadership by a talented 10 percent of a nation or racial group. According to Corn', Du Bois's strategic efforts suffer from historical misconceptions (his failure to mention and analyze "the two most effective political forms of organizing among black people ... the black women's club movement ... and the migration movement" (*Reader*, p. 95; *Future*, pp. 67–8)) and intellectual defects (assumptions regarding the inherent humanizing effects of what Corn' terms "highbrow culture": "that exposure to and immersion in great works produce good people" (*Reader*, p. 95; *Future*, p. 68)).

I think Corn' much closer to hitting the mark himself in his critique of Du Bois's failure to attend to the Black women's club movement, to his Black women peers more generally, in his writings especially. A much fuller, more informative, and rather persuasive critique of Du Bois's shortcomings in this important area has been carried out by Joy James in her *Transcending the Talented Tenth: Race Leaders and American Intellectualism*,[3] to which I will defer. But I am not persuaded by Corn's effort to make the case that Du Bois's considerations and articulations regarding the leadership of a "talented tenth," how they were talented such that they should lead, were defective in the way he contends. He interprets Du Bois as having believed the "educated elite" (Corn's phrase) can more easily transcend class and personal interests and act on behalf of the common good than the uneducated masses (*Reader*, p. 95; *Future*, p. 68). He makes the claim that Du Bois "wisely acknowledges" the problem of the "petty political games as well as ... the all-too-familiar social exclusions of the educated elite" of which Du Bois was both "villain and victim" (*Reader*, p. 95; *Future*, p.69) in his revisiting of his notion of leadership in his 1948 "Talented Tenth Memorial Address."[4] And in a footnote (number 21, *Reader*, p. 573; *Future*, p. 185) in support of his interpretive critique, Corn' quotes Du Bois from *Dusk of Dawn* as likewise "acknowledging" the fact that exposure to "highbrow culture" does not produce good persons as an automatic and necessary outcome. However, in the passage from the memorial address that Corn' quotes, Du Bois sets the time of his realization of the prospect that those he thought best able to lead might well see more to their own interests than the well-being of the race as "when I came out of college into the world of work" (*Reader*, p. 95; *Future*, p. 69). This would have been in 1894, when Du Bois left Harvard University to begin working at Wilberforce University (Ohio). And *if* Du Bois's retrospective is both honest and historically accurate autobiography,[5] then what Corn' terms his "acknowledgment" actually *precedes* the 1903 publication of "The Talented Tenth" by nearly a decade, and the *Dusk of Dawn* "acknowledgement" of a problem is not a *subsequent* realization that corrects a prior "intellectual defect."

Along this same line, for Corn', Du Bois's conception of leadership is defective in yet another important respect: "There is still [even in the 1948 memorial address] no emphatic call for accountability from below, or any grappling with the evil that lurks in the hearts of all of us. He recognizes human selfishness as a problem without putting forth adequate philosophical responses to it or institutional mechanisms to alleviate it" (*Reader*, p. 96; *Future*, p. 69). Is the problem of human selfishness to be resolved by "philosophical responses"? Elsewhere in *Reader* Corn' quotes Karl Marx favorably as declaring that philosophers have only interpreted the world, while the task is really to *change* it. I'm not sure what Corn' would have from Du Bois in the way of "adequate philosophical responses." Nor of "institutional mechanisms" to alleviate the evil "lurking in our hearts." If it is appropriate to fault Du Bois for not providing either adequate philosophical responses or alleviating institutional mechanisms, then should we expect Cornel to hit the mark where Du Bois failed to do so? More importantly, does Corn' set himself the challenge of doing so?

I think he does. That, in my judgment, is a substantial part of the mission of "Black Strivings in a Twilight Civilization": to set, and hit, a mark of a kind with, but higher than, that of which Du Bois fell short. Which is why the critique of Du Bois's alleged "Victorian" strategies, regarding leadership in particular, is so central to Corn's essay: they require "not piecemeal revision, but wholesale reconstruction" (*Reader*, p. 96; *Future*, p. 71). That reconstruction is disclosed, as I read "Black Strivings . . .," in Corn's positioning of and task-setting for the public intellectual:

> The fundamental role of the public intellectual – distinct from, yet building on, the indispensable work of academics, experts, analysts and pundits – is to create and sustain high-quality public discourse addressing urgent public problems that enlightens and energizes fellow citizens, prompting them to take public action. This role requires a deep commitment to the life of the mind . . . which serves to shape the public destiny of a people. Intellectual and political leadership should be neither elitist, nor populist; rather it ought to be democratic, in that each of us stands in public space, without humiliation, to put forward our best visions and views for the sake of the public interest. And these arguments are presented in an atmosphere of mutual respect and civic trust. (*Reader*, p. 97; *Future*, p. 71)

There is much to ponder seriously and to agree with in this. I have, and I do. But is this a "wholesale reconstruction" of Du Bois's approach to leadership? I think not.

First of all, Corn' takes *no* note in "Black Strivings . . ." of Du Bois's especially thoughtful critique of the leadership of Booker T. Washington in his "Of Mr Booker T. Washington and Others"[6] while he sketches out a broader account of the emergence among Black folk of leaders and leadership strategies – what Du Bois terms "the choosing of group leaders" – in an environment constituted by natural conditions ("sticks and stones and beasts") and "men and ideas." And Du Bois is on the mark in addressing the issue of "accountability from below," as it were, regarding undue curtailment of public critique of Washington's leadership:

the hushing of the criticism of honest opponents is a dangerous thing.... Honest and earnest criticism from those whose interests are most nearly touched – criticism of writers by readers, of government by those governed, of leaders by those led – this is the soul of democracy and the safeguard of modern society. ("Of Mr Booker T. Washington and Others," in *Souls*, p. 47)

Mindful of this important essay, each time I read and consider Cornel's critique of Du Bois's approach to leadership and what he (Corn') proscribes for a properly functioning public intellectual I am left perplexed. For not only is his proposal not a "wholesale reconstruction" of Du Bois's alleged intellectually defective Victorian strategies, centered on a talented tenth – which Corn' critiques with seemingly obvious disdain, given the terms and tone of his discussion – I find little in his proscription that differs substantially, if at all, from what Du Bois put forth. Note the requirement set by Corn' that a proper public intellectual *create* and *sustain* "high quality" public discourse (*Reader*, p. 97; *Future*, p. 71). Apparently, such public discourse does not, cannot, exist and persist without public intellectuals who, in addition to creating it, must also insure that its quality is "high." Which means that discourse produced and sustained by persons who neither are, nor are assisted by, Corn's public intellectuals is of "low" quality. What do we make, then, of Corn's critique of what he terms Du Bois's "mild elitism," a characterization which Corn' never bothers to define in "Black Strivings..."? But what he proposes for a public intellectual, on my reading, is of little difference from Du Bois's ideas and ideals for the talented tenth.

Corn's difficulty is compounded when, even further, he requires that the proper public intellectual "enlighten" and "energize" fellow citizens, thereby "prompting" them to "take public action" (*Reader*, p. 97; *Future*, p. 71). In reading this, I am to conclude, it seems, that without the specified interventions by Corn's public intellectual, citizens would be unenlightened and without either the energy or motivation to engage in appropriate public action. As already noted, in his essay Corn' criticized Du Bois for his alleged "inability to immerse himself fully in the rich cultural currents of black everyday life" (*Reader*, p. 89; *Future*, p. 56), and criticized his "elitism" for proposing that the most talented and well educated 10 percent of the race lead and save the rest. Note the terms and tone of Corn's characterization of Du Bois's proposal: "The educated and chattering class – the Talented Tenth – are the agents of sophistication and mastery, while the uneducated and moaning class – the backward masses – remain locked in tradition; the basic role of the Talented Tenth is to civilize and refine, uplift and elevate the benighted masses" (*Reader*, p. 91; *Future*, p. 60). Given the place in "Black Strivings..." at which these sentiments are expressed, and within the essay taken as a whole, I am convinced that the most appropriate interpretation to make of them is as an intended disdainful critique by Corn' by which, in taking the measure of Du Bois, he positions himself as opposed to Du Bois and better disposed toward those whose lives he represents Du Bois as being unable to appreciate fully enough: "He certainly saw, analyzed and empathized with black sadness, sorrow and suffering. But he didn't feel it in his bones deeply enough, nor was he intellectually open enough to position himself alongside the sorrowful, suffering, yet striving ordinary black folk. . . . Instead, his own personal and intellectual distance lifted him above them even as he addressed their plight in his progressive writings" (*Reader*, p. 90; *Future*, p. 58). Note, again, how different the tone and terms of characterization of "ordinary" Black folk when Corn' speaks of them in his own behalf compared to how he speaks of them in supposedly representing Du Bois's regard for them. Yet Corn' would have the proper public intellectual, on his terms, be the creative and sustaining source of "high" quality public discourse that "enlightens" other citizens, energizing and prompting them to take public action. How is it, then, that Corn' is not here being another instance of the figure in terms of which he characterized Du Bois and, apparently, does not take himself to be compelled to regard himself as "a good Enlightenment *philosophe*" (*Reader*, p. 91; *Future*, p. 60)? Because, I believe, he regards himself as continually and strenuously, humbly and in good faith, submitting himself to the effort to hit the proper mark for intellectual and political leadership: it should be "neither elitist, nor populist; rather it ought to be democratic, in that each of us stands in public space, without humiliation, to put forward our best visions and views for the sake of the public interest. And these arguments are presented in an atmosphere of mutual respect and civic trust" (*Reader*, p. 97; *Future*, p. 71).

Nonetheless, I remain unconvinced by Corn's characterization of Du Bois, and quite convinced that his own description of and proscriptions for a proper public intellectual *do not* amount to a "wholesale reconstruction" of Du Bois's strategy for intellectual and political leadership. In significant part this is because Corn' has not probed the matter of "leadership" as seriously and frankly as did Du Bois, who seemed compelled by his scientific efforts to produce *truthful* critical historical, sociological, cultural, and political-economic understandings of the situation and prospects of Black folk, to speak and write candidly of what in summary might be termed class differentiations among Black folk, while assessing which class could and should supply (was already supplying) the agents to conceive of developments that would bring about enhanced civilizational living for Black folk, and then to motivate, organize, and lead efforts to accomplish what was to be done. With regard to these intraracial distinctions and roles, particularly what roles and responsibilities *he* should take up, Du Bois was not ambivalent in the least. Quite the contrary. Even "self-assured" doesn't capture quite fully enough his steely, self-assured confidence in his own intellectual capabilities, in what he produced in exercising them and in the value of these productions to a world capable of appreciating them, and in the belief that his gifts of talent, when combined with his abiding love for and devotion to the very idea and ideal of "the Negro," conferred on him, required that he take up, the mantel of leadership along with others among the talented tenth of the race. Du Bois, in the words of one of my high school friends, wasn't conceited. Just convinced. It is my own sense of Du Bois, developed over years of reading and re-reading, considering and reconsidering a number of pieces of his work (nowhere near all of them), and aided greatly by David Levering Lewis's biography and works on Du Bois by other scholars, that "The Doctor," as he was called, took care to manifest his self-confidence as the first order of self-mastery. It was this self-presentation, I think, in addition to the aura that developed around Du Bois in the various social worlds of folks Negro and White, that made for the situation regarding which Cornel wrote, "there seemed to be something in him that alienated ordinary black people," on the way to concluding that "he was reluctant to learn fundamental lessons about life – and about himself – from them" (*Reader*, p. 90; *Future*, p. 58). Corn's conclusion, I think, is wrong.

In "Black Strivings . . .," however, Cornel does not pose and ponder the vexing question Du Bois did ponder – was *compelled* to ponder, I believe – and set forth his answer in his essay on the talented tenth: whether there had been, or could be, a historical instance when a race or people were able to develop and save themselves from life-threatening conditions and less than full realization of the possibilities for enhanced, artful, "civilized" living without the leadership of an especially capable and determined segment from among them (10 percent? 15 percent?) devoted to leading the way. Corn' criticizes Du Bois for his response, and condemns his response. Yet Corn' tries to best Du Bois in proposing leadership that, on my reading, is hardly distinguishable from that proposed by Du Bois. With Corn', it seems, there is an unacknowledged, lingering ill-at-ease, an ambivalence, toward leadership, about aspiring to be and declaring oneself to be a "leader," even a "leading public intellectual" – though aspire he most certainly does, and work especially hard to be – which feelings he would salve by recourse to resources from his home-training and nurturing Black cultural and communal life, especially certain elements of Black Christian religious traditions (e.g. the role of "humble servant"), and recourse to convictions and praxes with regard to democratic accountability "from the bottom up."

But Du Bois, too, from the outset, thought the talented tenth should *serve* by leading and, as he made explicit in his "Of Mr Booker T. Washington and Others," seemed convinced that critical accountability "from those whose interests are most nearly touched" is "the soul of democracy and the safeguard of modern society" (*Souls*, p. 47). Corn', then, must do a better job than he has to this point in his essay if he is to make a persuasive case for a need for a "wholesale reconstruction" of Du Bois's so-called "elitist" and "Victorian" approach to leadership as "inadequate for our time," which, in Corn's estimation, requires "democratic" leadership. For Du Bois, in *his* time, more than ninety years before the publication of Cornel's "Black Strivings . . .," set forth the very normative mark for leadership Corn' charges him with failing to hit. Here Corn' fails to take proper measure of Du Bois and, in the process, mismeasures himself to the extent that he believes himself to be making an offering – proposing democratically sanctioned leadership as the mark to be hit – which is a corrective to, and thus an advance on, Du Bois's conception of leadership. On both counts Corn' is wrong.

Does he do better in his critique of what he terms Du Bois's "American optimism" (*Reader*, pp. 97ff; *Future*, pp. 71ff)? Du Bois, Corn' says, was a progressivist (believed betterment via human effort possible and to be preferred) and an optimist (believed in, and worked to lead the realization of, ideals and real possibilities for betterment of "the Negro," within the US American civilizational project, first off, and the betterment of peoples of color, and of white folks, throughout the world). But, this optimism, in Corn's estimation, would prove to be one of Du Bois's shortcomings, since he did not fully understand and appreciate "the strong . . . black nationalist strain in the black freedom movement" (*Reader*, p. 97; *Future*, p. 72).

According to Corn', and I'm much inclined to agree with him, "The most courageous and consistent of twentieth-century black nationalists . . . adamantly rejected any form of American optimism or exceptionalism" (*Reader*, p. 98; *Future*, p. 74), a portrait he works hard to paint Du Bois into (i.e. as an optimist who believes in "American exceptionalism"). For Corn', it seems, had Du Bois fully understood and appreciated Black nationalists currents – as, apparently, Corn' does – the consequences for him would have been momentous, psychologically and existentially:

> Du Bois feared if they [courageous black nationalists such as Marcus Garvey and Elijah Muhammad] were right, he would be left in a state of paralyzing despair. . . . Du Bois's American optimism screened him from this dark night of the soul. His American exceptionalism guarded him from that gray twilight between "nothing to be done" and "I can't go on like this." . . . Du Bois's response to such despair is to say "we surely must do something." . . . So, he seems to say, let us continue to wait and search for Godot in America. (*Reader*, pp. 98–9; *Future*, pp. 74–5)

I find these stunning interpretive judgments since Corn' does not provide a shred of textual evidence, autobiographical or biographical, in support of them, though he will make much of them. There is no quote from or reference to any essay, book, or letter written by Du Bois, nor by anyone else in whom Du Bois confided in expressing such fear as Corn' attributes to him. Nothing. And for him to go even further and represent Du Bois as even *seeming* to counsel "let us continue to *wait* and search for Godot in America" strikes me as almost absurd after my having just re-read, once more and again, Du Bois's critique of Washington in "Of Mr Booker T. Washington and Others."

This is an especially challenging, even troubling, portion of Corn's "Black Strivings . . .," for his poignant psychologizing critique of Du Bois serves as his segue into what I interpret as his making the full-faced effort to position himself as providing what he regards as the "intellectual and political weaponry" required to give the appropriate account of, and strategy for alleviating, Black social misery as we enter the twenty-first century. Very much like The Doctor, in my estimation, Brother Corn' is, indeed, *convinced*. This segue, and Corn's positioning of himself by taking stock of "black strivings" *vis-à-vis* the efforts of Du Bois, gains its self-assigned, self-assured height through his penultimate taking the measure of Du Bois and showing him to be well short of the mark.

And what is the mark here? For Corn' it has not been set, or hit, by either Du Bois or Black nationalists, no matter how courageous the latter. (For Corn' the "militant despair" of Black nationalists leads to either suicidal rebellion or the "quixotic" notion of a separate Black nation (*Reader*, p. 98; *Future*, p. 75). Why, then, does he regard Black nationalists as so threatening to Du Bois?) Rather, as Corn' goes on to make abundantly clear, the mark has been set by others, specifically by Leo Tolstoy (Russia), Franz Kafka (Prague), *especially*, for Corn', by Anton Chekhov (Russia), and by a host of other Russian and Central European Jewish figures: Dostoyevsky, Turgenev, Herzen, Shestov, Brod, Tucholsky, Broch, Bergmann, Kraus (*Reader*, p. 99; *Future*, p. 76). Here we get to the crux of the matter, to the yardstick by which Corn' takes the measure of Du Bois: Du Bois is "the towering *black* scholar of the twentieth century" whose "scope of . . . interests, . . . depth of insights and the sheer majesty of his prolific writings bespeak a level of genius unequaled *among modern black* intellectuals" (*Reader*, p. 88; *Reader*, p. 55; emphasis added). However, these Russian and Central European Jewish writers (and Corn' takes particular care to identify these intellectuals in this way, regarding their being Russian and Jews of and in Central Europe during a particular phase of history as factors of great significance) "put forward profound interpretations of the *human* condition [not just of Russian or Central European Jewish conditions]. . . . They composed many of this century's most probing and penetrating novels, short stories, autobiographies and letters" (*Reader*, p. 99; *Future*, p. 76, emphasis added). It is among Black intellectuals of the USA that Du Bois is *the* towering figure; he does not measure up to Corn's *world*-class Russian and Central European Jewish intellectuals. And why not? Corn' is quite explicit: "my major intellectual disappointment with the great Du Bois lies in the fact that there are hardly any traces in his work of any serious grappling with the profound thinkers and spiritual wrestlers in the modern West from these two groups – major figures obsessed with the problem of evil in their time" (*Reader*, p. 99; *Future*, p. 76). And why, in Corn's judgment, should Du Bois have to grapple with the Russian and Central European Jewish thinkers on his list? Because in concentrating on the problem of evil, "the towering figures in both groups were struggling with political and existential issues similar to those facing black people in America" (*Reader*, p. 99; *Future*, p. 76).

If the issues with which these writers struggled were similar to those confronting Black folk in the USA, why should it be *required* of Du Bois – or of any intellectual of African descent exploring political and existential issues of Black life – that his or their efforts include taking note of the similar efforts of Russian and Central European Jewish intellectuals? Most importantly, why should Du Bois – or other intellectuals of African descent – be judged as less "towering" figures for not engaging their works? Furthermore, if the political and existential issues in the lives of Black people in the USA were, indeed, so relevantly similar to the lives of Russians and Central European Jews as to compel critical exploration, why is there no apparent reciprocal, respect-conferring requirement imposed by Corn' on his select group of Russian and Central European Jewish writers to have *them* engage the writings of towering Black intellectuals in order to better justify and legitimate them (the Russian and Central European Jewish intellectuals) as producers of "*world*-historical works" (*Reader*, p. 99; *Future*, p. 76, emphasis added)?

On what terms, by what means, by whom, do works come to have the status and position of "world's greatest," especially during what Corn' regards as the ghastly "Age of Europe" that was shot through with white racial supremacy? What Corn' wrote regarding what he took to be Du Bois's "patriarchal sensibilities" (manifested in Du Bois, in speaking of the "talented tenth," proclaiming that the saving of a race would be done by its exceptional *men*) is an especially appropriate critical judgment to be leveled against him regarding his standards for "world greatness" in intellectual productions: "they are unargued for, hence unacceptable" (*Reader*, p. 94).[7] I need much more in the way of argument to convince me that these writers set the standards by which Du Bois should be judged rather than their being his peers of towering accomplishments who explored in their works their senses of the life-conditions and experiences of those in their worlds for whom they cared a great deal, and that affected their own lives and sensibilities, thus their intellectual work, in profound ways such that, as Corn' notes, "fruitful comparisons may be made between the Russian sense of the tragic and the central European Jewish sense of the absurd and the black intellectual response to the African American predicament" (*Reader*, p. 100; *Future*, p. 77).

What is really at issue here is Corn's preparing the way for the section of his essay ("On Black Strivings": *Reader*, pp. 101–15; *Future*, pp. 79–107) in which he will turn to making his bid to best Du Bois at probing Black efforts under conditions that he (Corn') thinks best characterized as "absurd," efforts that Corn', borrowing directly from Du Bois, characterizes as "strivings":

> Black strivings are the creative and complex products of the terrifying African encounter with the absurd *in* America – and the absurd *as* America. Like any other group of human beings, black people forged ways of life and ways of struggle under circumstances not of their own choosing. They constructed structures of meaning and structures of feeling in the face of the fundamental facts of human existence –

death, dread, despair, disease and disappointment. Yet the specificity of black culture – namely, those features that distinguish black culture from other cultures – lies in both the *African* and *American* character of black people's attempts to sustain their mental sanity and spiritual health, social life and political struggle in the midst of a slaveholding, white-supremacist civilization that viewed itself as the most enlightened, free, tolerant and democratic experiment in human history. (*Reader*, p. 101; *Future*, p. 79)

Corn' will do his best to paint a portrait of Black folks' strivings heavy with their pathos and with his own genuine effort to feel it "deep in his bones" and, understanding how and why it came to be, to convey, in their behalf, in the writing (as well as in his engagements), his sense of their souls and of what ought to and can be done to relieve their suffering and to mitigate its causes. Corn' seeks assistance for his efforts by drawing on his list of towering Black intellectuals of music, art, and letters – John Coltrane and James Baldwin, among others, Toni Morrison above all – who, for him, are to Black strivings what Chekhov and his other favored Russian and Central European Jewish intellectuals were to the pressured and striving Russians and Jews of their times and places. His efforts deserve close scrutiny, especially in comparison to those of Du Bois.

III

What am I to say, then, of Corn's take on Du Bois, though my grappling with "Black Strivings . . ." is only half done? After commenting on Du Bois's leaving the USA for Ghana and quoting from his departing letter ("I just cannot take any more of this country's treatment. We leave for Ghana October 5th and I set no date for return. . . . Chin up, and fight on, but realize that American Negroes can't win" (*Reader*, p. 117; *Future*, p. 111)), Corn' concludes: "In the end, Du Bois's Enlightenment worldview, Victorian strategies and American optimism failed him. He left America in militant despair – the very despair he had avoided earlier – and mistakenly hoped for the rise of a strong postcolonial and united Africa" (*Reader*, p. 117; *Future*, p. 111).

Now, why conclude that Du Bois's worldview, strategies, and optimism had failed him? Why not direct the charge of failure, if appropriate at all, elsewhere – at a variety of persons and organizations, policy-makers and implementers in philanthropic and governmental agencies who comprised the Black and white talented tenth and who failed to have either the courage or wisdom to do the best and right for Black folk and the nation in ways envisioned by Du Bois? Why not, indeed, if having concluded that Du Bois quit the USA "After ninety-three years of the most courageous and unflagging devotion to black freedom witnessed in the twentieth century" (*Reader*, p. 117; *Future*, p. 111)? Because, I have concluded, doing so enables Corn' to better position himself to take up the role of Black public intellectual *par excellence*, who, having taken the measure of Du Bois as "the towering black scholar of the twentieth century" (*Reader*, p. 88; *Future*, p. 55) and determined his shortcomings while endeavoring to appreciate (fully?) his achievements and contributions, will, while knowingly and willfully standing on Du Bois's shoulders, with the assistance of others, take up where The Doctor left off ("For those of us who stand on his broad shoulders, let us begin where he ended . . . with his militant despair" (*Reader*, p. 118; *Future*, p. 112)) and endeavor to hit the mark that Du Bois, he thinks, fell short of. It is too soon to conclude whether and to what extent Corn' will be fully and consistently successful at doing so.

Notes

1   First published in Henry Louis Gates, Jr and Cornel West, *The Future of the Race* (New York: Alfred A. Knopf, 1996), pp. 53–112, endnotes pp. 180–96; republished in Cornel West, *The Cornel West Reader* (New York: Basic Civitas Books, 1999), pp. 87–118. Hereafter these two works will be referred to as *Future* and *Reader*, respectively.

2   W. E. B. Du Bois, *The Souls of Black Folk* (New York: The Modern Library, 1996, originally 1903), pp. 62–75.

3   New York: Routledge, 1996

4   Reprinted in *The Future of the Race*, pp. 159–77.

5   David Levering Lewis, in his biography *W. E. B. Du Bois: Biography of a Race* (New York: Henry Holt, 1993), has persuaded me that Du Bois should definitely not always be taken at his word when reading his recountings of his life.

6   *The Souls of Black Folk*, pp. 43–61, at p. 48.

7   This sentence is not in the original version of "Black Strivings . . ." published in *The Future of the Race*. It was added by Corn', apparently to the version published in *The Cornel West Reader* to end the paragraph which, otherwise, is republished without alteration.

15

The Political Philosophy and Humanism of Cornel West

Howard McGary, Jr

I am pleased that I have been invited to be one of the contributors to this volume devoted to the writings of Cornel West. In some respects my task is made easier given that I am one of a number of scholars who will comment on West's thinking, but in another sense my task is more difficult given the high standard that has been set by my fellow contributors.

Cornel West, like Paul Robeson, another important activist/scholar, has been characterized as a humanist. In this chapter, I shall briefly describe the various ways that humanism as a philosophical concept has been understood. I shall begin with the Renaissance period and move to a discussion of how humanism reflects itself in modern doctrines like communism and existentialism. Finally, in the light of these remarks, I shall try to gain a better sense of what it means to say that West is or is not a humanist.

What Is Humanism?

Humanism is the philosophical and literary movement that originated in Italy in the latter part of the fourteenth century. This movement eventually spread to other parts of Europe. By the late fifteenth century, humanists were teachers of grammar, rhetoric, history, poetry, and moral philosophy. Humanism as a movement took seriously the idea of the dignity of human beings and attempted to make humans the measure of all things.

Humanism was a basic aspect of the Renaissance. Renaissance thinkers attempted to integrate man into nature and history. Humanism in this sense is derived from the older term *humanitas*, which during the time of Cicero meant the education of man. The basic idea here was that the liberal arts were instruments that enabled us to distinguish men from other animals. These humanists during the Renaissance felt that through the liberal arts there could be a rebirth of the glory of the human spirit found in the classical age, which had been lost during the middle ages. This form of humanism can be seen as a return to antiquity. The movement was characterized by a rejection of the medieval heritage in favor of a return to the classical idea that the liberal arts educated man and put him in a position to exercise his freedom. In fact, the idea of human freedom was and continues to be one of the major themes of humanism.

Humanist thinkers during the Renaissance rejected the institutions of medieval society like the empire, the church, and feudalism because these institutions were thought to be things that man had to accept without modification. The humanists argued for human autonomy because they felt this autonomy was more indispensable to the good of man than the rigid institutions and hierarchies of the middle ages. Pico's (1463–94) work *Oration on the Dignity of Man* clearly expresses the humanist commitment to the importance of human freedom and man's capacity to shape his own world, to make it better.[1] The importance of human autonomy was also characteristic of French and Italian humanism.

Another important theme for the Renaissance humanist was the idea that man is a part of nature; the point being that an important aspect of man is his body, needs, and sensations. These things are seen as essential to him, and as such, he should not attempt to ignore or abstract himself from them. This is not to say that these humanists did not exalt the immaterial soul, but in doing so they did not ignore the body. There was a widespread acceptance of the value of pleasure. You found humanist thinkers in the fifteenth century maintaining that pleasure is the sole good for man or at least that social usefulness should be the end of arts like medicine, jurisprudence, and poetry. The recognition of the importance of pleasure and the value of satisfying man's physical needs and desires led these humanists to define man as a social and political animal and to emphasize the active life over the life of contemplation.

Even though Renaissance humanism stressed autonomy and the importance of naturalistic or bodily pleasures, it was not antireligious or anti-Christian. The Renaissance humanists engaged in the same debates as the medieval thinkers did about problems of God's nature and the human soul, and they reached many of the same conclusions reached by the medievalists, but they introduced two important themes to this discussion: (a) the civil function of religion; and (b) religious tolerance. The first theme pointed to the importance of religion in achieving earthly happiness and the role of religion in civic life and political activity. The second theme emphasized the possibility of the peaceful coexistence of different religions and what this can contribute to human happiness.

Finally, Renaissance humanism is thought to have contributed to the birth of modern science by exposing the firm commitment that man is a natural being, and as such, he can question and understand nature with the equipment that nature provides, namely the human senses. We also gained from Copernicus and Galileo the view that nature can be understood by humans through the language of mathematics.

Humanism in the Modern Age

Humanism in the modern age has not been a creed. There have been a wide variety of meanings given to humanism. However, as the philosopher Paul Kurtz has said, there are four themes that are most often emphasized. First, humanists express a great deal of confidence in human beings and they insist that the only basis for morality is human experience or human needs. Second, many, but certainly not all, are opposed to supernaturalistic or authoritarian forms of religion. Third, many believe that reason and science can assist us in constructing our moral and political values. Finally, humanism is concerned with the good life and social justice. All who have called themselves humanist have not accepted all of the themes above, but they all share a concern for humanity and agree that our moral and political ideals must constantly be reexamined and revised in accordance with present human needs.[2]

I would now like to turn to some important philosophical doctrines that have been labeled humanistic. Communism is one such doctrine. Although social theorists like Bruno Bauer and Ludwig Feuerbach discussed the importance of human needs in making political and social judgments, Karl Marx is recognized as the first major thinker to critically examine the notion of humanism. In the *Economic and Philosophic Manuscripts of 1844*, Marx claimed that there are three kinds of humanism: theoretical humanism or atheism, practical humanism or communism, and positive humanism, the view that humankind is its own product. In this early work, Marx attempts to explain the system of alienating relationships which result from private property and capitalistic society.

Marx claims that humans cannot satisfy their species' needs as humans in capitalistic society. No amount of reform or revision of capitalistic society will end this alienation. Humans can only reach their true human potential in a communist society. In a passage from *On the Jewish Question*, Marx writes:

> Objectification is the practice of alienation. Just as man, as long as he is engrossed in religion, can only objectify his essence by an alien and fantastic being; so under the sway of egoistic need, he can only affirm himself and produce objects in practice by subordinating his products and his own activity to the domination of an

alien entity, and by attributing to them the significance of an alien entity, namely money.[3]

Existentialism is another important philosophical doctrine that is said to embody humanism. Jean-Paul Sartre, the famous French philosopher, claimed existentialism as humanism. By this he meant that human beings should be placed at the center of history. Sartre rejected any form of humanism that viewed the human being as an end in itself. He rejected the idea of a human essence. According to Sartre, humans are constantly defining their nature through their choices. Sartre said that only man can realize himself as truly human. For the existentialist, there is no other realm or universe than the universe of human subjectivity.[4]

West and the Humanist Tradition

West has been widely identified as a brilliant, caring, and sensitive human being. These admirable qualities are attributed to his humanism and his humanistic outlook is said to manifest itself in his philosophy and politics. As a philosopher, I am interested in gaining a better understanding of how or if humanism as a philosophical doctrine is reflected in West's thinking. Clearly being a caring smart person does not make one a humanist in any philosophical sense of the term. So when West is described as a humanist what exactly does this mean?

One might simply mean that West is a person immersed in the liberal arts; a person who sees the liberal arts as playing a crucial role in the development of healthy individuals, and just and robust communities. This is an appeal to the old Renaissance idea that the liberal arts were instruments that enabled us to distinguish human beings from other animals. West's firm commitment to liberal education in general, and his struggle to show how important art, music, and literature are to the masses, provide us with good reasons for seeing him as a humanist in this sense. West, like Paul Robeson, believes that art, film, literature, and music are vehicles for revealing to diverse groups of people just how similar they really are. This is one of the reasons he takes such great delight in sharing American Black music with the world, and in pointing out the similarities between great American Black musicians and their counterparts in other parts of the world. He attempts to use his vast talents to educate and bring people who had been taught to see themselves as different together in a common struggle for human dignity.

Clearly, West can be identified as a humanist in this sense, but we should not stop there. West's humanism reveals itself in his commitment to certain doctrines and political struggles. As an activist and scholar, West champions the idea of autonomy, but not in the narrow sense of liberal bourgeois autonomy that views individuals as atomistic. West embraces the existential idea that humans choose and make themselves. Put in the words of the existentialist philosopher Jean-Paul Sartre, "in creating the man we want to be, there is not a single one of our acts which does not at the same time create an image of man as we think he ought to be."[5] Sartre, in his early life, strongly believed that the existential view of man did not commit one to a pessimistic view about man's destiny. Quite to the contrary, it asserts that the destiny of human beings lies within each human. So on this reading of existentialism, existentialism is an ethics of action and involvement.

However, there was and still is a widespread belief that existentialism is a pessimistic view of man and the world, a philosophy that turns a person's gaze inward, far from the political and social concerns of the outside world. This view led, for example, many young student activists in the Student Nonviolent Coordinating Committee (SNCC) during the American Civil Rights struggle to see existentialism as a philosophy of the self-indulgent. Sartre vigorously rejected this characterization of existentialism. However, later in his life, as he more closely identified himself with the struggles of the Algerian people against French colonization, he relegated his existentialism to a subphilosophy in favor of Marxism. I think it is fair to say that West does not embrace existential humanism even though he shares some of its ideas. He is a person who is committed to action and he certainly believes that human choices and the responsibility entailed are important, but unlike the atheistic existentialists, he believes that humans can be deeply shaped by religious convictions.

Socialism is another doctrine that has been strongly identified with West and with humanism. There is a long Marxist tradition in the African-American experience. Early African-American Marxists like Peter Clark, Edward D. McKay, and Hubert Harrison were the forebears to the Democratic Socialist Party (DSP) embraced by West. Some prominent African Americans in the late 1920s and 1930s were attracted to the Leninist version of communism because of the party's commitment to the Third Communist International resolution supporting the right of self-determination for African-Americans in the South.

Even in the middle of the twentieth century, the activist/artist/scholar Paul Robeson made no apologies for his friendship with the Soviet Union and other socialist countries.[6] Robeson clearly shared the early Marx's conviction that capitalist society creates a system of alienating relationships that estrange man from himself, from his fellowmen, and from the product of his labor. However, Robeson, although a supporter of socialist principles, strongly believed that the freedom of African-Americans would not be achieved without the struggle of people with a variety of political views who could unite around a common program of action. Robeson, like many other African-Americans who were sympathetic to socialist ideas, did not believe that achieving socialism was sufficient for creating a nonracist society. He insisted that communists as well as capitalists had to struggle with the evils of racism.

West, although highly critical of many versions of Marxist thought, seems to take a position akin to the position taken by Robeson. West's active role in the Democratic Socialists of America and his call for interracial coalitionary politics is quite reminiscent of the stance taken by Robeson.

Race and Humanism

A popular criticism of people giving credence to race and racial identities is the claim that doing so robs people of their humanity. In other words, to acknowledge race is to recognize a morally, politically, and socially irrelevant characteristic of persons. In fact, some people even claim that the concept of race is meaningless and harmful, and as such, the goal of any good society should be to eliminate all distinctions on the basis of race (Douglass, Appiah).

West, like Frederick Douglass, is a strong advocate of respecting the dignity of all human beings, but unlike Douglass he is not a biological amalgamationist. He does not hope for a time when it would be biologically impossible to make distinctions on the basis of race. West believes that cultural distinctions rooted in racial distinctions can have value, so he does not want to get rid of races *per se*; his goal is to get rid of racism. Given this goal, West believes that a socialist society is a necessary step toward this end.

However, West's commitment to socialism and humanism has caused some Blacks to criticize him for not being more closely identified with African-Americans. Some see this as a general problem for Black academics because of the demands placed upon them to succeed in the white academy. A similar criticism has been levied against Black artist/performers. Harold Cruse, in *The Crisis of the Negro Intellectual*, wondered whether Robeson and other Black artists of the Harlem Renaissance, who were commited to communism and humanism, had become blind to the pitfalls of racial assimilation schemes.[7]

Even during slavery there was a debate among African-Americans about what was the most appropriate means to achieve freedom. The debate centered on two positions: assimilation or separation. Could or should African-Americans attempt to assimilate into the larger white society or should they embrace some form of racial separatism? Robeson's commitment to humanism and socialism led him to reject racial separatism. In chapter 2 of *Here I Stand*, he wrote:

> This belief in the oneness of humankind, about which I have often spoken in concerts and elsewhere, has existed within me side by side with my deep attachment to the cause of my own race. Some people have seen a contradiction in this duality: white people who have seen me as a "citizen of the world" singing the songs of many lands in the languages of those people, have wondered sometimes how I could be so

partisan for the colored people; and negroes, on the other hand, have wondered why I have often expressed a warm affection for people who seem to be remote and foreign to them. I do not think, however, that my sentiments are contradictory; and in England I learned that there truly is a kinship among us all, a basis for mutual respect and brotherly love.[8]

West points out the similarity between the Black oppressed in America and oppressed people in other lands, and the fact that people in other lands are able to identify with and support the struggles of oppressed Blacks in America, but he thinks that racists and capitalist governments have a vested interest in keeping citizens of the world ignorant of these things.

West is right about this, but his response fails to appreciate the full complexity of the issues. Many people who have a warm sentiment for humankind nonetheless believe that there are situations where the interests of human beings innocently conflict. Furthermore, they believe that these conflicts are often racially based or if they are not it is extremely difficult to see why they are not. W. E. B. Du Bois felt that African-Americans faced a dilemma. He endorsed the brotherhood of man and the ideal of racial assimilation, but he believed that some form of racial self-segregation was necessary in order to eventually achieve racial assimilation.

Historically, we find significant segments of the Black, women, and gay liberation movements accepting the need for some form of self-segregation. Du Bois believed that even if we endorsed the idea of cultural pluralism, we face this paradox or dilemma. By cultural pluralism he meant: (a) each race has its own distinct and peculiar culture; (b) different races can share a common conception of justice and live at peace within one nation-state or world; and (c) no race or culture is superior to any other. Many African-Americans embraced this version of cultural pluralism. Some notable examples in the 1930s and 1940s were Du Bois, Booker T. Washington, and Paul Robeson. However, Du Bois also believed that individuals must develop close and strong ties with other members of their race in order to preserve those qualities that mark their culture off from others. He strongly expressed this position in his now famous paper "The Conservation of Races."[9] Moreover, he continued to believe this in his later life.

Does West endorse this position? I don't think so. West does not believe that Blacks, by relying on their own resources, can overcome racism even if the educated Black middle class felt a natural obligation to help their less fortunate brothers and sisters.

Must West reject all forms of racial solidarity in order to remain consistent with his humanism? It depends upon what this position entails. If racial solidarity entails that African-Americans categorically have a special obligation to advance the interests of other African-Americans when those interests conflict with the interest of members of other racial groups, then the position is not consistent with his humanism. But if the position is that African-Americans have a prima facie obligation to advance the interests of African-Americans then the position can be consistent with humanism. The second view only maintains that African-Americans are obligated to other African-Americans unless some stronger obligation presents itself. On this reading, human needs can override commitment to things like racial solidarity and Black pride. But the problem for people who embrace this view is to clearly articulate when race matters and when it does not. As the work of gifted thinkers like Du Bois, Robeson, and West demonstrates, this is not an easy thing to do.

West, in his first book *Prophesy Deliverance!* and his best selling book *Race Matters*, praises those African-American scholars who fall within what he describes as the humanist tradition in African-American social and political thought. According to West, the humanist tradition

> accents the universal human content of Afro-American cultural forms. It makes no ontological or sociological claims about Afro-American superiority or inferiority. Rather, it focuses on the ways in which creative Afro-American cultural modes of expression embody themes and motifs analogous to the vigorous cultural forms of racial, ethnic, or national groups. This tradition affirms Afro-American membership in the human race, not above it or below it.[10]

In *Race Matters*, West applauds those leaders who are labeled "race transcending prophets."[11] According to West, these prophets adopt what he calls a prophetic framework over a framework of racial reasoning. Within this framework race does matter, in that we don't ignore or minimize racist abuse, but the framework does not deify or demonize others. Instead of a closing-ranks mentality, a prophetic framework encourages a coalition strategy that solicits genuine solidarity with those deeply committed to antiracist struggle.[12] West identifies Robeson as a person who embraced this prophetic framework.

West's remarks are instructive, but I don't think they have silenced those who think that race is all that matters. Nor has he convinced those who believe that race should not matter at all. So as we have seen, Robeson and West both struggle to make sense of the claim that race matters within a humanist framework.

From his first book, *Prophesy Deliverance! An Afro-American Revolutionary Christianity* (1982), through his *The American Evasion of Philosophy* (1989), *The Ethical Dimensions of Marxist Thought* (1991), and his critique of African-American leadership (1999), West gives centrality to the value of all human beings. For West, the value of human beings is not given mere lip service, but it must shape our conduct. Our respect for humanity must be reflected in our practices.

What does it mean to say that humanism must be reflected in our actions and practices? In *Prophecy Deliverance!* West gives us a clue. For West, a person acting from humanistic motives is not simply motivated by kindness or sympathy. People can feel kindness and sympathy for nonhuman animals. When an action is

288 Howard McGary, Jr

humanistically motivated, then love or respect for human beings is the source of the kindness or sympathy, not some other principle like one's own happiness or the promotion of social utility. The utilitarian, for example, under the appropriate circumstances, can endorse actions that advance the interest of all or most human beings, but in such cases their end is the promotion of social utility and not a categorical and unequivocal love and respect for all human beings.

West is well aware that consequentialist arguments of the utilitarian variety have been used to devalue and subjugate some human beings. A rejection of this way of thinking is an important aspect of West's humanism. Before I examine his views on this matter, however, I want to examine another important component of West's humanism.

West also claims that a humanistic outlook is always an honest appraisal of the human condition. By this he means that a humanist does not devalue or romanticize the strengths and weaknesses of any group of human beings. In numerous places in his writings, he criticizes what he sees as a misguided humanism. For him, a clear example is the Black nationalist who valorizes the uniqueness of Black people; not to put down white people, but to help cure or mitigate the damage done to the self-concepts of African-Americans because of years of racial oppression. He believes that such valorizations are understandable, but not morally justifiable from a humanistic perspective.[13]

He clarifies this position in *Race Matters*. Here he criticizes what he calls the "pitfalls of racial reasoning." According to West, when Black leaders employ racial reasoning they claim that there are authentic Black people, that authentic Black people have Black solidarity, and that certain subgroups (like Black women) must subordinate their particular interests and rights for the general good of the Black community in an anti-Black racist society.[14]

For West, no matter how well intentioned such reasoning is, it is incompatible with a genuinely humanistic outlook. Racial reasoning, for West, always requires certain humans to tolerate violations of their human rights so that the group as a whole can prosper. Such sacrifices in the name of the common good of the group treat some group members as if their interests and rights are not equally worthy. For West, this is a profound moral wrong no matter how important our goals might be.

One might think, however, that it is rooted in the natural rights tradition that was developed by contractarian writers in the seventeenth and eighteenth centuries and refined by the supporters of human rights in the twentieth century, but I believe that this would be a mistake. According to the natural or human rights traditions, rights cannot be trumped by consequences. One of the most stringent defenders of rights was Immanuel Kant. He offered a strong nonconsequentialist account of rights that was rooted in the idea of impartial reasoning. For Kant, clear and impartial reasoning would not support using some humans as means to bring about good consequences for others. What is paramount in Kant's moral thinking is the reasons that autonomous individuals advance in support of their moral actions and conclusions.[15]

West has in numerous places criticized Kant's way of thinking about morality.[16] As a critic of foundationalist accounts of knowledge and morality, West is unwilling to endorse the idea of categorical, transcendental, and universal moral norms that are above history and culture. All of our norms are historically situated. Furthermore, as a pragmatist, these norms are not true with a big T, but they are said to be true because we have found them to be socially useful.

Christianity, Humanism, and Pragmatism

In the closing passage of *Prophesy Deliverance!* West writes:

> Revolutionary Christian perspective and praxis must remain anchored in the prophetic Christian tradition in the Afro-American experience which provides the norms of individuality and democracy; guided by the Afro-American humanist tradition which promotes the vitality and vigor of black life; and informed by the social theory and political praxis of progressive Marxism which proposes to approximate as close as humanly possible the precious values of individuality and democracy as soon as God's will be done.[17]

But what should we as philosophers make of West's preferences? Is he merely claiming that this perspective and way of acting allows him to proceed in the world in an efficacious way or is he recommending this perspective and way of acting to others? If it is the latter, then what exactly is he proposing and why? But before we can answer these questions, we need to gain a better understanding of how West's views on humanism, pragmatism, and religion are said to work together.

West's humanism is rooted in progressive action. For West, genuine humanism is incompatible with the toleration of any form of human oppression. He tells us time and time again that his philosophical outlook (prophetic pragmatism) and his religious commitment (prophetic Christianity) must be based upon action. In fact, in the preface to *The Cornel West Reader* he writes:

> To be human is to suffer, shudder, and struggle courageously in the face of inevitable death. To think deeply and live wisely as a human being is to meditate on and prepare for death. The quest for human wisdom requires us to learn how to die – penultimately in the daily death of bad habits and cruel viewpoints and ultimately in the demise of our earthly and temporal bodies. To be human, at the most profound level, is to encounter honestly the inescapable circumstances that constrain us, yet muster the courage to struggle compassionately for our own unique individualities and for more democratic and free societies. This courage contains the seeds of lived history –

of memory, maturity and melioration in the face of no guaranteed harvest. Hence my view of what it means to be human is preeminently existential – a focus on singular, flesh and blood persons grappling with dire issues of death, dread, despair, disease and disappointment. Yet I am not an existentialist like the early Sartre, who had a systematic grasp of human existence. Instead, I am a Chekhovian Christian who banks his all on radical – not rational – choice.[18]

Is West claiming that in order to be genuinely human one must be a progressive action-oriented pragmatic Chekovian Christian? Clearly, West thinks that such an outlook is morally permissible and useful, but is it required if one is to be truly humanistic? Obviously, liberals would have problems with requiring others to take such an outlook. But clearly West is not proposing that the state or any other body use force to make people adopt such a perspective. However, since he is a pragmatist, in what ways can or should he persuade others to adopt this perspective?

Liberals give great weight to freedom of thought and expression. They believe that people should be free to develop their own outlooks, especially their political religious commitments. Liberals give great weight to the value of tolerance. They believe that people who value justice should tolerate some things that are morally offensive provided that these things do not cause harm to innocent others.

What does West think about the value that liberals assign to tolerance? As a democratic socialist, West clearly rejects capitalism as a just system. However, he emphasizes over and over again that he does not accept what he calls vulgar Marxism; a Marxism that does not give appropriate regard to the individual. He rejects many legal reforms on the grounds that they still leave many individuals unable to live a decent existence. In fact, he believes that changing laws within the present structure of the liberal American legal system will not address "the plight of the ill-fed, ill-clad, and ill-housed."[19] West believes that, in actuality, many of these changes have often led to the conditions of the downtrodden becoming worse. According to West, big business or corporations control the nature and extent of liberal legal reforms. And no amount of liberal legal reform will address the plight of the truly disadvantaged, or the fact that this group is comprised of a significant segment of the African-American population.

West recognizes the efforts of the critical legal studies activists and theorists. They realize that some more radical reform is called for, but West appreciates the difficulties that they face in trying to change the system. He argues that their posture has primarily been defensive and reactive rather than proactive.

In this chapter, I have not assessed whether West is right or wrong about the general inadequacy of liberal reforms. Clearly he is not the first person to claim that we cannot achieve an egalitarian society in an economic system where corporate interests are seen as primary. What is not so clear is why West believes that one must adopt a humanist perspective in order to achieve a more egalitarian society.

What West does not do is to provide us with compelling reasons for thinking that a humanistic perspective is the only perspective that will allow us to frame laws and policies that will address the needs of all. Why are those who believe that we can achieve a more egalitarian and democratic society by acting from enlightened rational self-interest wrong? Remember, even Marx believed that the move from capitalism to socialism follows from workers acting in their own self-interest. Even prominent liberals like John Rawls have claimed that free and rational people can choose a socialist mode of production out of individual rational self-interest.[20] It would prove instructive if West could clearly explain how his justification for a more radical egalitarianism differs from the humanism we find in the early Marx and from the liberal idea of treating all in a fair and impartial way as expressed in the work of John Rawls.

West's humanism is clearly tied to his pragmatist perspective on economics, politics, and religion. It is crucial for West that religion and politics always be tied to concrete acts of the human will. Although he recognizes that these acts will be shaped by historical forces and institutional design, he gives the human will primacy. As a pragmatist, West does not attempt to show that humanism is true in a metaphysical sense. By embracing humanism and acting as humanists, more human beings will be able to satisfy their enlightened aims, interests, and purposes. For West, there are no truths about morals, politics, and religion in the same way that we find in epistemologically centered philosophies like Descartes's.

Conclusion

What I think we can learn from West's provocative ideas is that moral progress, like any other human progress, involves commitment and struggle. This commitment and struggle will not always be polite and free of emotional turmoil (we are human beings with emotions), but hopefully these interactions will be humane. West's historicist perspective has taught him that this is how it is likely to be. However, his deep religious faith allows him to hope that we will reach a time when every human is valued and respected. His hope is not tied to any fact about our natures or some overarching truth about our destinies, but rooted in the belief that human beings can find ways to create genuine democratic control over the major institutions that regulate their lives. As I have written in my own work on interracial coalitionary politics,[21] such coalitions to achieve laws and policies that will require a standard of treatment for all human beings are fraught with mine-fields built up by centuries of maltreatment, distrust, and misunderstandings. Whether we can find a common toehold to raise us to a higher plateau is not something that I can say that I am optimistic about, but having known such a remarkable human being as Cornel West makes me unwilling to bet against it.

Notes

1 See Della Mirandola Pico, *On the Dignity of Man* (Indianapolis: Bobbs-Merrill, 1965).
2 See Paul Kurtz, "What is humanism?" In Paul Kurtz (ed.), *Moral Problems in Contemporary Society* (Englewood Cliffs, NJ: Prentice Hall, 1969).
3 Karl Marx, "On the Jewish question." In Robert C. Tucker (ed.), *The Marx-Engels Reader* (New York: W. W. Norton & Co., 1972), p. 50.
4 See Jean-Paul Sartre, *Existentialism and Human Emotions* (New York: Wisdom Library, 1957).
5 Ibid., p. 17.
6 See Martin B. Duberman, *Paul Robeson* (New York: Alfred A. Knopf, 1989), pp. 415–19.
7 See Harold Cruse, *The Crisis of the Negro Intellectual: A Historical Analysis of the Failure of Black Leadership* (New York: Quill, 1984).
8 See Paul Robeson, *Here I Stand* (Boston: Beacon Press, 1988), pp. 48–9.
9 See W. E. B. Du Bois, "The Conservation of Races." In H. Brotz (ed.), *Negro Social and Political Thought 1850–1920* (New York: Basic Books, 1966).
10 Cornel West, *Prophesy Deliverance!* (Philadelphia, PA: Westminister Press, 1982), p. 71.
11 Cornel West, *Race Matters* (New York: Beacon Press, 1992), pp. 31–32, 43.
12 Ibid., p. 28.
13 West, *Prophesy Deliverance!*, pp. 72–8.
14 West, *Race Matters*, pp. 24–5.
15 See Immanuel Kant, *Foundations of the Metaphysics of Morals* (Indianapolis, Bobbs-Merrill, 1959).
16 See Cornel West, *The American Evasion of Philosophy: A Genealogy of Pragmatism* (Madison: University of Wisconsin Press, 1989), pp. 91–2, and *The Ethical Dimensions of Marxist Thought* (New York: Monthly Review Press, 1991), pp. 121–4.
17 West, *Prophesy Deliverance!*, p. 146.
18 West, *The Cornel West Reader* (New York: Basic Civitas Books, 1999), pp. xvi–xvii.
19 Ibid., p. 273.
20 See John Rawls, *A Theory of Justice* (Cambridge, MA: Harvard University Press, 1971), pp. 272–4.
21 See Howard McGary, *Race and Social Justice* (Cambridge, MA: Blackwell, 1999).

Part IV
Cultural Studies

16

"It's Dark and Hell Is Hot:" Cornel West, the Crisis of African-American Intellectuals and the Cultural Politics of Race

Peniel E. Joseph

Prologue: Reconceptualizing Black Liberation Struggles, 1954–1976

Historically, the cultural politics of race has been a central theme of the Black experience in American society. At the dawn of a new millennium African-American cultural production navigates a tightrope between commodification and discursive insurgency. Forms of cultural expression generated by Black youth during the post-Black Power era have become the subject of vigorous debates within American society.[1] For many the "Hip-Hop" generation represents the example *par excellence* of the lure and loathing historically tied to Black cultural production. At the heart of these debates over the "culture wars" is the crisis over color and democracy in American and global civil society. Philosopher Cornel West has argued that "nihilism" represents the most basic fundamental threat facing Black Americans, especially young Blacks living in poverty. According to West, this oppressed class of Black inner-city dwellers are trapped within bitter cycles of self-destructive behavior that are based, at least in part, on self-loathing and despair. For a Black social democrat whose influence in liberal-democratic circles has increased exponentially since the 1980s, West's focus on the behavioral aspects of the cultural politics of race reflects a crisis of interpretation among Black intellectuals engaged in cultural and political criticism. The role of Black intellectuals in contemporary social movements, most famously explored in Harold Cruse's 1967 classic *Crisis of the Negro Intellectual*, remains no less a subject of debate today.[2] The intense debates surrounding the role of Black intellectuals, leadership, and culture in Black liberation struggles illustrate contestation regarding the very idea of radical social, political, and economic transformation in American society.[3] West's simultaneous and self-righteous criticism of contemporary Black leadership and intellectuals effectively silences Black radicalism by ignoring alternative interpretations of Black cultural production in postindustrial American society. This chapter interrogates the ways in which West's approach to the cultural politics of race has impacted intellectual and political discourses. From an Ivy League trained intellectual of considerable stature, West's political thought has expanded the terrain of traditional criticism while setting its ideological parameters. Therefore, this chapter seeks to critically explore West's impact on the cultural aspects of race matters while traversing beyond this vision to reveal alternative modes of interpretation. Facile debates over culture separated from politics and social movements occur in a vacuum that is both acontextual and ahistorical. A major implicit and explicit theme surrounding debates over Black leadership, culture, intellectuals, and youth – central components of the contemporary Black Public Sphere – is connected to the problematic legacy of post-Second World War Black liberation struggles. The "movement era" represented an over two decades long protracted struggle for radical democracy in American and global civil society.[4] Achievements of the movement's "heroic period" (1954–65) remain comfortably enshrined in the nation's historical memory through symbolic holidays and smug celebration regarding the "workings of democracy."[5] In contrast, Black Power (1965–76) radicalism that mandated radical democratic transformation has been erased from the nation's collective memory. Narratives of Black Power radicalism are depicted as lurid, ridiculous, and venal, leading to bizarre accusations that scapegoat radicalism for the decline of the New Left, the emergence of the urban "underclass," and the specter of white "backlash."[6] Therefore, a major hindrance to the analysis of contemporary Black politics has been the antiradical biases of "left-progressive" critics.[7]

Black Power and Black Culture

One of the most striking aspects of the post-Black Power era has been the profound effect on Black culture and its practices and productions. As Edward Said has noted, cultural politics are always historically specific and informed by unique circumstances.[8] Black cultural production since the early 1970s has been marked by several converging phenomena taking place against a backdrop of: global transnational capital reorganization; the decline of Black-led antiracist political struggles; domestic political realignments that resulted in the diminishment of labor, inner-city, and civil rights constituencies; the fall of the Soviet

Union and seeming failure of socialist-modeled revolutionary movements; and, perhaps most importantly, the triumph of a neoliberal political perspective that placed constraints on the possibilities for radical democracy. It is within this context of rapidly changing political circumstances that the cultural politics of race, the political thought of West, and the contemporary crisis of Black intellectuals must be discussed. Black cultural productions and practices emerged as a global industry during the twentieth century. Indeed, as Robin D. G. Kelley illustrates, Black music, sports, style, and aesthetics function both as an alternative to minimum wage labor in the private sphere and as a vehicle for profit and entertainment.[9] The most striking development in the arena of Black cultural practices during the past twenty-five years has been the exponential growth in popularity, profit, and dialogue over Hip-Hop. More then just rap music, Hip-Hop represents Black urban cultural practices, including break dancing, graffiti art, and style politics.[10] Starting out as a predominantly urban Black male vehicle for pleasure, dialogue, and status, Hip-Hop, specifically rap music, has come to define a generation of American and global youth during the 1990s. However, this embrace has been, in many ways, ironic. The acceptance of Black cultural forms and practices represented by Hip-Hop corresponded with a litany of socio-economic indicators that revealed increased Black immiseration in American society. Even amid the economic growth periods of the 1980s and 1990s, Black rates of poverty, illness, unemployment, and incarceration remained disproportionately high. This phenomenon, what political scientist Clarence Lusane calls the "Black paradoxical moment," underscores the dynamic of lure and loathing that is at the core of the African-American experience.[11] According to Lusane, the irony of contemporary Black life is located in the juxtaposition between increased Black visibility, wealth, and power in the public sphere and the continued poverty and dislocation endemic to much of the Black community. In the midst of increasing social and economic dislocation engendered by deindustrialization and state-sanctioned political violence, much of the discussion of Black culture centered on notions of an urban "underclass."[12] Although criticized by radicals as racist and historic victim-blaming pseudo social science, the "underclass" thesis remains embedded in popular and academic discourses regarding the poor.

Cornel West and the Cultural Politics of Race in the Post-Black Power Era

A central theme in both social science discourse and the writings of West has been a focus on the presumed cultural roots of African-American misery, especially in the urban terrain. On this score, West's writings have been, in intellectual circles at least, the philosophical equivalent of sociologist William Julius Wilson's work that places race as a secondary factor in the continued marginalization of the Black urban poor.[13] However, whereas Wilson stresses the effects of deindustrialization in negatively impacting Black life chances, West has focused on issues of alienation and isolation in his discussion of the Black poor. In his best selling *Race Matters* West outlines his cultural vision of poor Blacks in "Nihilism in Black America." Criticizing both "liberal structuralists" and "conservative behaviorists" as ineffectual and shortsighted, West defines the greatest threat facing Blacks as the "experience of coping with a life of horrifying meaningless, hopelessness, and (most important) lovelessness."[14] Citing Black self-loathing as the number one threat to Black survival, West argues that the reasons for marked increases in rates of Black suicide and crime are the direct result of rapacious market forces and the crisis of Black leadership. According to West, the "shattering of black civil society" and the seemingly moribund state of Black leadership are intrinsically connected.[15] Moreover, West argues that in the aftermath of the hopeful optimism associated with 1960s-based liberation movements the "cultural structures that once sustained black life in America are no longer able to fend off the nihilistic threat."[16] In short, the post-Black Power era has witnessed the demise of cultural vehicles that supported the Black poor and a political vision that legitimated a previous cultural vision of Black life. The end result has been "a kind of collective clinical depression in significant pockets of black America."[17] For a self-proclaimed advocate of "Gramscian democratic socialism," it may seem curious that West, although mentioning the crucial role played by the state in exacerbating Black oppression, focuses primarily on the cultural politics of race matters in American society. However, West's victim-blaming and excoriation of contemporary Black leadership is indicative of larger conceptual blinders that plague both Black politics and Black political thought. From this vantage point West's obsessive focus on Black "nihilism," devoid of a corresponding critical posture against the state, has led critics such as Stephen Steinberg to describe West as the "left-wing of the backlash" against racial democracy in contemporary American society.[18] In a stinging rebuke, Steinberg criticizes West for focusing on Black alienation rather then radical political economic redistribution; themes that were of major importance just one generation ago and articulated by an eclectic array of individuals that included Frances Beal, Huey P. Newton, and Martin Luther King, Jr.[19] Similarly, Nick De Genova has raised important questions regarding West's cultural vision and its merits with respect to Hip-Hop culture, specifically "gangsta rap" music.[20] Both Steinberg's and De Genova's criticisms of West are cogent examples of both the profound limitations and the implications of West's cultural vision in the larger American public sphere. While these critics have illuminated crucial aspects of West's cultural vision, it is not my intent to cover the same ground. Rather, the discussion that follows attempts to place West's cultural politics in a larger political, theoretical, and cultural context.

Perhaps the most consistent aspect of West's explorations into the pitfalls of contemporary African-American culture has been his disparagement of Black leadership. In his best selling *Race Matters*, West begins his critique by placing Black leadership into three groupings: race–effacing managerial leaders; race–identifying protest leaders; and race–transcending prophetic leaders.[21] While critical of the first two for their respective narrow identification with corporate capital and Black nationalism respectively, West embraces the last category. Unfortunately, these types include only deceased figures such as Harold Washington and Martin Luther King, Jr. If West finds no salvation for the souls of Black folk in contemporary Black political leaders, his outlook on Black intellectuals is equally bleak. West's criticism of contemporary Black intellectuals is worth quoting in its entirety:

> There are few race–transcending prophets on the current black intellectual scene. James Baldwin was one. He was self-taught and self-styled, hence beholden to no white academic patronage system. He was courageous and prolific, a political intellectual when the engaged leftist Amiri Baraka was a petit bourgeois Bohemian poet named Leroi Jones and the former Black Panther Eldridge Cleaver became a right-wing Republican. He was unswerving in his commitment to fusing the life of the mind (including the craft of writing) with the struggle for justice and human dignity regardless of the fashions of the day or the price he had to pay. With the exception of Toni Morrison, the present generation has yet to produce such a figure.[22]

This passage is instructive for several reasons. First, West conflates history by suggesting that Amiri Baraka's pre–Black Power beat period and Eldridge Cleaver's post–Black Power reactionaryism exist in the same continuum. Second, as he is often in the habit of doing, West structures the parameters of "legitimate" Black political thought through both demonization and invocation. The former is witnessed in his lament over the dearth of "race–transcending" intellectuals on the contemporary scene. The latter is exhibited in his naming of Toni Morrison as the lone exception to West's "rules of racial leadership." Finally, and perhaps most egregiously, this statement is noteworthy for its silences. Despite coming of age amid radical Black-led social movements of the 1960s and 1970s, West fails to regard individuals such as Angela Davis, Huey Newton, Fred Hampton, and Vicki Garvin as advocating a philosophy and practice of Black radicalism that was, at its core, radical humanism. The work of historical anthropologist Michel-Rolph Trouillot is instructive here. Trouillot has argued that "silencing" is a constitutive part of the production of history.[23] West's nostalgia for charismatic political and intellectual leadership rests on a selective mediation of political elites. This tendency to focus on deceased and martyred individuals to articulate the contemporary state of African-Americans substitutes the "rough draft of history" for a more substantive analysis.[24] According to critic Adolph Reed, "This tendency underwrites political passivity through supporting a defeatist rhetoric that bemoans the absence of such heroes in our time."[25] The perpetuation of a selectively canonized, supposedly "race-transcendent" (and mostly deceased), cadre of Black political and intellectual leaders is intrinsically tied to West's cultural politics of race.[26]

Hearts of Darkness: Black Power as Pandora's Box

The Black Power Movement represents a quandary for progressives in the post-Black Power era. Vilified by both radicals and conservatives, narratives of Black Power are depicted as absurd, leading to the demonization of Black radicalism. [27] When not being scapegoated for the proliferation of contemporary crises, Black Power is most often actively forgotten. This is to say that this movement has been the victim of a curious type of historical amnesia; one that is premised on the act of remembering to forget. Although one of the most significant moments in post-war American and world history, this era is only beginning to come under the critical gaze of scholars.[28] During this time period efforts to end America's nightmarish history of racial, economic, and political exploitation reached a breaking point. Building on the discourses of radical underground activists in Harlem, New York, Monroe, North Carolina, and Oakland, California, Black activists and organizations situated the struggle for Black citizenship within a global context. Moreover, radicals redefined conceptions of citizenship, democracy, and nation-states to advocate a radically humanistic conception of contemporary affairs that called for the abolition of political oppression in all of its manifestations. The results were both unequivocal and far-reaching. Creatively utilizing tenets of Marxism, Black nationalism, and socialism, the Black public sphere, during the late 1960s and early 1970s, was dominated by radical Black internationalists who explicitly challenged state power on several fronts. This included efforts to end police brutality led by the Black Panthers; a radical prison movement personified by George Jackson and Angela Davis; groundbreaking second-wave Black feminist discourses such as Toni Cades's edited anthology *The Black Woman*, and political organizations including the Third World Women's Alliance; poor people and welfare rights movements led by Beulah Sanders and Johnnie Tilmon of the National Welfare Rights Organization; and the Black Convention Movement, which attempted to redefine Black politics through the creation of the National Black Political Assembly.

Revealingly, all of the above organizations and movements articulated a philosophy of radical humanism that is at odds with conventional portraits of the Black Power Movement and Black nationalism. Mentioning these movements acts as both an exercise in historical narrative and an attempt to exorcize the litany of cliches situated around the "crisis of Black leadership." West was a student at Harvard during the height of Black Power radicalism, and his ambivalence toward this era is marked through both silences and observations:

In the early 1970s, varieties of Black nationalism were predominant at Harvard. Imamu Amiri Baraka's Congress of African People (CAP), Ron Karenga's early writings, the politics of the Republic of New Africa (RNA) and, to some extent, the Nation of Islam were attractive to black student activists. As a product of the black church I have always acknowledged some of the tenets of black nationalism, namely black intelligence, beauty, character and capacity, and their subjection to vicious attack by white-supremacist practices. The fundamental issue of black identity – the affirmation of African humanity and ability – is a precondition for any black progressive politics. Yet my Christian universalist moral vision and my progressive international perspective – derived from my readings of Frantz Fanon, Kwame Nkrumah and Karl Marx (promoted by the Black Panther Party over what Huey Newton called "porkchop nationalism") – made me deeply suspicious of the politics of black nationalists. I worked with them on antiracist issues – and we discussed, laughed and partied together weekly – but I always staked out my Christian version of democratic socialist values.[29]

This passage illustrates West's skepticism toward, and misunderstanding of, the Black nationalist tradition. West's puerile "I knew black nationalists, but I didn't believe in them" stance recalls condescending liberal bromides such as "some of my best friends are black." Simplistically reducing Black nationalism to a focus on racial pride undermines both the depth and complexity of the Black nationalist tradition. In essentializing Black nationalism West both ignores the history of what Cedric Robinson has referred to as the "black radical tradition" in American society and commits the analytical sin (that of totalizing individuals and historical epochs) that postmodernism rhetorically disavows. The notion that Black nationalism is somehow at odds with "universalism" is ridiculous. As the work of Rod Bush and Kevin Gaines has recently illustrated, Black nationalism is far from a monolithic discourse.[30] Thus, teleological portraits of Black nationalism that stress an unbroken, race-essentializing, and male vision of "Great Black Nationalist Leaders" that range from Martin Delaney to Malcolm X are ahistorical. Historically, Black nationalists engaged in race, class, and gender struggles in an attempt to radically reconstruct democratic institutions in American society.[31] From West's narrow perspective it is easy to see why Black nationalism remains removed from mainstream discussions of Black leadership. However, radical Black nationalism's banishment from arenas of "respectable" discourse reveals the force and power of its focus on issues of color and democracy since the Second World War. Black Power radicalism comprised an eclectic mix of Black nationalism (what Huey Newton called "revolutionary nationalism"), Marxism, and internationalism. Contrasting the rhetorical bromides of self-help and Black pride that define current conceptions of Black nationalism (and more accurately reflect the conservative nationalism of Louis Farrakhan), Black Power (inter) nationalism mandated a radical reconstruction of American and global society. In short, radical discourses that emanated from and were seemingly crushed by state-sanctioned violence, internal struggles, and historical transformations represent a Pandora's Box for Black intellectuals. Intriguingly, "progressives" such as Henry Louis Gates and West either overtly reject or publicly distance themselves from Black Power radicalism.[32] In contrast to Gates's unabashed devotion to liberalism, West disingenuously laments the dearth of Black leadership (and its potential restorative effect on cultural institutions and practices), while ignoring the radical humanism that characterized the political brinkmanship waged between Black radicals and the state just one generation ago. This is absolutely necessary given West's scapegoating of Black nationalism. In a haphazard discussion of Black nationalism during the Black Power Movement (one that includes no citations), West argues that:

> black nationalist rhetoric contributed greatly to the black freedom movement's loss of meaningful anchorage and organic ties to the black community, especially the black church. In short, besides the severe state repression and the pervasive drug invasion, the black petit bourgeois nationalist perspectives and practices were primarily responsible for the radically decentered state of the black freedom movement in the seventies and eighties.[33]

With Black nationalism serving as a universal, monolithic, and ever-present straw man, it is not surprising that West must take pains *not* to discuss the breadth of Black radical politics during the "movement" era. Distancing himself from the radical humanism (and the strident historical materialism of the Marxist tradition) of the Black radical (and nationalist) tradition, West has emerged as a self-styled radical democrat whose "solutions" to the myriad crises facing Black populations in American society converge with neoliberalism's ritualistic blame-the-victim philosophies that disparage Black folks, especially young people.

Soulless Black Folk? Cultural Visions and Political Culture

As we have seen, several major themes inform West's cultural politics, including: a focus on perceived Black "nihilism" among the poor; a critique of the ineffectualness of Black political and intellectual leadership; skepticism toward Black nationalism; and, perhaps most pointedly, silence regarding relatively recent and globally informed Black radical liberation struggles. That West's criticisms converge with conservative characterizations of the Black poor and silences surrounding Black radicalism is indicative of a larger *conceptual* and *interpretive* crisis regarding Black politics. This conceptual crisis is reflected in the failure to search the lower frequencies[34] of African-American history to fashion a contemporary liberation narrative. The interpretive crisis suggests evading, ignoring, or failing to grapple with the meanings of Black radical social movements. West's writings, simultaneously problematizing and pathologizing Black politics, illustrate this conceptual and interpretive crisis. West's "Black Strivings in a Twilight Civilization" represents a brilliant and deeply flawed example of this. In discussing West's self-professed favorite essay,[35] I will juxtapose West's apocalyptical tone with a brief analysis of rapper DMX. My purpose here is to illustrate aspects of alienation in West's writings and DMX's lyrics that reveal a political defeatism that reflects the seeming demise of revolutionary political possibilities. In a critical assessment of W. E. B. Du Bois, West criticizes the dean of Black intellectual activism for "his inadequate grasp of the tragicomic sense of life – a refusal candidly to confront the sheer absurdity of the human condition."[36] Framing Du Bois as a turn of the century progressive, West finds him lacking the complexity to analyze the "absurd" situation that Blacks face in contemporary times.[37] The most revealing aspects of this essay are found in West's idiosyncratic view of Black history. Situating Du Bois as an "optimist" who held out hopes for salvation from American racism, West posits Black nationalism's critique of white supremacy as the direct opposite:

> Even when Du Bois left for Africa in 1961 – as a member of a moribund Communist Party – his attitude toward America was not that of an Elijah Muhammad or a Malcolm X. He was still, in a significant sense, disappointed with America, and there is no disappointment without some dream deferred. Elijah Muhammad and Malcolm X were not disappointed with America. As bona fide black nationalists, they had no expectations of a white supremacist civilization; they adhered neither to American optimism nor to exceptionalism.[38]

This is a curious intervention for several reasons. First, it ignores the richness of Black nationalism by positing it as intrinsically pessimistic. Second, it conjoins Elijah Mohammad's religious sectarianism with Malcolm X's explicitly secular political denunciations intended to radically alter unequal power relations domestically and internationally. Finally, it clings to the false binaries that haunt critical discussion of Black leadership and history. The catchphrases are all too familiar: "separation" versus "integration"; "violence" versus "nonviolence"; and "Martin" versus "Malcolm." For West, "Of all the hidden injuries of blackness in American civilization, black rage is the most deadly, the most lethal." Further stating that "black culture is... inseparable from black rage," West situates "black love" as the antidote to the "namelessness" associated with being Black. Revealing a nostalgia for the "good old days," West recites a litany of cultural production that, presumably, reflects the best that the race has to offer:

> Like the "ur-texts" of the guttural cry and wrenching moan – enacted in Charlie Parker's bebop sound, Dinah Washington's cool voice, Richard Pryor's comic performances, and James Brown's inimitable funk – the prophetic utterance that focuses on black suffering and sustains a hope-against-hope for black freedom constitutes the height of black culture. The spiritual depth (the how and what) of Martin Luther King's visionary orations, Nat Cole's silky soul, August Wilson's probing

plays, Martin Puryear's unique sculpture, Harold and Fayard Nicholas's existential acrobatics, Jacob Lawrence's powerful paintings, Marvin Gaye's risky falsettos, Fannie Lou Hamer's fighting songs, and, above all, John Coltrane's *A Love Supreme* exemplify such heights.[39]

What is both fascinating and unfortunate here is that this litany constitutes the best that West can prescriptively offer amid contemporary social and political crises. For all of its rhetorical flourishes and dramatic insistence of the redemptive power of Black love, a sense of political defeatism permeates the essay. The possibility of political revolution and simultaneous cultural revitalization is never mentioned. Instead, political transformation must come from within using "ur-texts" that form the basis for a canon of legitimated Black cultural production. Indeed, from this perspective Black liberation through cultural revitalization simply requires listening to a substantial record collection while viewing old episodes of "Good Times."

Regarded by some as reflecting a contemporary example of "spiritual strivings," rap music represents a quandary for Black critics and intellectuals. While some applaud rap music's iconization of the dispossessed living in predominately Black and brown urban communities,[40] others have focused on the contradictory, at times predatory, nature of rap lyrics.[41] Historian Robin D. G. Kelley, while observing the political and social content of rap music, has highlighted the politics of pleasure and play intrinsic to Hip-Hop and often ignored by critics.[42] While all of these approaches offer insights into both the creative genius and shortcomings of Black youth culture, the following examination of New York based rapper DMX takes a more unusual approach. I do not utilize DMX's lyrics to delve into the *mentalité* of Black youth in the conventional sense. Nor do I suggest that the rapper represents the authentic or corrupted voice and image of the Black poor. What I do suggest, however, is that both West's and DMX's apocalyptical vision of American civil society reflects the narrow ideological boundaries of the contemporary political arena. Lacking an alternative political imaginary (that has been historically utilized by Blacks to dream impossible and outsized dreams), DMX's violent imagery is simply the flip-side of West's more urbane *fin de siècle* declarations regarding the possibilities of radical political transformation.

At first glance, Earl Simmons, a.k.a. DMX, or the "X-Man" as he is reverently referred to by thousands of young Black and white Hip-Hop fans, provides a perfect example of West's "nihilism" thesis. With his gruff delivery and darkly comic narrative style, DMX has made a name for himself spinning particularly gruesome tales of murder, violence, sex, and seemingly endless acts of retribution and revenge. Upon closer examination, however, the "X-Man's" lyrics reveal both the resilience and tragic depths of African-American immiseration in the urban terrain. More importantly, DMX, similar to West's cultural vision of race, sees no way out of the contemporary crisis. Consider the chorus of the song "Look Thru My Eyes":

> Look thru my eyes and see what I see
> do what I do be what I be
> walk my shoes they would hurt your feet
> you know why I do dirt in the street[43]

DMX sets the tone by proclaiming that he's "Burning in hell but don't deserve to be,"[44] and his visceral imagery provides a tour (both real and imagined) of urban America's underground economy and its myriad effects on Black men and women. However, DMX's lyrical proclamations regarding drug-dealing, violent retribution, and love in postindustrial America are provocative for both the explicitness of their illicit narrative and their implicit knowingness regarding the perceived futility of Black existence. As a Black postindustrial urban-warrior, DMX represents the modern exemplar of the "brothers on the block" that Huey P. Newton, among others, sought to politicize during the heyday of the Black Power era. Lacking ties to political possibilities beyond racial symbolism (Malcolm X hats, MLK holiday), DMX narrates the opportunities found and lost in a dog-eat-dog world where escape is impossible. Indeed, from such a vantage point an untimely death is, if not a *fait accompli*, almost surely inevitable. For DMX, this public recognition of political oppression is evoked through private conversations with God:

> You tell me that there's love here
> but to me it's blatant
> that with all the blood here
> I'm dealin with Satan
> plus with all the hatin
> it's hard to keep peace
> Thou shall not steal
> but I will to eat

What is striking about DMX's cultural and political world-view is not its both real and imagined horrors. Nor is it the paradoxical nature of Earl Simmons's delivery: a rapid fire admixture filled with both ironic detachment and a frightening sense of urgency. Indeed, the salient feature of DMX's ruminations on life and death in inner-city America is their frightening acceptance of the status quo (albeit on terms deemed wholly unacceptable to normative institutions and critics). Whereas West posits love as the solution to cultural decadence, DMX embraces crass materialism and Old Testament retribution as a shield against increasing social, political, and economic crises.

Conclusion

Both West and DMX revel in, while simultaneously revealing, the profound limitations of conventional race rhetoric. According to scholar Joy James, part of this rhetoric justifies and legitimates structures of inequality:

> Conventional race rhetoric is able to foster a sense of "community," one predicated on segregation and the denial of its resurgence as both a racial and economic phenomenon. It also functions as a form of policing, multifaceted in its scope and intent and capable of setting borders for those "worthy" and "unworthy" of participating in the political economy of a bourgeois democracy.[45]

James's provocative insights might also address the limitations of West's cultural vision. Reflecting the contemporary skepticism toward the possibilities of radical or socialist inspired democracy, West's cultural vision lacks the imaginative aspirations that have, historically at least, provided a leitmotif for Black cultural production and practices. While West is ostensibly a pragmatist, his apocalyptic worldview masks a politics of defeatism that, ironically, converges with the cultural mind-set that he has made a career of both disavowing and pathologizing. As this chapter argues, both West's political thought and DMX's cultural practices are related to a larger set of historical and conceptual limitations that have their foundation in antiradicalism. In short, the "playa hating" that Black Power radicalism receives in contemporary discourses is evocative of the defeatism espoused by cultural critics such as West and cultural producers such as DMX. Both subscribe to a doomsday vision of Black life that hides behind itself through a focus on unrelenting pain. However, this grim portrait of Black life remains only partially accurate. Alternative political, intellectual, and cultural practices, traditions, and perspectives of Black life abound. After all, recent African-American social movements, despite major shortcomings, trumpet the possibilities of freedom, democracy, and liberation. Indeed, Vincent Harding's characterization of the radically humanistic legacies of recent Black social movements serves as an antidote to contemporary perspectives on culture and politics articulated by intellectuals and cultural workers:

> Yet there was a time, not long ago, a time in our own generation when humane passion and revolutionary commitment seemed to flood the streets of America. There was a time when men, women, and children believed in the imminent coming of radical, compassionate change in this country, and gave their lives, their fortunes and their honor for it. There was a time when ambivalent American presidents were forced to take up the marching songs of a freedom-possessed Black people. There was a time, not long ago, when talk of revolution and justice was as common as discussion of apathy.[46]

Notes

1   For examples see S. Craig Watkins, *Representin: Hip Hop Culture and the Production of Black Cinema* (Chicago: University of Chicago Press, 1998); Robin D. G. Kelley, *Yo Mama's Dysfunktional: Fighting the Culture Wars in Urban America* (Boston: Beacon Press, 1997); Michael Eric Dyson, *Race Rules: Navigating the Color Line* (New York: Addison-Wesley, 1996) and Tricia Rose, *Black Noise* (Hanover, NH: Wesleyan University Press, 1993).

2   Harold Cruse, *The Crisis of the Negro Intellectual* (New York: William Morrow, 1967). For a contemporary discussion see Joy James, *Transcending the Talented Tenth: Black Leaders and American Intellectuals* (New York: Routledge, 1997). See also Adolph Reed, "What are the drums saying Booker? The current crisis of the black intellectual." *The Village Voice*, April 11, 1995, pp. 31–6, and the debate it precipitated, "Discussion: black intellectuals in conflict," which included Danny Postel, "In defense of Adolph Reed," Norman Kelley, "Notes on the niggerati," Peniel E. Joseph, "In the post Civil Rights era," Reed, "Protect the legacy of the debate," and Manning Marable, "Manning Marable responds." *New Politics*, 5(4), 1996.

3   Some important works dealing with the role of black intellectuals include James, *Transcending the Talented Tenth*; Lewis R. Gordon, *Her Majesty's Other Children: Sketches of Racism from a Neocolonial Age* (New York: Rowman and Littlefield, 1997); Jerry Gaffio Watts, *Heroism and the Black Intellectual: Ralph Ellison, Politics, and Afro-American Intellectual Life* (Chapel Hill: University of North Carolina Press, 1994); Cornel West, *Race Matters* (Boston: Beacon Press, 1993) and *Keeping Faith* (New York: Routledge, 1993); Michael Eric Dyson, *Race Rules: Navigating the Color Line* (New York: Addison-Wesley, 1996); Michael Hanchard, "Cultural politics and black public intellectuals." *Social Text*, 14(3), 1996, pp. 95–108; and Adolph L. Reed, Jr, *W. E. B. Du Bois and American Political Thought: Fabianism and the Color Line* (New York: Oxford, 1997).

4   The notion that black liberation struggles were part of a larger movement that confronted white supremacy on an international level was forcefully articulated by black radicals during this era. See W. E. B. Du Bois, *Color and Democracy: Colonies and Peace* (New York: Harcourt, Brace and Company, 1945); Richard Wright, *The Color Curtain: A Report on the Bandung Conference* (Cleveland, OH: World Publishing Company, 1956) and *White Man Listen!* (New York: Anchor Books, 1957); Penny Von Eschen, *Race Against Empire: Black Americans and Anticolonialism, 1937–1957* (Ithaca, NY: Cornell University Press, 1997); Robin D. G. Kelley, *Race Rebels: Culture Politics and the Black Working Class* (New York: The Free Press), and " 'But a local phase of a world problem': black history's global vision, 1883–1950." *Journal of American History*, 86(3), 1999, pp. 1045–77); and Michael L. Clemmons and Charles E. Jones, "Global solidarity: the Black Panther Party in the international arena." *New Political Science*, 21(2), 1999, pp. 177–203.

5   For a discussion of the uses and abuses of racial symbols in the post-Black Power era, most notably Martin Luther King, Jr, see Derrick Bell, *Faces at the Bottom of the Well: The Permanence of Racism* (New York: Basic Books, 1992); and Michael Eric Dyson, *I May Not Get There with You: The True Martin Luther King Jr* (New York: The Free Press, 2000).

6   Scholars are just beginning to take the politics of this era seriously. See Komozi
    Woodard, *A Nation within a Nation: Amiri Baraka (LeRoi Jones) and Black Power Politics*
    (Chapel Hill: University of North Carolina Press, 1999); Charles E. Jones (ed.), *The
    Black Panther Party Reconsidered* (Baltimore: Black Classic Press, 1998); Timothy B.
    Tyson, *Radio Free Dixie: Robert F. Williams and the Roots of Black Power* (Chapel Hill:
    University of North Carolina Press, 1999); Rod Bush, *We Are Not what We Seem: Black
    Nationalism and Class Struggle in the American Century* (New York: New York University
    Press, 1999); Joy James, *Shadowboxing: Representations of Black Feminist Politics* (New
    York: St Martin's Press, 1999); Adolph L. Reed, Jr, *Stirrings in the Jug: Black Politics in the
    Post-Segregation Era* (Minneapolis: University of Minnesota Press, 1999); and Robin
    D. G. Kelley and Betsey Esch, "Black like Mao: Red China and black revolution."
    Souls, 1(4), 1999, pp. 6–41.
7   Ironically, this is where the works of Cornel West and Adolph L. Reed, Jr converge.
    Both are dismissive of black radical traditions connected to black nationalism and
    Marxism, while failing to substantively explore these traditions or offer viable political
    and intellectual alternatives. West routinely depicts black nationalism as a monolithic
    ideology centered on black pride. Moreover, from West's interpretation of history, the
    Black Power Movement was dominated by a "new" black professional class (students,
    politicians, administrators) that "manipulated the movement for their own benefit,"
    while the black poor "became dependent on growing welfare support or seduced by the
    drug culture." From this bizarre and monumentally wrongheaded distortion of the era,
    it is easy to see why West both is dismissive of this time period and takes pains to distance
    himself from black nationalism. See West, *Keeping Faith*, p. 283; and *Race Matters*,
    pp. 35–46. Reed's criticism of the Black Power Movement, while more in-depth
    than West's, has been even more dismissive. According to Reed, Black Power radicalism
    failed due to an ideological romanticism that hindered pragmatic confrontation with
    state institutions, especially by the early 1970s amid the incorporation of black elected
    officials. For Reed, "The global, axiomatic narratives of pan-Africanism (eight points),
    cultural nationalism (Seven Principles), and the potted Marxism-Leninism (mechanistic
    laws of 'scientific' socialism) that collectively defined the discursive arena of black
    radicalism offered neither conceptual space nor analytical tools that could be brought
    to bear to make sense of the dynamics shaping the new black politics." The major flaws
    of Reed's analysis center on a failure to acknowledge the very real gains made by Black
    Power radicals coupled with a schematic conceptualization of Black Power ideologies.
    To be sure, radicals made errors and flaws. However, as recent case studies by Komozi
    Woodard and Timothy Tyson illustrate, black radicals stretched the political and prac-
    tical terrain of American and global democracy by dreaming outsized dreams. Rather
    than punishing, demonizing, and dismissing them for daring to challenge state-sanc-
    tioned violence and racism, scholars would do better to critically examine the successes
    and shortcomings of this period. Interestingly, in the tradition of Harold Cruse's bruising
    polemics of the 1960s, Reed fails to fully disclose his own personal political involvement
    in the political radicalism of the 1960s and 1970s that he now so readily disparages. See
    Reed, *Stirrings in the Jug*, pp. 1–52; and "Why is there no black political movement?"
    The Village Voice, November 18, 1997, pp. 36–7.
8   Edward Said, *Culture and Imperialism* (New York: Alfred A. Knopf, 1993), p. xii.

9 Kelley, *Yo' Mama's Dysfunktional*, pp. 43–77.

10 Tagging or graffiti art was a major source of creative outlet for New York based black and Latino youth and simultaneously a bane to city officials and residents during the late 1970s and 1980s. See Kelley, *Yo' Mama's Dysfunktional*, pp. 60–1.

11 Clarence Lusane, *Race in the Global Era: African Americans at the End of the Millennium* (Boston: South End Press), p. xvi.

12 The scholarship that explores and criticizes concepts of the underclass is voluminous. Some exemplary examples include Michael Katz (ed.), *The Underclass Debate: Views From History* (Princeton, NJ: Princeton University Press, 1993); Adolph Reed, *Stirrings in the Jug*; and Kelley, *Yo' Mama's Dysfunktional*.

13 See William Julius Wilson, *The Truly Disadvantaged: The Inner City, the Underclass, and Public Policy* (Chicago: University of Chicago Press, 1987).

14 West, *Race Matters*, p. 14.

15 Ibid., p. 16.

16 Ibid., pp. 15–16.

17 Ibid., p. 17.

18 Stephen Steinberg, *Turning Back: The Retreat from Racial Justice in American Thought and Policy* (Boston: Beacon Press, 1995), pp. 126–34.

19 This point is underscored in recent work on Martin Luther King, Jr that stresses his radical humanism and unapologetic criticisms against white supremacy during the final, increasingly bitter, years of his life. For a remarkable discussion see Dyson, *I May Not Get There with You*.

20 Nick De Genova, "Gangsta rap and nihilism in black America: some questions of life and death," *Social Text*, 43 (Fall), 1995.

21 West, *Race Matters*, p. 39.

22 Ibid., p. 43.

23 Michel-Rolph Trouillot, *Silencing the Past: Power and the Production of History* (New York: Beacon, 1995).

24 Charles Payne's monumental study of the Mississippi movement underscores this point. See *I've Got the Light of Freedom: The Organizing Tradition and the Mississippi Freedom Struggle* (Berkeley: University of California Press, 1995), pp. 39–405.

25 Reed, *W. E. B. Du Bois and American Political Thought*, p. 184.

26 It should be noted that West's definition of leadership as emanating from "deeply bred traditions and communities that shape and mold talented and gifted persons" is, at best, ambiguous and problematic. Uncritical constructions of black leadership narrow the breadth and scope of black politics while reifying the heroic roles of race men and women who have received legitimation as the presumed "President of Black America." For a critical discussion of the pitfalls of an uncritical approach to the notion of black leadership see Reed, *Stirrings in the Jug* and *W. E. B. Du Bois and American Political Thought*; and Kevin Gaines, *Uplifting the Race: Black Leadership, Politics, and Culture in the Twentieth Century* (Chapel Hill: University of North Carolina Press, 1996).

27 Nikhil Singh provides a brilliant discussion of these antiradical discourses. See Nikhil Singh, "The Black Panther Party and the 'underdiscovered country' of the left." In Charles Jones (ed.), *The Black Panther Party Reconsidered* (Baltimore: Black Classic Press,

1998), pp. 57–105. Progressive Adolph Reed adds to the dismissal and demonization of this era by black radicals for being too naive, theoretically deficient, and ideologically dogmatic to understand the complexities of the emerging postindustrial political order. Instructively, Reed reserves his most scathing criticism for the young black men and women who dared to challenge white supremacy, monopoly capital, and state violence, rather than the systemic and illegal machinations (COINTELPRO, murder, violence, intimidation, threats, etc.) used to undermine the movement. See Reed, *Stirrings in the Jug.*

28   Recent works that deal with Black Power radicalism include Jones, ed., *The Black Panther Party Reconsidered*; Woodard, *A Nation within a Nation*; Tyson, *Radio Free Dixie*; Bush, *We Are Not What We Seem*; and Joy James, *Shadowboxing: Representations of Black Feminist Politics* (New York: St Martin's, 1999).

29   Cornel West, "The making of an American radical democrat of African descent." In Cornel West, *The Cornel West Reader* (New York: Basic Civitas Books, 1999), p. 6.

30   Bush, *We Are Not What We Seem*; and Kevin Gaines, *Uplifting the Race.*

31   The political activism of Hubert Harrison, the "father of Harlem radicalism," is instructive here. Harrison was a humanist, radical socialist, and militant black nationalist. However, his advocacy of "race first" does nothing to undermine his commitment to humanism. Rather, Harrison's black nationalism was a response to the politics and practices of white supremacy that made black claims to moral universalism illegitimate. Black nationalism has been a historical response against white supremacy's illusory claim to hold the key to ideas of citizenship, democracy, and humanity. The conflation of black nationalism as somehow being antiuniversalist or a corollary to white supremacy is ahistorical and false. However, this does much to explain the antinationalist sentiment that permeates the writings of West and other black progressives. For a discussion of Harrison see Jeffrey B. Perry, "An introduction to Hubert Harrison, 'the father of Harlem radicalism,'" *Souls*, 2(1), 2000, pp. 38–54.

32   Originally airing in 1998, the Henry Louis Gates narrated PBS *Frontline* documentary "The two nations of black America" lampooned the Black Panthers and ridiculed the very notion of black radical politics, while conveniently forgetting the fact that black radicalism had engendered the very black studies programs that Gates (among many others) has benefited from.

33   West, *Keeping Faith*, p. 286.

34   I borrow this term from Ralph Ellison's meditation on the inner workings of black life. See Ralph Ellison, *Invisible Man* (New York: Random House, 1952).

35   *The Cornel West Reader*, p. 87.

36   Cornel West, "Black Strivings in a Twilight Civilization." In Henry Louis Gates and Cornel West, *The Future of the Race* (New York: Alfred A. Knopf, 1996), p. 57.

37   Ibid., p. 64.

38   Ibid., pp. 72–3.

39   Ibid., p. 90.

40   DeGenova, "Gangsta rap and nihilism in black America," p. 127.

41   Ernest Allen, Jr, "Making the strong survive: the contours and contradictions of message rap." In William Eric Perkins (ed.), *Droppin' Science: Critical Essays on Rap Music and Hip Hop Culture* (Philadelphia: Temple University Press, 1996).

42 Kelley, *Yo Mama's Dysfunktional!*, pp. 44–77.
43 DMX, "Look thru my eyes." *It's Dark and Hell Is Hot* (Def Jam, 1998).
44 Ibid.
45 James, *Shadowboxing*, p. 16.
46 Vincent Harding, "The misplaced bicentennial: of history, revolutions and hope." *Black World View*, 1(1), 1976, p. 3.

17

Reading Cornel West as a Humanistic Scholar: Rhetoric and Practice

Clarence Shole Johnson

Introduction

A survey of Cornel West's writings cannot but reveal the diversity of his pre-occupations. The issues West engages with range from philosophy and theology to literary and cultural criticism. Specifically, they include: an elaboration of the genesis and development of American pragmatism; a critique of neopragmatism; an analysis of postanalytic philosophy; an examination of the rise and decline of the philosophy of religion in the academy; the place and role of humanistic studies in the academy and society at large; race and social theory; critical legal theory; cultural studies; issues affecting people of color generally and other unrepresented groups; and Black–Jewish relations.

The ease with which West traverses traditional disciplinary boundaries in some ways is proof that these boundaries are largely artificial and only promote intellectual parochialism. For West, a significant consequence of such parochialism is that it disconnects the intellectual life from praxis. And in his view this disconnection is inconsistent with the role of the intellectual, especially the humanistic scholar, to society. West's own examination of the role and significance of the humanistic scholar to society may be read, therefore, as a reaction, if not indeed a corrective, to intellectual parochialism and isolationism. At the very least, he implicitly considers the separation of the theoretical and the practical life as partly responsible for the failure of academics, especially those in the humanistic disciplines, to define their relevance to society. This disconnectedness underlies his comment in "The Dilemma of the Black Intellectual" about "common perceptions [in the Black community] of the impotence, even uselessness, of black intellectuals."[1] And it is also against this background that West's speculation about the resurgence of neopragmatism in contemporary America is to be understood. In "The Limits of Neopragmatism," he attributes this resurgence of neopragmatism to what he claims is "the crisis of purpose and vocation in humanistic studies and professional schools." And he adds:

> the recent hunger for interdisciplinary studies – or the erosion of disciplinary boundaries – promoted by neopragmatisms, poststructuralisms, Marxisms and feminisms is not only motivated by the quest for truth, but also activated by power struggles over what kinds of knowledge should be given status, be rewarded and be passed on to young, informed citizens in the next century. *These power struggles are not simply over positions and curriculums, but also over ideals of what it means to be humanistic intellectuals in a declining empire* – in a first-rate military power, a near-rescinding economic power and a culture in decay. (Emphasis added)

Thus, he endorses Richard Rorty's attack on academic professionalization and specialization, saying that Rorty's *Philosophy and the Mirror of Nature* is, among other things, "a challenging narrative of how contemporary intellectuals have come to be contained within professional and specialized social spaces, with little outreach to a larger public and hence little visibility in, and minimal effect on, the larger society" (KF, p. 138). In light of the foregoing observations, I submit that what drives West's diverse intellectual engagements is the quest to define his own relevance to society as a humanistic scholar. Furthermore, it is toward the realization of this quest that his most significant discourses are geared. My aim in this study, therefore, is to elaborate how West, by employing his theory of prophetic pragmatism, endeavors to establish himself as a humanistic scholar. I shall engage this task by addressing two key questions: (a) what does it mean to be a humanistic scholar; and (b) how, if at all, is West a humanistic scholar?

I

Humanism is first and foremost an antiestablishmentarian philosophical position that stresses the value of the individual over those institutions in society that often have primacy and ascendency over individual life.[2] Humanism is motivated by challenge and crisis, and it is animated by a critical temper. The establishments to which humanism is reacting may be religious; or economic, in the sense of the etherealization and transcendence of market forces that affect the life of the ordinary individual and over which he or she has no control; or political, in the sense of the primordial and immanent institutions of power that determine the lives of ordinary citizenry, but over which the ordinary citizen has no control. The net effect of this controlling influence of the institutions on individual life is that it renders the individual powerless and thus dispossesses her or him of the agency to determine the direction of her or his life. Humanism thus seeks to liberate individuals from such dominating and oppressive forces that deprive them of individuality so that they can realize their potential. Paul Kurtz aptly expresses this point as follows:

> The problem for the humanist is to create the conditions which would emancipate man [woman] from oppressive and corruptive social organization, and from the denigration and perversion of his [her] human talents, which would liberate him [her] from one-sided and distorted development, and which would enable him [her] to achieve an authentic life. (Kurtz, p. 11)

Kurtz identifies four distinctive features of humanism, some or all of which any variant form of the doctrine may espouse. First, humanism rejects a supernaturalistic conception of the universe and denies the claim that humans have a privileged and special place in the cosmos. Alternatively put, humanism conceives of both the human being and the rest of the entire cosmos as a part of nature; consequently, everything that happens both to human beings and to the rest of the cosmos can be given a naturalistic explanation, one grounded in experience (Kurtz, p. 3). Second, humanism affirms that moral values have no meaning in the absence of human experiences. Indeed, a necessary and sufficient condition for the existence of morality is that there are human beings and hence human experiences. It follows from this view that humanistic ethics reject the notion that morality originates from and even requires religion. On the contrary, as Kurtz points out, humanistic ethics "asks that we, as human beings, face up to the human [experiential] condition" (Kurtz, p. 4).

But is not the rejection of the supernatural just what it takes to say that life is meaningless and hopeless, especially when the individual is pitted against the inscrutable, overwhelming and ever-revolving forces of nature? In other words, does not a subscription to a humanistic philosophy entail a pessimistic outlook on life? The answer, according to Kurtz, is "no." Although some humanists have adopted a pessimistic outlook on life in view of a rejection of a theistic universe, "most humanists have found a source of optimism in the affirmation that value is related to man" (Kurtz, p. 4). This optimism derives from a proper appreciation (or cognition) of the human condition, its challenges, problems, and hence its possibilities. Through a proper deployment of her or his powers of thought and intelligence, the human being is able to build a good (or better) life for herself or himself.

The third principle to which at least some humanists subscribe is that ethical judgments are open to rational scrutiny and that such judgments can be given empirical warrant. This principle is consistent with the rejection of a religious-based conception of ethics. Whereas a religious-based conception of morality, such as the Divine Command Theory, advances an absolutist and hence universalistic principle of morality, one that is grounded on *a priori* considerations, a humanistic ethic views moral norms as general guides which are to be applied and modified in light of the contingent (or empirical) circumstances and conditions of individuals. The role of reason in the moral domain is limited to scrutinizing the circumstances in which humans find themselves and determining whether or not existing norms need to be applied or modified in the quest to provide at least a provisional basis for action.

The fourth and final attribute of humanism is that it involves some form of social humanitarianism. What this means is that humanists often are committed to a form of social justice principle in which they seek at least to promote the happiness of the greater number of people and at most the happiness of humanity as a whole. This humanist concern with social justice derives from the belief that all human beings are members of the same human family; thus it is the humanist's obligation to advance the welfare of human kind (Kurtz, p. 9). Humanistic positions with a humanitarian strain include liberal, democratic, utilitarian, and socialist. Each of these positions is driven by a double humanist ideal of the development of individual potentialities and of the promotion of social harmony and justice. To quote Kurtz:

> If liberal, Renaissance and Enlightenment humanisms emphasized the perfectability of the individual and had faith in the instrumentality of reason and education, utilitarian, democratic, and especially socialist humanism have emphasized that many or most of the problems of man can only be resolved by social action, by changing the social system, the underlying economic structure, the forces and relationship of production. Humanists today attack all those social forces which seek to destroy man; they deplore the dehumanization and alienation of man within the industrial and technological society, the conflict and tension, poverty and war, racial discrimination and hatred, inequality and injustice, overpopulation and waste, the emphasis on the mere quantity rather than on the quality of life. In effect, they condemn all the contradictions of modern life, and the failure of modern man to achieve the full measure of his potential excellence. (Kurtz, pp. 10–11)

It is clear from this passage that humanism emphasizes the value of human life and human dignity as an end.[3] Thus, a humanistic scholar is an intellectual who is concerned with defending the dignity of humanity against the abusive and oppressive societal power structures that alienate, dehumanize, and denigrate the individual. To that end, a humanistic scholar is not only antiestablishmentarian, but also motivated by ethical and sociopolitical concerns. Given these considerations, how then, if at all, is West a humanistic scholar?

There is no question that West's views are antiestablishmentarian, as is clear from the theme of social justice that permeates his writings. In both his philosophical and theological writings, West consistently bemoans what he deems the social injustice that is meted out to the ordinary individual in society, especially in a capitalistic environment, by the dominant institutions of power. For instance, in the essay "Prophetic Theology," he elaborates the doctrine of *imago Dei*, the doctrine that humans are made in the image of God, as espousing among other things an egalitarian principle in which God identifies with all stripes of humanity. In this connection, he says, the doctrine targets "those who are denied dignity and a certain minimum of humane treatment." He explains humane treatment in terms of "a Christian mandate for identification with the downtrodden, the dispossessed, the disinherited, with the exploited and the oppressed."[4] And in the essay "The New Cultural Politics of Difference," West declares that the aim of the new cultural politics of difference is that of "locating the structural causes of unnecessary forms of social misery, [of] depicting the plight and predicaments of demoralized and depoliticized citizens caught in market-driven cycles of therapeutic release – drugs, alcoholism, consumerism – and [of] projecting visions, analyses and actions that proceed from particularities and [to] arrive at moral and political connectedness" (KF, p. 30). In particular, he declares that the purpose of the new cultural politics of difference is to "expand the scope of freedom and democracy" in a civilization that revolves around market forces (KF, p. 31).

I will examine some of the issues West addresses in the essay "The New Cultural Politics of Difference" if only to demonstrate why, in my view, this concern establishes him as a humanistic scholar. For the present, it is only worth emphasizing that the principal target of his critique is the sociopolitical and economic forces that are reified in Western societies. These are the forces that shape the life and the existential circumstances of ordinary individuals and over which the latter have little or no control. This means that the philosophical position within which West treats the issues he raises, namely prophetic pragmatism, evidently satisfies at least the fourth characteristic of humanism – i.e. the concern with social justice.[5] Indeed, for West, the whole point of prophetic pragmatism is that it "analyzes the social causes of unnecessary forms of social misery, promotes moral outrage against them, organizes different constituencies to alleviate them, yet does so with an openness to its own blindnesses and shortcomings" (KF, p. 139).

But to the extent that West's engagements are generally articulated through his doctrine of prophetic pragmatism, they also satisfy the other requirements of humanism. For instance, implicit in most forms of humanism is an optimistic outlook on life. There certainly is no shortage of optimism in West's sociopolitical engagements. West often articulates this optimism in the notion of hope and in his advocacy for improving the life and lot of the ordinary individual. To illustrate, the solution he proposes to the nihilistic threat that he believes afflicts the Black community, even with its limitations, is meant to occasion hope and optimism as against despair and meaninglessness.[6] And the hope and optimism he wishes to inspire is not just for Black America, but instead is for all of "the working-class and underclass American communities."[7] The reason is that it is this entire group that constitutes "the wretched of the earth" within America.

Although West grounds this optimism in his Christian background, so that in a sense he anchors his humanism in religion, he does not consider religion a necessary prerequisite for optimism. Nor for that matter does he consider religion a requirement for morality. He states that prophetic pragmatism is perfectly compatible with a nonreligious outlook (*Evasion*, p. 233). What this means is that prophetic pragmatism is only contingently related to a religious outlook. It follows therefore that although prophetic pragmatism embodies a moral outlook, that outlook too is perfectly compatible with a nonreligious perspective. But even if West did not assert that prophetic pragmatism is compatible with a nonreligious outlook, it is doubtful that he would claim that moral values have meaning in the absence of human experiences. The empirical grounding of prophetic pragmatism would certainly argue against such a position. It is a contingent fact that humans exist and hence *that human societal experiences* call for moral valuation. From this it would follow that morality would be absolutely unintelligible for human beings in the absence of human experiences.

The third characteristic of humanism noted above is that ethical judgments are open to rational scrutiny and they can be given empirical warrant. It is clear that the humanism I am attributing to West, based as it is on his prophetic pragmatism, would uphold this characteristic. Consider that West is constantly calling for a critique of the status quo. This call is motivated by what he deems a moral outrage against the perceived suffering of and injustice meted out to others. Implicated in this call, then, is a demand that we deploy our rational faculty to analyze the cause of human suffering and to search for solutions to human misery. One can assume that, for West, the ethical judgments we form at any given moment are subject to the Emersonian empirical principles of revisability, contingency, and experimentalism. After all, he tells us that it is these principles that undergird American pragmatism, of which prophetic pragmatism is a contemporary variant (*Evasion*, chapter 1). I turn now to West's discussion in "The New Cultural Politics of Difference" for further amplification of this thesis.

II

The central idea in "The New Cultural Politics of Difference" is that, at any given historical period, cultural critics are responding to the numbing crisis of their time. For example, in the mid-nineteenth century, a period West describes as the decline of the Age of Europe, Matthew Arnold, one of the cultural giants of the time, proposed a way of addressing the crisis of a potential conflict between, on the one hand, the rapidly eroding aristocracy and an emerging arrogant middle class and, on the other hand, a massive, restless working class with anarchic tendencies. According to West, Arnold's proposal consisted in a dissolution of classes and the establishment of a secular humanist culture. Arnold believed that the secular reconceptualization of culture – that is, wresting culture away from the dominant religious-based institutions to secular institutions – "could play an integrative role in cementing and stabilizing an emerging bourgeois civil society and imperial state" (KF, p. 6). In this regard, Arnold conceived of cultural critics as "the true apostles of equality" (KF, p. 7).

Arnold's response is significant because it expresses his belief that a revision of culture, consisting in a reconstitution of the power structure, would ensure stability (as against anarchy) and hence preserve European civilization. West quotes Arnold as saying, "Through culture seems to lie our way, not only to perfection, but even to safety" (KF, p. 7). The operative words here are "our" (versus their), "perfection" (versus imperfection and ugliness), and "safety" (versus barbarism and mob conduct). As West correctly observes, the questions that immediately arise are: who are the "we" whose "perfection" and "safety" must be preserved; and who are the "they" whose imperfection and barbarism must be guarded against? These questions are significant because, says West, they exhibit the typical Euro-centric white male character of the cultural critic's response to the crisis of the period. The "us" to whom Arnold refers were the white males and the "them" referred to others. Indeed, the us/them distinction in Arnold's response is clearly exclusionary, says West, especially in light of Arnold's "negative attitudes toward British working-class people, women and especially Indians and Jamaicans in the Empire" (KF, p. 8). West thus concludes correctly that, for Arnold, culture was meant to be a weapon for bourgeois white (read European) male safety (KF, p. 8). In West's view, it is this Arnoldian conception of culture that has come to inform Western society. And it is this conception of culture that motivates and infuses the new cultural politics of difference. In other words, it is this conception of culture that provides the crisis to which the new cultural politics of difference is respond-ing in contemporary society.

According to West, the major crisis of contemporary society is the misrepre-sentation and marginalization of the Other – i.e. peoples of color, women, homosexuals, the elderly, and Jews – by the established institutions of power. The various forms of representation of these groups (or their members) as "different" has led to a depoliticization and exclusion of their members from so-called mainstream society. For West, it is these forms of representations and their consequences that comprise the crisis to which the new cultural politics of difference is responding. And the object of the response from marginalized peoples is to overhaul or dismantle the very institutions of power responsible for the crisis in question. As West puts it, the objective is "to empower and enable social action and, if possible, to enlist collective insurgency for the expansion of freedom, democracy and individuality" (KF, p. 4).[8]

West identifies what he characterizes as three distinct challenges confronting the practitioner of the new cultural politics of difference: intellectual, existential, and political. The intellectual challenge is: how does the cultural critic respond, at least in terms of proposals put forward, to the crisis of the period? The existential challenge is: how does the practitioner of the new cultural politics of difference acquire the "self-confidence, discipline and perseverance necessary for success without an undue reliance on the mainstream for approval and acceptance?" (KF, p. 25). And the political challenge is of making relevant to the larger society one's intellectual engagements by forming alliances with, and utilizing, those extraparliamentary organizations whose sole purpose is to agitate and advocate on behalf of the less fortunate. I shall treat his discussion of these challenges in turn.

To the extent that the new cultural politics of difference is responding to the crisis of marginalization and downright exclusion in contemporary society, con- tends West, its inception can be traced to the post-Second World War period. This period marked the end of the Age of Europe, with much of Europe ravaged by war and the former European colonies agitating for and gaining political independence. But the period also marked the birth of the United States as a major Western power, for while Europe was struggling economically to recover from the war, the United States was enjoying tremendous economic success. This success in turn occasioned a new American middle class. Of significance, though, is that tempor- ally contiguous with the emergence of this new mass middle class, says West, was "the first major emergence of subcultures of American non-WASP [i.e. non White Anglo-Saxon Protestant Christian] intellectuals: the so-called New York intellec- tuals in criticism, the Abstract Expressionists in painting, and the bebop artists in jazz music" (KF, p. 11). According to West, the emergence of these new sub- cultures signaled a challenge to the dominant American white male elite that was still loyal to an older and eroding European culture. Outside of the United States, Blacks in the former European colonies were challenging white hegemonic cultural practices.[9]

It is not difficult to see why both New World and Old World Blacks would be mounting intense challenges to white hegemonic practices. Since colonialism (and its predecessor slavery) was legitimated on a deliberate white supremacist denial of the humanity of Black people and an attendant blatant and systematic (mis)repre- sentation of Blacks, post-Second World War Black cultural critics, both within and outside the United States, were driven, therefore, by the quest to validate Black humanity against the preponderant racist cultural practices. In other words, the early Black cultural critics embarked upon the task of reconstituting Black iden- tities and articulating Black humanity.[10] However, West considers highly deficient the intellectual response of the early Black cultural critics within the United States. He alleges that those critics were driven by a moralistic motivation to combat white supremacist and racist misrepresentations of Black peoples, and in light of this motivation they posited what they considered positive images of Blacks.[11] But he thinks that this strategy is problematic for two reasons. First, he says, the positing of the so-called positive images presupposes a moral judgment about what exactly constitutes a Black positive image. In other words, the notion of a positive Black image is value-laden. But, then, whose value judgment was being used as the norm for determining positive Black image(s)? No doubt, it was the value judgment(s) of those critics. What this all means, concludes West, is that the early Black cultural critics betrayed the same tendency of the dominant white male power elite, namely to universalize their own experiences as the experiences of all peoples. In the present situation, the early Black cultural critics universalized their own conception(s) of positive Black images as that (those) of all Black people.

Second, these critics, according to West, betrayed a homogenizing impulse in representing Black peoples as of a kind. This means that they essentialized Blackness or, what is the same thing, dissolved Black specificities and so elided differences among Black peoples. West attributes this essentialization of Blackness to a fundamental assumption of these early critics, namely that every Black person was an equal candidate for the same kind of racist characterization and treatment. Given this assumption, together with the additional assumptions – (a) that Blacks were of a kind, (b) that Blacks were psychologically similar to whites, and (c) that whites considered themselves human – the critics then concluded that Blacks too were human. But West thinks the generalization that Blacks are of a kind is false because, even though in principle every Black person was (and is) an equal candidate for the same kind of racist treatment, in practice considerations of class, gender, sexual orientation, and the like often influenced (and still influence) the way one Black person was (and is) treated in contrast to another. For example, a lower-class Black person was (and is) often treated less favorably than her or his middle-class Black counterpart. Of course, West is not contesting the claim that Blacks are similar to whites *qua* humans in light of psychological make-up. It is only the claim about the similarity of Black experiences that he is challenging. To that end, he explains what he considers the supposed facile generalization of the early Black cultural critics by saying that such a generalization was motivated by the critics' preoccupation with gaining white acceptance. Consequently, they advanced an assimilationist account of Black humanity by creating a mythological reified Black homogeneity. In short, West's contention is that the early Black cultural critics uncritically accepted the prevailing norms in their defense of Black humanity (KF, pp. 16–19).

There is no doubt that West is sympathetic to the antiracist motivations of the early Black cultural critics. Nevertheless, I believe that his criticism is unfair at best and misses the point at worst. Let us begin by considering closely the charge of essentializing Blackness or, as he puts it, of dissolving Black particularities. West's criticism seems rooted in the belief that the critics in question *should have been* concerned with drawing attention to Black specificities as they defended Black humanity. But the question is: why should they be concerned with Black specificities at all? An elaboration of Black specificities presupposes Black humanity in the first place. And since the point at issue was not whether there were specific kinds of Blacks – gays or lesbians, rich or poor, men or women – but instead the larger question of whether or not Blacks were humans, to elaborate Black particularities would have been to lose sight of the crucial objective, namely the representation of Blacks as *human*. Thus, West's criticism seems to miss the point.

To uphold my claim, consider how we normally proceed with the task of *classifying* objects (in the broadest sense of the term). Here we may invoke the Aristotelian concepts of *genus* and *species*, whereby the former is broader in extension than the latter.[12] To begin, I can classify myself as an animal and go on to say that I belong to the same genus as horses, cows, cats, dogs, owls, etc., for these too are animals. But then I may go on to point to the characteristics, whatever they are, that differentiate me from these other animals and in virtue of which I classify myself further as human and classify them as beasts. Then, further, within the human *species* I may go on to identify those specific features that distinguish me (and others like me) as male from those that distinguish a female. And so on. What this all means is that to classify oneself as X, Y, or Z is to identify oneself as a member of the class of entities that belong to X, Y, or Z. It is to say that one instantiates (or exemplifies) those attributes that are essential to, and thus are shared by, all the members of the class of X, Y, or Z.

Now, since the racist misrepresentation to which the early Black cultural critics were responding was not whether any Black was male or female, rich or poor, gay or lesbian, *but instead whether Blacks belonged to the same species as whites* – namely the human species – it was imperative, therefore, that the response be directed at this specific issue and not whether within the species some members had other traits. Of course, it follows that if a thing is human, *ceteris paribus* it also is either male or female, gay or lesbian (or may be neither), rich or poor, etc. But the converse is not true. It does not follow, for example, that because a thing is male or female it is therefore human. Thus, West's criticism simply does not apply.

Suppose, however, one assumes that West was correct in his criticism. Still, I believe that one can make the case for treating the response of the early Black cultural critics more sympathetically than he seems to allow. To do this, let us turn to the existential challenge that West suggests the new cultural politics of difference should meet. The challenge, recall, is how the cultural critic of a marginalized, misrepresented, and disenfranchised group can develop the psychological fortitude, in the form of self-confidence, discipline, and perseverance, necessary for success without an undue reliance on the mainstream for acceptance and approval (KF, p. 25).

The most significant effect on African diasporic peoples of the assault on Black humanity is the undermining of their self-confidence and the questioning of their abilities and potentialities. Roy D. Morrison, II, makes this point very poignantly in respect of postemancipation Black Americans, writing: "Postemancipation blacks had social and economic inferiority imposed upon them by Jim Crow laws and racism. In many cases, they internalized such negative notions and came to regard themselves as innately inferior to whites."[13] West is fully aware of this problematic of Black existence, for he reminds us that "To be a black artist in America is to be caught in what I have called elsewhere 'the modern black diasporan problematic of invisibility and namelessness.' This problematic requires that black people search for validation and recognition in a culture in which white-supremacist assaults on black intelligence, ability, beauty and character circum-scribe such a search" (KF, p. 59; compare p. 74). This psychological damage of racist practices is much more visible and protracted in the West because of mass media — movies, television, radio, etc. — through which popular culture is disseminated. And contemporary Western societies still propagate "old" stereotypes of Blacks as intellectually inferior to whites even in somewhat sanitized ways but often with a pretended intellectual sophistication.[14] To be sure, such stereotypes are regularly and quickly challenged. But that is beside the point. The point, for my present purpose, is that a casual reflection upon contemporary racist practices cannot but lead one to imagine the kind of nearly insurmountable odds with which the early Black cultural critics had to contend in their endeavor to defend Black humanity, *especially in the absence of a cultural infrastructure or apparatus of their own*. One can assume, for example, that if their views were deemed "too radical" those views would not be given an avenue for expression. On the contrary, if those views gave a semblance of credence to the standard stereotypes and beliefs about Blacks, then they would readily find expression. It is pertinent to note, for instance, the circulation in the white academy of Leopold Senghor's absurd declaration that emotion is to Blacks as reason is to whites, and of John Mbiti's erroneous assertion that the African conception of time is limited to the past and the present and that Africans have no conception of the future.[15] These remarks perfectly harmonize with the prejudices that inform white denial of Black intelligence, rationality, and ultimately humanity. It is not surprising therefore that they were so readily circulated by mainstream intellectual outlets.

Against this background, then, it would seem that the early Black cultural critics who endeavored to defend Black humanity had little choice but to do so within the very cultural apparatus through which Black humanity was assaulted. In other words, it was impossible for the early Black cultural critics to pursue the task in question outside of the mainstream cultural apparatus, given that they did not have a cultural infrastructure of their own. They had to challenge the mainstream "from within," a method that West himself endorses in his frequent calls for transracial alliances with white liberals and others to address issues. (See my discussion of West's view in "Cornel West as Pragmatist and Existentialist.") Moreover, the early cultural critics had to engage the task without at the same time antagonizing the custodians of the apparatus. In sum, the early Black cultural critics had to practice political reticence — to adapt West's characterization of Dewey's maneuvering tactics in affiliating with humanitarian organizations that were sympathetic to the plight of the industrial underclass while still himself under the patronage of the very middle-class establishment that was largely responsible for the status quo (*Evasion*, pp. 80–1; compare p. 108).

I have highlighted this difficulty that the early Black cultural critics had to negotiate because I believe that it provides a basis for understanding and appreciating the alleged assimilationist and homogenizing impulses (to use West's terminologies) of those critics. It is in this light that I consider unfair West's condemnation of the motivations of the critics as originating simply from "a quest for white approval and acceptance and an endeavor to overcome the internalized association of blackness with inferiority" (KF, p. 16). Indeed, a contemporary variant of the predicament of the early Black diasporan cultural critic can be seen in the endeavor of Black studies and women's studies to gain recognition and acceptance in the academy. These studies arose largely as a result of sociopolitical agitations in the 1960s. Before these studies were recognized as legitimate areas of intellectual inquiry, however, they had to go over many hurdles, the most fundamental of which was to be sanctioned by the various curriculum committees of academic institutions. To be sanctioned means to be accepted and approved by those committees. And the politics of gaining such acceptance and approval involved, among other things, modifying and moderating the rhetoric in which the arguments were made for the legitimacy of those studies as genuine areas of intellectual inquiry. Sometimes the politics of gaining acceptance and approval may even require diluting the content of the proposed syllabi of the studies so as not to offend the custodians of the academic "cultural" apparatus.

Notice that the curriculum committees here are analogous to the cultural apparatus in society whose approval and acceptance needed to be won by the early Black cultural critics. The strategic maneuverings of the pioneers of women's studies and Black studies are similar to those of the early Black cultural critics. And the difficulties that confronted the pioneers of women's studies and Black studies – e.g. that of making credible their various programs as legitimate areas of inquiry against the backdrop of hostile criticism and virulent opposition from the custodians of the academic cultural apparatus – correspond to the predicament of the early Black cultural critics. If, therefore, it would be disingenuous to condemn the pioneers of women's studies and Black studies for their strategic political maneuvers, it would similarly be disingenuous to condemn the early Black cultural critics for their strategic maneuverings in defending Black humanity within the very racist institutional structure that they sought to challenge. The need for sympathy and understanding that I am advocating is accented when one recalls West's own observation about the negotiating that even the prophetic critic, the new cultural worker situated within the umbrella of the new cultural politics of difference, has to undertake.[16]

III

This brings me to the political challenge that West says must be addressed by a practitioner of the new cultural politics of difference. Indeed, it is through his discussion of this challenge that West's humanistic scholarship most poignantly reveals itself. The challenge, to repeat, is for the practitioner to make relevant to society at large her or his intellectual engagements by working with extraparliamentary groups whose purpose is to advocate for the less fortunate in society. Examples of extraparliamentary groups are the church and similar religious organizations, trade unions, the National Association for the Advancement of Colored People (NAACP), academic organizations such as the American Association of University Professors (AAUP), and similar types of civic organizations. A condition for being a practitioner of the new cultural politics of difference, for West, is that the individual be affiliated both with the academy and with extraparliamentary groups of the kind mentioned above. *Qua* intellectual, the practitioner necessarily functions within the academy in order to stay "attuned to the most sophisticated reflections about the past, present and future destinies of the relevant cultures, economies and states of our time" (KF, p. 102) and to gain exposure to the "paradigms, viewpoints and methods" that the mainstream has to offer (KF, p. 27). On the other hand, in being affiliated with extraparliamentary organizations, the practitioner of the new cultural politics of difference grounds herself or himself in what West describes as subcultures of criticism – that is, those "progressive political organizations and cultural institutions of the most likely agents of change" (KF, pp. 27, 102–3). This simultaneous positioning is essential for the intellectual to connect the life of the mind to praxis. In particular, the ultimate goal of this dual and complementary positioning is to help promote "greater democracy and freedom" (KF, p. 103) in society. And the intellectual accomplishes this feat through providing systematic criticism that demystifies existing power structures and by implementing in praxis the ideas garnered from the academy. In this connection, a subtext in West's discussion is that the new cultural worker should conceive of herself or himself as a kind of Socratic gadfly to the society and even to the very institutions to which she or he belongs within and outside the academy. As a Socratic gadfly, the new cultural worker must bring to bear all of her or his analytical skills to interrogate existing power structures, institutions, issues and communal relations in the hope of improving them. The crucial issues on which she or he should focus attention are political, economic, and social – or, more generally, existential. The new cultural worker should be prepared to engage issues such as the following:

> how to help generate the conditions and circumstances of such social motion, momentum and movements that move society in more democratic and free direc-

tions. How to bring more power and pressure to bear on the status quos so as to enhance the life chances of the jobless and homeless, landless and luckless, empower degraded and devalued working people, and increase the quality of life for all? (KF, p. 102)

West captures this political role of the intellectual in the concept of the intellectual as a critical organic catalyst of change in society (KF, pp. 27, 102), a concept he obtained from the critical thought of the Italian Marxist Antonio Gramsci.[17] Following Gramsci, West distinguishes between "organic" and "traditional" intellectuals. The former, he says, are those individuals who are "linked to prophetic movements or priestly institutions, [and] take the life of the mind seriously enough to relate ideas to the everyday life of ordinary folk." For West, organic intellectuals are "activistic and engaged." In contrast, traditional intellectuals "revel in the world of ideas while nesting in comfortable places far removed from the realities of the common life." As such, traditional intellectuals are "academic and detached" (KF, p. 87).[18] In light of this distinction one can appreciate the severity of West's criticism of Black intellectuals. The thrust of his criticism is that Black intellectuals have little or no respect in the Black community precisely because they are largely "traditional" intellectuals. Thus, their intellectual engagements have little or no instrumental value to the day-to-day predicament that confronts the Black community. What this means, in effect, is that Black intellectual engagements are not humanistically oriented. Yet, before I determine whether or not West's own practice is congruent with his rhetoric, it may be worthwhile to examine the reasons he gives for this lack of humanistic orientation of Black intellectual engagements, and thus whether or not he is justified in condemning Black intellectuals as he does.

West traces the supposed irrelevance of Black intellectual activities, and hence what he perceives as the impotency of Black intellectuals, to the nonexistence of the necessary infrastructure in Black institutions to sustain intellectual life (KF, pp. 70–1; compare RM, p. 64). He attributes this state of affairs to two factors: (a) Black integration into mainstream postindustrial elite American universities even as these institutions have shown a tendency to question the abilities and capabilities of Black students as potential scholars (KF, p. 74; compare p. 70); and (b) a lack of creative imagination among Black scholars themselves to originate and sustain indigenous institutional mechanisms that promote criticism and self-criticism (KF, p. 70). These two factors, for West, conjunctively inhibit the development of the intellectual apparatus that will yield and sustain the kind of culture that defines intellectual life. Given that Black intellectuals, like other professionals in society, seek fame, recognition, status, and power, the kind of climate in which they function, with little to sustain them intellectually, has made the bulk of them inconsequential to the wider academy (which often marginalizes them) and to the Black community itself.[19] And the situation is exacerbated by an endemic tension and distrust between Black intellectuals on the one hand and the larger Black community on the other, especially since the former refuse to be "organically linked with African American cultural life" (KF, p. 71) in visible ways. According to West, this refusal is effected through exogamous marriages, abandonment of Black institutions, and a "preoccupation with Euro-American intellectual products [that] are often perceived by the black community as intentional efforts to escape the negative stigma of blackness or [that] are viewed as symptoms of self-hatred" (KF, p. 71).

But what are the sociological factors that account for this lack of infrastructure to promote and sustain intellectual activity in the Black community? This question is of the utmost importance since, as West observes, at least two main intellectual traditions are endemic (even intrinsic) to African-American life: (a) the Black Christian tradition of preaching, i.e. Black orality and oratory; and (b) the Black musical tradition of performance (KF, pp. 72–3). To characterize as "traditions" the Black practice and methodology of preaching and musical performance is to say the following: (a) that the respective forms of activity in each tradition are executed within an institutional infrastructural framework; (b) that there is a culture which both sustains and in turn is sustained by the infrastructure; (c) that there are very rigid criteria for excellence, criteria that are applied ruthlessly but very objectively; and (d) that there is an intolerance for mediocrity. It is because of these factors, says West, that the "traditions" in question have been able to produce and immortalize legendary figures in both music and the Black church.[20] Yet we do not find a similar or equivalent tradition in Black intellectual life. According to West, this is partly because the Black community as a whole conceives of intellectual life as having *only* instrumental value. Thus, they celebrate the intellectual who is a political activist or cultural critic (KF, p. 71).

Assuming that West is correct, his diagnosis suggests that there has been a monumental failure of the Black institutions themselves to define their relevance to the Black community. After all, Black intellectuals are members of academic institutions. Accordingly, the larger Black community's belief that Black intellectuals are useless to their needs, if true, is more a reflection of the failure of the Black institutions than of the Black intellectuals. In other words, the phenomenon West describes is more a statement about the Black institutions themselves than about the Black intellectuals.[21] Of course, the supposed perception of impotence of the Black intellectual, again if true, is a post-Civil Rights phenomenon. The 1960s witnessed all stripes of Black people, intellectuals and non-intellectuals, men and women of different classes and stations in life, banding together at the grassroots level in the advocacy and demand for human freedom and dignity. There was institutional commitment to the struggle for civil rights. But above all, there was *a service ethos* that Black institutions fostered, encouraged and transmitted. Somehow, this spirit that linked the individual with the larger community via the institutions in question seemed to evaporate with post-Civil Rights gains. The importance of institutions has now become subordinate to the (self-) importance of the individual. Consequently, except only nominally, there has been an "erosion of the service ethos," as West calls it, at both the institutional and the individual levels. Echoing a similar sentiment, bell hooks states: "We have experienced . . . a change in that communal ethic of service that was so necessary for survival in traditional black communities. That ethic of service has been altered by shifting class relations. . . . A certain kind of bourgeois individualism of the mind [now] prevails."[22]

This is certainly not to deny that particular individuals, specifically academic intellectuals, sometimes make the effort to be involved with local groups or organizations in their communities. In his challenge of West's attack on Black intellectuals, Lewis Gordon provides instances of academic intellectuals as political activists.[23] Indeed, Gordon faults West's criticism of Black intellectuals on two counts. First, he questions what he deems West's subscription to a postmodernist restrictivist concept of the intellectual as an academician and, consequently, West's claim that Black academic intellectuals detach themselves from their communities. Gordon thinks, on the contrary, that there are nonacademic intellectuals who are also involved in their communities. Second, and more importantly, Gordon charges that West wrongly identifies (all forms of) political activity with the consensus-building type that West himself practices and its *modus operandum* of "speech and agreement" (or dialogue). Gordon then construes West's charge that academic intellectuals have failed to make themselves relevant to the Black community to mean that, for West, academic intellectuals have failed to perform the *only* kind of political activity, the dialogic, that can lead to change in the community. To counter West's position, Gordon proceeds to identify another form of political activity, the instrumental (or functional), that, he says, emphasizes "building up institutions or simply responding to immediate problems" in the community. In Gordon's view, it is this latter form of political activity that is mostly practiced by Black academics. And it is in this context that Gordon gives examples of Black academic intellectual who are politically active in their local communities (Gordon, pp. 200–1). Unfortunately, says Gordon, the political activity of this type of academic intellectual is not as "visible," except of course in the community itself, as is the political activity of what he calls the celebrity-type of intellectuals – meaning people like West.[24]

Yet I do not think that Gordon's examples of political praxis constitute a refutation of West's thesis about the general impotence of Black intellectuals as such.[25] What Gordon demonstrates through the examples is that academic intellectuals *may sometimes* be involved in their communities. By means of these examples, Gordon thus highlights a dimension of political activity that West often downplays or subordinates to the dialogic method of addressing political concerns. Thus, it is not so much that West narrowly conceives of political activity as consensus-building as that he seems to privilege the consensus-building form over other forms of political activity. It is this privileging that leads him to envision political activity of the individual within an institutional framework whose operative methodology is speech and dialogue. Accordingly, he advances the thesis about the general absence of a coherent and systemic involvement of individuals as a call of duty. And he attributes this absence to the nonexistence of the necessary infrastructure in the Black institutions. Of course it does not follow that there are infrastructural problems of the kind West alleges or that individual academic intellectuals may not be active in their communities. And this is what Gordon demonstrates. But the two positions are not contradictory; they are complementary.[26]

While I believe that West is quite right in condemning the nature of Black intellectual life *as a function of major infrastructural problems in Black academic institutions*, I think that his criticism is misdirected. He should have directed his criticism at the Black institutions, especially their leadership, however that is defined, not at the intellectuals. The reason is that it is the leadership that has failed to take initiatives to cultivate and promote the kind of culture and climate that drives intellectual activity of the kind exhibited in elite white schools. The caliber of Black faculty (indeed of any scholar) and the nature and scope of their intellectual endeavors (however defined) are all a function of the kind of leadership provided. And where such leadership is found wanting in its function the results show in the intellectual life of the community. To illustrate, few Black institutions have taken initiatives to launch a serious African-American studies program or an African(a) studies program as part of their core curriculum. Yet it is these academic areas that speak directly to life in the Black community, and it is via these academic areas that a connection can be made with the ground-level activities in the community.[27] It seems that for most Black schools, African-American studies or African(a) studies exist only nominally. Thus, until the situation is corrected, Black intellectual activity will have no organic link of the kind West envisions, and so, assuming West is correct in his criticism, Black intellectuals will continue to be perceived collectively as useless to the larger Black community. Since it is the leadership that is vested with the authority and responsibility to create and/or alter the climate in which intellectual activity takes place, it is that body that West should have targeted for criticism, not the Black scholars themselves. It is that body that must generate and support the ethos of service in the collective consciousness of Black academics, an ethos that informs praxis in the form of duty.

IV

The preceding discussion of West's attack on Black intellectuals within the context of his analysis of the new cultural politics of difference clearly helps to bring into focus the humanistic orientation of his scholarship. The existential, intellectual, and political concerns that he thinks drive the new cultural politics of difference also inform his castigation of the Black intelligentsia. It is of course arguable that West is justified in his criticism of Black intellectuals or even that his claim of the perception of their supposed impotency is accurate. Gordon's criticism is meant to show that West got it all wrong. Regardless of how one interprets West's views, however, there can be no doubt that his concerns are humanistic, especially since they are inscribed within the parameters that govern humanistic enterprises. After all, his targets in both "The New Cultural Politics of Difference" and "The Dilemma of the Black Intellectual" are specific kinds of structures that delimit the scope of individual agency. In "The new cultural politics of difference," these are structures that incapacitate the individual from participating effectively in political, economic, and other forms of social activity. In "The Dilemma of the Black Intellectual," his critique is of the absence of those structures that he considers vital to empowering individuals so that they may realize their duty in the Black community.

Obviously, West wishes to contrast the nature of his own intellectual activity with those of other Black intellectuals, especially those in Black institutions. He considers his own scholarship and intellectual life to be directly relevant to the Black community and indeed to the larger American society, and believes that he establishes this relevance through an organic link with the community. By "organic link" he means participating in organizations that are concerned with addressing issues that pertain to the Black community. He states:

> when I think of my own organic link with the black community, it's not that I am somehow thoroughly immersed in the black community, in some pantheistic way. Rather, I'm simply working in a particular organization or institution in which we are contesting among ourselves how we can best generate visions, analysis, and forms of political action I want to say "be organized," rather than "be organic."[28]

The specific way in which West says he is organically linked to the Black community is through "black organizations and institutions, from united fronts to churches" (*A Critical Sense*, p. 136). And he lists among these organizations the Congressional Black Caucus and the Democratic Socialist Party of America. Germane to the present discussion is West's remark that he and other members of the Democratic Socialist Party of America had "tried to make health care a major public issue in America for nine years and . . . were unable to do it for the first six or so. Then boom, it just took off [under the Clinton administration, even though without success]" (*A Critical Sense*, p. 142). In typical Deweyan fashion, West's membership in the kind of organizations mentioned earns him a voice, he says, in the discussions that shape public policy. And to the extent that whatever public policies are adopted affect different constituencies, West thus says he sees "the need for multicontextualism." By this he means traversing the different kinds of constituencies "from working people to very poor people, to the academy, as well as other professions" (*A Critical Sense*, p. 136), all of whom are affected by public policy of one kind or another.

The foregoing catalogue of West's affiliation with groups whose operations and workings have a direct bearing on public policy cannot but lead one to conclude that his practice as a humanistic scholar is congruent with his rhetoric. One can even safely generalize that many of his writings and public engagements are but first-person expressions of the concept of the intellectual as an organic catalyst in society. This generalization is sustained by the kind of issues West addresses in works such as *Race Matters*, *Prophetic Fragments*, *Prophecy Deliverance!*, and *Keeping Faith*, to name a few.

To sum up, West's diverse engagements, articulated within his theoretical framework of prophetic pragmatism, establish him as a humanistic scholar. A humanistic scholar is an intellectual who endeavors to give practical application to her or his theoretical engagements in order to uphold the dignity of humanity. West's immediate concern is with the downtrodden in American society. By examining among other things two of West's essays, "The New Cultural Politics of Difference" and "The Dilemma of the Black Intellectual," I have shown how West pursues his humanistic endeavor. Of importance is that West's challenge that scholars relate the life of the mind to praxis is, indeed, a call for scholars to be humanistic in their orientation.

Acknowledgments

I wrote the first draft of this chapter during a one-semester sabbatical leave from Spelman College in spring 1997, which I spent at New York University under the auspices of the Faculty Resource Network. I wish to thank the administrators and staff of the Faculty Resource Network Program for making my stay worthwhile. I also wish to thank my faculty host, Professor Robert Gurland of the Philosophy Department of New York University, for those stimulating and very engaging trial periods for some of my ideas. I also wish to acknowledge the Faculty of Graduate Studies and Research at Middle Tennessee State University for the award of a Faculty Research Grant that enabled me to transform this chapter from its original form to the finished product that it is. Finally, I thank Abioseh M. Porter, Sheldon Wein, George M. Carew, Thaddeus Smith, and, as always, Tina Johnson for their very helpful comments and suggestions.

Notes

1   Cornel West, *Keeping Faith* (New York and London: Routledge, 1993), p. 71. This text is referred to hereafter as KF.

2   For accounts of humanism see the following: Paul Kurtz, "What is humanism?" In Paul
     Kurtz (ed.), *Moral Problems in Contemporary Society* (Englewood Cliffs, NJ: Prentice
     Hall, 1969), pp. 1–14 (referred to hereafter as Kurtz); Corliss Lamont, *The Philosophy of
     Humanism*, 7th edn (New York: Continuum, 1990); Nicola Abbagnano, "Humanism."
     In *The Encyclopedia of Philosophy* (New York: Macmillan, 1972); and F. C. S. Schiller,
     "The definition of pragmatism and humanism." In *Studies in Humanism* (Freeport, NY:
     Books for Libraries Press, 1907, reprinted 1967). My account of humanism as a
     philosophical position is based largely on Kurtz's discussion.
3   Kurtz goes on to sum up humanism as "an attempt to enoble and enrich human
     life, whether in individual terms as each human being satisfies his [her] ideals and
     dreams, or in social terms, where we seek to develop rules and norms of justice"
     (Kurtz, p. 5).
4   See Cornel West, "Prophetic theology." In Willis H. Logan (ed.), *The Kairos Covenant*
     (New York: Friendship Press, 1988), p. 115. It is to be remarked that West char-
     acterizes the essays that comprise *Prophetic Fragments* as his "response to one basic
     question: How does a present-day Christian think about and act on enhancing the
     plight of the poor, the predicament of the powerless, and the quality of life for all in a
     prophetic manner?" See his *Prophetic Fragments* (Trenton, NJ: Africa World Press,
     1988), p. xi.
5   I have discussed West's doctrine of prophetic pragmatism in my "Cornel West as
     pragmatist and existentialist." In Lewis R. Gordon (ed.), *Existence in Black: An Anthol-
     ogy of Black Existential Philosophers* (New York: Routledge, 1997).
6   See Cornel West, *Race Matters* (New York: Vintage Books, 1993), chapter 1 on the
     issue of Black nihilism (this work is referred to as RM hereafter). I discuss West's
     account in my "Cornel West as pragmatist and existentialist."
7   *The American Evasion of Philosophy* (Madison: University of Wisconsin Press, 1989), p. 7
     (hereafter abbreviated as *Evasion*).
8   West points out that the new cultural worker is not necessarily a marginalized member
     of society. On the contrary, she or he may be among the very privileged elite either by
     birth or by some other kind of social phenomenon. Yet, even in spite of the privilege
     that she or he enjoys, such a worker, through a Humean sympathetic consciousness,
     identifies with the predicament of the so-called Other, and so aligns herself or himself
     with the Other in challenging the status quo. Dewey showed a similar sympathy with
     the underclass of nineteenth-century America.
9   I have narrowed my discussion of the new cultural politics of difference to Black
     challenges of white hegemonic practices because, as will be seen, West criticizes the
     early Black response to such practices and I have doubts about the veracity of his
     criticism.
10   This endeavor may be described as the historical ancestor of the new (read con-
     temporary) cultural politics of difference. Minus the anachronism one could even
     say that the early Black response constitutes at the very least the intellectual
     challenge that West suggests a practitioner of the new cultural politics of difference
     should meet.
11   It is curious, even if beside the point, that West does not identify the critics to whom he
     is referring. In his discussion of the art of Horace Pippin (KF, chapter 4), he directs his

criticism at the protagonists of the Harlem Renaissance. He denounces the Harlem Renaissance, calling it "a self-complimentary construct concocted by rising, black, middle-class, artistic figures to gain attention for their own anxieties at the expense of their individual and social identities, and to acquire authority to impose their conceptions of legitimate forms of black cultural productions on black America" (KF, pp. 62–3). West accuses the protagonists of the Harlem Renaissance of the crime of denigrating the art of the ordinary self-taught Black folk (Horace Pippin, etc.). And, for West, the alleged denigration consists in the characterization of the art of the ordinary folk as an expression of "primitivism" because the artists lacked formal training. In so characterizing their art, charges West, those champions of the Harlem Renaissance meant both to distance themselves from the "uncouth" Black artists and to call attention to themselves as the sophisticated "new" negro whom the white establishment should find acceptable. It is very likely that West has the same group of cultural workers in mind in his discussion in the essay "The New Cultural Politics of Difference." In any case, it suffices for my purpose that West's criticism may apply to individuals as diverse as Alain Locke, Du Bois, James Weldon Johnson, George Schuyler, and Richard Wright. For an account of the politics of Black representation in the arts see, for example, Abby Arthur Johnson and Ronald Maberry Johnson (eds), *Propaganda and Aesthetics* (Amherst, MA: University of Massachusetts Press, 1979), especially chapters 2, 3, and 5. I consider below the veracity of West's criticism.

12   By the expression "broader in extension" I mean that the number and kinds of things that are subsumable under the concept *genus* are wider than those subsumable under the concept *species*.

13   Roy D. Morrison, II, "Self-transformation in American blacks." In Lewis R. Gordon (ed.), *Existence in Black* (New York: Routledge, 1997), p. 38.

14   The recent publication of J. Herrnstein and Charles Murray (eds), *The Bell Curve: Intelligence and Class Structure in American Life* (New York: Free Press, 1994) is proof of this claim.

15   See John Reed and Clive Wake (eds), *Senghor: Prose and Poetry* (London: Heinemann), pp. 34–5. For a sympathetic reading of Senghor's view see Abiola Irele, *The African Experience in Literatures and Ideology* (Bloomington and Indianapolis: Indiana University Press, 1990), chapter 4, especially. pp. 76–8. John Mbiti's view is expressed in his *African Religions and Philosophy* (London, Ibadan, and Nairobi: Heinemann Educational Books, 1969). For discussions of Mbiti's view see George Carew, "A critique of John S. Mbiti's traditional African ontology." *Quest: An International Journal of African Philosophy*, 8 (June), 1993, pp. 170–89, and my "An analysis of John Mbiti's treatment of the concept of event in African ontologies." *Quest: An International Journal of African Philosophy*, 9(2) and 10(1), 1996, pp. 139–57.

16   See PF, p. 42. I have already discussed West's observation in my "Cornel West as pragmatist and existentialist."

17   See Cornel West, "On Christian intellectuals." In PF, pp. 271–2.

18   This distinction underlies West's preference for Dewey's form of pragmatism over those of Emerson and Pierce (see *Evasion*, pp. 5–6). For West, Dewey was an organic intellectual. West gives Martin Luther King, Jr as another example. He says that King "linked the life of the mind to social change." See his "Martin Luther King, Jr:

prophetic Christian as organic intellectual" (PF, pp. 3–12). In this essay, West illumin-
ates the intellectual and existential influences on King's prophetic vision for social
change.

19   In general, faculty in Black institutions are often saddled with very heavy teaching
loads; they often lack the necessary research and support facilities to pursue scholarship;
and their remuneration and benefits are anything but congruent with the demands on
their time. It would thus be quite fair to say that they are often demoralized.

20   West gives as examples of musical legends Louis Armstrong, Sarah Vaughn, Charlie
Parker, Nat King Cole, etc., and in preaching, figures such as the Rev. Manuel Scott
and Gardner Taylor (KF, p. 73).

21   I suggest that this is the reason why Black institutions do not gain support from the
Black community, especially the Black middle class, and not that (as West claims) the
paucity of Black infrastructures for intellectual activity "results ... from" the inability
of Blacks to gain respect and support from the community (KF, p. 71). It is the other
way around.

22   bell hooks and Cornel West, "Black women and men: partnership in the 1990s." In
bell hooks and Cornel West, Breaking Bread: Insurgent Black Intellectual Life (Boston:
South End Press, 1991), p. 15.

23   See Lewis Gordon's Her Majesty's Other Children (Lanham, MD: Rowman and
Littlefield Publishers, 1997), pp. 194, 200–1. This work is referred to hereafter as
Gordon.

24   Gordon mistakenly thinks the distinction in question is between public intellectuals
and popular/celebrity intellectuals. His discussion rightly suggests, however, that both
celebrity and noncelebrity intellectuals are varieties of public intellectuals. But this is not
a major issue.

25   I shall ignore Gordon's mistaken ascription of a restrictivist/exclusivist conception of
the intellectual to West. I have already noted West's characterization of Martin Luther
King, Jr as an organic intellectual (note 18) even as we know that King was not an
academic intellectual. As if to anticipate Gordon, West describes King as "the most
significant and successful organic intellectual in American history" (PF, p. 3, original
emphasis). Furthermore, we saw that West distinguishes "two organic intellectual traditions in African American life: the black Christian tradition of preaching and the black
musical tradition of performance" (KF, pp. 72–3, emphasis added). He contrasts these
two forms of intellectual traditions to the academic intellectual tradition. Although all
three traditions are "linked to the life of the mind," the former two, he says, "are
rooted in the black life and possess precisely what the literate forms of black intellectual
activity lack" – namely, a culture and mechanism to sustain it (KF, p. 73). The
expression "rooted in black life" translates, in my view, into being connected with praxis.

26   Admittedly, West sometimes seems ambivalent in his critique of the Black intelligentsia. One gets the impression that he vacillates between two claims: (a) that it is the
absence of the necessary infrastructure in the Black community that is responsible for
the impotence of the Black intellectuals; and (b) that it is the Black academic intellectuals themselves who are detached from the community and in turn receive the
contempt of the community. This ambivalence/vacillation on his part leaves him
open to a variety of interpretations each of which has some measure of plausibility.

Nevertheless, I believe that it is the first of these claims that is central to his discussion. The reason is that West generally considers the existential predicament of the individual as a function of certain forces and structures against which the individual is to struggle. The forces and structures may be political, social, economic, or, as in the case of the Black community, institutional malaise. In his view, it is these factors that need always to be reconfigured in order to improve the life and lot of the individual.

27   One exception is Spelman College in its African Diaspora and the World (ADW) course. Inaugurated in 1993, this course was designed with the express objective of serving as a core curriculum identity-marker that should distinguish the institution from all others of its kind. Even so, the college has not envisioned the course beyond the freshman level in spite of overwhelming evidence (based on positive student reactions) of its value. Besides, there is an abysmal failure on the part of the college to provide the necessary resources to support the course and incentives to entice faculty out of their narrow specializations to be interested in teaching the course. Not to mention that the college has been extremely reluctant to commit the resources to recruit faculty whose formal training is in interdisciplinary studies with emphasis on the African Diaspora.

28   "American radicalism." In Peter Osborne (ed.), *A Critical Sense: Interviews with Intellectuals* (New York and London: Routledge, 1996), p. 136. Subsequent references to this text are to the page numbers of this volume.

18

Cornel West's Representations of the Intellectual: But Some of Us Are Brave?

Nada Elia

The choice of becoming a black intellectual is an act of self-imposed marginality in the black community; it assures a peripheral status in and to the black community.

Cornel West, *Keeping Faith*

Exile means that you are always going to be marginal, and that what you do as an intellectual has to be made up because you cannot follow a prescribed path. If you can experience that fate not as a deprivation and as something to be bewailed, but as a sort of freedom, a process of discovery in which you do things according to your own pattern, as various interests seize your attention, and as the particular goal you set yourself dictates· that is a unique pleasure.

Edward W. Said, *Representations of the Intellectual*

When one renders black intellectualism synonymous with black academics, the intelligentsia increasingly distances from past and present material, democratic struggles for social justice.

Joy James, *Transcending the Talented Tenth*

Cornel West is a pragmatist philosopher – as much a social reformer as a lover of ideas. A scholar with a political commitment to justice, he does not shy away from confronting the prejudices of his readers. By denouncing the pervasive presence of racism among "liberals," the myopia of Afrocentrists, the voracious greed of corporate capitalism, and numerous other social ills plaguing contemporary society, West has prodded our consciousness, challenging us to acquire greater insights into the plight of the majority, the have-nots. Yet as he reaps one professional laurel after another, West's tone, in his articles, interviews, and public addresses, becomes gloomier, as he writes that his academic achievements have "inescapably" alienated him from the African-American community he sprang from, whose members' circumstances he seeks to represent and ameliorate.

West opens his meditative essay "The Dilemma of the Black Intellectual" with the observation that "The contemporary black intellectual faces a grim predicament. Caught between an insolent American society and an insouciant black community, the African American who takes seriously the life of the mind inhabits an isolated and insulated world."[1] According to West, there are (only) two organic intellectual traditions in African-American life: the Black Christian tradition of preaching and the Black musical tradition of performance. Practitioners of these traditions are blessed with community ties that are reinforced with every exercise of their vocation. Black literate intellectual activity, on the other hand, is the product of secular Euro-American education; hence a Black intellectual scholar's inevitable alienation from the Black community, despite the desire "to dedicate one's life to the activities of reading, writing, and conversing for the purposes of . . . political enhancement of black (and often other oppressed) people."[2]

West is laudable for his persistence in denouncing the oppression of Black America, even as he personally escapes its harsher direct impact. In doing so, he differs, for example, from such Black thinkers as Shelby Steele, who questions whether racism can still be considered an impediment to the professional advancement and success of African-Americans, and who, in "On Being Black and Middle Class," for example, polemicizes the end of a feeling of group victimhood among Blacks. But West should not be compared to the likes of Steele, an outspoken critic of affirmative action, and the darling of Black and white conservatives.

Our examination of West's feelings of forlornness will benefit instead from comparisons with two sets of intellectuals: Black scholars, activists, and academics, with whom he shares race; and those he has called "race-transcending intellectuals," (as opposed to "nationalists" and "race-erasing intellectuals"), who are nevertheless committed to improving the circumstances of their less privileged community members. I wish to argue two points. One is that West's narrow definition of the intellectual is in conflict with his own professed revolutionary ideals, as it fails to recognize genius outside the elite academy. My second point is that, even by his very narrow definition (which may indeed translate at times into marginalization), West need not suffer from the existential angst he is experiencing, for, as Edward Said argues in *Representations of the Intellectual*, to be an exile, literally or metaphorically, is to have greater freedom to espouse various ideologies, beliefs, movements, and to reside, in some ways, in the "site" of one's choice, while the native who has never left her or his community is mired in confining traditions.

Yet one must address the very real estrangement that West experiences. West's gloom has at least two sources, one personal, the other racial. The personal comes from his believing he is representative of the "Black intellectual," a claim that, fortunately, is erroneous. I say fortunately not because I do not wish a progressive, highly erudite, extremely successful scholar to represent the "Black community," but rather because I agree with the numerous Black scholars who acknowledge that this community is now, and always has been, an "imagined community."[3] More correctly, while the homogenizing "commonalities" were imagined, the "community" has historically been united by the negatives: the absence of freedom of physical movement and open religious beliefs, the denial of political rights, the vicious and continuing attacks on the Black person's very integrity and humanity. In terms of its positive achievements, however, the Black "community" has never been monolithic, and while it has occasionally been fruitful to gloss over differences in order to secure a greater good, those differences have never been erased. The very attempt to push them into the background has backfired at key moments in the history of Black struggles, as evidenced by the disagreements between Sojourner Truth and Frederick Douglass, Mary Shadd Carey and Henry Bibb, W. E. B. Du Bois and Booker T. Washington, Martin Luther King, Jr and Malcolm X, Martin Luther King, Jr and the Student Nonviolent Coordinating Committee (SNCC) leadership, as well as the denunciation, by Black feminists/womanists, of the sexism of Black revolutionaries.

As far as the racial reason for concern goes, West is certainly justified in his fears for "the future of the race." Black Americans are still among the poorest communities in the USA – comparable indeed to poor "Third World" communities – with the country's highest unemployment rates. As the "national unemployment rate" dipped to a thirty-year low in 1999, hovering at 4 percent of the "American population," it was a staggering 12 percent among Blacks, a figure that, as Black economist Julianne Malveaux points out, would be considered a crisis requiring immediate attention if it were among whites.[4] And while the career opportunities of female Black academics are greater than they have ever been, they remain confined in many ways that do not apply to white women. Strong white women are viewed as super-achievers, for example, but a strong Black woman is deemed "threatening," a much greater danger to the institution than her pale sister. And while many academic departments (attempt to) have a Black woman among their members, very few actively seek two Black women, even among those departments that would find it unacceptable to have only one white female.

One could argue further that West's melancholy comes from a correct reading of the situation of African-Americans at the end of a century which failed to deliver on its many promissory notes, "a ghastly century whose levels of barbarity, bestiality, and brutality are unparalleled in human history."[5] As that century neared its end, West felt he was facing "the frightening abyss – or terrifying inferno – of the twenty-first century,"[6] when corporate profiteering drives an ever wider wedge between the haves and the have-nots. This comes at a very high cost to Blacks generally, and a more personal one to the token few, the successful talented tenth who have joined the "haves":

As this Talented Tenth comes to be viewed more and more with disdain and disgust
by the black working class and very poor, not only class envy but class hatred in black
America will escalate – in the midst of a more isolated and insulated black America.
This will deepen the identity crisis of the black Talented Tenth – a crisis of survivor's
guilt and cultural rootlessness.[7]

But the majority of Blacks, from various walks of life, do not feel that way.
Nell Irvin Painter, herself a professor at Princeton University, is "fascinated" by
what she describes as West's "apocalyptic tone" when he describes the present
circumstances, comparing them to the recent past, and reminiscing on what
he views as more favorable circumstances for Blacks some fifty years ago.
Painter differs significantly from West, who claims that "in all honesty, there
were relatively more and better black intellectuals then than now,"[8] explaining
that:

> the present-day academy and contemporary literate subcultures present more obs-
> tacles for young blacks than those of decades past. This is so for three basic reasons.
> First, the attitudes of white scholars in the academy are quite different from those in
> the past.... Second, literate subcultures are less open to blacks now than they were
> three or four decades ago.... Third, the general politicization of American intellec-
> tual life ... constitutes a hostile climate for the making of black intellectuals.[9]

A Black intellectual herself, and one who finally has a forum for the exercise of her
talent, Painter argues that, as for her, "I wouldn't go back seventy-five years or to
any previous time. In fact, I wonder whether I was born a few years too early to
take full advantage of opportunities open to educated black women. . . . I place my
hopes in the future."[10] Similarly, bell hooks, who co-authored *Breaking Bread:
Insurgent Black Intellectual Life* with West, argues that she does not share West's
feeling of estrangement from the "black community":

> In fact, I think that a lot of the bridges that have been built between various black
> communities have been formed by black women thinkers. But our work does not
> receive attention. So many people say there is a lack of intellectual leadership, part of
> that lack is the refusal of the masses of people to take on the work that many black
> women have already done, and raise us to the level of leaders.... I don't come here
> as an intellectual who's been estranged from her community.... I feel I don't know
> that estrangement. I feel that a lot of black women don't. We nurture both in the
> academy and beyond.[11]

Both Painter's and hooks's arguments come from a feminist perspective, which
proposes that intellectual Black women's work, their leadership, as well as the
significant improvement in their circumstances, "in the academy and beyond," fail
to be recognized. In their denunciation of the invisibility of Black women's
achievements, they echo to some degree the thesis behind the groundbreaking

and appropriately titled 1981 anthology *All the Women Are White, All the Men Are Black, But Some of Us Are Brave.*

Most Black college students also feel their lives are pregnant with a myriad of opportunities, despite the racism that they acknowledge still affects their social lives, a racism they do not fail to recognize in the anti-Affirmative Action crusade that would rob them of the chance to go to college – a chance the vast majority of them have today, but which they did not have half a century ago. And if West's tone strikes an unduly apocalyptic note with (mostly women) fellow scholars, and both male and female students, it also rings an unfamiliar tune for many younger Blacks outside the academy, who believe things have never looked brighter for them. Popular, nonintellectual Black magazines such as *Essence* and *Ebony* regularly feature positive portrayals of Black people, even as they acknowledge that "the system" continues to downpress them. *Essence* and *Ebony* do not claim to address or represent the subaltern – and illiteracy, for example, is rampant among the poor who have slipped through the cracks – but West writes about marginalization from the majority of Blacks, not only the least privileged among them.

Beyond the academy, Malveaux points out that, in 1940, about 70 percent of Black women worked as domestics, while in 1998, 45 percent of African American women held jobs that paid less than $7.50 per hour, compared to 38 percent of white women. Malveaux correctly deplores the hardship of these women, yet the figures she gives, while dismal, reveal a significant narrowing of the racial divide, itself an indicator of an improvement in Black women's circumstances. In an interview, white feminist Susan Faludi explained that, in recent years, women's circumstances have nudged up, while men's circumstances have remained stagnant or even slightly deteriorated during times of national economic depression. Recognizing that, despite the media's efforts to convince us otherwise, "it's hardly a time of jubilation for anyone," Faludi nevertheless writes:

> The truth is, of course, that women are moving from the subbasement to the basement. By any objective measure – pay, representation in boardrooms, status – men are still ahead. But psychologically it's much harder to fall than to climb, even if you land at a higher point than those who are just beginning to rise.[12]

I suggest that, *as a middle-class male*, West feels he is confronting what he has described as "a hostile climate for the making of black intellectuals," while Painter, for example, is seeing greater opportunities than ever for her and other women scholars.

Another Black feminist scholar, Joy James, argues that West's feeling of estrangement as an intellectual comes from the nature of his elitist academic scholarship, adding that many intellectuals are in no way estranged from their Black community, although they may not actually be recognized as "intellectuals" when one uses the narrow academic definition of a scholar with numerous books published by university presses. "When one renders black intellectualism synonymous with black academics," James warns, "the intelligentsia increasingly distances from past and present material, democratic struggles for social justice."[13] James gives Charlene Mitchell as an example of "an activist intellectual without degrees, book contracts, or university appointment."[14] She argues that Mitchell's early years call for a rethinking of "the scant attention paid to the political thought and agency of youth,"[15] for Mitchell was only in her teens when she mobilized Black and white patrons to desegregate Chicago theaters, joined the Communist Party, and convinced people in cold homes that mine owners, not the striking mine workers, were to blame for the strike.

Even as he writes of his alienation, West recognizes, in "The Dilemma of the Black Intellectual," that his is indeed a "bourgeois model," whose "linchpin . . . is academic legitimation and placement."[16] To him, this is: "inescapable for most black intellectuals. This is so because most of the important and illuminating discourses in the country take place in white bourgeois academic institutions and because the most significant intellectuals teach in such places."[17]

The above citation is representative of West's conflation of two terms that are not synonymous, though they may overlap, namely the scholar and the intellectual. It does not accommodate the likes of Mitchell, whose erudition is impressive though she has never studied or taught in white elite institutions, or Mumia Abu-Jamal, whose prison letters reveal a critical mind that years behind bars have failed to dull. Mitchell and Abu-Jamal certainly produce "important and illuminating discourses," and neither feels alienated from or by her community.

James's analysis, in *Transcending the Talented Tenth: Black Leaders and American Intellectuals*, of some of the factors behind the political ineffectualness of professional elites, provides what I believe to be among the best readings of West's feelings of isolation. "It is logical," James writes, "but not anti-intellectual, that oppressed people prioritize the productions of intellectuals they find useful and enlightening, and that they make value judgements relevant to their estimation of intellectuals' ability to deliver even a brief respite from oppressive conditions."[18] Thus, if West does not have the recognition he covets among oppressed Blacks, it is not because of his intellectualism, but rather because of the elite nature of his endeavors, endeavors which can, *at best*, produce an excessively slow trickle-down effect. Radical intellectual activists, however, maintain, as Frantz Fanon explained in *The Wretched of the Earth*, that the successful revolutionary struggle requires "a whole social structure being changed from the bottom up."[19]

In "Giving back," Walter Mosley speaks of "the blues" as the unbreakable bonds that link all Black Americans:

> The blues are the black man's culture, the black woman's race. They are our identity and why we recognize each other in all our hues and features, religions and origins. The high yellow socialite from a well-respected Atlanta clan knows the pain and

emptiness of the coal-colored cowboy riding the lonely north Texas range. She knows because their lot is the same.... They both see a world that is invisible to most of white America. To them, the beating of Rodney King wasn't a crime; it was the picture of a common history that started centuries ago.[20]

The soft-spoken, three piece suit clad, light-skinned West lives those blues too, shares that common history. In the introduction to *Race Matters*, he tells how he was reminded of it on numerous occasions, as he tried unsuccessfully to hail a taxi cab in New York, as he was repeatedly arrested by the police for driving "suspiciously slow" on a residential Princeton street with a posted speed limit of 25 m.p.h., and as he was arrested in Western Massachusetts on fake charges of trafficking heroin.[21] He is a brother, and Black Americans know it, and look up to him as a positive role model.

Why, then, does West feel so isolated? Why does he feel that his alienation, as he achieves academic success, is absolutely inevitable? Why does he feel it to be any different from the alienation of any intellectual from the laypeople? I must now address the second part of my argument, namely that intellectuals need not deplore their "marginal status," for it can indeed be viewed as a privileged position, allowing one "a double perspective that never sees things in isolation."[22]

The USA is not an intellectual country, as West himself recognizes in "The Dilemma of the Black Intellectual," where he observes:

> The quest for literacy indeed is a fundamental theme in African American history and a basic impulse in the black community. But for blacks, *as with most Americans*, the uses of literacy are usually perceived to be for more substantive pecuniary benefits than those of the writer, artist, teacher, or professor. (Emphasis added)[23]

Historically, this country's heroes have been successful entrepreneurs, business tycoons, entertainers, and their fellow-entertainers, the athletes. We may elect actors, singers, real estate or business tycoons, former wrestlers or basketball players as our "representatives," we vote them into our top political offices, but an intellectual for president is, quite simply, inconceivable in the USA. The "average American" can name countless athletes past and present, but not five philosophers. Intellectuals are not a visible part of the American people: in fact, only a small minority of Americans seek a higher education. According to the National Center for Educational Statistics, in 1995, some 15 million Americans were enrolled in institutions of higher education. Of these, 11 percent were African-Americans, a figure that compares well with the national 12 percent of the population. However, only 2 percent of the total degrees granted in any given year since 1985 are doctorates, across racial lines.

American people are not an intellectual people; their scholars are not household names. But that too is across all racial lines. A first-rate white scholar, say Eve

Kosofsky Sedgwick, is alienated from working-class white people. Asian-American shopkeepers or restaurant workers may value education highly (as do Blacks, indeed), yet they do not relate to, identify with, an Asian-American nuclear scientist. And a first-rate Black philosopher will remain an unknown entity among Blacks, unless she or he inscribes herself or himself into their lives as the person who led a march, organized a national boycott, and daily harassed the politicians, not fellow academics, with the urgent need to improve the circumstances of the suffering poor. One must remember that, to this day, Du Bois is better known for his political activism in the NAACP than for *Dusk of Dawn*. Similarly, the quality of her scholarship notwithstanding, Angela Davis is a cultural icon because of her political activism among subaltern communities: prison inmates, the illiterate, unemployed and unemployable urban poor, youth at risk.

In "Intellectual Exile: Expatriates and Marginals," Edward Said maintains, "exile is also . . . a *metaphorical* condition. . . . Even intellectuals who are lifelong members of a society can, in a manner of speaking, be divided into insiders and outsiders".[24]

> Every scene or situation in the new country necessarily draws on its counterpart in the old country. Intellectually this means that an idea or experience is always counterposed with another, therefore making them both appear in a sometimes new and unpredictable light: from that juxtaposition one gets a better, perhaps even more universal idea of how to think, say, about a human rights issue in one situation by comparison with another.[25]

In comparison to what West views as his "peripheral status in and to the black community," an intellectual such as Said, also from a privileged background, the product of private schooling, department chair at a prestigious university, and president of his discipline's largest international organization, the Modern Language Association, has immense and immediate recognition among oppressed members of his own Palestinian community. (I choose Edward Said as representative of the privileged insider, "race-transcending intellectual," because of numerous similarities in his and West's personal backgrounds.) Said has immediate recognition, despite the fact that he is an American citizen, a Christian speaking for a mostly Muslim community (Christian Palestinians have generally fared better than Muslims), and a nonresident of the usurped land. The majority of Palestinians have never read Said's scholarly work, do not know him to be a music critic as well as an academician. Most do not even know him as the author of *Orientalism*, a book that no humanities or social sciences scholar can ignore. They know him as the man who has received death threats for his pro-Palestinian stance in hostile territory, and for denouncing Yasser Arafat's nepotism. They know him as the man who spoke truth to power, when he had nothing to gain, and everything to lose from it. Without having read him, they know his writings have placed him on the Jewish Defense League's hit-list. Certainly an intellectual in every sense of the word, Said avers his vocation comes with inevitable publicity. "There is no such thing as a private intellectual, since the moment you set down words and then publish them you have entered the public world."[26]

Said, like West, belongs to the privileged among his native communities. Although a dispossessed exile, as West is an Afrodiasporan, Said was born into a wealthy family that nurtured his scholarly ambitions, as indeed West was born to a middle-class Black family who did not rent an apartment but owned their own home, and he was nurtured by a civilian air force administrator father and a schoolteacher mother. Said's college education, just like West's, consisted of Ivy League schools; in fact, both studied at Harvard and Princeton and visited at a number of elite universities before taking up high-ranking positions at these same elite institutions. And just as Said has been spared life under Israeli occupation, West, from his early childhood, has been spared life in the urban projects. On the other hand, Said's scholarship does not even address issues particularly pertinent to the Palestinians, while West has consistently written about issues directly related to Black existence. Yet Said does not feel alienated. In *Representations of the Intellectual*, Said says that he makes it a point to always accept, when possible, invitations to speak at Palestinian venues. In doing so, he cements his connections with underprivileged community members he is unlikely to meet at Columbia, or at other American universities where he lectures.[27] Said's practice is similar to that of bell hooks, who, when she gives lectures to overwhelmingly white audiences outside of her home institution, prearranges to find out where Blacks tend to hang out, and spends a few hours at restaurants, diners, or other popular venues frequented by Black patrons, so she can address their nonacademic concerns, such as dealing with alcoholism, drug addiction, or violence in the family, thus always reaching out.

In conclusion, I confess that my reading of West may be deemed a little harsh, yet I hope it will mostly be understood for what it is, a wake-up call for all our academic leaders of the left. West's intentions, as always, are blemishless. I have nonetheless tried to emphasize that his distance from the people who need his activism is not as "inescapable" as he believes. Surely, to be alternative is to recognize genius in ways not necessarily acknowledged by the dominant discourse. Recognizing Black genius outside the academy is also empowering and hope-inspiring, for it sees agency and resistance among those the dominant discourse had deemed helpless. In order to broaden our appreciation of Black intellectualism, we must change the criteria by which "intellectualism" is gauged. And, as we do so, US scholars may find it more acceptable to espouse "low culture" causes, and they will no longer be so isolated. As a highly respected scholar at what may well be the world's leading university, West is in a prime position to advocate this change.

Writing about Du Bois, "the towering black figure of the twentieth century," whom he holds in reverent awe, West commented:

Du Bois was never alienated by black people – he lived in communities where he received great respect and admiration. But there seemed to be something in him that alienated ordinary black people. In short, he was reluctant to learn fundamental lessons about life – and about himself – from them. Such lessons would have required that he – at least momentarily – believe that they were or might be as wise, insightful, and "advanced" as he; and this he could not do.[28]

If West could acknowledge the intellectualism of grassroots activists, the future of the Black intellectual will undoubtedly appear brighter to him. An undisputed leader, West can overcome the predicament of the Black intellectual in the elite institution. He should do so, as we are speeding down a slippery road, and cannot afford to sleep at the wheel. For I believe these are indeed the worst of times, when a country's president locks up the Blacks, keeps out the browns, harasses the women, and is the darling of Blacks, browns, women, and "the left."

Notes

1   Cornel West, *Keeping Faith: Philosophy and Race in America* (New York: Routledge, 1993), p. 67.
2   Ibid., p. 68.
3   See Benedict Anderson's discussion of that expression in the introduction to his *Imagined Communities: Reflections on the Origin and Spread of Nationalism* (New York: Verso, 1991).
4   Ironically, there is an advantage to the invisibility of black unemployment: at least the USA is not mounting a major war against a convenient enemy, simply to revive the national economy.
5   "Black Strivings in a Twilight Civilization." In Henry Louis Gates, Jr and Cornel West (eds), *The Future of the Race* (New York: Knopf, 1996), p. 56.
6   Ibid., p. 112.
7   Ibid., p. 110.
8   West, *Keeping Faith*, p. 68.
9   Ibid., pp. 68–9.
10 Nell Irvin Painter, "A different sense of time" (review of *The Future of the Race*), http://www.thenation.com/issue/960506/0506pain.htm
11 Comments made at a forum on "The Responsibility of Intellectuals in the Age of Crack" at the Massachusetts Institute of Technology, hosted by Eugene Rivers, and reproduced in *The Boston Review*, 19(1). Participants included West, hooks, Henry Louis Gates, Jr, Margaret Burnham, Glen Loury, and Anthony Appiah.
12 Susan Faludi, interviewed by Sue Halpern in *Mother Jones*, September/October 1999, p. 37.
13 Joy James, *Transcending the Talented Tenth: Black Leaders and American Intellectuals* (New York: Routledge, 1997), p. 156.
14 Ibid., p. 176.

15   Ibid.

16   West, *Keeping Faith*, p. 75.

17   Ibid., p. 76.

18   James, *Transcending the Talented Tenth*, p. 159.

19   Frantz Fanon, *The Wretched of the Earth* (New York: Grove Press, 1963), p. 35.

20   Walter Mosley, "Giving back." In Walter Mosley, Manthia Diawara, Clyde Taylor, and Regina Austin (eds), *Black Genius: African American Solutions to African American Problems* (New York: W. W. Norton & Co., 1999), p. 38.

21   West, *Race Matters* (New York: Vintage, 1994), p. xv.

22   Edward Said, *Representations of the Intellectual* (New York: Pantheon, 1994), p. 60.

23   West, *Keeping Faith*, p. 68.

24   Said, *Representations of the Intellectual*, p. 53.

25   Ibid., p. 60.

26   Ibid., p. 12.

27   I have personally read many of these "interviews" or reports of comments made at social occasions Said attended, and am occasionally dismayed at how commonplace they are, addressing, in a most elementary way, such basic and rehashed issues as "the American reception of *Orientalism*," or "Arab-bashing in the American media." Professionally, Said cannot conceivably benefit from granting them, yet he continues to do so. Indeed, what these "social comments" demonstrate without the shadow of a doubt is how well Said can address widely differing audiences, ranging from literary scholars to nonintellectual dabblers.

28   West, "Black Strivings in a Twilight Civilization," p. 56.

Afterword: Philosophy and the Funk of Life

Cornel West

> To hell with the philosophy of the great men of this world! All great wise men are as despotic as generals.
>
> Anton Chekhov

How sweet it is to be taken seriously by one's colleagues and friends in our fast-paced world of superficial praise and supercilious putdown! How joyous it is to encounter critics who actually have read one's work in a careful and cautious manner! So I salute the scholars who have contributed to this volume. And I especially thank the brilliant editor, my dear brother George Yancy.

I shall use this unique opportunity to not only respond to the major criticisms of my work put forward in these essays, but also couch my responses in the form of a pithy interpretation of my life and thought. First and foremost I am a *reader* – of works and lives – in order to survive and thrive. My addiction to the life of the mind is existential. I must read profound books in order to stay sane. My love of the world of ideas is erotic. I gain great pleasure from immersing my life in the lives and times of creative thinkers. Yet, in addition to sanity and pleasure, I read in order to enhance the art of living and expand the scope of democracy.

I consider my writings as by-products of and secondary to my readings of unsettling texts and disarming contexts. Hence most of my books are existential dialogues, or intimate conversations, with major figures who provoke my vision, challenge my viewpoint, or console my soul. The radical improvisational character and the existential dialogical content of my hybrid synoptic orientation and heterogeneous synthetic disposition appears on the surface as an undisciplined eclecticism. But this seems so primarily because the inspiration for my intellectual enactments, in written and spoken word, is as much or more music as philosophy. As with Walt Whitman, Mark Twain, James Baldwin, and Toni Morrison, my fundamental aim as an intellectual is to create a distinctive *presence* as voice and body in order to be seen, heard and felt in the cacophony of past and present voices in the grand dialogue of humankind. And I am in the American and New World African grain owing to my deep temperamental roots in two grand US art traditions: Black music (spirituals, blues, jazz, rhythm & blues and rap) and Black religious rhetoric. The painful laughter of blue notes and the terrifying way of the cross, of tragicomic darkness and of world-transforming compassion constitute indispensable elements of my Chekhovian Christian mode of thinking and being. This is why my existential soulmates and intellectual sources are more life-wrestling artists than academic philosophers – poetic geniuses like Montaigne, Pascal, Emerson, Kierkegaard, Ruskin, Du Bois, Lorde, instead of philosophic giants like Leibnitz, Kant, Frege, Carnap, Husserl, Strawson, and Quine. Critical engagement with both lineages is crucial. In the perennial quarrel between poetry and philosophy I embrace both, but tip my hat toward the poets, especially the musical poets (Beethoven described himself as a "poet of tones"). Yet since my Chekhovian Christian voice is filtered through two highly *unmusical* streams of thought, the progressive Marxist tradition and the radical democratic version of American pragmatism, the subterranean tragicomic darkness and substantive world-transforming compassion of my vision may appear muted.

Radical Historicism and Philosophy

We human beings are fundamentally featherless, two-legged, linguistically conscious creatures of biological inheritances and historical traditions. We are organisms of desire whose first day of birth makes us old enough to die yet whose ingenuity and curiosity make it possible to forge visions and hopes for more free and democratic possibilities. Our basic desires for protection, association, and recognition under circumstances not of our own choosing render us creatures of nature and creators of history. Of course, we can create new versions of nature or remain deferential to historical conditions. But we are contingent and fragile organisms in the face of the horrors of nature, the terrors of history, and the cruelties of fate and fortune. My Chekhovian Christian voice embraces a radical historicism with its concomitant fallibilism, contextualism, and experimentalism. Needless to say, my fallibilism promotes a piecemeal, not wholesale, skepticism. Therefore I reject any form of relativism. Instead my contextualism posits reliable, though not absolute (or transcendental), courts of appeal to adjudicate between scientific theories, moral viewpoints, aesthetic evaluations, and religious claims about the world. And my experimentalism accents the dialectical interplay of tradition and innovation, settled belief and unsettling doubt, status quo and unpredictable transformation. In this sense, the grand philosophic traditions in search of absolute certainty, indubitability, and necessity are suspect – voices to learn from and be challenged by but, in the end, contested – in the name of historical revision and open-endedness.

My obsession with modernity and evil, with forms of unjustified suffering and unnecessary social misery in modern times, propels me to put a premium on the analytical understandings of the causes of this social misery and the cultural sources for resistance to this suffering. My initial starting point is courage in the face of death, of social death, civic death, psychic death, and physical death. In short, I begin with Black existence in the American past and present in which the white supremacist threat of the variety of deaths has been prominent and paramount in the lives of people of African descent (slavery, Jim Crow, lynching, nobodiness, disease or destruction). Black culture is a distinctive modern culture primarily because it is preoccupied with coming to terms with the most devastating death-dealing forces in the most death-denying of modern civilizations (the USA). No other modern people has had to confront so many forms of violence and disrespect in a country that prides itself for its freedoms and civilities. My Chekhovian Christian voice – a voice obsessed with forms of death, courage and freedom – accents the transfigured cries, moans, and groans that enact existential agency and enable political insurgency in the face of overwhelming historical odds and weighty white supremacist forces. Yancy is right to view my work through the lens of existential and democratic hope (though I reject the language of "vanguard" on democratic grounds). Yet, like the blues, my hope has little to do with American optimism. Instead, it is rooted in the ever-changing capacity of each one of us to forge vision and courage to empathize, organize, and sacrifice for radical democracy and freedom. And this is an existential question as well as a political challenge.

Putnam, my dear teacher, colleague, friend, and brother, is right on the mark in his powerful and poignant essay. During our thirty-year conversation, Putnam has rightly noted my stress on the existential dimension of American pragmatism (given the emphasis on the social, aesthetic, and psychological dimensions by Peirce, Dewey, and James, respectively). My Kierkegaardian attention to death, despair, and disappointment and my Chekhovian concern with icy incongruity and dark absurdity – both (Kierkegaard and Chekhov) shot through with deep compassion – may undercut my Emersonian sense of possibility. Like James, Gramsci, and, at times, even Dewey, I candidly confront the nightside of our lives and societies. And like them, I do not fetishize evil or freeze its forms into natural phenomena. Yet I do have a darker and bleaker view than them, without succumbing to a fatalist or defeatist position. I simply acknowledge that the left has been defeated, with some discernible effects, and that human beings perennially wrestle with the historically mediated threats to being (anxiety), meaning (absurdity), and community (insecurity). Putnam's persuasive close reading of *The American Evasion of Philosophy* – the best I have seen – grasps the Gramscian intention of the text; to see the ways in which this rich though imperfect tradition can provide resources of existential and democratic hope for radical democrats in the USA. It is no accident that the work was inspired, in part, by the magisterial writings of Raymond Williams, who tried to do the same thing for post-war Britain.

Gordon, a young brilliant philosopher and radical Black activist, fully understands the existential and political dimensions of my project. He rightly grasps that I am not primarily a pragmatist, though he believes I have too great a faith in American society. More fundamentally, he believes I underplay or even ignore the Black intellectual tradition (with exceptions of Toni Morrison, W. E. B. Du Bois, James Baldwin, and a few others). Although he wrongly charges me with elevating Morrison to the status of greatness owing to her white recognition, i.e. Pulitzer Prize of 1987 and Nobel Prize of 1993, even though the essay he invokes appeared in 1985, I get his point. He, and others, understandably challenge my tendency to downplay the achievements of Black scholars and writers when compared with canonical European ones or Black musicians.

I have great respect for Black scholarly accomplishments. And I have examined some of them on various occasions. I also acknowledge that we must build on the best work they have done. Yet we must not be limited by them. And we must be intellectually honest. For example, my stream within the Marxist tradition – the radical democracy of council communists (soviets without Bolsheviks!) like Pannenkoek, Gorter, or Korsch – has few Black figures, e.g. like the great St Clair Drake in the 1930s' American Workers Party of A. G. Muste. Most of the grand Black Marxists, like most Marxists in the world, were Leninists (of some sort). And as much as I respect pioneering figures such as the legendary Alain Locke (encouraged by the pathblazing work of Leonard Harris and others) and the brilliant Sylvia Wynters (due to my brother Glenn Jordan and my brief moments in her powerful presence at Stanford decades ago), I find the notion of Locke as a towering *philosophic* figure suspect and the idea of Wynters as the intellectual counterpart of Sarah Vaughan laughable. And I even reject the notion that the great Du Bois was the Duke Ellington of the Black intellectual tradition.

I read Locke's Harvard dissertation and many other writings in preparation for a Harvard conference in 1974 on Locke with papers by Ralph Ellison, Harold Cruse, and Nathan Huggins. I concluded then that he was a towering man of letters with a fine training in philosophy. Yet he never fulfilled his great promise in either philosophy or criticism. Sylvia Wynters is a highly talented thinker in a white, patriarchal academy who also left much of her talent unrealized. Sarah Vaughan is an undisputed genius, one of the greatest artists of the twentieth century, whose achievements go beyond Du Bois in the realm of sheer creativity. Similarly, Duke Ellington, like Louis Armstrong, had no intellectual counterparts in the humanities of any color in America. So here, with regard to Vaughan, Armstrong, or Ellington, even the great Du Bois is out of his league.

My dear brother Gordon simply does not want to acknowledge that the
intellectual (not experiential!) achievements of Black musicians like Ellington,
Armstrong, Tatum, Monk, Parker, Davis, Vaughan, Holiday, Coltrane, Gillespie,
and others are on a different level and scale than Black scholars and writers – with
rare exceptions like Morrison and Ellison. And white recognition has nothing to
do with it! Furthermore, the sheer heroic will of an individual intellectual, like
myself or himself, will not do either. C. L. R. James or Frantz Fanon are not giants
because they aspired to be the next Marx and Sartre or Ellington and Armstrong.
They aspired to be themselves and remained true to themselves as they were
inspired by others. Yet both intellectual titans fall far short of the genius of
Armstrong or Ellington. Gordon wrongly believes I aim to save American civilization or achieve greatness owing to white recognition. My popularity, like that of
anyone, is transient and momentary. I plan to speak the same fallible truths and
bear the same imperfect witness come what may – even as the times and applause
change. And, to put it crudely, since when does one who defends the insights of
Minister Louis Farrakhan, Al Sharpton, Edward Said, Ralph Nader, and
Angela Davis make one so popular in America? If this makes me a tragic figure,
I'll take it!

My radical historicism deeply upsets Headley, the passionate defender of disin-
terested professionalism. His love of "cognitive models," "claims of Reason," and
"dispassionate execution of arguments" leads him to reduce and traduce my work
to religious inspiration, political slogans, and "spiritual coalition" (whatever that
is!). Given his rigid positivistic dualisms of reason/passion, discipline/irrationalism,
logic/emotive rhetoric, it is not surprising that he would so flagrantly misconstrue
my writings. Since so much is required in order for us to engage in a constructive
conversation, a first step is for him to read closely Mendieta's superb essay – in
order to get Headley to see the value of thinking historically as opposed to
philosophizing transcendentally.

Mendieta's historicist interpretation of my historicist interpretation of American
pragmatism as a reconstituting and reframing of US identity at the end of the
twentieth century is a gem. It captures the spirit of the book itself! In fact, one of
the central aims of my work, since *Prophesy Deliverance!* (1982), has been to
examine critically the soul of American civilization – its distinctive institutions,
practices, and ideas – in order to disclose its democratic possibilities. And I have
attempted to do this by putting the USA on the world stage against the backdrop
of the fall of European empires, rise of new nations, and revolt of subaltern
peoples. So which pragmatism I choose means not only which America but also
which world, especially given the probable Americanization (McDonaldization,
Disneylandization, or radical Democratization) of the world.

In this sense, prophetic pragmatism is a particular historicist interpretation of
American pragmatism put forward after such developments as the decolonization
of Third World peoples, the second wave of feminism, and the collapse of

American apartheid; it is a specific historicist philosophic intervention into our postmodern moment after the rise of analytic philosophy, structuralism, deconstruction, and Western Marxism. The "prophetic" in prophetic pragmatism refers to both the Protestant sources of the philosophical movement and my own attempt to be true to the blue notes in American history (its own forms of evil and death and its wrestling with tragicomic darkness). As Putnam and Mendieta rightly see, the prophetic has little or nothing to do with prediction. Instead, it has to do with identifying, analyzing, and condemning forms of evil and forging vision, hope, and courage for selves and communities to overcome them. Radical democracy is visionary plebodicy – the grand expression of the dignity of the doxa of the suffering demos.

Yet my Chekhovian Christian voice is neither reducible to nor identical with radical democratic politics. In their extraordinary essays, Anderson and Yancy wonder aloud whether I reduce truth to utility, religion to politics, and Christian faith to radical democracy. In fact, I am *radically anti-reductionist* on these matters, but I tend to be rather silent on the philosophic "more" beyond utility, the religious "more" beyond politics, and the Christian "more" beyond world-denying love. To engage in sustained talk about this "more" tends to open the door to the forms of metaphysics, ontology, and theology I reject. Yet some of my favorite thinkers, from whom I've learned so much and felt so deeply, boldly walk through these doors – Plato (of the rich dialogues, not textbook Platonism), Augustine, Kant, Whitehead, Heidegger, Marcel, Barth, Tillich, Daly, and Cone. And much more is at stake here than the status of transcendence in my religious thought. It comes down to the slippery issue of the role and function of *mystery* in my philosophical anthropology. Or, more loosely, my picture of the human in the natural and historical world. How do we talk about mystery – its shudderings and ecstasies – without falling into the traps of unwarranted metaphysics, ontology, and theology? As the early Wittgenstein intimated, can we be "true" to the mystery of our lives and histories within the confines of metaphysical, ontological, and theological discourses, or ought we to remain silent owing to the preciousness, elusiveness, and sheer complexity of mystery? I am suspicious of these discourses precisely because I value the *irreducible mystery* of what is, who we are, and where we are going.

Yet I am no mystic – whose infallibility often resides in intuition or selfless union with the Absolute – nor an irrational anti-reductionist whose sense of mystery is so ubiquitous or promiscuous that a dose of science is required to set some things straight. Copernicus, Newton, Darwin, Faraday, Einstein, and Heisenberg do have important fallible yet acceptable points to make!

When I say I am a Chekhovian Christian I mean that as a radical historicist I refuse to foreground my view in metaphysical, ontological, or theological terms, though in every conceivable view there are such operative terms in the background. This simple and profound point motivates the work of my favorite living philosopher (and my former teacher at Boston College in 1975), Hans-Georg Gadamer. It is no accident that the sequel (or volume II) to his masterpiece, *Truth and Method* (1960), focused on the greatest post-Second World War poet of Europe – Paul Celan.

For me, the foreground consists of a *dramatic* site of dialogical contestations and clashing narratives over which blood, sweat, and tears flow. This existential and intellectual agon is always already shot through with forms of transcendence and immanence, logos and eros, dialectic and rhetoric, foundationalist metaphors and antifoundationalist (or even skeptical) operations. And each site bears heavy marks of the biographical, political, social, and psychosexual. Part of the greatness of American democratic thought – of which James, Dewey, Hook, and Rorty are one grand stream – is the acknowledgement of the messiness and dirtiness of our foregrounds and the inescapable backgrounds that shape them. This is, in part, what Ezra Pound meant when he said that Walt Whitman was an exceeding great stench but he is America. And there is much stank and stench in the grandest of the tragic pragmatist figures who took philosophy to the streets – William James.

But only with the tragicomic blues do we get the funk, the funk of America and the funk of life on the underside of America. My prophetic pragmatism speaks of this funk and tries to give it weight in the philosophic tradition of pragmatism. My Chekhovian Christian voice tries to make this funk center stage of American intellectual life, to make the tragicomic darkness and forms of evil and death in Black life central to the drama of an incomplete democratic experiment called the USA.

To take this funk seriously is to stress the dramatic and dialogical over the metaphysical and ontological (or theological). Surely, death and disease, sadness and sorrow, agony and anguish, unemployment and homelessness are real. Yet they result from conflicts and struggles existentially felt and politically circumscribed. Historically, artists have been more willing to confront this funk than philosophers and theologians. Melville and Twain had grasped the early stages of American funk – already articulated in the great American art of the spirituals – before most American philosophers and theologians acknowledged its reality. The "funky" existential insights of David Walker, Frederick Douglass, and Ida B. Wells-Barnett informed the "funky" artistic genius of William Faulkner, Tennessee Williams, and Richard Wright. And, of course, Black philosophers like the legendary Alain Locke encountered this funk more in artists than in his philosophic colleagues.

I consider Chekhov the greatest literary artist of late modernity because he is the pre-eminent poet of the funk of life, its tragicomic darkness, mystery, and incongruity, with a blues conclusion: keep lovin' and fightin' for justice anyhow, i.e. regardless of the situation. He has a secular and agnostic viewpoint permeated with an inexhaustible compassion of resilience and resistance to evil. And he has a mastery of craft and technique that only the greatest of blues-filled jazz musicians – like Coltrane – can fully appreciate!

My Chekhovian Christian voice permits the possibility of the shadow of the divine (Anderson) or the chance of a crypto-fideism (Yancy) because crucial narratives of my dramatic site invoke the doings and sufferings of Jesus of Nazareth. Jesus, as rendered in the synoptic gospels as well as the non-canonical ones of Thomas and others, is for me neither an ethical model (his sense of the comic is too weak), a political model (his failure to condemn slavery or include women in his first-order group of disciples), nor a familial model (his relative lack of eros for intimate significant others or even philia for relatives). Rather, he is Existential Exemplar owing to his life of compassion or world-denying love: one who first introduced and enacted a mode of being in the world that put loving service to others – all others – at the center of being human. Since radical democracy for me is not simply an institutional arrangement or form of governance but also a way of life and struggle, the world-denying love of Jesus and the world-transforming love of the radical democrat are closely related (though not identical). Both drink from the well of life's mystery and are not reducible to mere utility, politics, or democracy. For Jesus Christ, the language of God-centeredness and the coming of the kingdom animated his world-denying love, and his confidence in God's sovereignty sustained him (even given his blues-question (psalm 22:1) on the cross about God forsaking him!). For the Chekhovian Christian, the language of love-centeredness, the tragicomic character of the flowering of radical democracy, the anxiety-ridden leap of faith in the possibility of God's goodness, yield a blues-ridden gospel. The Chekhovian Christian voice accents the cross more than crown, Good Friday more than Easter, love through the darkness of life more than triumphant bliss at the end of life. Ours is in the trying – the rest is not our business. The Chekhovian Christian voice puts a premium on the powerful passion and poignant compassion of Jesus and less on the ultimate consolation and eschatological comfort of orthodox Christian theology.

What makes the Chekhovian Christian a Christian? Why not just be a Chekhovian radical democrat without the Christian baggage? As a radical historicist, I view a particular interpretation of the Christian tradition as the most profound understanding of the human predicament. It is a view that includes the placement of the tragic and majestic among everyday people and ordinary folk, the dignity of each and every person, love as agency and justice as aim, perennial dissatisfaction with mendacity and forms of un-freedom as catalyst for personal and historical transformation. All these elements are requisite for radical democrats. Yet even this sketchy Christian viewpoint is inadequate; it lacks a strong sense of the comic and the body, i.e. it does not possess enough funk like the sermons of John Donne. Many of the dark spirituals – almost Sophoclean in outlook – provide the "funkiest" version of modern Christianity, lifting the voices of common people in the face of the terrors of the social death of slavery trying to devour them. Yet the comic dimension stressed by the blues out-funked even the funky Christianity of the dark spirituals. The civic death-grip of Jim Crow after the broken dreams of emancipation in the Gilded Age pushed Black thought toward the Chekhovian pole. To put it crudely, my distinctive voice and unique vision try to mediate the dark way of the cross in the funky Christianity of the spirituals with the tragicomic dark laughter in the funkier blues for the aims of wise living and democratic expansion.

This is why my brother, teacher, and former colleague James Cone hits the nail on the head in his moving personal essay. He understands that my passion for play, as in Huizinga's classic work *Homo Ludens*, is inseparable from my conception of life as dramatic agon. And my devotion to fun – a word coined in modernity by Americans, is part of my California frontier humor. Since some of the aims of professionalism in the academy are to tame the comic, domesticate the subversive, and conceal the funk – even as we teach Lucian, Rabelais, Chekhov, Twain, Marx, Morrison, and I hope Richard Pryor – I resist professional incorporation even as a highly visible voice in the academy. My Muse of subversive memory and democratic tradition, along with existential anguish and intellectual curiosity, enables the improvisational style that my dear sister and fellow scholar Copeland pinpoints so acutely. The insightful theologian Josiah Young rightly highlights the links of my improvisational Chekhovian Christian voice with that of the great Emmanuel Levinas with regard to the reality of the Other and the unconditional obligation to the Other. I first encountered these Levinasian themes in the essays of Simone Weil, the works of Iris Murdoch, and, above all, the prose fiction of Dostoevsky. In fact, I see the shadow of the incomparable Russian writer over Levinas (especially given his debts to that German philosopher obsessed with Dostoevsky, Heidegger) as much as his rich Judaic traditions. How ironic to see the greatest late twentieth-century Jewish philosopher shaped by the atheistic ex-Nazi Heidegger – both with common roots in that Slavophilic Christian critic of the decadent West, Dostoevsky!

Pittman accuses my improvisational style of being downright irresponsible. Do I not interpret Marx as a mirror image of my radical historicism? Do I impose metaphilosophical debates of the 1970s and 1980s on the Germany of the 1840s and 1850s? There is no doubt that my interpretation of Marx (along with Engels, Kautsky and Lukács) is influenced by my neopragmatic leanings. Yet any insightful reading of a complex thinker like Marx is guided by background prejudgments and presuppositions. Lukács's Hegelian lens, Kojeve's Heideggerian lens, or Althusser's structuralist lens come to mind here. Yet each of these interpretations does some hermeneutical violence to Marx's texts. Some interpretations are more persuasive than others, yet most of the serious ones have some insights to offer.

The fundamental aim of my book on Marx was to tease out the ethical dimensions of Marx's thought against the dominant Marxist forms of determinism, inevitablism, and vulgar utilitarianism. This turn toward the ethical within the

Marxist camp and historicist school in the 1970s and 1980s was unpopular and atypical. I arrived at this turn – now more widely accepted (even by Derrida in his fine new book on the Marxist tradition!) – after writing an aborted thesis on T. H. Green's neo-Hegelian thought and another dead-end project on the Aristotelian bases of Marxist thought. I was wrestling with my own radical democratic identity over against the Marxist tradition and reading Marx in light of neopragmatic lenses. Are these lenses distorting at times? Indeed. Do they utterly destroy the integrity of Marx's thought? Not at all. Contrary to Pittman's interpretation, Marx had deep metaphilosophical concerns – from his dissertation on post-Aristotelian philosophy to his unpublished *The German Ideology*. These concerns are not identical with those of Dewey, Hook, or Rorty, but they do have some elective affinities. My aim was to accent the latter, which is the best we late moderns can do. Needless to say, the tensions within Marx's own work between his positivism and historicism, his scientism and hermeneutical stance, remain unresolved. And when Pittman grossly misreads my heroes, Pascal and Kierkegaard, as promoting subjective conceptions of certainty and covert rationalistic foundations of faith, his own narrow positivism, realism, and even scientism surface in the name of a dialectical philosophy.

Pittman rightly pits me against the grandest dialectical project in contemporary criticism – the hermeneutical Marxism of Fredric Jameson. And though he tends to conflate my interpretation of Nietzsche (historicist, Hobbesian, individualistic) with my critique of Jameson's Derridean interpretation of Nietzsche (poststructuralist, textualist, trans-individualist), Pittman correctly accents my defense of moral discourse without transcendental grounds in contrast to Jameson's sophisticated attempts to go beyond such discourse. What Pittman misses is my immanent critique of Jameson – namely, how Jameson's deep Hegelian Marxism pits him against his own poststructuralist attempt to go beyond ethical discourse based on a misreading of Nietzsche as exemplary poststructuralist. Instead, Pittman falls back on the predictable defense of the cognitive function of philosophy, in contrast to my improvisational use of philosophic traditions. And like Gordon and Headley, Pittman reduces prophetic witness bearing to mere experience without *critical* reflections or existential identification with those who suffer without *analytical* operations. Hence, their flagrant misconstruals of my dialogical and dramatic conceptions of philosophy, critical theory, and the arts.

This dialogical and dramatic orientation surfaces most clearly in my treatment of Du Bois, a highly controversial treatment brilliantly examined by my dear brother and colleague Lucius Outlaw. In his provocative – and troubling – essay, Outlaw rightly discusses my ambivalence toward Du Bois, elitism, and my present notoriety. A major drumbeat throughout his piece is my implicit attempt to measure myself against Du Bois, and, indeed, go beyond him. And in one sense Outlaw is right. I distinguish between Du Bois as scholar and Du Bois as philosophical anthropologist, Du Bois as historical sociologist and Du Bois as the late Victorian

Enlightenment visionary. In my essay, I focus on the latter designations and criticize him in light of my tragicomic blues sensibilities. Outlaw correctly takes me to task for not specifying the criteria for my desirable tragicomic viewpoint. I simply assert and assume that those who fail to linger on the night side of the human predicament have inadequate conceptions of this predicament. Then I try to show how and why Du Bois's conception of the human condition reflects this failure to linger. The grand irony of the great Du Bois is that his magnificent scholarship focuses on the night side of European modernity and American society, yet his Goethean (cloudless-sky symbol) shunning of the funk of life leads him away from the tragicomic darkness of the blues of the very people whose freedom he heralds. In short, Outlaw admonishes me to put it bluntly. My Chekhovian Christian voice simply cuts deeper and thereby is more truthful than Du Bois's Goethean Enlightenment view that undergirded his marvelous scholarship.

Outlaw is even more exacting in his lengthy examination of my ambivalence about elitism, Du Bois's and mine. Du Bois was a nineteenth-century Victorian elitist whose democratic sentiments led him to acknowledge the capacity of ordinary people to develop. I promote a more radical democratic leadership that respects talent, discipline, and insight – hence it is in a certain sense elitist – yet I view this leadership already at work among all classes, genders, and groups. Hence, I stress democratic mutuality and reciprocity more than Du Bois's dynamic hierarchy and verticality. I understand that self-confidence may appear as arrogance, yet self-criticism and accountability are the go-cart of democratic leadership.

My own ambivalence about my own notoriety has little to do with any feeble attempts to outdo the great Du Bois. My own ambivalence about Du Bois prevents me from desiring to imitate him despite his grand achievements. This is so because his conception of greatness differs so radically from mine – at the existential (not political) level. His devotion to the freedom of oppressed peoples greatly inspires me. But he enacts a more aristocratic mode of being wedded to Goethean conceptions of the great man who sits high, looks low, and solicits deference. I embody a more democratic mode of being tied to a Chekhovian Christian view of the great person who resides in the funk, alongside the folk searching for a way out of the dark with a smile and a tear.

Outlaw rightly takes me to task for highlighting Du Bois's failure to engage in a sustained encounter with Chekhov and Kafka – or the rich Russian and Central European literary traditions – without criticizing the Russians or Europeans for overlooking the Black intellectual traditions. And much more work needs to be done to examine this cross-cultural contrast, as in the fertile scholarship of Dale E. Peterson. I simply tried to show how Du Bois's disparaging of the blues and jazz reflects his own distancing from the tragicomic voices and viewpoints *within* African-American culture. And even Outlaw calls for "close scrutiny" of this point. Yet this is no small point. The very linchpin of my voice and vision hangs on the insightfulness and truthfulness of the rich traditions of tragicomic darkness and world-transforming compassion linked to radical democratic practices and struggles.

Radical Democracy and Modernity

Decay, decadence, and decline are major tropes in my work because of the relatively weak presence or feeble power of radical democratic struggles in modernity. Despite the undeniable victories of liberal capitalist democracies in modern times, radical democratic projects remain on the cross – fugitive efforts rendered nearly impotent and trapped in plutocratic, pigmentocratic, patriarchal, and heterosexist constraints. My frequent references to the twilight of capitalist civilization is not a harkening to some golden age in the past or to an apocalyptic collapse in the future but rather a terrifying near eclipse of the very vision of radical democracy in a self-congratulatory present. To be a radical democrat is to confront the tragicomic character of a commodified and bureaucratized world of icy polar darkness and hardness that reduces world-transforming compassion to naive utopianism given the fashionable indifference to social misery of pervasive consumerism and hedonism.

My Chekhovian Christian embrace of radical democracy is rooted in a prophetic critique of prevailing forms of dogmatism and domination. The dogmas (and embodied forms of domination) of the market, method, technology, reason, empire, nation-state, race, gender, and straightness not only blind us from their dark side, they also encourage us to fetishize them as solutions to pressing problems or crisis. These dogmas often lead us to deny or evade the forms of domination that impede radical democratic practices. They tend to render us apathetic, complacent, or too downright cowardly in the face of heroic challenges of expanding democracy in the political, economic, and existential spheres.

In a fascinating and sympathetic critique of my work, *Cornel West and the Politics of Prophetic Pragmatism*, Mark David Wood traces my move from revolutionary socialist to progressive reform. In a probing and challenging text on my corpus to be published soon, Rosemary Cowan shows how a prophetic Christian vision guides this radical democratic politics, be it revolutionary or reformist. I think both writers have some truths to tell.

Three major misunderstandings becloud my radical democratic project. First, too much attention has focused on my "Nihilism in Black America" essay in *Race Matters* (a mere 14 pages in a 16-book corpus!) that accents existential agency *alongside* structural constraints. Yet despite claims in the chapter about the centrality of corporate market institutions and racist stereotypes in shaping nihilistic responses or how these responses are not forms of pathological behavior but rather efforts "of a people bereft of resources in confronting the workings of US capitalist society" (p. 25), critics insist on characterizing my position as a conservative blaming-the-victim perspective. Even close readers like Mills and Gordon, along with less reliable ones like Headley, Hayes, and Joseph, perpetuate this gross misreading. And given my trenchant critiques of conservatism and liberalism, especially their reluctance to give weight to capitalist market forces and white supremacist bombardment, throughout my corpus, I find it bizarre that this sophomoric reading persists. Maybe the very language of nihilism suggested a downplaying of structural realities, hence a leftist knee-jerk designation of a blaming-the-victim perspective. Yet even an uncharitable yet close reading would see my focus on existential agency within a capitalist, white supremacist civilization, not a self-blaming victimization with no historical contexts.

Headley, Hayes, and Joseph fall squarely into this trap. They spend much time recycling this myth with little textual evidence or references to other essays or chapters in my work. A mere glance at my piece "Race and Social Theory" would cure them of much of their gross misunderstanding. Yet even this treatment would not suffice for Joseph. His charges of my political defeatism, scapegoating of Black nationalism, and dismissing of Black radicalism and Marxism are even more ludicrous. DMX can speak for himself, but Joseph's flat-footed analyses of his music and my work would give the blues the blues. He overlooks the existential agency in the form and content of the music and work and sees only the bleak truths independent of the oppositional aspirations and practices of the music and work. My critical appreciation of the Black nationalist tradition goes back to *Prophecy Deliverance!*, where the African Blood Brotherhood, Black Panther Party, and League of Revolutionary Black Workers are heralded as high moments in the Black Freedom Struggle. This stance has been consistent in my work, as witnessed by my sustained engagement and debates with the Dean of Contemporary Black Nationalism, my dear brother Maulana Karenga, the leading Black nationalist, the beloved Minister Louis Farrakhan, the towering scholar of Pan-African Studies, the late and great John Henrik Clarke, and the famous theorist of Afro-centrism, my fellow co-teacher Molefi Asante. Lastly, the dismissing of Black radicals and Marxists bespeaks such an ignorance of my work that one can only plead in humility and hope: please do more homework my brother before one enters a serious dialogue! My review of Cedric Robinson's classic text *Black Marxism* or my nearly $10,000 gift to the founding of the Black Radical Congress is a good place to start.

Mills surely has done his homework. And as in his superb two volumes on political philosophy and white supremacy, Mills provides a brilliant reading of my project. His major insight is that my hybrid formulation of prophetic pragmatism attempts to Americanize left-wing theory and practice; his main criticism is that my corpus does not contain a sustained analysis of white supremacy inscribed in the state and economy. He is correct on both points. My Gramscian concerns lead me to accent the specificity of American left possibilities and my writings on race pull from the works of others on the macrostructural level (Du Bois, Cox, Patterson, Wilson, Kilson, Bobo, and others) yet fail to engage this level on my own with original research. This is primarily because the latter requires the very empirical research that I have little time to do. Hence I rely on the research of others, and throw out speculative hypotheses to be validated or refuted by such research. Needless to say, my book *The War Against Parents*, written with the sophisticated economist Sylvia Ann Hewlett, is full of empirical data and social scientific inquiry. Yet it is atypical of my corpus.

Iris Young addresses this text as well as my work with Roberto Unger, *The Future of American Progressivism*, in a provocative manner. She perceives a genuine tension between my hard-hitting feminism in *Race Matters* (or *Breaking Bread* with bell hooks) and my "antifeminist" nostalgic idea of the family in *The War Against Parents* − or the social constructivism of earlier years and the biologism of later years. In addition, she suggests, wrongly I think, that the West–Unger book is "only slightly more radical than the mainstream of the Democratic Party." Our text is much closer to Nader's Green Party than Gore's Democratic Party.

The second major misunderstanding of my work on radical democracy is my conservative gender politics. This charge is made because Hewlett and I defend the progressive possibilities of egalitarian (not patriarchal or heterosexist) marriage and the post-Second World War conditions of government support and economic undergirding of strong families, and we reject the ugly results of narcissistic (not appropriate or necessary) divorces on children. We also highlight the crucial role of dads and fathers in shaping the destinies of children. The kind of democratic feminism Hewlett and I promote is hard to discern and detect on the current ideological spectrum.

Young rightly notes the weight we put on the workplace and economic sphere. Our sustained treatment of managerial greed, wealth inequality, and declining workers' power is often overlooked. What bothers Young is the alleged lack of attention to the racial segregation and sexist subordination in the 1950s. Yet throughout our analysis we acknowledge and condemn these ugly realities (pp. 36, 98, 104, 134, 197). What really upsets Young is our critique of libertarian feminism that elevates autonomy and choice over social responsibility and community. We do not claim that family breakdown is caused by the women's movement. Our multidimensional analysis prevents such a reductionist claim. And even Young suggests we are too economistic at times, which militates against her charge of culturalist reductionism.

Furthermore, our stress on two parents, especially the biological parents, as best for children strikes Young as biologistic and homophobic. Yet we make it clear that this does not stigmatize single mothers and fathers, disqualify loving gay or lesbian parents, or preclude successful adoption of children. We simply want transformed workplace accommodations, government policies, and attitudes in the variety of families to put a premium on the well-being of children. And this motif is the constant drumbeat of our progressive text. And again, even Mills – in a brief footnote – reinforces this second myth based on Young's misreading.

The third misunderstanding of my radical democratic politics is that it is too Americentric. In this way, I am accused of ignoring the rest of the world and endorsing a narrow American nationalism. I confess that a distinguishing feature of my work, as philosopher and cultural critic, is the centrality of the multilayered realities of white supremacy in modern Black existence within the USA. So my point of entry is Americentric, yet my radical democratic project is militantly international. As the West–Unger book shows and the West–Lerner text (*Jews and Blacks*) demonstrates, my suspicions of nationalisms run deep on radical democratic grounds. So my preoccupation with American civilization is neither chauvinistic nor nativistic; it simply grounds the universality of radical democracy within the particularity of my specific context of lived experiences and political struggles.

Radical Intellectuals and the Academy

My dear friend and brother Howard McGary and brother Clarence Johnson both rightly situate my work and life in the modern humanist tradition. My intellectual heroes – from Erasmus to Raymond Williams, Jonathan Swift to Aime Césaire – often fall within this precious intellectual heritage. My Chekhovian Christian voice is located on the radical pole of modern humanism. Like those of Frantz Fanon, C. L. R. James, and June Jordan, my focus is on the existential agency and political insurgency of "the wretched of the earth," especially in the USA. To be a radical humanist intellectual is to be not solely an academic with left-wing politics, but a public figure and visible force for radical democratic ideals and causes. Like my brothers Edward Said and Noam Chomsky or my sister Barbara Ehrenrich, all exemplary radical humanist intellectuals, I have a desire to share the passion and action of my time. To be a radical intellectual is to speak painful yet fallible truths to the powers that be as well as to bear witness in the face of those powers. My quest for poetic eloquence is rooted in my desire to communicate with others in order to unsettle their prejudgments, challenge their presuppositions, and unhouse their souls. This desire flows from a deep respect for others. This is why speaking outweighs writing in my intellectual praxis, and also why reading is more important than both activities. For me, to be a radical humanist intellectual is to be a man or woman of letters obsessed with close readings of texts and contexts and eager to share those readings with others.

My intellectual journey has been unique in the history of the American academy. My sheer level of privilege and scope of exposure is unprecedented. I have matriculated from the riches of a Black family, church, public schools, and streets to Harvard, Princeton, Union Theological Seminary, Yale, then back to Princeton and Harvard – with prolonged teaching posts in prisons, adult education, workers' schools, as well as the University of Paris. And the towering academic figures I studied closely with are incredible, including John Rawls, Hilary Putnam, Stanley Cavell, Roderick Firth, Israel Scheffler, Hans-Georg Gadamer, Bernard Williams, Robert Nozick, Preston Williams, Samuel Beer, H. Stuart Hughes, Talcott Parsons, Richard Rorty, Thomas Kuhn, Carl Hempel, Paul Benaceraf, Walter Kaufman, Thomas Scanlon, Peter Gomes, Malcolm Diamond, Thomas Nagel, Sir Arthur Lewis, Gregory Vlastos, Terry Irwin, Sheldon Wolin, Richard Grandy, Raymond Geuss, David Hoy, G. A. Cohen, Joel Porte, Daniel Aaron, Thorkild Jacobsen, Paul Hanson, G. Ernest Wright, and above all Martin Kilson. And I encountered these figures during my undergraduate and graduate years! My teaching years at Union with the late great James Washington, James Cone, James Forbes, Beverly Harrison, Donald Shriver, Tom Driver, and so many others; at Columbia with Edward Said, Paul Bové, Jonathan Arac, Sidney Morgenbesser, Stanley Aronowitz, Margaret Ferguson, and others only deepen my fortunes. And words fail to convey the depths of my teaching years at Yale, Princeton, and Harvard. In short, the academy has been an indescribable source of empowerment for me.

Yet my writing and teaching have been markedly anti-academic not out of explicit opposition to academic professionalism but from an allegiance to humanistic intellectual work I ironically nurtured in the academy. Most of my literary sources of inspiration have been anti-academic in spirit – Emerson, Whitman, Melville, James, Twain, Du Bois, Niebuhr, Rorty, Kierkegaard, Schopenhauer, Nietzsche, Morrison, Wittgenstein, and above all Chekhov. Yet I do have great respect for my academic teachers and mentors from whom I have learned so much.

I give much weight to teaching in the academy and in the larger society. In fact, the priority I give to reading and speaking is closely related to the centrality of teaching in my intellectual vocation. In this sense, I am more a public teacher than public intellectual (a phrase I have never used to describe myself, though I have also never rejected it!), more interested in Socratic probing of the public than pronouncing blueprints for the public.

This kind of Socratic activity requires some degree of marginality in society. In her essay, Elia suggests that I scorn this marginality. Instead, I revel in it. But this marginality is not to be equated with estrangement. I do not feel estranged from the Black community or American culture. I do know my radical democratic politics and Chekhovian Christian voice are marginal to both. I definitely do not consider myself representative of the "Black Intellectual" – a xenophobic formulation confined to Negrophobic journals like *The New Republic*. Nor do I confine intellectuals to the academy, as seen in my treatments of Black intellectuals like Martin Luther King, Jr, Malcolm X, Mumia Abu-Jamal, Black musicians, and preachers. And my aim is not to be recognized among one's people or in one's society – something I have too much of at the moment. Rather my goal is to make my vision and viewpoint more credible and convincing among fellow human beings. And this requires the uses of all media of technology (radio, TV, video,

Internet, films, newspapers, magazines, books) and the uses of one's celebrity status for one's vision. My new music CD, *Sketches of My Culture*, exemplifies this commitment.

In conclusion, my radical historicist orientation and radical democratic politics breed a radical intellectual project that takes the form of a Chekhovian Christian voice – a dark voice that combines the blood-stained way of the cross in the funky Christianity of the spirituals with the tear-soaked tragicomic laughter in the funkier blues in order to enhance the art of wise living and enlarge the scope of democracy. Just as learning how to die unleashes courageous energy to live and living compassionately encourages democratic ways of struggle – so, too, taking philosophy seriously immerses us into the funk of life and bids us to find our distinctive voice and share our unique vision.

Select Bibliography of Cornel West's Works

Books

The *African-American Century: How Black Americans Have Shaped Our Country* (with Henry Louis Gates, Jr). New York: Free Press, 2000.

The Cornel West Reader. New York: Basic Civitas Books, 1999.

Courage to Hope: From Black Suffering to Human Redemption (with Quinton Hosford Dixie). Boston: Beacon Press, 1999.

The Future of American Progressivism: An Initiative for Political and Economic Reform (with Roberto Unger). Boston: Beacon Press, 1998.

The War Against Parents: What We Can Do for America's Beleaguered Moms and Dads (with Sylvia Ann Hewlett). New York: Houghton Mifflin Company, 1998.

Restoring Hope: Conversations on the Future of Black America. Boston: Beacon Press, 1997.

The Future of the Race (with Henry Louis Gates, Jr). New York: Random House, 1997.

Struggles in the Promised Land: Towards a History of Black–Jewish relations in the United States (with Jack Salzman). New York: Oxford University Press, 1997.

Jews and Blacks: A Dialogue on Race in America, and Culture in America (with Michael Lerner). New York: NAL/Dutton, 1996.

Jews and Blacks: Let the Healing Begin (with Michael Lerner). New York: Grosset/Putnam, 1995.

James Snead's White Screens, Black Images: Hollywood from the Dark Side (edited with Colin MacCabe). New York: Routledge, 1994.

Keeping Faith: Philosophy and Race in America. New York: Routledge, 1993.

Beyond Eurocentrism and Multiculturalism, Volume 1: Prophetic Thought in Postmodern Times. Monroe, ME: Common Courage Press, 1993.

Beyond Eurocentrism and Multiculturalism, Volume 2: Prophetic Reflections: Notes on Race and Power in America. Monroe, ME: Common Courage Press, 1993.

Race Matters. Boston: Beacon Press, 1993.

Breaking Bread: Insurgent Black Intellectual Life (with bell hooks). Boston: South End Press, 1991.

The Ethical Dimensions of Marxist Thought. New York: Monthly Review Press, 1991.

Out There: Marginalization and Contemporary Cultures (with Russell Ferguson, Martha Gever, and Trinh T. Minhha). Cambridge, MA: MIT Press, 1990.

The America Evasion of Philosophy: A Genealogy of Pragmatism. Madison, WI: University of Wisconsin Press, 1989.

Prophetic Fragments. Grand Rapids, MI: E. William Eerdmans Publishing Company, 1988.

Post-Analytic Philosophy (with John Rajchman). New York: Columbia University Press, 1985.

Prophesy Deliverance! An Afro-American Revolutionary Christianity. Philadelphia: The Westminster Press, 1982.

Theology in the Americas: Detroit II (with Caridad Guidote and Margaret Coakley). Maryknoll, NY: Orbis Press, 1982.

Select Articles, Chapters and Book Reviews

"The moral obligations of living in a democratic society." In David Batstone and Eduardo Mendieta (eds), *The Good Citizen*. New York: Routledge, 1999.

"Black critics and the pitfalls of canon formation." In Robert Davis and Ronald Schleifer (eds), *Contemporary Literary Criticism: Literary and Cultural Studies*. New York: Longman, 1998.

"The Million Man March." *Dissent*, 43(1), 1996, pp. 97–8.

"After OJ and the Farrakhan-led Million-Man March: is healing possible?" (interview with Michael Lerner), *Tikkun*, 10(6), 1995, pp. 12–21.

"The left after forty years." *Dissent*, 41(1), 1994, pp. 15–16.

"10 events that shook the world: Reaganism, racial tension, and the rise of the underclass." *The Utne Reader* (Minneapolis), Issue 62, March 1994, p. 67.

"The deeper threat to Black America." *Education Week* (Washington, DC), 123(1), 1993, p. 46.

"Diverse new world." In Paul Berman (ed.), *Debating PC: The Controversy Over Political Correctness on College Campuses*. New York: Laurel Press, 1992.

"Learning to talk of race." *New York Times Magazine*, August 2, 1992, p. 24.

"Black leadership and the pitfalls of racial reasoning." In Toni Morrison (ed.), *Race-ing Justice, En-gendering Power*. New York: Pantheon Books, 1992.

"The legacy of Raymond Williams." *Social Text*, 30–3, 1992, pp. 6–8.

"Black anti-Semitism and the rhetoric of resentment." *Tikkun*, 7(1), 1992, pp. 15–16.

"Theory, pragmatism, and politics." In Jonathan Arac and Barbara Johnson (eds), *Consequences of Theory*. Baltimore, MD: Johns Hopkins University Press, 1991.

"Why I write for Tikkun." *Tikkun*, 5(5), 1990, pp. 59–60.

"Leaders to meet an international challenge." *The Progressive*, 54(11), 1990, pp. 37.

"Black–Jewish dialogue: beyond rootless universalism and ethnic chauvinism." *Tikkun*, 4(4), 1989, p. 95.

"Imperatives of seminary reform." *Christianity and Crisis*, 49(5/6), 1989, pp. 104–5.

"CLS and the liberal critic." *Yale Law Journal*, 97(5), 1988, pp. 757–71.

"Rethinking Marxism: struggles in Marxist theory. Essays for Harry Magdoff and Paul Sweezy." *Monthly Review*, 38, 1987, pp. 52–7.

"Metaphysics." In Mircea Eliade (ed.), *The Encyclopedia of Religion, volume 9*. New York: Macmillan Publishing Company, 1987, pp. 485–7.

"Neo-Aristotelianism, liberalism and socialism: a Christian perspective." In Bruce Grelle (ed.), *Christianity and Capitalism: Perspectives on Religion, Liberalism and the Economy*. Chicago: Center for Scientific Study of Religion, 1986.

"Unmasking the Black conservatives." *The Christian Century*, 103 (July 16), 1986, pp. 644–8.

"Contemporary Afro-American social thought." *Over There* (American Studies Journal in Britain), Winter 1986, pp. 11–16.

"Leszek Kolakowski's *Religion*." *Old Westbury Review*, 2 (Fall), 1986, pp. 147–53.

"Foreword." In Franz J. Hinkelammert, *The Ideological Weapons of Death*. New York: Orbis, 1986, pp. v–vii.

"Realign the left." *Democratic Left*, 13(1), 1985, pp. 4–5.

"Not-always-perfidious Albion." *Christianity and Crisis*, 45(1/2), 1985, pp. 5–6.

"Violence in America." *Christianity and Crisis*, 45(10), 1985, pp. 222–3.

"On visiting South Africa." *Christianity and Crisis*, 45(17), 1985, pp. 412–14.

"Review of Naison Mark's *Communists in Harlem During the Depression*." *Monthly Review*, 37 (December), 1985, pp. 48–51.

"Reconstructing the American left: the challenge of Jesse Jackson." *Social Text*, 11 (Winter), 1984/5, pp. 3–19.

"On Black–Jewish relations." *Christianity and Crisis*, 44(7), 1984, pp. 149–50.

"Red/green smokescreen." *Democratic Left*, 12(2), 1984, p. 15.

"Black politics will never be the same." *Christianity and Crisis*, 44(13), 1984, pp. 302–5.

"Religion, politics, language." *Christianity and Crisis*, 44(16), 1984, pp. 366–7.

"Christian theological mediocrity." *Christianity and Crisis*, 44(19), 1984, pp. 439–40.

"The paradox of the Afro-American rebellion." In Sohnya Sayres (ed.), *The 60s without Apology*. Minneapolis: The University of Minnesota Press, 1984.

"Religion and the left: an introduction." *Monthly Review*, 36(3), 1984, pp. 9–19.

"Review of James Bentley's *Between Marx and Christ: The Dialogue in German-speaking Europe 1870–1970*." *Commonweal*, 111 (February 24), 1984, p. 24.

"Review of Juan Luis Segundo's *Faith and Ideologies*." *Commonweal*, 111 (January 27), 1984, pp. 27–57.

"Review of Richard Wightman Fox and T. J. Jackson Lears (eds), *The Culture of Consumption: Critical Essays in American History 1880–1980*." *Christianity and Crisis*, 44(3), 1984, pp. 66–70.

"Philosophy, politics and power: an Afro-American perspective." In Leonard Harris (ed.), *Philosophy Born of Struggle*. Dubuque, IA: Kendall/Hunt, 1983, pp. 51–9.

"The Black church and socialist politics." *Third World Socialists*, 1(2), 1983, pp. 16–19.

"Black theology of liberation as critique of capitalist civilization." *Journal of the Interdenominational Theological Center*, 10(1/2), 1982/3, pp. 67–83.

"Fredric Jameson's Marxist hermeneutics." *Boundary 2: A Journal of Postmodern Literature* (special issue on Marxism and postmodernism), 11(1/2), 1982/3, pp. 177–200.

"Lukacs: a reassessment." *The Minnesota Review*, 19 (Fall) 1982, pp. 86–102.

"The Black struggle, the Black church and the US progressive movement." In Linda Unger and Kathleen Schultz (eds), *Seeds of a People's Church: Challenge and Promise from the Underside of History*. Detroit: Seeds of a People's Church, 1981.

"Socialism, religion and the Black struggle." *Religious Socialism*, 4(4), 1980, pp. 5–8.

"Socialism and the Black church." *New York Circus*, 3(5), 1979, pp. 5–8.

"Black theology and Marxist thought." In Gayraud Wilmore and James Cone (eds), *Black Theology: A Documentary History 1966–1979*. Maryknoll, NY: Orbis Press, 1979.

"Schleiermacher's hermeneutics and the myth of the given." *Union Seminary Quarterly Review*, 34(2), 1979, pp. 71–84.

"Philosophy and the Afro-American experience." *The Philosophical Forum*, 9(2/3), 1977/8, pp. 117–48.

Select Commentary on West's Work

Anderson, Jervis, "The public intellectual." *The New Yorker*, 69(46), 1994, pp. 39–48.

Anderson, Victor, "The wrestle of Christ and culture in pragmatic public theology." *American Journal of Theology and Philosophy*, 19(2), 1998, pp. 135–50.

Appiah, Kwame Anthony, "Review of *The American Evasion of Philosophy: A Genealogy of Pragmatism*." *The Nation*, 250(14), 1990, pp. 496–8.

Banks, William M., *Black Intellectuals: Race and Responsibility in American Life*. New York: W. W. Norton and Company, 1996.

Beardslee, William A., "Cornel West's postmodern theology." In David Ray Griffin, William Beardslee and Joe Holland (eds), *Varieties of Postmodern Theology*. Maryknoll, NY: Orbis Press, 1995.

Brown, Bill, "Interview with Cornel West" (includes Brown's commentary and an excerpt from West's Chicago Humanities Institute Symposium talk). *Modern Philology*, 90(4), 1993, pp. 142–66.

Collins, Patricia Hill, "Review of *Breaking Bread: Insurgent Black Intellectual Life*." *Signs*, 20(1), 1994, pp. 176–9.

Cose, Ellis, "A prophet with attitude: Cornel West talks of race, love and rage." *Newsweek*, June 1993, p. 71.

Donovan, Rickard, "Cornel West's new pragmatism." *Cross Currents*, 41(1), 1991, pp. 98–106.

Dyson, Michael Eric, "Review of *Prophetic Fragments*." *Theology Today*, 45(4), 1989, pp. 451–3.

Goldberg, David Theo, "Whither West? The making of a public intellectual." *Review of Education, Pedagogy, Cultural Studies*, 16(1), 1994, pp. 1–13.

Gooding-Williams, Robert, "Evading narrative myth, evading prophetic pragmatism: Cornel West's *The American Evasion of Philosophy*." *The Massachusetts Review*, 32(4), 1991/2, pp. 517–42.

Gooding-Williams, Robert, "Review of *Keeping Faith: Philosophy and Race in America*." *Philosophical Review*, 104(4), 1995, pp. 601–3.

Gordon, Lewis, "Black intellectuals and academic activism: Cornel West's 'Dilemmas of the Black intellectual.'" In Lewis Gordon (ed.), *Her Majesty's Other Children*. Lanham, MD: Rowman and Littlefield, 1997.

Select Bibliography 367

Gordon, Lewis, "Review of Cornel West's *Race Matters.*" *Political Affairs*, 73(2), 1994, pp. 34–7.

Griffin, David R., "Liberation theology and postmodern philosophy: a response to Cornel West." In David Ray Griffin, William Beardslee and Joe Holland (eds), *Varieties of Postmodern Theology*. Maryknoll, NY: Orbis Press, 1995.

Hart, William, "Cornel West: between Rorty's rock and West's hard place." *American Journal of Theology and Philosophy*, 19(2), 1998, pp. 151–72.

James, Joy, *Transcending the Talented Tenth: Black Intellectual Leaders and American Intellectuals*. New York: Routledge, 1997.

Johnson, Clarence Shole, "Cornel West as existentialist and pragmatist." In Lewis Gordon (ed.), *Existence in Black: An Anthology of Black Existential Philosophy*. New York: Routledge, 1996.

Kazi, Kuumba Ferrouillet, "Cornel West: talking about race matters." *The Black Collegian*, 24(1), 1993, pp. 24–35.

Little, Danielle K., "Does truth depend upon the audience to whom one is speaking?" *QBR*, November/December 1999, p. 18.

Miller, D. W., "In the race for the White House, does race matter? Why Harvard's Cornel West couldn't save Bill Bradley's presidential campaign." *Chronicle of Higher Education*, 46(29), 2000, pp. A21–2.

Morris, Walter S., "West maligns Black conservatives." *The Christian Century*, 103(29), 1986, pp. 863–4.

Nichols, John, "Interview with Cornel West." *The Progressive*, 61(1), 1997, pp. 26–9.

Osborne, Peter, "American radicalism: Cornel West." In Peter Osborne (ed.), *A Critical Sense: Interviews with Intellectuals*. New York: Routledge, 1996.

Painter, Nell Irvin, "Review of *The Future of the Race.*" *The Nation*, 262(18), 1996, pp. 38–40.

Pittman, John, "Postphilosophy, politics, and race." In Emmanuel Chukwudi Eze (ed.), *Postcolonial African Philosophy: A Critical Reader*. Cambridge, MA: Blackwell, 1997.

Quin, Eli, "A battle plan to vanquish the demons of US racism." *The Philadelphia Inquirer*, May 9, 1993, p. N2.

Quirk, Michael J., "Review of *Keeping Faith: Philosophy and Race in America.*" *Cross Currents*, 44(4), 1994, pp. 535–9.

Reed, Adolf, "What are the drums saying, Booker? The current crisis of the Black intellectual." *Village Voice*, April 11, 1995, pp. 31–6.

Romano, Carlin, "Philosopher express." *The Philadelphia Inquirer*, June 23, 1993, pp. F1 and F8.

Rorty, Richard, "The philosopher and the prophet." *Transition*, 52, 1991, pp. 70–8.

Sundquist, Eric J., "Review of *The Future of the Race.*" *Commentary*, 102(1), 1996, pp. 60–3.

Van Leeuwen, Mary Stewart, "Parenting and politics: giving new shape to 'family values.'" *The Christian Century*, 115(21), 1998, pp. 719–21.

West, Charles C., "Review of *The Ethical Dimensions of Marxist Thought.*" *Theology Today*, 49(3), 1992, p. 439.

Wieseltier, Leon, "The unreal world of Cornel West: all and nothing at all." *The New Republic*, March 6, 1995, pp. 31–6.

Wood, Mark David, *Cornel West and the Politics of Prophetic Pragmatism*. Chicago: University of Illinois Press, 2000.

Yancy, George, "Review of *Jews and Blacks: Let the Healing Begin*." *Philadelphia Tribune Magazine*, July 1995, 11.

Yancy, George, "Interview with Cornel West." In George Yancy (ed.), *African-American Philosophers, 17 Conversations*. New York: Routledge, 1998.

Yancy, George, "Review of *Restoring Hope: Conversations on the Future of Black America*." *Philadelphia Tribune Magazine*, February 1998, pp. 11 and 20.

Index